A HISTORY OF THE INDIANS OI

The Civilization of the American Indian Series

UNIVERSITY OF OKLAHOMA PRESS : NORMAN

A HISTORY OF THE

INDIANS

OF THE UNITED STATES

by Angie Debo

BY ANGIE DEBO

The Historical Background of the American Policy of Isolation (with
    J. Fred Rippy) (Northampton, Mass., 1924)
The Rise and Fall of the Choctaw Republic (Norman, 1934; New edi-
    tion, Norman, 1967)
And Still the Waters Run (Princeton, 1940)
The Road to Disappearance: A History of the Creek Indians (Norman,
    1941)
Oklahoma: A Guide to the Sooner State (Ed., with John M. Oskison)
    (Norman, 1941)
Tulsa: From Creek Town to Oil Capital (Norman, 1943)
Prairie City: The Story of an American Community (New York, 1944)
Oklahoma: Foot-loose and Fancy-free (Norman, 1949)
The Five Civilized Tribes of Oklahoma (Philadelphia, 1951)
The Cowman's Southwest, Oliver Nelson (Ed.) (Glendale, Calif., 1953)
History of the Choctaw, Chickasaw, and Natchez Indians, by H. B.
    Cushman (Ed.) (Stillwater, Okla., 1962)
A History of the Indians of the United States (Norman, 1970)
Geronimo: The Man, His Time, His Place (Norman, 1976)

For my young neighbors
HUGH AND RAMONA O'NEILL
Who Read and Understand

LIBRARY OF CONGRESS CATALOG CARD NUMBER: 73-108802

ISBN: 0-8061-1888-1

Copyright © 1970 by the University of Oklahoma Press, Norman, Publishing Division of the University.
Manufactured in the U.S.A. First edition, 1970; second printing, 1971; third printing, 1972; fourth print-
ing, 1974; fifth printing, 1977; sixth printing, 1979; seventh printing, 1984; eighth printing, 1985.

A History of the Indians of the United States is Volume 106 in **The Civilization of the American Indian**
Series.

PREFACE TO THE SEVENTH PRINTING

It is, of course, impossible to carry on original research for a book of this scope. It is based on general knowledge of the work of many historians. When I discovered errors, I corrected them in subsequent printings. This time I am making a major change by disentangling the Sauk and Fox Indians. These allied but distinct tribes were erroneously designated as the "united Sac and Fox tribe" in their first treaty, which was negotiated with the Sauks alone in 1804; and this error was maintained in spite of Fox protests in all government relations with them during the century and three quarters following. Thus historians, basing their research on official statements and archives, have accepted it as fact. Only recently has the true history of these tribes begun to emerge. I am glad to correct my own account in accordance with these findings.

ANGIE DEBO

Marshall, Oklahoma
March 25, 1983

PREFACE TO THE FIRST PRINTING

From the landing of the first European on its shores until comparatively recent years, the history of the United States has been influenced by its aboriginal inhabitants to a degree far out of proportion to their numbers. "We have led the vanguard of civilization in our conflicts with them for tribal existence from ocean to ocean," said Chief Pleasant Porter of the Creeks. Even yet, although they are the smallest of minority groups, their welfare rests more heavily upon the American conscience than that of any other people. The dominant race can never forget that they were here first, and that they are entitled to survival rather than extinction. But this sense of obligation is not always supported by knowledge.

It is understandable that the average intelligent non-Indian American is uninformed about Indian (or Alaska native) affairs, as uninformed as I myself would have been if my research and writing had been done in some other field. Indian history is a highly specialized subject, and it never gets into the books on general history. I began my own studies for no better reason than that the sources were available; and I remember how surprised and shocked I was when I began to uncover the facts, and how my lightly held assumptions were proved wrong.

It is not so easy to forgive the readiness of the uninformed to burst out in shrill speech or rush into shriller print to demand the solution of problems he has made no effort to understand. Much of the wrong the Indians have suffered was motivated by naked greed and ruthlessness; but only the student of their history knows how much was done by well-meaning people with preconceived notions which they never bothered to submit to the test of facts. And the latter were the unconscious allies of the exploiters.

A few years ago some recommendations of a church official were referred to me for evaluation. He had reported to a mission board on the feasibility of some proposed work, and then gone on to general pronouncements on Indian policy. In them he blithely confessed: "Of course I have a definite bias—"; "I have always believed—"; "So I am prejudiced"; "However, this is only a personal opinion, made without too much knowledge of the facts." My comment still stands: "He has disqualified himself, and anything he says is suspect."

I am thinking of another experience. Some fullblood Oklahoma Creeks asked me to meet them at an Indian church. They gave directions but added, "Anybody can tell you where it is." I turned at what I thought was the right corner, but after driving through hills and blackjacks I feared I had missed the road. I came to a large, well-equipped school. It was recess and the children were out on the playground. About half of them were Indians. I found several teachers gathered in one of the rooms visiting, and asked them where the church was. Not one of them had ever heard of it. Then I went outside and found out from some Indian children on a teeter board that it was on top of the next hill about a quarter of a mile away. The only reason that it did not show from the school was that the undergrowth was too thick. It was set in an extensive clearing with camp houses and brush arbors all around it. No doubt it had been an important community meeting place two generations before the white people ever came to that locality. The brush hid it from the schoolhouse, but there was a denser thicket in the minds of those teachers of Indian children obscuring their intellectual and spiritual view.

Two years ago I taught a course in Indian history to thirty-six men and women, teachers of Indian children in public schools, Indian Bureau schools, and mission schools, who had come for seven weeks of intensive training in the Indian field through lectures, seminars, tours, reading, and the exchange of experiences. They were a selected group, with a mental attitude very different from the closed mind of the church official or the mindlessness of the teachers in the Creek settlement. One would think that with their sensitivity and understanding and their firsthand knowledge, they had no need of further insights, but I have never seen any other students so eager to learn more. They listened avidly to the lectures, read in the library far beyond their assigned six hundred pages a week, and purchased armloads of books to carry home. It is through their insistence that I am presenting my course in book form.

I hope it will give basic information, not only for persons who work with Indians, but for all Americans of good will. For as Oliver La Farge once wrote, "We, the United States, have undertaken a serious experiment. Belatedly, we have set out to help some four hundred thousand people [550,000 now]—reared in a totally different culture under utterly different circumstances, the remnant that has survived our aggression—to adapt themselves to our culture with benefit to themselves and to us."

To carry out this task we need all the resources we can acquire, something more than preconceived prejudices or comfortable ignorance. I have written this book because I believe the best way to begin is by a general historical survey. Naturally I have had to rely on the work of many scholars in specialized areas. Documentation was not only impractical, but impossible. Instead I have suggested further readings, selected mainly, I must confess, on the basis of my personal preferences. If I have recommended too many books by my own publisher, it may be due partially to my greater familiarity with them, but I like to think it is because of the surpassing achievements of the University of Oklahoma Press in the Indian field.

I have an even stronger justification for what might seem an undue emphasis on the history of Oklahoma Indians. This state had the largest Indian population of any state in the Union—one third of the total in the whole country—until the rapidly growing Navaho tribe brought Arizona to the lead; but the reason lies deeper than that. It had been set aside as an Indian Territory, the focus of Indian policy through most of the nineteenth century. It became the home of tribes representative of the diverse life ways of the entire United States except those of the Pueblos, the desert dwellers, and the Alaska natives. The liquidation of tribes and reservations that began in 1887 reached its climax here: in its completeness and finality, in the value of the property, the dispersion of the people, and the violence and strength of the supplanting regime. Thus in many ways the history of Oklahoma Indians is an epitome of Indian history.

What have we learned from these centuries of cruelty or blundering on the one side and tragedy on the other? In the dark days of the 1950s I tried to sum up the essence of it all in an attempt to formulate an enlightened policy.

"These principles are: protect the Indians' land (including timber, minerals, water, all natural resources) and give them a chance by revolving credit to develop it; provide them with vocational and educational training equal to that of other citizens; assist Indians who *choose* to leave their own neighborhoods in *voluntary* relocation; encourage instead of thwarting tribal organization, and recognize the Indians' need for their own social groupings; resist the temptation to direct Indians' private lives; consult Indians freely in formulating policies and reject any that are not approved by the tribes involved. (With regard to the last, it is remarkable in looking back two hundred years to see how Indians have been almost uniformly right in their judgment of policies affecting their interests.)

"The result would be: some people living happily and prosperously on their own land and making an economic contribution to our common country; and some individuals living an adjusted life in white society. This is as far as we need to go with them. Whether or not it would result eventually in complete amalgamation—the disappearance of Indians as Indians—is immaterial. Give them a chance to live now, and the future will depend on natural evolution."

Subsequent experiences have not caused me to change these conclusions.

ANGIE DEBO

Marshall, Oklahoma

CONTENTS

Preface to the Seventh Printing   *page v*
Preface to the First Printing   *vii*
1. The Indians in Their Homeland   3
2. The White Man Comes   19
3. The White Man Stays   36
4. Caught in the Power Struggle   69
5. A New Power Rises   84
6. The New Power Advances   101
7. An "Indian Territory" Is Established   117
8. History Repeats Itself   150
9. The Indian Territory Joins the White Man's War   168
10. The White Man's War Affects the Frontiers   184
11. Reconstruction in the Indian Territory   201
12. Hunters of the Plains Settle in the Indian Territory   215
13. North Plains and Northwest Tribes
    Fight for Their Homelands   233
14. The Apaches Make Their Last Stand   267
15. Now the Reservations   284
16. Breaking Up the Reservations   299
17. What Happened to the Indians?   316
18. The White Man Repents   332
19. Back to the Old Bad Days   349
20. The White Man Gets a New Chance   383
21. The Indians Find New Hope   405
    Selected Readings   423
    Index   429

ILLUSTRATIONS

Natchez life	*page* 51
Indians found by Raleigh	52
Pocahontas	53
Wichita grass house	54
Mandan village	55
Indians of the Northwest Coast	56
Aleuts	57
Onondaga village	58
French Castle	59
Kickapoo bark house	60
North Plains Indians moving camp	61
Rendezvous on Green River	62
Sioux hunting buffalo	63
Sioux camp at Pine Ridge	64
Ba-da-ah-chon-du	65
Hopi pueblo of Walpi	66
Apache family group	131
Joseph Brant	132
Little Turtle	133
Tecumseh	134
Tenskwatawa	135
Opothle Yahola	136
Osceola	137
Rabbit Skin Leggings	138
No Horns on His Head	139
Tilaukait	140
Tamahas	141
Sequoyah	142
John Ross	143
Stand Watie	144
Oktarharsars Harjo, or Sands	145
Navaho woman and baby	146

George Bent and his wife   *page* 243
Cherokee capitol   244
Potawatomi girls   245
Satanta   246
Satank   247
Chief Joseph   248
Sitting Bull   249
Little Wolf and Dull Knife   250
Geronimo   251
Young Apache prisoners   252
Comanche girls   253
Chitto Harjo   254
Jason Betzinez   255
Pleasant Porter   256
Niganithat   257
Okmulgee Council   258

Modern Florida Seminoles   355
Children of Tesuque Pueblo   356
Fort Apache cattle   357
Guy Okakok   358
John Wooden Legs   359
Howard Rock and La Verne Madigan   360
Chief Andrew Isaac   361
Successful urban Indians   362
Third Annual OIO Youth Conference   363
Church of Taos Pueblo   364
Paul Bernal on the shore of Blue Lake   365
Governor Severino Martinez of Taos Pueblo   366
Navaho capital at Window Rock   367
Regents of Navajo Community College   368–69
Zuni women baking   370

MAPS

Western Trails   *page* 152
The Indian Territory, 1888   206
Alaska   384
Indian Reservations in the "Lower 48," 1969   406

xiv

A HISTORY OF THE INDIANS OF THE UNITED STATES

"They wanted my country and I was in trouble defending it."—CHITTO HARJO

CHAPTER ONE

THE INDIANS IN
THEIR HOMELAND

They were a people beginning—
With beliefs,
Ornament, language, fables, love of children
(You will find that spoken of in all the books.)
And a scheme of life that worked.[1]

Although these aboriginal Americans varied widely from the "western" stereotype—they did not all live in tipis, wear Sioux war bonnets, or speak one "Indian language"—yet they had many common characteristics. These have influenced their history, persist to the present day in their descendants, and form their unique contribution to the American spirit.

Notable was their adaptation to their physical environment. While the white man sought to dominate and change the natural setting, the Indian subordinated himself to it. Geronimo, the wild Apache raider, looking back on his loved homeland after years of exile expressed it thus:

"For each tribe of men Usen created He also made a home. In the land for any particular tribe He placed whatever would be best for the welfare of that tribe.

"When Usen created the Apaches He also gave them their homes in the West. He gave them such grain, fruits, and game as they needed to eat. . . . He gave them a pleasant climate and all they needed for clothing and shelter was at hand.

"Thus it was in the beginning: the Apaches and their homes each created for the other by Usen himself. When they are taken from these homes they sicken and die."

Incidentally, this upside-down logic, this reversal of cause and effect as the white man would see it, is also typically Indian. The Indian

---

[1] From *Western Star*, by Stephen Vincent Bénét (published by Holt, Rinehart & Winston, Inc.). Copyright 1943 by Rosemary Carr Bénét; reprinted by permission of Brandt & Brandt.

3

thought with his emotions instead of his mind. But his feelings were—and are—true. He had an integrity of spirit deeper than conscious reasoning.

Geronimo's statement hints at another Indian characteristic, his love for his homeland, which amounted to a mystical identification with it. This is difficult for the white man to understand. When Garry, of the Spokanes of eastern Washington,[2] said, "I was born by these waters. The earth here is my mother," he was not using a poetic figure of speech; he was stating what he felt to be the literal truth. Toohoolhoolzote, a chief of the Nez Percés, fighting to keep his land, said, "The earth is part of my body and I never gave up the earth." Fifteen hundred miles away in embryo Oklahoma, a region as remote to Garry and Toohoolhoolzote as the other side of the moon, Eufaula Harjo exhorted the participants in the ceremonials of the old Creek town of Tulsa, "The mountains and hills, that you see, are your backbone, and the gullies and the creeks, which are between the hills and mountains, are your heart veins." When the white man cut up this living entity with his surveying instruments, the Indian felt the horror of dismemberment.

All this, in a way not subject to analysis, was a part of the Indian's religion, for he was deeply religious. The familiar shapes of earth, the changing sky, the wild animals he knew, were joined with his own spirit in mystical communion. The powers of nature, the personal quest of the soul, the acts of daily life, the solidarity of the tribe—all were religious, and were sustained by dance and ritual.

Out of all this grew the feeling for beauty that makes the modern Indian superbly gifted in the various art forms. It is not an accident that a disproportionate number of Indians are among the great American dancers. The steps and discipline of the ballet are foreign to native experience, but the feel is there. Indian laborers are in demand as strawberry pickers in the Oklahoma Ozarks, for nobody but an Indian would arrange a box of berries with an eye to artistic effect. The beautiful penmanship of beginning Indian children is well known. A freighter on the Chisholm Trail visiting the Cheyenne school at Concho, Indian Territory, in 1880, recorded his impressions: "Their writing and drawing would beat the Kansas schools, but in spelling and

---

[2] Throughout this book I have used the modern names of states and locations except where clarification is needed. This saves the repetition of "present-day Washington" or "what is now Washington."

arithmetic they are lost." This of young Indians only five years removed from life on the buffalo plains.

The Indians' eloquence in the use of language, even when clumsily interpreted, has been marked throughout their history. Now this sensibility joined with education and skill in English usage is finding modern literary expression. In the Institute of American Indian Arts, a new specialized boarding school for Indian teenagers at Santa Fe, is a small class in creative writing. New Mexico State University conducts an annual Creative Writing Awards Program open to high school students throughout the state. In a recent year there were 816 entries, of which eighteen were selected by the university for publication; and of these eighteen, six were the contributions of Institute students. One-third of the eighteen who placed out of the 816!

Their teacher, Terry Allen of the T. D. Allen husband-wife writing team, started them out on a combination of fact and imagination for their first assignment: "The story of your life from the time you were born until you are thirty years old." A Navaho boy, who had known no English until he started to school, wrote with such perceptive insight that she encouraged him to complete the story and publish it. The resulting book[3] has been characterized as a succession of "sharp-edged images . . . providing glimpses of meaning that few non-Indians have ever seen before." Once, preparing to write, the young writer "got wound up" by dashing off a poem about a winged seed that drifted to his desk:

> The drifting lonely seed,
>   Came past my barred window,
> Whirling orbit, it landed before me,
>   As though it were a woolly lamb—
> Untouched, untamed, and alone—
>   Walked atop my desk, stepping daintily.

These young Institute students are not a selected group; or rather the selection is in reverse. In many cases they have been sent to boarding school because of a disrupted home situation. And their achievements in painting, sculpture, ceramics, design, music, and drama are as astounding as their literary expression.

This Indian creativity has received striking recent recognition in the awarding of the 1969 Pulitzer Prize in fiction to N. Scott Momaday

[3] Emerson Blackhorse Mitchell and T. D. Allen, *Miracle Hill*.

5

for his novel, *House Made of Dawn*. It depicts the adjustment problems of a returned Indian war veteran torn between his native heritage and the world outside. The thirty-five-year-old author is a former Oklahoman, the son of a fullblood Kiowa artist father and a French-English-Choctaw mother.

None of this helped the Indians in their encounter with the white man. On the contrary, their temperamental and personality traits were a handicap. Industrious and thrifty in their own way, they lacked the ruthless driving force of the invading race and they had no experience to meet it. In 1906, shortly before Oklahoma statehood, when all that new frontier was bursting with a frenzy of development and the Indians were left stranded and helpless, Pleasant Porter, the wise old mixed-blood chief of the Creeks, made a thoughtful analysis to a committee of the United States Senate. "It is a complex problem, gentlemen. . . . You are the evolution of thousands of years, perhaps. . . . We both probably started at the same point, but our paths diverged, and the influences to which we were subjected varied, and we see the result."

Even now Indian children do not want to "show off" in the classroom, and the Indian with a good job is pulled down by the needs of his numerous relatives. For 350 years an attempt has been made—a faltering attempt, but always present—to acquaint the Indians with the white Americans' economic techniques, but they have produced few business or industrial leaders. Even an organizing genius like Tecumseh depended upon emotional appeal and a mystical union with the unseen world rather than a drive for prestige.

There was one exception in many tribes—the attainment of distinction through war honors. Thus war as an exciting contest of courage and skill was a necessity. One time in 1724 the Creeks offered to mediate between the Senecas and the Cherokees, who were having a good time collecting each other's hair, but the Senecas explained that they could not afford to make peace, "We have no people to war against nor yet no meal to eat but the Cherokees." In their more deadly wars with the white man, chiefs convinced that peace was their only salvation always complained that they could not restrain their "crazy young men." Actually that was the only way in which these youths could rise to advancement in the tribe. This warriors' code probably accounts for the admiration they often felt for army officers and their willingness to enlist as scouts, sometimes even against their own people. But the thirst for military glory was not universal. Many tribes, like the seden-

6

tary Pueblos, fought bravely, but only in self-defense. Peace making was a highly emotional procedure involving beads and tobacco and other esoteric symbols.

In his relations with the white man the Indian had little capacity for compromise, for pliant yielding to the inevitable in order to salvage what he could. He entered into a treaty and learned its provisions and never admitted its abrogation. When the populous tribes of the Gulf and southern Appalachian region were removed to the present Oklahoma, their treaties guaranteed that their tribal autonomy would be perpetual. But conditions changed, their country was flooded with white settlers, and Congress liquidated the Indian regime in preparation for statehood. Two excerpts from many pages of testimony, taken through interpreters, before an unsympathetic senatorial committee illustrate the working of the fullblood mind—its dogged persistence, its strong religious trust (by this time these Indians were Christians), and, in spite of all evidence to the contrary, its ultimate dependence upon the good faith of the American government.

Redbird Smith, a Cherokee, showed the senators a photograph of the original patent to his tribe and an eagle feather that had been given to his great-grandfather at the negotiation of the removal treaty. He insisted, "I say that I will never change; before our God, I won't. It extends to Heaven, the great treaty that has been made with the Government of the United States. Our treaty wherever it extends is respected by the Creator, God. Our nations and governments all look to our God."

Said Willis F. Toby, a Choctaw fullblood, "I am still faithful to the Great Father of the United States, who made this treaty with the Indians, and I am faithful to that treaty, and the Almighty God that rules the world, I trust in him, and he will stand as the guardian of my people."

They never did change. Twenty-five years later they were still sending delegations to Washington working to erase the vigorous, growing state of Oklahoma from the map and restore the old untroubled life that had gone forever. Obviously, in view of the relative strength of the two races, the refusal to adjust to the irrevocable was very damaging to their own interests.

This same habit of quiet withdrawal was—and still is—used in other circumstances. The Indian wanted to be with his own people, to preserve his inner values, his cultural integrity. To this desire he owes his remarkable record of survival, the preservation of his distinctive

7

identity, through centuries of encroachment by a more numerous and aggressive race; but it has been baffling to well-meaning "civilizers" determined to throw him into the melting pot. White settlers come in to a thriving Indian Baptist or Methodist church and innocently attempt to integrate it. The result is a white congregation with no Indian members. A home demonstration agent has an enthusiastic club of Indian women—good housekeepers from primitive times, they are eager to learn more effective methods. Then an order comes from above to integrate them with the white home extension clubs of the community. They quietly quit.

Passive resistance was carried to the ultimate extreme. The Indian could die, simply because he would not adapt to what he could not willingly accept. Pleasant Porter, with a philosophical understanding that few white men have attained, explained it to investigators from the Board of Indian Commissioners in 1903:

". . . There is no life in the people that have lost their institutions. Evolving a thing out of itself is natural, transplanting it is a matter of dissolution, not growth. . . .

"Q. You told us a moment ago they were dying off pretty fast?

"A. Yes, sir, the older people are.

"Q. Is there any special cause for that?

"A. Nothing; there is no new disease; I don't see anything other than the want of hope."

This trait accounts for the appalling loss of life when Indians were torn from their homeland. Tribes migrated voluntarily with no damage, and in times of emergency the efficiency and dispatch with which they could travel long distances is almost incredible; but any forcible uprooting carries the same dreary statistics. For example: 418 Nez Percés brought from their mountain homeland in 1877 to be imprisoned briefly at Fort Leavenworth and then settled in the Indian Territory, 367 survivors allowed to return in 1885; 24,000 Creeks enumerated by name and town before their forced removal in 1836, only 13,537 by the census of 1859, after they had begun to recover somewhat from their grief and despair. The same story can be repeated many times with widely separated tribes. Geronimo was statistically correct when he said of the Apaches, "When they are taken from these homes they sicken and die."

This universality of intellectual and spiritual traits is surprising in view of the Indians' great diversity in language and physical characteristics. It is impossible to determine whether this divergence origi-

8

nated before they crossed from Asia to the American continent, or whether it developed during the uncounted millenniums when they settled and intermarried in small bands apart. It is readily observed wherever a fullblood group congregates, whether in church or council or dance. Within each is a uniformity of feature and body structure never found in a similar assembly of white Americans; but these groups differ widely from each other. For convenience they are usually classified according to language families known as linguistic stocks. The tribes within these larger groupings did not necessarily recognize their relationship. Although ethnologists may find traces of common beliefs and customs, these tribes were sometimes separated by great distances or even by traditional enmity.

Among the most important linguistic stocks are the Iroquoian, the Algonquian, the Muskhogean, the Siouan, the Caddoan, the Athapascan, the Shoshonean, the Piman, the Yuman, the Salishan, the Shahaptian, the Lituamian, and the Koluschan. Besides these are the Euchees, which are not known to have a linguistic relationship to any other tribe; the Pueblos, who although of four diverse linguistic stocks are usually classed as one group; and the Kiowas, distantly related to one Pueblo stock. Non-Indian natives of Alaska are the Eskimos and the Aleuts.

Among the Iroquoian tribes was the powerful League of the Iroquois of central and western New York. It consisted of the Five Nations—Mohawks, Oneidas, Onondagas, Cayugas, and Senecas—later the Six Nations when joined by the Tuscaroras of North Carolina. Other Iroquoians were the Hurons, on the upper St. Lawrence and the area east of Lake Huron, and the Cherokees, of the southern Appalachian region and the adjoining areas of Georgia and Alabama.

Surrounding these Iroquoian enclaves were the many Algonquian tribes extending along the Atlantic seaboard from Virginia north to the St. Lawrence and west to the Mississipi and beyond. It was Algonquian tribes that first met the Jamestown and Plymouth colonists, and an Algonquian tribe, the Delaware, that made the treaty with William Penn. Around the Great Lakes were the Ottawas, the tribe of the celebrated Pontiac; and in the Ohio country lived the Shawnees, the tribe of the great Tecumseh. The allied Sauk and Fox tribes first lived in Wisconsin, but moved southward. Black Hawk was a Sauk leader, and the Kickapoos and Potawatomis were their friends. The Chippewas (or Ojibwas) extended into northern Minnesota and Wisconsin from Canada. The Cheyennes and Arapahos moved from

Wisconsin and Minnesota to the buffalo plains; and the Blackfeet, most westerly of Algonquian tribes, lived on the upper Missouri and the adjoining part of Canada.

The Muskhogean people included the populous tribes of the Gulf region. Among them was the Creek Confederacy occupying most of Georgia and Alabama. Its nucleus consisted of several tribal towns of the Muskogees proper, who had a tradition of western origin with high mountains forming "the backbone of the world," a migration toward the sunrise, the crossing of a great and muddy river, and the occupation and conquest of their eastern home. Later they were joined by their relatives, the Alabamas, the Coushattas, the Hitchitees, and the Tuskegees. Then as the great Confederacy grew in power and influence, it was joined by fragments of unrelated tribes, refugees from white encroachment or Indian wars. Among these were the Euchees and several bands of Algonquian Shawnees. Survivors of the Natchez also fled to the Creeks. This was a distinctive Muskhogean tribe of the lower Mississippi, which had an elaborate system of sun worship, a hereditary nobility, and a royal family of divine attributes and prerogatives.

An offshoot of the Creeks was the Seminole tribe of Florida. The name, *Seminole*, means "wild," or "those who camp at a distance," a term equivalent to the white American's "frontiersman." For a time the Seminoles remained members of the Creek Confederacy, but being separated from their kinsmen by the white man's international boundary, they became an independent tribe.

West of the Creeks were the numerous and prosperous Choctaws, also a Muskhogean people with a tradition of western origin. They lived in Mississippi and adjoining regions of Louisiana and Alabama. North of them were their traditional kinsmen, the Chickasaws, of northern Mississippi and western Tennessee. These two tribes had separated so recently that they spoke an almost identical language.

The Siouan people may have circled along the Gulf and southern Atlantic, for the small Biloxi tribe of Mississippi and the Catawbas of the Carolina region spoke a Siouan language. (Both joined the Creek Confederacy, and some Catawbas are still living in Oklahoma.) But the main Siouan tribes lived in the great central area: the Winnebagos in Wisconsin; the Sioux proper (or Dakotas) first in Minnesota and finally on the northern buffalo plains; the Osages in Missouri, but hunting and sometimes establishing settlements on the prairies of Oklahoma; the Quapaws in Arkansas; the Iowas, Otos and Missouris, Kansas (or Kaws), Poncas, and Omahas on the Missouri River and its tributaries in Iowa and eastern Nebraska; the Crows ranging the region between the upper Platte and Yellowstone rivers; and the Mandans, who occupied two permanent villages on the Missouri near the present Bismarck, North Dakota.

The Caddoan linguistic stock comprises the Caddos proper, who lived on the lower Red River in northwestern Louisiana, southwestern Arkansas, and northeastern Texas; the Wichitas, between the Arkansas River in Kansas and the Brazos River of Texas; the Pawnees, on the Kansas River in Kansas and the Platte and Republican rivers in Nebraska; and the Arikaras (often called Ricarees or Rees), who lived along the Missouri River south of the Mandans.

The Shoshonean people includes the Shoshonis proper, extending from the desert regions of southern California through the Great Basin to the rivers and mountains of southern Idaho and western Wyoming; the Paiutes of the Great Basin; the Utes from the eastern edge of the Great Basin through western and central Colorado; the Bannocks of southern Idaho; the Hopi Pueblos of Arizona; and the Comanches, an offshoot of the Shoshonis, who came out on the Great Plains and migrated southward ranging from southwestern Kansas through western Texas and eastern New Mexico and raiding as far as Durango in Mexico. The Shoshonean forms one branch of a greater linguistic family, the Uto-Aztecan, which includes the Aztecs and other advanced peoples of Mexico and Central America. Another branch is the Piman of southern Arizona and northwestern Mexico, of which the Pima proper, the Papago, and the Yaqui are the most important tribes.

The Comanches' migration from the mountains to the Great Plains and southward was paralleled by a similar movement of the Kiowas, who came from the headwaters of the Missouri and Yellowstone in western Montana, lived for a time in the Black Hills of South Dakota, and eventually settled between the Arkansas and Red rivers in southwestern Kansas, western Oklahoma, and the Texas Panhandle. As they moved south they fought the Comanches until the two tribes made peace about 1790, from which time they were closely associated.

The Athapascan people consists of several Apache tribes of the plains and mountains of New Mexico and Arizona and the Sierra Madre of Mexico; the Kiowa-Apaches, who formed an integral part of the Kiowa tribe; the Navahos of New Mexico and Arizona; and many tribes occupying an immense area in Alaska and western Canada. Islands of stability set among the widely ranging Athapascans of the Southwest were the permanent villages of the Pueblos.

Less advanced than the Pueblos were the Indians of the Yuman linguistic stock, who lived in the deserts and canyons close to the lower Colorado in Arizona and Nevada and adjacent parts of California. The most important tribe is the Yuma proper. Others are the Mohave, the Hualapai, the Yavapai, and the Havasupai.

Indians of the Salishan linguistic family occupied most of Washington and neighboring areas of Idaho, Montana, and British Columbia. The most important tribe was the Flathead of western Montana. The Kalispels and Coeur d'Alenes lived in Idaho and eastern Washington west of the Flatheads, and the Spokanes west of *them* in eastern Washington. Other tribes lived along the coast (the Nisqualli at the south end of Puget Sound) and along the central Columbia.

The Shahaptian people occupied the lower Columbia east of the Cascades and the lower reaches of the Snake River. The principal tribe was the Nez Percé of the beautiful plateau country of central Idaho and eastern Oregon and Washington. Close Shahaptian neighbors were the Walla Wallas and Palouses, who lived northwest of the Nez Percé country, the Umatillas in north-central Oregon, and the Yakimas of south-central Washington. Other inhabitants of the Pacific Northwest were the Indians of the Lituamian linguistic stock, comprising the Modocs and Klamaths, whose home was in northern California and south-central Oregon.[4]

In Alaska, besides the widespread Athapascans, there were the Tlinget tribes of the Koluschan linguistic stock of the islands and coastland of the southeastern strip that runs along British Columbia. The Haidas, an unrelated people of the Queen Charlotte Islands, also extended into the tip of this Alaskan strip. The non-Indian Eskimos live mainly in the northern and western areas, on Kodiak Island, and in a few settlements scattered through other parts of the state. The Aleuts inhabit the Alaska Peninsula and the chain of Aleutian Islands extending beyond its tip, and a strip along the coast to the east. They speak an Eskimauan language, but in other respects are more Indian than Eskimo.

[4] The most convenient reference for a large proportion of these tribes is Muriel H. Wright, *A Guide to the Indian Tribes of Oklahoma*. This book is not so limited in scope as might be implied; its sixty-five entries include not only Indians from the eastern seaboard to the Rocky Mountains, but a few from the Far West.

With so great a range of climate, topography, and flora and fauna, people conforming as did the aboriginal inhabitants of the United States to their physical background developed a great diversity of culture. It should be noted that none of them had any domestic animals except the dog, and of domestic fowls, turkeys were raised only by the Pueblos. Most of them made pottery and baskets, and many practiced agriculture—raising corn, beans, squashes, pumpkins, and tobacco, all New World products. But their practices differed widely.

Most of the area east of the Mississippi was a rich country heavily forested. There the Indians lived in settled villages of substantial houses made with a framework of poles covered with mats or bark or plastered with mud mixed with straw. Many of them protected their villages by palisades of closely set poles driven into the ground. They cleared the land by girdling the larger trees and burning the underbrush and planted their crops. They also picked and stored quantities of the nuts and wild fruits with which their country abounded; and they killed deer, bear, and other animals, and caught fish from their streams and rivers. They had many ceremonials, of which the most important centered around the harvesting of the corn.

They traded extensively with each other, traveling by established trails or on their many rivers, using birchbark canoes in the north, dugouts or rafts in the south. They had well-defined patterns of war and friendship, usually based on traditional relationships in a legendary past. (For example, the Delawares were regarded as the "grandfather" by other Algonquian woodland tribes.)

The League of the Iroquois was formed in the sixteenth century according to historical records, much earlier by archeological evidence. Each tribe retained its identity, but the union was strong enough to bind them together throughout their separate history. The Creek Confederacy was made up of fifty or more towns with outlying villages. Each town had a smoothly functioning local government, and the town chiefs came together in council to decide matters of interest to the whole. The Confederacy was loosely organized (it had two main divisions—the Upper on the Coosa and Tallapoosa rivers and the Lower on the Flint and Chattahoochie—which sometimes acted separately, and smaller sectional groupings were sometimes formed) but, in general, it acted with surprising unanimity.

The Creek town is typical of the economic and social life of the populous tribes of the Southeast. At its center were the public buildings, set on terraces in the more important towns. Here was the "square," formed of four shed-like structures enclosing an open space of hard-packed earth with the sacred communal fire in the center. In these the men sat in council, seated according to official rank, to decide matters of war and peace, planting and hunting, disputes between citizens, and other affairs of the town. Just off the corner of the square was a tall conical building, the "hot house," where the people met for business or recreation during inclement weather. Close by was the chunkey yard, a level sunken rectangle surrounded with banks for the seating of spectators; this was the place for games and informal dancing. Grouped around the public center with some semblance of a street arrangement were the individual dwellings, each usually consisting of from one to four separate buildings—cook room, winter lodging house, granary, and so on—arranged around a little square similar to the town square.

Close to each dwelling was a private garden plot tended by the women, but the main food supply was grown on a large field belonging to the town. It was laid out in family plots, but the planting and cultivating was done by the whole town working together under the orders of the chief, who worked side by side with the other citizens. The town also turned out together for the harvesting, but each family gathered the produce of its own plot and placed it in its own storehouse. Each also contributed voluntarily to a public store which was kept in a large building in the field and was used under the direction of the town chief for public needs.[5]

The Cherokee town had a similar economic, social, and political organization. Of particular authority were the seven "mother towns," in earliest times the headquarters of the seven clans. Each served as a sort of capital of the towns of the surrounding area. Over the whole tribe were officials with headquarters in an important town, but this central authority was very weak. With the small, warlike Chickasaw tribe the central organization overshadowed the town, while the peaceable, materially minded Choctaws began early to spread out from the towns into the surrounding countryside.

Just as the religious and ceremonial life of the woodland Indians centered around the corn, that of the Plains tribes centered around the buffalo and the worship of the sun, which was so conspicuous in their big sky. Members of the Coronado expedition in 1541 recorded the

[5] Many books have been written about the customs of these Southeastern tribes. The description of Creek life is taken from Angie Debo, *The Road to Disappearance.*

14

first description of the life way of these people when they encountered the Apaches on the High Plains of the Texas Panhandle.

"These Indians subsist . . . entirely on cattle [buffalo], for they neither plant nor harvest maize. With the skins they build their houses; with the skins they clothe and shoe themselves; from the skins they make ropes and also obtain wool. From the sinews they make thread, with which they sew their clothing and likewise their tents. From the bones they shape awls and the dung they use for firewood, since there is no other fuel in all that land. . . .

"They are a gentle people, not cruel, faithful in their friendship, and skilled in the use of signs. [Remember, the writer was describing Apaches!] They dry their meat in the sun, cutting it into thin slices, and when it is dry they grind it, like flour, for storage and for making mash to eat. They cook it in a pot, which they always manage to have with them. When they put a handful in the pot, the mash soon fills it, since it swells to great size." The chronicler admired their skill in tanning buffalo hides and deerskins. They had an active trade with the Pueblos, trading skins and dried meat for corn and cotton cloth. The writer described their manner of setting up their tipis and their habit of moving from place to place—"for they have no permanent residence anywhere, since they follow the cattle to obtain food"—using their dogs as pack animals or making travois from their trailing tipi poles.

As time passed, the Indians acquired horses from the Spaniards, and life on the Plains became glorious. Their clothing of deerskin dripping with fringe made a striking effect as they rode. All were superb riders, and the men spent much time perfecting their skill and training special mounts for buffalo hunting and war. If they needed to cross a river, they quickly made a frame of branches and covered it with buffalo skin to make a fragile tub-shaped boat.

As life on the Plains became more inviting with the use of horses, more tribes moved out there, the Sioux and Cheyennes and Arapahos from the east, the Comanches and Kiowas from the west. Some abandoned their agriculture entirely and based their economy on the buffalo herds—"We lost the corn," say the Cheyennes. Others like the Osages maintained their fixed residences, where they planted their crops, rode out to the Plains for their supply of meat, and returned to harvest their corn and settle down for the winter.

The economic rhythm of the Kiowa year is typical of the buffalo-hunting culture and of the proud individualism of the Plains tribes. Their great fall hunt in early October was their time of harvest. Runners were sent ahead to select suitable campsites. Then the men killed, and the women prepared and dried the meat and stretched and pegged the hides. The Kiowas then went into winter camp, setting their tipis by a stream. There the men worked over their year's supply of weapons, braided their lariats and bridles, and fashioned their saddles; and the women tanned and decorated the skins and made the clothing. The winter camp was also a time of relaxation and recreation. When spring came, the Kiowas packed their tipis and began their summer wandering over the prairies, breaking up into small groups and killing only enough game for their immediate needs. The summer was also the time for military exploits, with bands of young men carrying out horse stealing and raiding projects of their own. At times they met as a tribe for ceremonials (especially the sun dance) and the settlement of important matters in council. Then certain leaders stood out as head chiefs, maintaining their ascendancy through wisdom in council and bravery in war. Meanwhile the buffaloes were fattening, and with October came another time of laying in the year's supply of skins and meat.[6]

Strangely enough, there were Plains tribes that never adopted the typical Plains culture. These included the Caddoan tribes and the Mandans. Although they hunted buffalo, they lived in permanent villages and practiced agriculture. The Wichitas made their dwellings of grass woven on a frame of poles and withes; the Pawnees, Arikaras, and Mandans lived in strong houses of timber covered with earth.

Randolph B. Marcy described a Wichita village on Rush Creek, near the present Rush Springs, Oklahoma, which he visited in 1853. "Their lodges are about twenty-five feet in diameter at the base, twenty feet high, and in the distance have very much the appearance of a group of hay-stacks." He characterized the interior arrangements as "such, that every person has a bunk, raised from the ground and covered with buffalo-hides, forming a couch which is far from being uncomfortable. When seated around the fires in the centre of the lodges, they have an air of domestic happiness about them which I did not expect to find."

In the Southwest the Pueblos lived in multistoried houses of stone or adobe, remaining in the same location for centuries and growing their crops by irrigation. They obtained their meat by hunting, but raised and wove cotton for their clothing and excelled in pottery. Their

[6] An account of Kiowa life as told by old-time Kiowas is given in Alice Marriott, *The Ten Grandmothers*.

ceremonials and artistic decorations stressed—and still stress—the importance of rain.[7]

The Navahos were distributed over great reaches of desert, planting crops where they could on the floors of canyons and arroyos. They brought logs long distances from their timbered mountain slopes to build solid circular hogans, covering the roofs and sometimes the walls with earth. They acquired sheep from the Spaniards and became great shepherds, and they learned weaving from the Pueblos and became skilled weavers of the wool. They had—and have—a complex ceremonial life based on harmony with unseen spiritual forces, but until recently they had no organized government. Their Apache relatives were pursued with such implacable hostility by the Spaniards that they took refuge in the mountains, living largely by raiding, traveling incredible distances when pursued, building slight wickiups of brush that could be easily abandoned, but pausing when they could to raise corn and to gather and store edible wild plants.

The Piman and Yuman tribes practiced a frugal agriculture, carefully irrigating from the few streams of their desert land. Some of the tribes along the Colorado lived in canyons. The Havasupai, especially, lived—and still live—at the bottom of a branch of the Grand Canyon, where they had their houses and storage places. In the fall they made the difficult climb to the upland and spent the winter there gathering native products and killing small game.[8]

The Indians of the Great Basin and the California desert utilized all the resources of their poor country. They wandered over it in small family groups, gathering seeds and nuts, digging roots, and snaring rabbits and other small animals. They made their clothing from the desert plants, weaving strings of sagebrush or desert willow into a sort of mat to serve as a scanty garment and weaving a winter wrap from strips of rabbit fur. Their dwellings were temporary, made of branches covered with bunches of grass or desert bushes, and in winter they covered the whole with earth. Above all other Indians they excelled in basketry. A sociable people, they occasionally gathered in larger groups for ceremonials, dances, and communal rabbit drives, but they had no organized tribal governments.[9]

[7] An interesting description of Pueblo life and the making of pottery is Alice Marriott, *Maria: The Potter of San Ildefonso*.

[8] An account of their life may be found in Flora Gregg Iliff, *People of the Blue Water*.

[9] Their life way is conveniently summarized in the first chapter of Virginia Cole Trenholm and Maurine Carley, *The Shoshonis*.

17

Elsewhere in California lived many—perhaps 250—small, self-sufficient tribes, with life ways corresponding to the great diversity of physical setting. They practiced no agriculture, gathering and storing wild products, whether of inland valley, rugged upland, or forest. They killed deer or water fowl where these abounded, or caught and dried the salmon that came up the northern rivers. Living in a warm climate, they built the lightest of shelters and wore the scantiest of clothing. From tribelet to tribelet they differed widely in physical characteristics and social customs and beliefs, developing poise and responsible conduct from life in a small, ingrown society.[10]

The Indians of the Pacific Northwest lived in a land of rich natural resources. They depended largely on the salmon runs, catching the great fish in skillfully made traps. They killed elk, deer, mountain sheep, and bear, and some tribes made trips over the mountains to the buffalo plains. Their country abounded in wild fruit and succulent roots, and their camass meadows were greatly valued. Some of them lived in pit houses, sunk four feet below the surface of the ground with an overhead framework of poles covered with mats or hides. Among their dances was the *chinook*, which was supposed to bring the warm wind to melt the snow. A distinctive institution was the *potlatch*, a give-away ceremony that brought pleasure to the recipients and status to the giver. These Indians had distinct social classes based on ancestry, and the royal blood of the chiefs set them apart from the common herd.

A separate culture along the coast extended north through British Columbia and included the Tlingets and Haidas of southeastern Alaska. These people felled the great trees and fashioned them into planks with their crude tools and built houses fifty or more feet long, surprisingly like the white man's farm buildings, and divided into compartments to shelter several families. They also made boats, beautifully shaped and decorated, carrying thirty men and capable of ocean voyages for whaling or fishing. They carved the soft cedar into grotesquely shaped totem poles that stood by their houses.

Thus the United States was inhabited by a self-sufficient people before the coming of the white man.

[10] An interpretation of California Indian culture may be found in Theodora Kroeber, *Ishi*. This is the poignant story of a wild Indian who strayed from the Stone Age into the twentieth century and found sympathy and understanding from anthropologists at the University of California.

CHAPTER TWO

THE WHITE MAN COMES

In 1906, Chitto Harjo, a Creek fullblood, gave his own interpretation of Indian history. Using an Indian rhetorical device, he traced the relations between his people and the invading Europeans as a dramatic confrontation between two individuals—"I" or "I and my people" and "Columbus" or "he." "My ancestors and my people were the inhabitants of this great country from 1492. . . . It was my home and the home of my people from time immemorial, and is to-day, I think the home of my people.

"Away back in that time—in 1492—there was a man by the name of Columbus came from across the great ocean, and he discovered this country for the white man. . . . What did he find when he first arrived here? Did he find a white man standing on this continent then. . . . I stood here first, and Columbus first discovered me. . . . I want to know what did he say to the red man at that time? . . . He told him, 'The land is all yours; the law is all yours.'"

When Columbus returned to Spain with his story of a gentle people living on new green isles, the resulting stampede was like a later-day gold rush or oil boom. The Spaniards using the West Indies as a base, fanned out in three directions across the Caribbean Sea and the Gulf of Mexico. John Cabot sailed for England along the Atlantic coast from Newfoundland to as far south probably as Delaware in 1497. The Portuguese explorer, Gaspar Corte-Real, reached Labrador and Newfoundland in 1500. The next year he kidnaped two shiploads of the natives to be sold as slaves. (Labrador means "the place of labor material.") Very soon the ships of many nations were fishing on the Newfoundland Banks. In 1524, Giovanni da Verrazano, a Florentine in French service, explored the coast from Cape Fear northward. He entered New York harbor, "a pleasant place between steep little hills, and among those hills a mighty, deep-mouthed river ran into the sea." His men launched a small craft and heard a friendly greeting from the shore. Then a crowd of men "clad in the feathers of fowls of divers hues" sprang into canoes and came to meet the strangers, but a change of wind forced the Europeans to move away. Ten years later Jacques Cartier discovered the St. Lawrence and sailed up the river to Montreal, claiming that area for France. The first encounter of the Indians with these explorers falls into a pattern: friendly curiosity and helpfulness, then, with greater experience, deepening distrust and active hostility.

In spite of these stray voyages of other Europeans, the sixteenth century of exploitation belongs to the Spaniards. Their first colony was established early in 1494 on Hispaniola by Columbus on his second voyage, and a sizable amount of gold was shipped back to Spain at the same time. By 1515 there were seventeen Spanish towns on the island; mines were being worked, and crops of grain, cotton, and sugar cane were growing, all by the labor of enslaved Indians, the same people who had welcomed Columbus so innocently on his voyage of discovery. In twenty-one years their population on this one fertile island had shrunk from a quarter of a million to fourteen thousand; in a few more years they had become extinct. But it was in 1515 that the great Bartolomé de Las Casas, the first Catholic priest to be ordained in the New World, went to Spain to intercede with Ferdinand in their behalf.

To be interested in saving souls was nothing new. Extending Christianity had been one of the chief motivations that had launched Columbus on his great adventure. The conversion of the natives was officially declared to be the prime object of his second voyage, and six priests were sent along to accomplish it. But saving souls did not include measures to keep body and soul together. The missionaries had to work fast if they were to convert any Indians before the Spanish policy of enslavement and gold tribute should wipe them out. Las Casas was the first one to accept it as part of his religious duty to influence the government to protect them.

He kept up the fight for the rest of his long life, carrying on investigations and fearlessly publishing his findings, lobbying at the court, and drafting laws for the king to sign. All this had its effect. The acts of the conquistadors were not completely restrained by the orders of the distant home government, but they were somewhat ameliorated. Almost as important to the historian—and Las Casas was a historian— he put the facts on record. The exploitation of the Indians by the other imperial powers had no Las Casas to record it.

In 1513, Juan Ponce de León, a member of Columbus' first colony, sailed from Puerto Rico with a royal patent to settle new lands and distribute the natives among the colonists. (This was the encomienda system, by which the land grant included the people to work it, an evil that was finally discredited in the era of reform.) He sailed around the east, south, and west of an "island," which he named Florida, landing at several places and finding the Indians hostile. One wonders—the Indian grapevine being what it was—whether news from the West Indies had reached the mainland. He was succeeded by a number of slave catchers. When he returned in 1521 with a second colonizing expedition, he was attacked by the Indians and killed. But by 1525 through voyages of slave hunters, explorers, and would-be colonizers, the Spanish had mapped the entire eastern and southern coast of the United States.

Meanwhile, Cortés had conquered Mexico and plundered the fabulous wealth of the Aztecs, and other Spaniards hoped to duplicate his experiences in the lands to the north. In 1528, Pánfilo de Narváez with four hundred colonists landed at Tampa Bay on the west coast of Florida. The Indians fled from their village at sight of his sails. The next day they returned and "made signs and menaces, and appeared to say we must go away from their country." Some of his colonists turned back with the ships, but he plunged inland with three hundred men, including forty armored horsemen. The Indians abandoned their villages, attacking the intruders as they advanced to the north and west. At Apalachee Bay the Spaniards decided they had had enough. They killed their horses and made frail boats of the hides, subsisting on horseflesh and the corn they found in the villages, while the watching Indians harassed them as they worked. Finally, with their force reduced to 242 men, they put to sea; and the Indians could feel that they had got rid of these particular Spaniards.

The retreating colonists skirted the coast hoping to reach Mexico. They were finally wrecked in the vicinity of Galveston Island, Texas. Here the Indians, unacquainted with the white man's way, wept at their plight, warmed them at driftwood fires, fed them with roasted fish and nuts, and sang and danced about them. Then winter came, food became scarce, and a pestilence attacked their hosts. The Span-

21

iards succumbed to various misfortunes until as time passed only five were left.

Among the survivors were the resourceful and kindly Álvar Núñez Cabeza de Vaca, who had been the treasurer of Narváez' expedition, and a Negro slave named Estevanico, or Stephen. The five were reduced to a sort of informal slavery by the Indians. Vaca became so capable a servant that the Indians entrusted him with trading trips to the interior, where he first saw the buffalo.

Vaca also became a medicine man. During that first plague-stricken winter, the Indians in desperation decided "to make us physicians, without examination or inquiring for diplomas." The Spaniards protested that they had no such power; but the Indians answered that "extraordinary men" must have such endowments and if they would not use them they should not eat. After starving for several days, Vaca decided upon a blend of Indian and Christian prayer. He blew on his patients and passed his hands over them as he had seen the witch doctor do, made the sign of the cross, and recited a paternoster and an Ave Maria. The sick recovered and Vaca devoutly thanked God.

After six years Vaca and three other captives escaped to a tribe he had met on one of his trading trips. (The fifth chose to remain with the Indians on the coast.) In this village was a very sick Indian, and again Vaca's powers were tested and his patient recovered. Here they remained with the grateful Indians until the following summer. Then they struck off across the country to the west. Everywhere they were treated with kindness, and as their fame as medicine men spread, the Indians of each village escorted them to the next settlement. Vaca humbly attributed his cures to divine intervention, but Estevanico swaggered and strutted, shaking a gourd rattle and accepting the acclaim of the Indians.

On the Río Grande in the vicinity of El Paso the travelers were told of a people upstream who wore cotton fabrics and lived in big towns with immense houses. They struck west across southern New Mexico and Arizona and northern Mexico. Finally they came to a trail leading south down the Sonora Valley, the highway of a lively commerce: bright parrot feathers from the south, turquoise and dressed skins from the "great cities" of the north. They turned down this trail, still escorted by relays of admiring Indians. On the Yaqui River they reached the frontiers of Spanish Mexico, where they began to see evidence of slave-catching raids—deserted villages with remnants of the terrified population hiding outside and, on the Sinaloa River, a party of mounted Spaniards driving slaves southward. The four wanderers "gave many thanks to God" for their deliverance, but Vaca was saddened by the devastation "the Christians" had wrought among the Indians. Half the men and all the women and boys, he said, had been carried away; and in spite of his protests even the friendly band that had escorted the stragglers to this reunion was added to the collection of captives.

The travelers were taken to Mexico City, which they reached in July, 1536. Their story of rich cities to the north created a sensation. Vaca returned to Spain and applied for the governorship of Florida (which extended indefinitely westward and could include this fabulous region), but that office had just been given to Hernando De Soto. Of his two Spanish companions, one settled down in Mexico, the other returned to Spain. Only Estevanico, once more a slave, remained to guide an expedition to the land of wealth.

Three years passed before plans could be launched for this new conquest. The expedition was entrusted to Francisco Vásquez de Coronado. A reconnaissance was sent out under Fray Marcos de Niza, a Franciscan who had seen strenuous service in Peru and Guatemala, and Estevanico, with an escort of friendly Mexican Indians, was sent ahead to prepare the way. Once more the Negro became an important personage, preceded by Indian retainers carrying his rattle trimmed with feathers and little bells, and sending back word to Fray Marcos of the tales he was hearing of great cities in a land named Cíbola.

Eventually Estevanico's runners with his rattle of office arrived at Hawikuh, the westernmost pueblo of the Zunis. The Zunis still live at the same place, just east of the Arizona–New Mexico boundary. The Spanish always referred to the "Seven Cities of Cíbola," but only six are known to ethnologists. Hawikuh was a single apartment house of stone and adobe, wide at the base and receding towards the top, where it reached a height of six stories. The roofs of the lower stories formed terraces, which could be manned by defenders and from which stones could be rolled down on invaders. The lowest story was used only for storage and had no entrance except through the roof. Each terrace was reached by ladders, which could be pulled up, and the entire pueblo was surrounded by a stone wall.

When Estevanico's messengers presented his symbol of authority to the headman, the latter became very angry at sight of the bells. Did he connect these Spanish trinkets with the Spanish slave hunters, of which he no doubt had heard? He threw them on the ground and ordered the messengers to turn back. But Estevanico advanced to the pueblo and was killed there. The Zunis still have a legend about the death of the "Black Mexican with chili lips [lips swollen from chili]." His terrified companions fled back to Fray Marcos, and Fray Marcos returned to Mexico "with more fear than food," as he expressed it. But he reported that he had found a settlement larger than Mexico City in a "land, which, in my opinion, is the largest and best of all those discovered." Larger and better than Mexico or Peru!

The expeditionary force was mustered at Compostela in the present Mexican state of Nayarit. Coronado was a bare thirty years old and his cavaliers were young hotbloods fresh from Spain in their teens and early twenties. They and their horses were splendidly accoutered. They were followed by foot soldiers and a body of Indian allies brave in war paint. Fray Marcos and other Franciscans walked with the army. Sheep, cattle, goats, and swine had been collected to drive along as food and to stock the projected settlement. Hernando de Alarcón was to sail up the coast paralleling their march with shiploads of provisions.

The expedition left Compostela in February, 1540. Two months later it reached Culiacán, from which place Coronado set out ahead with an advance party of about eighty horsemen, twenty-five or thirty foot soldiers, a large number of Indian allies, and all the friars. As second in command of this detachment he chose the able and experienced García López de Cárdenas.

By his own humane inclinations and by strict orders from the home government, Coronado was committed to do no harm to the Indians he should find—except to invade and possess their country. He carried an ample supply of trinkets and trade goods, for he would take nothing—except their liberty—without paying for it.

The expedition encountered some hostility as it passed through the slave-hunting frontier. Beyond that, the Indians, remembering Vaca and Fray Marcos, exerted themselves in hospitality, inviting the Spaniards into their towns and supplying them with provisions. But the trail was not as smooth as Fray Marcos had described it, and the coast was much farther than he had reported. As a consequence, Alarcón's supplies were out of reach.

Alarcón did advance up the Gulf of California, and at the head he "found a mighty river with so furious a current that we could scarcely sail against it." But he worked his way up the Colorado to the vicinity of Yuma. The Indians along its banks helped him in every way, appreciating his presents and accepting his claim that he was the son of the sun. They were "large and well formed"—people of Yuman tribes, still noted for their athletic prowess. They planted their fields near the river, but went to the mountains, probably to hunt and collect wild fruits and nuts, after gathering their produce. A few of them had visited Cíbola (through mountains and deserts 350 miles as the crow flies) and added more details of its wealth. But Alarcón had to abandon the idea of making contact with Coronado.

Meanwhile, Coronado was toiling through the rugged terrain of eastern Arizona. If it had any inhabitants, he did not see them, and as the provisions gave out, his army suffered severely from hunger. The Cíbolans were aware of his coming and were preparing to defend themselves. They removed their women and children to a place of safety on top of a mesa and collected all their warriors and probably some nearby Apaches at Hawikuh. They sent out emissaries to meet Coronado, who sent them back with presents and a message of peace— which made no impression on the embattled defenders. They made a midnight attack on his advance guard—fighting "like valiant men," said Coronado—but they were driven off. Then as they withdrew they sent up columns of smoke to signal his approach.

When the invaders came in sight, two or three hundred of the warriors issued from the pueblo and formed in front. They rejected Coronado's peace signals and drew lines on the ground with sacred corn meal, warning the Spaniards not to cross. Coronado finally ordered a charge, and in the short, sharp battle that followed, Spanish weapons and armor proved superior to Indian valor. The warriors fled to join their comrades inside the pueblo, leaving several of their number dead on the field. The Spaniards then stormed the pueblo, while its defenders opposed them with flights of arrows and stones rolled down from the upper stories. Coronado was seriously wounded and borne away unconscious by his men, and other Spaniards were injured, but the pueblo was captured in less than an hour. The defenders withdrew, ignoring Cárdenas' assurance that they could remain there at peace. They met in council at Matsaki a few miles farther east and made plans for another defense.

The first sight of Cíbola had been a great shock to the Spaniards when, instead of a great rich city shining with gold and turquoise, they saw a little pueblo "all crumpled together"; but when they entered it in their desperate hunger, their reaction was decidedly un-Spanish. "There we found something we prized much more than gold or silver; namely plentiful maize and beans, turkeys larger than those in New

Spain,[1] and salt better and whiter than I have ever seen in my whole life," said one chronicler.

The Spaniards occupied the pueblo from July to early December. Coronado managed to bring the headmen into conference and make peace. They brought him presents of deer and buffalo skins and a few turquoises, and received trinkets in return. He sent an expedition northwest to the Hopi country, seven pueblos grouped on almost inaccessible mesas, with their fields and water supply at the foot. (The Hopis still live in that vicinity.) They knew, of course, what had happened to the Zunis, and drew up their warriors on the plain below the first mesa. Again the line was drawn on the ground with the sacred corn meal, again there was a battle in which the defenders were defeated, and the Hopis also submitted and brought presents to the invaders. At the Hopi towns the Spaniards learned of a great river to the west, and when they returned to Cíbola with their story, Coronado sent Cárdenas to investigate. Thus Spaniards with Hopi guides looked in awe down the Grand Canyon of the Colorado.

Coronado also learned of a river to the east, which was of course the Río Grande. The people of that distant area had also heard of the invaders. Whether from curiosity or fear a delegation came with presents from Cicúye (Pecos), beyond the river on the eastern Pueblo frontier. At the head were two chiefs whom the Spaniards called Bigotes and Cacique. They confirmed Vaca's story of the buffalo plains and offered to guide Coronado there, for they carried on an active trade with the Plains Apaches.

Coronado sent a detail of about twenty Spaniards under Captain Hernando de Alvarado back with the visitors to explore. They passed the sky-city of Ácoma perched on its rock, where the people came down to give them cotton cloth, skins of buffalo and deer, and turkeys and other food. They went on to the Río Grande, where north of the present Albuquerque was a cluster of twelve two-story adobe pueblos, which they called Tiguex. Again the people turned out to greet them, marching around their tent to the music of a flute and presenting gifts. Then "Indians from the surrounding provinces came to offer me peace," Alvarado reported. The Spaniards estimated that there were seventy or eighty such pueblos in the area. Still guided by Bigotes, they turned up the river, visiting friendly pueblos as far as Taos, then as now built on both sides of a clear-flowing stream spanned by wooden bridges. Alvarado sent back a report so favorable that Coronado decided to

[1] A reference to the domesticated turkeys of the Aztecs in Mexico.

winter in the Río Grande area. As one sees this land of peace and plenty, one can understand how rich it appeared to the more primitive tribes surrounding it.

Bigotes finally conducted the Spaniards to his own town of Cicúye. In our day an uninhabited ruin, it was at that time the strongest of all the pueblos, with about fifty adobe houses four and five stories high grouped around eight large plazas. Here the visitors were given a ceremonial welcome and presents. They estimated that it had about five hundred warriors.

At the pueblo were two slaves of Bigotes and Cacique, captives from the plains far to the northeast. One called Ysopete or Sopete was a Wichita (or from a closely related tribe); the other, whom the Spaniards called the Turk "because he looked like one," was apparently a Pawnee. These two guided the Spaniards east to the plains, where they found the buffalo "in such multitudes that I do not know what to compare them with unless it be the fish of the sea." Following down the Canadian, they came to a place where the trail turned northeast; there, the Turk told them, lay Quivira, a region of fabulous wealth in gold, silver, and fabrics. He said that he himself had owned a gold bracelet, but it had been taken away from him by his captors. This was, of course, a scheme to get passage back to his homeland, but the excited Spaniards abandoned their buffalo hunting, hurried back to Cicúye, and demanded that Bigotes and Cacique show them this ornament. When the chiefs answered that the Turk was lying, Alvarado enticed them into his tent and put them in iron collars and chains. He put the Turk and Sopete in chains also and returned with the four prisoners to Tiguex. Naturally he left a hostile pueblo behind him.

Meanwhile, Coronado had sent Cárdenas to prepare winter quarters for him at Tiguex. Cárdenas demanded that the Indians vacate one pueblo—Alcanfor—and he and his party moved in. The Indians complied, but their hospitality was becoming strained. Then one of the Spaniards raped an Indian woman. Her husband complained, but the culprit was not punished, either because he could not be positively identified or because he was the brother of a high Spanish official in Mexico. Coronado later said that he would have punished him if he had known about it. He was still at Cíbola.

Coronado's main army and the livestock reached him at Cíbola in late November, having suffered much from cold and hunger. Leaving the others to follow later, he took thirty of "the most rested men" to Tiguex. There he heard the Turk's story. By this time Quivira had become a fabulous land where everybody ate from gold and silver dishes and a powerful chief rested under a tree hung with golden bells. Coronado demanded to see the bracelet, and when the captive chiefs still denied that it existed, Alvarado, with Coronado's approval, took them outside the pueblo and set a vicious dog—or dogs—on them. Still no bracelet.

Coronado's party required much food and warmer clothing. He sent men to the eleven pueblos to collect supplies, meticulously paying for them with trinkets—but taking them. When their store of cloth was insufficient, the Indians were stripped of the garments they were wearing.

Soon messengers were running between Tiguex and Cicúye and other pueblos plotting resistance. They built palisades around the more distant of the Tiguex pueblos. Then they began by attacking the Spanish horse herd. Coronado sent Cárdenas to subdue them. He tried to induce them to make peace, but they scorned his overtures. Then he stormed one of the fortified pueblos, breaking down the walls with battering rams and smoking out the defenders, forcing them to surrender. He set up stakes, fastened the captives to them, and burned them alive. When Coronado in Alcanfor was informed of what was happening he had Bigotes, Cacique, Sopete, and the Turk taken there to see how the Spanish punished those who resisted them.

The next day Coronado's main army arrived from Cíbola and went into quarters at Alcanfor. It was now near the end of December. The Indians abandoned most of their pueblos and fortified themselves in two. Coronado besieged them, and they were finally reduced, one when its water supply gave out after a siege of three months. Then the other pueblos were burned so they could not become centers of resistance. Thus perished once-happy Tiguex. An appalling number of Indians were killed. Others, mainly women and children, were captured and became slaves. A few probably escaped and joined other settlements.

The Spaniards suffered some casualties, but they were protected somewhat by their armor and superior weapons. During the war Zia, a pueblo about thirty miles northwest, furnished them some food and clothing, either from fear or from hostility to Tiguex. Coronado restored Cacique to his people and tried without success to enlist them in the war. He sent messages to the other pueblos assuring them of his friendship, but their fear and hostility were apparent.

Finally, with Tiguex destroyed and the other pueblos, he hoped, neutralized, he set out on April 25, 1541, for Quivira. At Cicúye he released Bigotes, and all seemed forgiven. But the headmen managed to plot with the Turk to misguide the Spaniards and lose them. He accordingly led them southeast over the High Plains of the Texas Panhandle, a region so level that they saw nothing but "cattle and the sky." This great column of armored horsemen, foot soldiers, Indian allies and slaves, cattle, and sheep must have seemed a strange spectacle to the Plains Apaches. They were friendly, and the Spaniards recorded their customs, marveling at their skill in killing the buffalo on foot with bows and arrows. They came out of their tipis to look at the invaders and, coached by the Turk, joined in to misdirect them. Finally, at Tule Canyon, where a branch of the Red River cuts the High Plains, Coronado forced a showdown.[2] The Turk confessed his duplicity, and Sopete became the guide. Coronado sent most of his command back to Tiguex and with thirty picked mounted men turned sharply to the north, paralleling the western boundary of Oklahoma. The Turk was put in chains but allowed to live, since there might be some truth in his description of Quivira.

Following the compass as it inclined slightly to the east, the army finally reached Quivira, villages of grass-covered lodges along the Arkansas and Smoky Hill rivers in central Kansas. There was no great king, no gold, nothing worth the conquest. These were Sopete's people, buffalo hunters and farmers. They were terrified at the sight of the mounted, armored Spaniards, but Sopete reassured them while the Turk managed to advise them first to kill the horses and then finish off the stranded invaders.

The Turk also tried to lead the Spaniards still farther north, probably to his own tribe, the Pawnees, but Coronado had him garroted. Sopete was allowed to remain with his people. Coronado returned by the direct route through the Oklahoma and Texas panhandles to join the rest of his people at Alcanfor. There they spent the winter subsisting on food requisitioned from the intimidated pueblos up and down the river and on buffalo they had killed on the plains. In April, 1542, they started back on the long trail to Mexico. (One happy incident: before leaving they freed the slaves captured in the Tiguex war.) They paused at Cíbola, where the people appeared "pacified and calm" but

---

[2] Of the many accounts of Coronado's journey, I am following the route determined by Herbert E. Bolton because of his careful study of the terrain. See, especially, *Coronado on the Turquoise Trail*, which is probably his most interesting book.

followed the retreat picking up stray baggage and persuading some of the Mexican Indians to remain with them. With the departure of Coronado, Pueblo Land settled back to recoup its grievous losses and to hope that the Spanish nightmare had passed forever. It might have consoled them had they known that Coronado and Cárdenas had to stand trial for cruelties committed there. Coronado was acquitted, but Cárdenas was fined and condemned to a year of rigorous army service.

Meanwhile, De Soto had landed at Tampa Bay at about the time when Estevanico was killed at Cíbola. With 550 armed men, about 200 horses, and some workmen, including smiths to forge iron slave collars and chains, he fought his way up the peninsula as the Indians signaled his approach by relays of fires. He spent the winter in the vicinity of the present Tallahassee. In the spring, as Coronado was starting out from Mexico, he began his dark trail of rapine and murder through the Gulf country. Unlike Coronado he had no illusions about conquering the Indians without hurting them. When he arrived at a town in the interior, the inhabitants, unacquainted with Spanish methods, usually welcomed him. He seized their stored food and quantities of pearls, demanded carriers and women, and captured their chief to guide him to the next town.

He first went north through the eastern Creek country. A notable stop was at Cufitachiqui (Cusseta) on the Savannah River, where a woman chief, decked in furs and feathers and strings of pearls and followed by a fleet of canoes bearing presents, came across the river to greet him and escort him to her town. Cusseta, then and for more than three centuries following, was a leading town of the Creeks. Even now in Oklahoma are Creeks who trace their descent from it in unbroken historical sequence.

De Soto kidnaped this "queen" and carried her away on foot like the other captives. She managed to escape before he reached one of the great terraced towns of the Cherokees in western North Carolina. Turning southwest to the Creek country again, he entered Coosa, where the chief came out to meet him wearing a robe of marten skins and preceded by men playing on flutes. He seized more slaves and the chief himself and passed on. Entering the Choctaw country, he was hospitably welcomed by a chief named Tuskaloosa, "the suzerain of many territories, and of a numerous people." He demanded carriers and women, and Tuskaloosa promised to collect them at Mabila (the modern Mobile carries the name).

Actually, the chief had sent word to his warriors to assemble there and strengthen the palisade. In the ensuing battle the Spaniards came near to being wiped out, but they rallied and fired the town, trapping the Indians inside, where nearly all were burned to death or killed as they tried to escape. De Soto remained there a month to bury his dead and rehabilitate his wounded. Then he turned north to spend the winter in a Chickasaw town, the same winter that found Coronado subduing the pueblos of Tiguex.

In the spring when he was preparing to leave, he made his usual demand for carriers and women, and the outraged Chickasaws attacked, killing most of his horses and eleven of his men. As soon as he could recover, he went on to the northwest, and in May he reached the Mississippi. While he was building barges to cross it, some chiefs of Azuixo (Arkansas) came over in a fleet of canoes with two hundred warriors bearing furs, buffalo robes, dried fruit, and fish. The chiefs sat in the sterns under skin awnings while the warriors rowed. All were brightly painted, wore "great bunches of white and other plumes of many colors," and carried "feathered shields." They were "fine-looking men, very large and well-formed; and what with the awnings, the plumes, and the shields, the pennons, and the number of people in the fleet, it appeared like a famous armada of galleys." (These people were probably Quapaws, in our day a weak and broken tribe.) They set the presents ashore, but when the Spaniards came down to the river to meet them, they withdrew in fear and the Spaniards fired upon them, killing several.

The Spaniards effected their crossing in early June and advanced north and west through Arkansas, where the settlements were close together and well provisioned. The people fled as they approached, but they plundered the towns as they passed through, capturing men and women when they could. They probably came close to the Oklahoma border. Thus the invaders were closing in on the Indians from two directions; on June 29, the day that Coronado reached the Arkansas River in Kansas, the two expeditions were less than three hundred miles apart. When the disillusioned Coronado was spending his unhappy winter in the one remaining pueblo at Tiguex, the equally disillusioned De Soto, having lost half of his men and most of his horses, was spending *his* unhappy winter in Arkansas.

In the spring, like Coronado, De Soto set out on his return journey. He followed a river, probably the Arkansas or the Red, down to the Mississippi. At the mouth of this river was a village called Guachoya. The people fled and the Spaniards occupied their town. Here De Soto

31

fell ill, but he sent a messenger to a town on the other side of the Mississippi demanding carriers and provisions, for he was the "Child of the Sun" and "whence he came all obeyed him, rendering their tribute." The chief sent back word that the "Child of the Sun" should be able to dry up the river. De Soto was too weak to cross over and punish him, but as an object lesson he ordered his men to destroy an unsuspecting town some distance off. The attack came so suddenly that the inhabitants had no opportunity to resist. "The cries of the women and children were such as to deafen those who pursued them," said the Spanish chronicler. "About one hundred men were slain; many were allowed to get away badly wounded that they might strike terror into those who were absent."

This was De Soto's last atrocity. He died soon after, and his followers, fearing an Indian attack, buried him by night in the Mississippi so that his body would not be found and reported that he had ascended to the sun. Then they started west across Louisiana and the Caddo villages of east Texas, fighting off Indian attacks, capturing more slaves. In the fall of 1542 they turned back to the vicinity of De Soto's death, built boats, and, almost a year later, started down the Mississippi. They took along one hundred slaves, having freed the others. On their retreat they were attacked several times by Indians, and ten of their number were killed. They finally reached the Gulf and eventually landed near Veracruz in Mexico.

At the very time that these land expeditions were turning back in failure—June 27, 1542—Juan Rodríguez Cabrillo left Mexico by sea and beat his way up the west coast of California. He put in at a few places, finding the unwary Indians friendly and helpful. The expedition went as far north as the Rogue River in southern Oregon before it returned through storm and hardship to Mexico.

The bad news brought back by these three expeditions discouraged further expansion of the northern frontier. A few plans to establish missions or colonies in Florida were defeated by the hostility of the Indians. But during the latter half of the century the English and French made some attempts to break the Spanish monopoly of the New World.

In 1577, Francis Drake started out on his famous voyage around the globe. Sailing through the Strait of Magellan and coming up the West Coast, he made a landing on June 17, 1579, probably at the place still known as Drake's Bay just north of San Francisco, where Cabrillo had preceded him thirty-seven years before. He found the

Indians "people of a tractable, free and loving nature, without guile or treachery." They brought baskets filled with a certain herb and began to worship the Englishmen as gods. Drake took possession of the country in the name of the queen and her successors, accepting it as a gift from the uncomprehending natives—"WHOSE KING AND PEOPLE FREELY RESIGNE THEIR RIGHT AND TITLE IN THE WHOLE LAND UNTO HER MAJESTIES KEEPING," according to the brass plate he set up. It was not the first time nor the last when Indians gave away their land without knowing it.

Claiming possession was easy; making permanent settlements was something else. England and France both tried the latter and failed, but these early attempts brought a distinct pattern into Indian-white relations. First the Indians would share their food with the newcomers. Then the supply ships would be delayed and the settlers, having made no attempt to grow a crop, would become demanding. The Indians, with their stores depleted, would refuse further aid. Then would come bad feeling, even open hostility.

In 1562, Jean Ribaut set out to find a suitable place to found a colony of French Huguenots. Traveling north along the east coast of Florida with "unspeakable pleasure," he came to the mouth of St. Johns River. The Spanish apparently had not reached this place, for the Indians were unafraid. They showed Ribaut the best place to beach his boats and exchanged gifts with him. The women and children brought evergreen boughs for their chief and the visitors to relax on as they held council. Ribaut planted a stone column claiming the land for France. Then the Indians replenished his ship's stores with fresh fish, oysters, crabs, lobsters, beans, meal cakes, and fresh water.

Ribaut sailed on, coming to an even better location, "one of the goodliest, best, and fruitefullest countreye that ever was seene." It still bears the name he gave it—Port Royal, at the southern tip of South Carolina. Here the Indians were afraid, for the Spaniards had been there. "Yet after we had been in their houses and congregated with them, and showed curtesie . . . they were somewhat emboldened," said Ribaut. He planted another stone column and left some of his men there while he returned to France for colonists and supplies. But he was kept at home by the religious wars, and his discouraged garrison built a crude boat and put to sea. A few miserable survivors finally reached France.

In 1564 a second expedition was sent out under René de Laudon-nière, a young lieutenant of Ribaut's. He decided to settle with the friendly Indians at the mouth of the St. Johns. They were overjoyed to see him again. They had tended Ribaut's stone pillar as an object of worship, crowning it with garlands and placing baskets of food at the foot. But again the supply ships failed, and the Indians finally attacked a French foraging party, killing two and wounding twenty-two others. Said Laudonnière, "If wee had bene succoured in time & place, & according to the promise that was made unto us, the warre . . . had not fallen out."

Supplies and substantial reinforcements finally came in 1565, but almost immediately Pedro Menéndez de Avilés came from Spain with a fleet of warships and massacred the settlers. When the French were again ready to colonize, they had retreated to the St. Lawrence. The place Menéndez had fortified as his base of operations became St. Augustine, Florida, the first permanent white settlement in the United States.

Menéndez then established military posts and Jesuit mission stations in a line between Tampa Bay and Port Royal and in the Creek and Cherokee country in Georgia. But one was wiped out by a French avenger of Ribaut and Laudonnière, and the others were destroyed by the Indians or abandoned for lack of provisions. Menéndez also projected a settlement on Chesapeake Bay and sent out a party of Jesuits, who founded a mission near the head of the York River; but the Indians, remembering a previous kidnaping expedition, annihilated it. Then the captain of a Spanish relief ship retaliated by catching eight Indians and hanging them from the yardarm of his vessel. Except for his one post at St. Augustine, Menéndez' efforts had failed.

In 1584, Sir Walter Raleigh began his attempts to establish an English colony on the North Carolina coast. His explorers declared the new land to be "the most plentiful, sweet, fruitful, and wholesome of all the world," with unspoiled natives "such as live after the manner of the golden age." He planted his first colony there the next year on Roanoke Island at the entrance to Albemarle Sound. But his supply ships were late, and his settlers failed to plant crops, wore out the hospitality of the Indians, and finally hitched a ride back to England when Sir Francis Drake came by from one of his raids on the Spanish in the West Indies. Raleigh's last settlement was the famous "Lost Colony." Abandoned for three years while England faced the Spanish Armada, it had vanished when a supply ship finally reached the place. Twenty-seven thousand Lumbee Indians now quietly farming in the Carolinas believe themselves to be the descendants of these settlers and a hospitable native tribe that took them in. Certainly white characteristics in hair and features may be seen in Lumbees calling themselves fullbloods.

So much for French and English failures and a feeble Spanish foothold in Florida. Then near the turn of the century permanent colonies were established almost simultaneously by the Spaniards, French, English, and Dutch in the area north of Mexico. They brought a new dimension to the white man's encroachment.

CHAPTER THREE

THE WHITE MAN STAYS

Said Chitto Harjo: "At that time when we had these troubles it was to take my country away from me. I had no other troubles. . . . I could live in peace with all else, but they wanted my country and I was in trouble defending it."

For four decades after Coronado, Pueblo Land was unmolested. But the Mexican frontier was advancing, and from 1581 on, explorers and missionaries were once more crisscrossing the American Southwest. The Indians fled before them or killed them when they could. The Spanish retaliated savagely, leaving a trail of destruction and death and carrying away captives as slaves. Finally, in 1595, the government launched a serious plan of colonization.

Juan de Oñate was placed in charge, with his nephew, Vincente de Zaldívar, as second in command. It was 1598 before he got off from Santa Barbara in Chihuahua, with 130 soldier-colonists and their families, a band of Franciscans, a large body of Negro and Indian slaves, 7,000 head of livestock, and 83 wagons and carts to carry the women and children and the baggage. Advancing up the Río Grande, he hoped to surprise the Indians, but they learned of his coming, gathered up their supplies, and fled to the mountains.

At the pueblo now known as Santo Domingo north of Albuquerque he found the people at home. He summoned representatives of thirty-one pueblos there and made them subjects of the king of Spain. Then he proceeded north and established his headquarters at a pueblo renamed San Juan, north of the present Espanola. There on September 8 he celebrated the completion of a church, and the next day he assembled headmen from the surrounding pueblos and put them

36

through a ceremony in which they swore allegiance to God and to the king of Spain and received wands of office as his lieutenants. On the same day the country as far west as the Hopi pueblos and east to the Plains was divided into districts with friars assigned to each.

On October 6, Oñate set out for the western pueblos. At Ácoma he and his large party received a liberal "donation" of corn and fowls (turkeys), and these Indians also were put through the form of submission to the king. Six weeks later Juan de Zaldívar, the brother of Vicente, came by and demanded food and blankets for *his* party. This second assessment was too much, and the Ácomas refused. The Spaniards began to seize the supplies, and the Indians resisted and killed Zaldívar and fourteen of his soldiers.

Back in San Juan, Oñate sent Vincente de Zaldívar with seventy men to wage "war without quarter" on Ácoma. After two days of fierce fighting on the stone steps leading to the top of the mesa, the Spaniards destroyed the pueblo and massacred five hundred men and three hundred women and children in cold blood. About five hundred women and children and eighty men were taken alive. Probably a few escaped and fled to the mountains, possibly to the Navahos. At San Juan the prisoners were sentenced. All over twelve years of age were condemned to twenty years of slavery, the men over twenty-one having one foot cut off as an additional penalty. All girls under twelve were turned over to the friars to be distributed "in this kingdom or elsewhere," and the boys were given to Zaldívar.

The next victims were the Tompiros, who lived in a group of pueblos east of the Monzana Mountains and carried on a lively trade with the Plains Apaches. When Oñate came there for his tribute of food and blankets, they gave so grudgingly that he set fire to one pueblo and killed some of the people as they fled. Then he sent Zaldívar with a large force against them. In a six-day battle that followed, eight or nine hundred Indians were slaughtered, three pueblos were burned and leveled, and four hundred prisoners taken.

By 1601 the once prosperous Pueblo Land was a vast scene of desolation. Every month Oñate's soldiers made their rounds to collect the tribute. When the Indians saw them coming, they picked up everything they could carry and fled to the mountains, where thousands died from cold and starvation. Naturally the Spanish colonists suffered from the depopulation of the country and the scarcity of supplies, and they were disappointed over the absence of mines and rich sources of plunder. Many of them returned to Mexico in 1601. Probably the

37

colony was too weak to guard the enslaved Indians closely. Most of the Ácomas and Tompiros managed to escape and return home. The Ácoma pueblo was re-established on top of its mesa, and in 1603 or 1604 it made an uneasy peace with the conquerors.

Finally Oñate was forced out as governor, and in 1609, Pedro de Peralta was appointed to the position, with instructions to find a better site for the capital. Thus he founded Santa Fe about 1610, building the impressive governor's palace with its thick adobe walls, which still fronts the north side of the plaza. He brought the colonists there, 250 Spaniards and 700 servants. Most of the latter were Tlaxcalan Indians who had accompanied the settlers from Mexico. While the Spaniards lived around the plaza, these laborers settled on the hill south of the tree-bordered rivulet called the Santa Fe River. There the church of San Miguel, now the oldest church in the United States, was erected for their use.

Oñate and Zaldívar were convicted and punished for their cruelty to the Indians, but like Coronado and Cárdenas they could hardly have carried out their assignment without cruelty. No Spaniard expected to soil his hands with labor, and there was no gentle way of persuading the Indians to feed and clothe the settlers. Meanwhile, the French, English, and Dutch were finding *their* source of wealth in the fur trade.

In 1605 the French began by establishing a trading post at Port Royal, Nova Scotia (Acadia). Samuel de Champlain chose the location and was stationed there about two years. Marc Lescarbot, who came in 1606, wrote of the Indian trade, "When winter came the savages of the country assembled at Port Royal from far and near to barter . . . some bringing beaver and other skins . . . also moose skins, of which excellent buff jackets may be made, others bringing fresh meat."

In 1608, Champlain founded Quebec, and with that as a base he explored northern New York, the Ottawa River, and the Great Lakes. As the French moved up the St. Lawrence, they established Trois-Rivières in 1634 and Montreal in 1642. Soon their trade extended to the Great Lakes, the Illinois country, the upper Mississippi, and over the northern plains to the Rocky Mountains.

The Indians liked the French. The gentleman adventurers who visited their country accepted the hospitality of their wigwams with courtesy and consideration. The *voyageurs* and *coureurs de bois* learned their languages, married their women, and adopted their ways. Jesuit missionaries traversed the same paths and visited the same

38

wigwams, converting the Indians without subjecting them to alien rule. And the French settlers along the St. Lawrence were too few to push the Indians off the land and destroy the game. Champlain made one fatal mistake from the standpoint of French interests. In his eagerness to explore the country he joined a war party of the Hurons against the Iroquois. The Iroquois were dismayed and routed by their first experience with the white man's firearms, but from that time on their formidable Confederacy blocked French expansion to the south.

The same year that the French established Port Royal, an English captain, George Weymouth, sailed to Maine and explored the region around the mouth of the Kennebec, where he found "great plenty of fish." The following day "I traded with the savages all the forenoon upon the shore, . . . where for knives, glasses, combs, and other trifles to the value of four or five shillings, we had forty good beavers' skins, otters' skins, sables, and other small skins, which we knew not how to call." Two years later, in 1607, the English planted a settlement there, but the profits were disappointing and after two winters the settlers returned to England.

That same year, 1607, marks the date of the first permanent English settlement in the United States. "The six and twentieth day of April about foure a clocke in the morning," wrote Master George Percy, "wee descried the Land of Virginia: . . . faire meddowes and goodly tall Trees, with such Fresh-waters runninge through the woods as I was almost ravished at the first Sight thereof." They landed on the shore of "the Bay of Chesupioc" and "got good store of Mussels and Oysters, which lay upon the ground as thicke as stones. . . . We passed through excellent ground full of Flowers of divers kinds and colours. . . . Going a little farther, we came into a little plot full of fine and beautiful strawberries, foure times bigger and better than ours in England."

But a shower of arrows was loosed on them, wounding two. (Probably the Indians were remembering Menéndez.) And in the years of death and starving that followed their settlement at Jamestown, the Indians alternated between sudden attacks and gifts of food. Captain John Smith and other leaders spent most of their time chasing them, demanding corn, and neglecting to plant any of their own. It would have been easy to wipe out the settlement, but Powhatan, the chief of a strong confederacy of Tidewater tribes, managed to hold his people to an uneasy peace. Then another pattern was formed, which would soon become familiar. The colony eventually gained a firm foothold, immigrants of a sturdier breed were arriving, and new settlements and farms were spreading up and down the James River, As they placed the land under more intensive cultivation, the game was destroyed, and the Indians' little fields were being overrun by the settlers' livestock. Then the Indians decided too late to sweep away the intruders.

Powhatan died in 1618 and was succeeded by his warlike brother, Opechancanough. The latter laid his plans carefully. On March 22, 1622, groups of Indians drifted through the settlements. Then suddenly they struck, killing 347 of the 1,200 inhabitants, wiping out whole settlements and isolated farm families. One converted Indian revealed the plot to an English friend, who managed to warn Jamestown in time. The surviving settlers then went against the Indians, destroying their villages, crops, and canoes, reducing them—it was believed—to impotence. But in 1644 under the leadership of Opechancanough, now almost a century old, they struck again. Again the surprise was complete, and 300 settlers fell; but by this time the Indian cause was hopeless, for the colony had a population of 8,000. Opechancanough was captured and killed, and the great Powhatan Confederacy ceased to exist.

In its colonial policy England, like Spain, expressed concern for the conversion of the natives. As early as 1585, when Raleigh was projecting his colonizing venture, he enlisted Richard Hakluyt to urge his cause on the queen. In the paper Hakluyt prepared, he stated as a principal aim "the gayninge of the soules of millions of those wretched people, the reducinge of them from darkness to lighte, from false-hoodde to truthe, from dombe idolls to the lyvinge God, from the depe pitt of hell to the highest heavens."

There was also the aim of "civilizing" them. The first charter given by James I for colonizing Virginia expressed the hope not only of bringing them to "the true Knowledge and Worship of God," but "to human Civility, and to a settled and quiet Government." According to a pamphlet written in 1609, after garbled rumors had come back from the feeble Jamestown settlement, "The report goeth, that in Virginia the people are savage and incredibly rude, they worship the divell, offer their young children in sacrifice unto him, wander up and downe like beasts, and in manners and conditions, differ very little from beasts, having no Art, nor science, nor trade, to imploy themselves, or give themselves unto, yet by nature loving and gentle, and desirous to imbrace a better condition. Oh how happy were that man which could reduce this people from brutishness to civilitie, to religion, to Christianitie, to the saving of their souls."

In 1619 serious plans were made to put these purposes into effect. In its report of persons and provisions sent out to the colony that year, the London Company included along with one hundred "Boyes to make Apprentises" and fifty "Young Maydens to make wives," fifty "Men sent to beare up the Charge of bringinge upp thirty of the Infidles Children in true religion and Civilitie." Also there was a list of gifts in money sent to the colony. One by an anonymous donor consisted of £550 in gold "for the bringing up of Children of the *Infidels*: first in the Knowledge of God and the true Religion; and next in fitt Trades whereby honestly to live." Another came from a bequest of £300 "to the College in Virginia, to be paid, when there shall be ten of the *Infidels* children placed in it. And in the meane time foure and twenty pounds by yeers, to be distributed unto three discreet and Godlie men in the Colony, which shall honestly bring up three of the *Infidels* children in Christian Religion and some good course to live by."

People do not make gifts, especially anonymous gifts, unless they are sincerely committed. And although, as in Spain, this concern for the advancement of the natives was more apparent at home than at the point of contact, it was shown to some extent in the colony. That year, when elected burgesses met at Jamestown for the first representative assembly in America, they provided that "eache towne, citty, Borrough, and particular plantation do obtaine unto themselves by just means a certaine number of the natives' children to be educated by them in the true religion and civile course of life—of which children the most towardly boyes in witt and graces of nature to be brought up by them in the first elements of litterature, so to be fitted for the College intended for them, that from thence they may be sente to that work of conversion." The site chosen for this college was the thriving town of Henricus (sometimes called Henrico) about fifty miles upriver from Jamestown. The London Company granted ten thousand acres of land there for a university and one thousand for an Indian school.

As to how these children would be acquired, the suggestion was made in official documents from 1609 on that they should be kidnaped. This was not carried out except in one famous instance, when the friendly Pocahontas, favorite daughter of Powhatan, was abducted and held in a pleasant captivity that brought about her conversion to Christianity and her marriage, with her father's consent, to John Rolfe.

But except for Pocahontas, the gap between the opposing life ways was too vast to be bridged by giving the Indians Christianity, education, and vocational training, at least by the method conceived at the time. The thought never occurred to even the most enlightened Englishmen that the Indians might have something to give, and apparently they never suspected that the natives had lost "a scheme of life that worked."[1]

Plans for the university and the Indian school were advancing hopefully when the surprise attack of 1622 destroyed Henricus along with whatever good will had existed among the colonists. The settlement was never rebuilt and the Indian education project died; punishing the Indians seemed more practicable than civilizing them. Seventy years later, however, the idea was revived. The College of William and Mary was founded in 1693 with provision for teaching Indians; it was only when few Indians enrolled that this purpose lapsed.

In 1609, two years after the founding of Jamestown, Henry Hudson, an Englishman in the service of the Dutch East India Company, sailed up the river that now bears his name. He and his men were charmed with the lovely, unspoiled land, "as pleasant with grass and flowers and goodly trees as ever they had seen, and very sweet smells came from them." Except for two tragic incidents he found the Indians a "loving people." In the outer harbor of New York they boarded his ship and traded tobacco for knives and beads. Then he came ashore and they "all stood and sang after their fashion." But the next day a boat's crew sent to take soundings was attacked; one man was killed and several wounded by arrows. Apparently this attack was unprovoked.

Hudson reached the tip of Manhattan Island, then wooded to the water's edge, with an Indian village among the trees. Twenty-eight canoes full of men, women, and children met him there and sold him some oysters and beans. At a place farther up the river he went ashore with a chief in one of the Indians' canoes and was taken to a bark house made on a framework of poles bent to form an arched roof. Inside, two mats were spread for him and the chief to sit on, "and immediately some food was served in well-made red wooden bowls; two men were also dispatched at once with bows and arrows in search of game. . . . They likewise killed at once a fat dog and skinned it in great haste, with shells which they get out of the water."

1 Better than any history for an understanding of these events is Bénét, Western Star.

At this time or another, Hudson invited some chiefs on board and treated them to brandy. One fell into a drunken stupor and remained on the ship all night. When he recovered, he was ecstatic over the new experience. Two centuries later the Delawares still had a tradition of the supernatural awe felt at the sight of the great winged vessel, their grand welcoming dance, and a garbled account of the drinking incident. They said the name *Mannahattanik* meant "the place where we were all drunk." Possibly the tradition ties in with Hudson's account of the meeting in the harbor. This first taste of alcohol was more significant than anyone could have foreseen. The European had developed some immunity to its effects or restraint in its consumption through millenniums of use. To the Indian it was wholly ruinous. As tribe after tribe encountered it, it became a large factor in their history. Even today the "drunken Indian" is more than a stereotype.

At Stony Point, on Hudson's return, some Indians came aboard his ship, and one stole a pillow and some shirts from a cabin; and the mate shot and killed him. Instantly there was a wild mix-up as the Indians fled to their canoes. The next day a large party of them loosed a flight of arrows at the ship, but they were intimidated by one shot from its cannon and a volley of musketry. Hudson made his way down without further incident.

He was followed by Dutch merchants, who established a trading post on Manhattan Island as early as 1612. Soon the business spread along the coast between the Connecticut and Delaware rivers; a thin line of settlement advanced up the Hudson, and Fort Orange (Albany), founded in 1617, became the center of a flourishing trade with the Iroquois. The displaced Indians around the settlements on the lower river resisted sporadically, but the mutually profitable relations between the Dutch and the Iroquois were never disturbed.

Meanwhile, the English continued their fishing and trading activities in New England. John Smith came out from England and mapped the coast in 1614. He left a ship under a Captain Thomas Hunt to pick up a cargo of corn, beaver pelts, and other articles. Hunt put in at several points pretending trade, seized and bound about thirty Indians, and sold them as slaves in Spain. One of these was Squanto of the Patuxet tribe that lived at a place marked "Plymouth" on Smith's map. In 1605 he and two other Indians had been persuaded to go to England with Weymouth. There they came under the protection of the ardent colonizer, Sir Ferdinando Gorges, who taught them English and questioned them about their country and its inhabitants. He was impressed with their "great civility far from the rudeness of our common people."

Squanto returned home with Smith, only to be captured and sold by the treacherous Hunt. But he managed to get back to England, and in 1619 he started home again with an expedition sent out by Gorges. In Maine they picked up another Indian named Samoset, who had formed some acquaintance with English fishermen and traders there. They skirted the coast to Squanto's old home, only to find that every one of his tribe had died of a plague, probably smallpox brought on English ships. (Another pattern: As the white frontier advanced, tribe after tribe fell before new diseases to which they had developed no resistance.) Squanto and probably Samoset then went to live with the Wampanoags, a tribe about forty miles southwest on Narragansett Bay. Six months later the Pilgrims settled at the deserted site where the populous villages and cornfields of the Patuxets had once flourished.

The Pilgrims, as all Americans know, had been delayed, so that they made their landfall at the tip of Cape Cod on November 21, when "summer being done . . . ye whole countrie, full of woods & thickets, represented a wild & savage heiw."[2] They made several exploratory trips ashore searching for a favorable location. One night they camped on the beach, not noticing "through snow or otherwise" that they were in the midst of a settlement of Indians, seven of whose people had been carried away by Hunt. At dawn the Indians attacked with "a great and strange crie" and a flight of arrows. The Englishmen replied with their muskets and the Indians made off, with nobody hit on either side.

When the Pilgrims finally decided on Plymouth and began to build houses—and to die during that terrible winter—the Indians watched, appearing from time to time and then melting into the woods. Late in March, when the worst was over and the twenty-one surviving men were at work, Samoset came "along the houses" to greet them with "Wellcome" in broken English. "He was a man free in speeche, so farr as he could express his mind, and of seemly carriage." They "gave him strong water, and bisket, and butter and cheese, & pudding, and a piece of mallard, all of which he liked well." They lodged him in one of their houses that night and sent him away the next morning with a knife, a bracelet, and a ring; he promised to return with more Indians and some skins to trade.

The following day he came back with "five other tall, proper men,"

2 The most convenient collection of the Pilgrims' writings is George F. Willison, *The Pilgrim Reader*.

who also "did eate liberally of our English victuals" and "sang and danced after their manner." Later he brought Squanto and finally Massasoit, chief of the Wampanoags, with sixty of his warriors. The chief was "a very lustie man, in his best yeares, an able body, grave of countenance & spare in speeche." The Pilgrims met him formally and "conducted him to a house then in building, where we placed a green rug and three or four cushions." There with Squanto and Samoset as interpreters they made a pact of peace and mutual assistance. Massasoit assigned a trusted lieutenant named Hobomok to live at Plymouth as his representative; "a man of accounte for his valor & parts amongst ye Indians," he was able to further friendship and trade between the Pilgrims and the surrounding tribes.

Samoset soon went back to Maine. Squanto, literally a man without a country, remained with the Pilgrims "and was a special instrument sent of God for their good . . . He directed them how to set their corne, where to take fish and to procure other commodities, and was also their pilott to bring them to unknowne places for their profitt, and never left them till he dyed."

Their corn turned out well, while the seed they had brought from England "came not to good." Thus it was appropriate that they and the Wampanoags celebrated Thanksgiving together that fall. There would have been no harvest, no harvest festival, and probably no Pilgrims except for an Indian plant and an Indian's advice in growing it. Massasoit came with ninety men and stayed three days, contributing five deer to the feast.

That same fall the Pilgrims made a trading trip to the Massachusetts Indians, thirty miles north of Plymouth on the bay still called by their name. This tribe had been making hostile threats, but with Squanto and two other Indians as interpreters they made peace. The women became so eager to trade that they "sold their coats from their backs and tied boughs about them—but with great shamefastness, for indeed they are more modest than some of our English women are." A few weeks later a vessel, the *Fortune*, arrived from London with thirty-five new colonists, and the Pilgrims loaded it with furs for the return voyage. And there was not "any amongst them that ever saw a beaver skin till they came here and were informed by Squanto."

Shortly after the ship left, the Narragansetts, who lived across the bay from the Wampanoags, sent the Pilgrims a hostile message—a bundle of arrows tied with a snakeskin. The Pilgrims sent the skin back filled with bullets. The Narragansetts declined the challenge, but the

45

Pilgrims enclosed their village with a palisade of poles. Possibly Squanto helped by giving out word that they "kept ye plague buried in ye ground and could send it amongst whom they would."

In the spring the captain of a fishing ship brought the news of the massacre of the Virginia settlers, quoting the proverb, "Happie is he whom other men's harmes doth make to beware." This must have upset the Pilgrims. In a letter they had sent back on the *Fortune* they had characterized the Indians as "very trusty, quick of apprehension, ripe-witted, just," and "very faithful in their Covenant of Peace with us, very loving and ready to pleasure us . . . And we . . . walk as peaceably and safely in the woods as in the highways of England. We entertain them familiarly in our houses; and they, as friendly, bestowing their venison on us." Although some tribes had shown a hostile spirit, the Pilgrims had disarmed them by a combination of firmness and upright dealing. Still they must have reflected that they had fewer than one hundred people, men, women, and children, in the midst of a large Indian population. They built a blockhouse, "made with a flat roof & batllments on which their ordnance were mounted." And they sullied their good record by an unprovoked attack on the Massachusetts.

Bad relations had developed between these Indians and a disorderly trading settlement recently established near them. The Pilgrims suspected that they were plotting with other tribes to destroy this settlement and Plymouth also. Captain Miles Standish accordingly set out for the place with eight picked men and Hobomok as interpreter (Squanto had recently died) ostensibly on a trading trip. The Massachusetts were defiant and wary, but the English succeeded in killing seven of them. Then they carried the head of the leader back to Plymouth and set it up on the blockhouse.

Other small trading and fishing settlements were established along the coast between "the Dutch on one side and the French on the other." Then in 1630 came the great Puritan immigration to Massachusetts Bay and the beginning of Boston, Roxbury, Cambridge, and other towns. From this strong and prosperous colony the exiled Roger Williams found refuge with the Narragansetts, and with Quakers and other refugees founded Rhode Island. Others from Massachusetts settled along the Connecticut River and formed a colony there.

As the English frontier advanced to Connecticut, it encountered the powerful Pequot tribe, which lived west of Narragansett Bay. In 1636 the Pequots killed two English traders and their parties. Since both men were notoriously quarrelsome and arrogant, they probably invited their fate, but the Massachusetts Bay Colony sent a military force to demand the surrender of the killers and the payment of a large fine in wampum. The Pequots refused, and in the ensuing war a combined force from Massachusetts and Connecticut with some Narragansett allies went against the Pequots, and the tribe was virtually wiped out. Some women and children that escaped the massacre were taken as slaves and distributed in Massachusetts and Connecticut or sold in the West Indies.

The charter given by Charles I to Massachusetts had stated that the conversion of the Indians was "the principal ende of this plantation." In 1640 the General Court tardily requested the elders of the churches to consider the matter. John Eliot, the pastor at Roxbury, accepted the responsibility seriously. He took one of the Pequot captives into his family, learned the local Algonquian dialect, and began to preach to the Indians. He helped his converts form Christian villages, where they cultivated the land, made brooms, baskets, and eelpots for the colonists, and sold fish, venison, and berries. He furnished them with spades, axes, and other tools and taught the women how to spin. He started churches and schools in the villages and made preachers and teachers of his converts. He established an Indian college within the Harvard Yard, which numbered among its pupils the youngest of Massasoit's three sons and another youth who became the chief's secretary. He also translated the Bible into their language and had it printed by the Cambridge Press at the Indian college. In all these labors he was financed largely by philanthropic people in England, but the colony aided him by appointing an able layman, Captain Daniel Gookin, to superintend the work. By 1674 there were two established Indian churches, fourteen Indian towns, and 1,100 "Praying Indians." But the next year his plan for thriving settlements of Christian Indians living in peace and mutual economic benefits with their English neighbors went down in King Philip's War.

Conditions had changed since the barely surviving Plymouth Colony had made peace with Massasoit in 1621. Now there were probably forty thousand English between Long Island and the Kennebec, and only about half as many Indians. Also, a new generation conducted the relations between the two races. Hobomok had lived in the home of Miles Standish until he died in 1642. Massasoit had died in 1661. The early Pilgrim leaders had also passed from the scene.

Massasoit was succeeded by his sons, first by Alexander briefly,

47

then after Alexander's death by Philip, an able young man of twenty-four. The English farms and towns now surrounded the Wampanoags on all sides and were advancing relentlessly on their shrinking heartland. True, the colonists paid for the land they acquired, but still it was gone. Philip told an English friend, "But little remains of my ancestor's domain, I am resolved not to see the day when I have no country." He also complained, "The English are so eager to sell the Indians liquor that most of [them] spend all in drunkenness, and then raven upon the sober Indians."

He traveled or sent his messengers to unite all the tribes from the Hudson to the Kennebec. Most of them accepted. In the summer of 1675 he held a two weeks' war dance for the chiefs and leading warriors of his allies. One by one the names of the English towns were called; at each name a brave would pick up a brand from the central fire, dance with it in a ceremonial battle, and finally conquer it by quenching it in the earth.

Suddenly they struck. Town after town was put to flame and death from Connecticut to the outskirts of Boston, even part of Plymouth itself. Only Rhode Island was largely spared out of respect for the aged Roger Williams and the Quakers. Plymouth,[3] Massachusetts, and Connecticut fought Philip with a ferocity equal to his own. They offered the Narragansetts a bounty for Wampanoag scalps or captives, and when that tribe sided with Philip they attacked its stronghold, breached it in a desperate battle, and set fire to the crowded wigwams inside. Here 207 of the colonial militia were killed, but the Indians lost perhaps 500 warriors, and 500 women and children were burned to death. A few survivors were captured. Increase Mather wrote of them, "When they came to see the ashes of their friends, mingled with the ashes of their fort . . . where the English had been doing a good day's work, they Howl'd, they Roar'd, they Stamp'd, they tore their hair; . . . and were the pictures of so many *Devils* in Desperation."

Old Jethro, a preacher Eliot had trained, put on war paint and joined Philip. He was finally captured and hanged. When Philip burned Medfield, a town twenty miles from Boston, James the Printer, who had set the type for Eliot's Bible, posted this message on the bridge across the Charles: "Know by this paper that the Indians whom thou hast provoked to wrath and anger will warr these 21 years, if you

3 The historian will remember that the Plymouth Colony was not annexed by Massachusetts until 1692.

will. . . . You must consider that the Indians lose nothing but their lives, while you must lose your fair houses and cattle." However, sixty of the Praying Indians enlisted in the colonial militia as scouts, where their knowledge of woodcraft proved invaluable. Captain Gookin maintained that they "turned ye balance to ye English side."

It began to turn during the summer of 1676, as parties of Indians were hunted down and defeated after bitter fighting. Philip's wife and nine-year-old son were captured. "It must have been as bitter as death to him," Mather reflected gleefully, "to lose his wife and only son, for the Indians are marvellously fond and affectionate toward their children." Philip's other relatives were killed. Several times he himself missed death by a hair, only to escape and rally his warriors again. Finally they began to surrender. But when one of his braves suggested making peace, he killed him with his own hand. When he was again surrounded, it was this man's brother who shot him in revenge as he tried to slip away.

The heads of Philip and his relatives were set up on the Plymouth blockhouse, and his wife and child, in spite of Eliot's pleading, were sold into slavery in Bermuda, a melancholy end to the last of Massasoit's line. (Massasoit's statue fittingly stands on the hill overlooking the landing place of the Pilgrims. They could hardly have survived without his friendship.)

Hundreds of other captives, even those who had surrendered under promise of protection, were sold as slaves, some locally, but most in the West Indies or Spain. The land where an active native society had flourished half a century before was sold to settlers. Nobody listened to old John Eliot, "The design of Christ . . . is not to extirpate nations, but to gospelize them. To sell souls for money seemeth to me a dangerous merchandise." A few of his converts straggled back, but their hope was gone. He wrote, "There is a cloud, a dark cloud upon the work of the Gospel among the poor Indians."

Even if Philip had succeeded in destroying New England, there was now a stable line of English settlement from Maine to the Carolinas. New York was by this time under English control. The Virginians had spread from the Tidewater up to the Piedmont. Nathaniel Bacon defeated the Indians of that frontier the same year New England destroyed Philip's warriors. In 1682, William Penn founded Philadelphia and soon after made his famous treaty with the powerful Delaware tribe. The English succeeded to the Dutch trading relations with the Iroquois, who with English encouragement tortured and killed the French Jesuits from Canada. But these missionaries did make some converts, and in 1688 a Jesuit gathered them into a colony at Caughnawaga across the river from Montreal. Their descendants still live there except when their skilled workmen, famous for their balance on high girders, are employed in building the skyscrapers of New York and Chicago.

Soon after Philip failed to push back the English frontier of the Northeast, a similar united effort was made against the Spanish frontier of the Southwest. All through the century the Pueblos had been restive, with sporadic rebellions and flights to the Navahos and Apaches. The latter tribes became increasingly hostile because of Spanish slave raids. (Slave-catching was now forbidden by the home government, but prisoners taken in war could be enslaved legally and it was always easy to start a war.) All this hostility flamed up in the Great Pueblo Revolt of 1680.

It was planned by Popé, a medicine man who had been flogged and driven out of San Juan for witchcraft (i.e., practicing the native religion). He fled to Taos and sent messengers to the other pueblos, using knotted cords to indicate the chosen day. At the appointed time the Pueblos killed their resident friars and all the soldiers and colonists they could catch—over four hundred in all—and burned their churches. Then with their Apache allies they besieged Santa Fe, demanding the liberation of all Indian slaves, including the Mexican Indians, and the abandonment of New Mexico. The governor was defeated and forced to retreat with the entire Spanish population—about seventeen hundred—to El Paso (now Juárez).

For thirteen years Pueblo Land was free. An observation by a friar shows how completely the Indians threw off their eighty years of alien control: "They have been found to be so pleased with liberty of conscience and so attached to the worship of Satan that up to the present not a sign has been visible of their ever having been Christians."

During that time the Spaniards made several raids, burning some pueblos and killing or capturing some Indians before retreating. Then in 1692, Diego de Vargas, newly appointed governor, made a circuit of the province offering peace but finding little response. Returning the next year with a larger force, he recaptured Santa Fe and began to reduce the pueblos. If one submitted, officials and priests were stationed there to control it. If it resisted, it was stormed, the captured

50

Model showing Natchez life: king carried on litter, common house at right, corn storage bin at left, temple on mound in background.

COURTESY AMERICAN MUSEUM OF NATURAL HISTORY

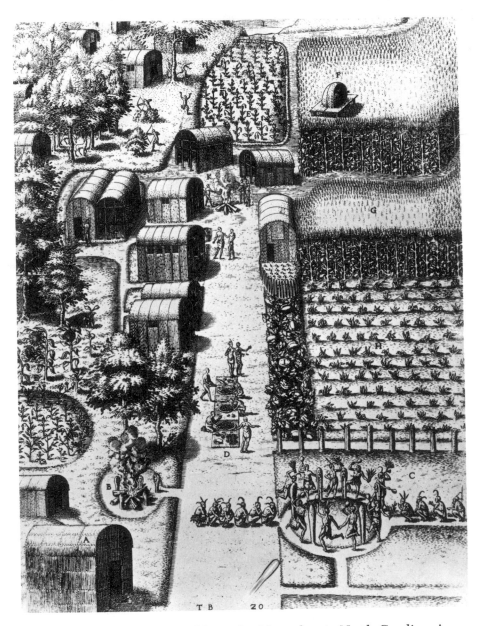

Life way of Indians found by Raleigh's settlers in North Carolina. A de Bry woodcut composite (from a water color by John White) showing agriculture, ceremonials, hunting, lodges.

Pocahontas of romantic legend, daughter of Powhatan. Portrait made in London in 1616, one year before her early death.

The gap in the opposing life ways was too vast to be bridged in the form conceived at the time.

Wichita grass house, about 1870.
Coronado found numerous villages of grass-covered lodges.
COURTESY W. S. NYE

Mandan village, by George Catlin, 1832. Note the palisade, buffalo-skin boats, central meeting place with tribal "medicine" on poles and in cylindrical container.

Indians of the Northwest Coast, by George Catlin, 1855.
*They felled the great trees and made boats, beautifully shaped and
decorated.*

Aleuts, by George Catlin, about 1855.
They lived in underground shelters and their women were skilled in basketry.

COURTESY AMERICAN MUSEUM OF NATURAL HISTORY

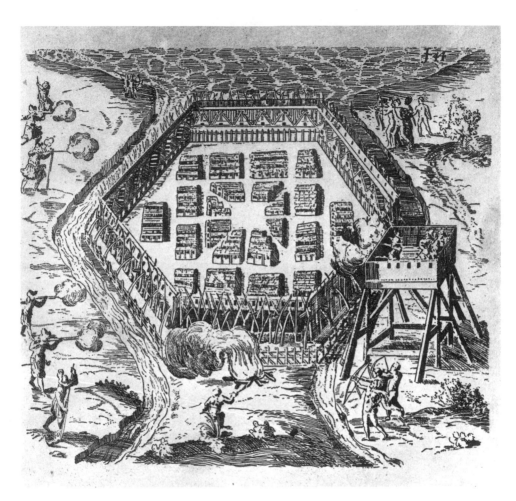

Attack on a palisaded Onondaga village in present New York by
Champlain and Indian allies, 1615, from early French engraving.
*Champlain made a fatal mistake from the standpoint of French
interests.*

French Castle at Old Fort Niagara, headquarters of Sir William Johnson at the close of Pontiac's War. Photograph by S. Grove McClellan.

Kickapoo bark house and storage platform.

The Kickapoos were living in an "elegant and substantially built little village of bark houses."

North Plains Indians moving camp, by George Catlin, 1832. Note the four mounted warriors at upper right protecting the laden train of women.

Rendezvous on Green River, by Alfred Jacob Miller, 1837. Shoshonis make a spectacular arrival in the foreground.

COURTESY WALTERS ART GALLERY, BALTIMORE

Sioux hunting buffalo, by George Catlin, 1832.

On the plains the Indians hunted the buffalo and gloried in their horse herds.

COURTESY NATIONAL COLLECTION OF FINE ARTS, SMITHSONIAN INSTITUTION

Sioux camp at Pine Ridge, 1891.
The last flare of the old Indian spirit had ended in surrender.

COURTESY NATIONAL ARCHIVES

Ba-da-ah-chon-du, or He Who Outjumps All, Crow chief, by George
Catlin, 1832.

*The Crows were "rich in everything an Indian required to make
him happy."*

Hopi pueblo of Walpi, located on a mesa with sheep pens below the
edge and a sandy waste of farmland in the distance.
Starving or prospering, they would remain free.
COURTESY AMERICAN MUSEUM OF NATURAL HISTORY

women and children were enslaved, and the men who surrendered were shot or hanged. Many pueblos were abandoned and the people fled to the Navahos or the Apaches or to pueblos that still held out. The revolt was not entirely crushed until the end of 1698. Even then, the Hopis were never subdued, but remained free through the rest of the Spanish period.

The Pueblos received some benefits from the Spaniards—domestic animals, peach trees, better farm implements. But they were under the spiritual control of the padres and the political control of nonresident alcaldes appointed by the governor. The pueblo had to pay its alcalde a tribute of sheep, butter, beans, corn, and other provisions. The men had to perform the labor of his fields and the women worked in his household. They were required to manufacture his cotton and wool into fabrics for his use. The governor's palace and his haciendas were also maintained by their labor.

The Apaches suffered most of all from the Spanish occupation. The reconquest broke the long-established trade relations between them and the settled Indians, for the Spaniards forced the Pueblos to join the campaigns against them. The Spaniards also created hostility between them and the Pimas, who had long been their friends and allies. Very early in the century they were paying the Pimas a bounty for Apache scalps. Thus the Apaches were forced into the predatory habits that distinguished them in later years. Even historians failed to notice that they had once entered creatively into the aboriginal economic life of the Southwest.[4] Their Navaho kindred also became addicted to raiding, but they benefited from the arts of the Pueblo refugees who settled among them.

During the same century Spanish officials and Franciscan friars from their base at St. Augustine were establishing control over the Indians of Florida and southern Georgia. In 1612, Father Pareja published the first of his books in the Timucuan language spoken by most of the Florida Indians. By 1634 there were thirty missionaries with forty-four stations and thirty thousand converts. A general revolt in 1656 was put down, and Florida, like New Mexico, remained under the Spanish system of tribute, personal service, and Christianity.

Meanwhile, in 1682, while the Indians of the Southwest were enjoying their brief freedom and William Penn was establishing his thriving English colony, Robert Cavelier de La Salle, starting from

[4] This misconception was corrected through the extensive research of Jack D. Forbes in *Apache, Navaho, and Spaniard.*

Canada, built a fort on the Illinois River and then descended the Mississippi to its mouth, claiming all the land it drained, under the name of Louisiana, for France. Two years later he attempted to secure this vast area by planting a settlement at the mouth of the river. He failed, but the plan persisted.

Thus the European territorial claims were approaching each other. During the ensuing years the scope of white encroachment upon the Indians was extended to diplomatic intrigue, and they became pawns in the game of imperial rivalry.

CHAPTER FOUR

CAUGHT IN THE POWER STRUGGLE

As the power struggle on the continent of Europe, so familiar to historians, extended to the New World, the imperial rivals used their colonies as footholds from which they worked to outdistance their adversaries and enlarge their dominions by bringing as many native tribes as possible into their spheres of influence—obtaining their trade, inciting them to war against their opponents or the Indian allies of their opponents, and reducing them to protectorates. But what would become of the aboriginal inhabitants in the process?

With the English there was the constant but seldom-expressed purpose of absorbing their land. With Spain it was to reduce them to serfdom. With the French in Canada there was not only the habit of fraternizing with them, but a clearly expressed policy of merging the two races. As early as 1603, even before he had founded Quebec, Champlain's journals show that he was inviting the Indians to move down the St. Lawrence so they could be nearer the French and their trade. In 1666–67, because French colonists were slow in arriving, the great minister Colbert advised the intendant at Quebec to strengthen the colony by inducing the Hurons, Algonquians, and others who had become Christians "to come and settle in common with the French, to live with them and raise their children according to our manners and customs" so that "having only one law and one master, they might likewise constitute only one people and one race." But when, after La Salle's failure, the French finally obtained a foothold in Louisiana, they followed there the same policy as their imperial competitors.

All intrigued to create a subservient party in each tribe, chiefs they had won to their interest by presents, high-sounding titles, medals, and professions of friendship. Chitto Harjo gave a good characterization of these overtures, clearly referring to the promises James Oglethorpe made to the Creeks in gaining their consent to the settlement of Georgia. "He told me that as long as the sun shone and the sky is up yonder these agreements will be kept. . . . He said as long as the sun rises it shall last; as long as the waters run it shall last; as long as grass grows it shall last. . . . He said, 'Just as long as you see this light glimmering over us, shall these agreements be kept, and not until all these things cease and pass away shall our agreement pass away.' That is what he said, and we believed it."

Besides the Indians' natural guilelessness, these empire builders had the convincing argument of trade. An Indian who had to cut down trees and build his house with stone tools and tend his corn with a crooked stick or the shoulder blade of a bison knew how to appreciate an ax or a hoe, or who had to kill his game and fight his wars with bows and arrows, to appreciate guns. His wife, accustomed to working skins into usable softness or cooking in pottery vessels, was equally eager for a length of red cloth or an iron pot. And the beads and bells and ribbons and nose and ear jewels were desirable luxuries, to say nothing of the rum or whisky that could reduce a whole band to happy insensibility. At the same time, the great Southern tribes and the Iroquois began to acquire domestic animals and to plant European fruit trees around their dwellings.

In 1689, France and England began the century and more of wars that were not to end until the final defeat of Napoleon in 1815. The names given to them by the English colonists are typical of the interests involved: the first three were dominated by dynastic and imperial ambitions; the fourth actually started between the colonials in America and continued for two years before their European rulers made a formal declaration. But in all of them Indians allied with the rival powers scalped each other or fell upon outlying white settlements with fire and death—all for the glory of some mythical king across the ocean. A list of the wars that occurred during the colonial period will show how continuous they were and how short were the periods of nominal peace between them:

King William's War (England entered War of the League of Augsburg), 1689–97

Queen Anne's War (War of the Spanish Succession), 1702–13

King George's War (first between England and Spain, merged with War of the Austrian Succession), 1739–48

French and Indian War (merged with Seven Years' War), 1754–63.

In King William's War, Spain was allied with England. Then in 1700, when the grandson of Louis XIV of France became king of Spain, the foreign policy of the two realms was joined.

In 1697, Louis XIV commissioned Pierre Le-moyne, Sieur d'Iberville, to carry out La Salle's interrupted plan for the settlement of Louisiana. He founded Biloxi in 1699. Two years later his brother, Jean Baptiste Le-moyne, Sieur de Bienville, was appointed governor. Bienville built a fort on Mobile Bay in 1702 and founded the present Mobile in 1711. His men explored up the Mississippi and Red rivers, while French traders from Canada and the Illinois country built posts down to the lower Ohio and explored several hundred miles up the Missouri.

In spite of the Spanish king's subservience to French interests, his war council undercut him when it could, and the rival empire builders —the Spaniards from the Southwest, the French from Louisiana—extended their boundaries against each other all the way from the Gulf to the Platte River. The French founded Natchitoches in the present Louisiana in 1713, and in 1716 the Spaniards established the mission of Los Adaes only fifteen miles west. Also in 1716, the French built Fort Rosalie in the country of the Natchez Indians. The Spaniards founded San Antonio, Texas, in 1718, and the friars began immediately to construct the Alamo. Later in the same year Bienville founded New Orleans and made it the capital of the province. At the same time, agents of the two powers worked to win the friendship of the Plains tribes.

In 1719, Bernard de La Harpe came up the Red River and proceeded north through Oklahoma. On September 3 he reached an Indian settlement on the Arkansas above the present Muskogee. He described the level prairie country with soil "fertile, black and light," and the location of the village on hills above a timbered creek. The Indians were of Caddoan stock, Tawakonis and possibly some other tribes closely related to the Wichitas. (Their descendants are now affiliated with the Wichitas in Oklahoma.) They lived in compact villages of dome-shaped houses "of straw and reeds covered with earth," and they raised an abundance of corn, beans, and pumpkins, and "prodigious quantities" of tobacco. They had excellent hunting in the vicinity—buffalo, bear, and deer—and good fish in the river, but they regularly left their villages in October for the buffalo plains to obtain their year's supply of meat and skins. The horse—unknown until Coronado—had become an essential part of their life way, for they had "very beautiful horses . . . being unable to do without them either in war or hunting." These were equipped with "saddles, bridles which are very well made [,] and wear even breastplates of leather."

"More than seven thousand persons, a part comprised of wandering tribes who came expressly from their villages to sing me the calumet" joined in the ceremonials of greeting to La Harpe. They gave him "a crown of eagle feathers decorated with little buds of all colors" and "two calumet plumes, one of war and the other of peace." Day and night they feasted and sang and danced and made speeches. He spent two days with them. Before he left he had one of his men "carve on a post the arms of the king and the company and the day and year of taking possession." He recommended the establishment of a permanent French outpost in the settlement to trade with the friendly Indians there and to win the Comanches and Apaches of the distant plains to the French interest.

This plan was never carried out, but at some unknown date a French trading post was eventually established on the Arkansas. The same year that La Harpe visited the Tawakonis an expedition under Charles Claude Du Tisné came from the Illinois country up the Missouri to the Osage River and entered into friendly relations with the Osages. Then, traveling southwest, he visited two Pawnee (or possibly Wichita) villages in northern Oklahoma on the Arkansas or the Verdigris River. He found these people also in possession of horses, and he traded with them for two horses and a mule marked with a Spanish brand. On September 27 he set up a flag between the two villages to claim the country for the king of France. It was probably in the 1740s that a trading post was established, possibly at the same site. Impressive remains have been discovered east of the present Newkirk. In a large circular area enclosed by a moat and fragments of a palisade are many articles of French manufacture—trade goods and implements used by the builders. Surrounding it are the remains of Pawnee and Wichita lodges with an immense number of the stone picks used by Indian women as dressing tools, an indication that the main object of the trade was buffalo robes.

An unrecorded phase of this French contact was the activity of the wandering *coureurs de bois,* who carried on an unauthorized trade with the Indians, bringing peltry and slaves to sell at Mobile. They were especially active among the Osages,[1] inciting them to raid the Plains tribes—their traditional enemies, the Pawnees, and the newly arrived Comanches—to bring back captives for this market. Indian slaves were not entirely satisfactory; they had a tendency to mope or even to die when uprooted. Bienville suggested sending them to the West Indies and trading them for Negroes on a three for two basis, but apparently this was not done.

In the main, however, the Indians who hunted over the prairies between the French and Spanish frontiers were relatively unharmed by white contacts. In some respects they had gained; they had acquired horses and entered into a desirable trade. The populous agricultural tribes of the Gulf and southern Appalachians were more directly affected by the three-cornered rivalry between the Spanish in Florida, the French in lower Louisiana, and the English along the coast.

Virginia traders reached the Cherokees in 1673. Carolina traders reached the eastern Creeks probably earlier than that, and by 1696 they were carrying on business with the Alabamas of the Creek Confederacy, who lived on the Alabama River just below the junction of the Coosa and Tallapoosa. English traders reached the Chickasaws by 1698 and the Choctaws by about 1714. Charleston became the main trading center. Pack horses carried the goods along the ancient Indian trails, and the traders married Indian women and settled permanently in the Indian towns. Many of them were rascals, but a few identified themselves with their adopted people and became leaders in the progress of their tribes.

The English had better goods and better prices than their French and Spanish rivals, and this circumstance handicapped the latter in their attempts to extend their control over the Indians. In 1703, after the outbreak of Queen Anne's War, English emissaries working among the Creeks incited the Alabamas to decoy a French party into their country and kill them. The French then began paying the Choctaws and Chickasaws a bounty for Alabama scalps, but Bienville soon managed to make peace with the Creeks. In 1714 he visited the Alabama towns. He could speak their language, and he made friends wherever he went. He received permission to build Fort Toulouse on the lower

[1] See John Joseph Mathews, *The Osages,* 98 ff., for the impression made on the people of that tribe by the first appearance of the "Heavy Eyebrows."

Coosa in a rich and beautiful region surrounded by populous towns. While it was under construction he went up the Tallapoosa to the heart of the Upper Creek country and then crossed on foot to the thriving towns of the Lower Creeks. But the French never succeeded in making the Creeks subservient, and the English continued to trade beneath the very guns of the post.

The French were even less successful in their relations with the Natchez. Iberville and other French officials had first visited this unusual tribe in 1700, when they were ceremonially received by the great chief, or Sun, surrounded by 600 of his warriors. The French later were present at an orgy of ritualistic human sacrifices upon the death of the Natchez' Great Female Sun. But perhaps the tribe was reached by English traders. There were hostile incidents when Fort Rosalie was established, and Bienville imposed a highhanded peace. In 1729 the commandant ordered a Natchez town to remove from the vicinity where he planned to build a settlement near the post. Their sacred temple was there, with the bones of their ancestors on shelves lining the walls, and a sacred fire that was never allowed to go out. The outraged Natchez thereupon massacred the unsuspecting garrison. The French enlisted the help of 700 Choctaw warriors, overpowered the Natchez in their strongholds, and almost annihilated the tribe. The ferocity of the revenge of the French shocked all the Indians of the region, even their Choctaw allies. Of the Natchez who survived the last desperate battles, 427 were captured and shipped to Haiti as slaves. Some escaped and found refuge with the Creeks, where they formed a small town in the Confederacy. (Their few descendants are still living in the hills southeast of Muskogee, Oklahoma.) Others fled to the Chickasaws, and when the French demanded their surrender, the Chickasaws defiantly refused.

The Chickasaws had come under the influence of the English traders and were firm allies of the English throughout the colonial period. Their tribe was small but very warlike, and their territory lay between the French settlements in Louisiana and Illinois. From the high point of Chickasaw Bluff where Memphis now stands, they attacked French boats going up and down the Mississippi. After vain attempts to make peace with them, the French decided on extermination, enlisting the help of the Choctaws. Bienville wrote in 1719, "The Choctaws, whom I had set in motion against the Chickasaws, have destroyed entirely three villages of this ferocious Nation, which disturbed our commerce on the river. They have raised about four hun-

74

dred scalps, and made one hundred prisoners. . . . [This] is a most important advantage which we have obtained, the more so, that it has not cost one drop of French blood, through the care I took of opposing those barbarians to one another. Their self-destruction operated in this manner is the sole efficacious way of insuring tranquility in the colony."

In 1733, after they received the Natchez refugees, Bienville incited the Choctaws under the chief Shulush Homma (Red Shoes) to make another expedition against them; but the Chickasaws met them and made peace. Then in 1736, Bienville himself took command, organizing a French-Choctaw army at Mobile and another of French and Indians in the Illinois country to attack the Chickasaws from both sides. But the two forces failed to arrive simultaneously, and the Chickasaws, from their fortified stronghold, beat off both. The French observed that an English flag was flying over the Chickasaw fort and that the defenders fought with English guns. A similar attempt to subdue the Chickasaws in 1739 also failed, although French reinforcements came from distant Canada. But the Chickasaws were becoming discouraged. Some of them left their country and settled in Carolina. The remaining portion finally sued for peace, but the Marquis de Vaudreuil, who had succeeded Bienville as governor, refused to grant it. In 1752 he led an expedition against this valiant people and suffered another defeat.

Early in the settlement of Louisiana, the French won the Choctaws to their interest, but a pro-English party, influenced by traders, was apparent by 1740. Shulush Homma, whose wife, it is said, had been seduced by a Frenchman, became the leader. A civil war ensued, in which many Choctaws died for the glory of France or England. Finally, the tribe called a council to compose their differences. In the interest of harmony they killed Shulush Homma, but his brother continued the war. Eventually, the pro-French party with the help of its European ally was victorious. In 1750 peace was made by the Treaty of Grandpré, which virtually reduced the Choctaw Nation to a French protectorate. The death penalty was prescribed for any Choctaw who should kill a Frenchman, for any Englishman who should enter a Choctaw village, and for any Choctaw who should invite him. The Choctaws would continue to make war on the Chickasaws; they would "never cease to strike at that perfidious race as long as there should be any portion of it remaining."

The Creeks were subjected to the machinations of all three imperial powers,[2] but they maintained their proud independence. They

---

[2] For an example of the involved English intrigues, see Debo, *The Road to Disappearance*, 28–31.

75

preferred the English trade, but they ignored the urging of the English to expel the French and Spanish agents. Once they joined the English in a pleasurable raid on northern Florida during Queen Anne's War. The Spanish missions had been the most successful with the Timucuas around St. Augustine and the Apalachees around Apalachee Bay. During the winter of 1703–1704, Governor James Moore of Carolina, with fifty British soldiers and one thousand Creeks, Catawbas, and other Indians, invaded the Apalachee country and destroyed missions, towns, churches, fields, and orange groves and virtually wiped out the tribe, killing hundreds of people and capturing fourteen hundred which they sold as slaves. The country was still a wild waste when the naturalist William Bartram visited it seventy years later. In 1706 a similar raid was made on the Timucuas. The Creeks gradually moved into Florida and united with some of the fragmented tribes they found there, thus becoming "Seminoles."

In 1733, when James Oglethorpe founded the colony of Georgia as an outpost against the Spanish, the Creeks were willing to make some concessions to secure a new and profitable trade: "We promise . . . to give no encouragement to any other white people but [the English] to settle amongst us, and that we will not have any correspondence with the Spaniards or French, . . . and do firmly promise to keep the talk in our hearts, as long as the sun shall shine or the waters run in the rivers." To the Creeks this meant only that they had obtained a closer market for their produce. The English settlement was limited to a narrow strip skirting the coast and bending in a right angle up the Savannah River. Oglethorpe visited their towns and joined in their exuberant ceremonials. They had no suspicion that his charter encompassed all their prosperous domain.

James Adair, the ablest and most unscrupulous of English agents, was living among the Chickasaws. In the spring of 1747 a party of more than fifty Creeks came through that country on their way to raid the Quapaws in Arkansas, and he persuaded them to join a Chickasaw raid on the French settlements down the Mississippi. The French then demanded that the Creeks punish them. The Creeks called a council— and how impressive these councils were with the chiefs from all the towns meeting together, the warriors listening and hastening on errands, the women preparing food, and the young people dancing for the entertainment of the visitors. There they drew up the defiant answer that they were all people of one fire and would stand together, and unless the French would cease their evil design to stir up a civil war among them as they had among the foolish Choctaws, Fort Toulouse would be wiped out and the river would carry the blood of the garrison down to Mobile.

Adair was convinced that if all the resident traders had co-operated at this time they could have incited a general war of the Chickasaws, Choctaws, and Creeks against the French that would have overwhelmed the whole of Louisiana. But he underestimated the French influence among the Choctaws and failed to understand the proud self-reliance of the Creeks.

The Carolina officials labored constantly to incite the warlike Cherokees to fight the Creeks—"well knowing," said Adair, "that one pack of wolves, was the best watch against another of the same kind"—but nothing came of their efforts but border raids. They succeeded better in fomenting wars between the smaller tribes of the area, fur-nishing guns and ammunition in exchange for captives, which they sold to the northern colonies or the West Indies. Thus many tribes were exterminated or survived only in fragments. Then as their settle-ments advanced, the Carolinians crowded the Tuscaroras and made a regular business of kidnaping their children for the slave market.

Apparently the harassed Tuscaroras had heard good reports of William Penn and the Quakers, for in 1710 they sent a delegation to the governor of Pennsylvania. Eight belts of wampum were presented one by one to the governor's commissioners, and with each a request. The first belt: The elder women and mothers asked the friendship of the Christian people, the Indians, and the governor of Pennsylvania so they might fetch wood and water without risk of danger. The second belt: The children born and about to be born implored room for sport and play without fear of death or slavery. The third belt: The young men asked the privilege of leaving their towns to hunt for meat for the mothers, the children, and the aged ones without fear of death or slavery. The fourth belt: The old men, elders of the people, asked for peace so the forest might be as safe as their palisaded towns. The fifth belt: The whole tribe asked a lasting peace. The sixth belt: The chiefs asked for peace with Pennsylvania, so they could be relieved from the fearful apprehensions of the past several years. The seventh belt: The Tuscaroras asked for a cessation of murder and capture so they would not fear "a mouse or anything that rustles the leaves." The eighth belt: The tribe, being strangers to Pennsylvania, asked for an official path (means of communication) with its people.

The tribe overestimated the humane spirit of the Quaker colony.

Its officials temporized, not wanting another Iroquoian tribe on their frontier. Then the discouraged Tuscaroras took the warpath against the Carolinians; in 1711 they struck the settlers on the Roanoke, killing 137. The Carolinians enlisted the Catawbas and other tribes, including 310 Cherokees, and went to war against them.

Some Senecas had been present at the Pennsylvania conference. They took the wampum belts to the council of the Confederacy, which decided to take the Tuscaroras in. The latter began moving northward. On September 25, 1714, the chiefs of the Five Nations notified the governor of New York in these words, "They were of us and went from us long ago, and now are returned and promise to live peaceably among us." In 1722 the tribe was officially recognized as a member of the Confederacy in a treaty made with the English colonists.

The Cherokees usually maintained an uneasy peace with the Carolinians. In 1721 they made an agreement with the governor, Sir Francis Nicholson, defining the boundary and making a small land cession. In 1730, Sir Alexander Cuming, an unofficial envoy, induced them to declare allegiance to King George II with much ceremony. He then took some of their chiefs to England, where they knelt before the king and "laid the Crown of the Cherokee Nation," with five eagle tails and four enemy scalps, at his feet and signed articles committing them to admit only English traders and to assist the English in any war with France.

The final conflict, as everyone knows, came from French-English rivalry over the land north of the Ohio. The name, "French and Indian War" given to it by the English colonists indicates that the Indians were allied with the French, but Indian participation was not as simple as that. The French were extending their fur trade east from the Illinois country, winning, after their fashion, the friendship of the Indian tribes. The Iroquois, never subservient to the English but valuing their trade, also hunted for furs in this area and sometimes even served as middlemen, buying or seizing the catches of the Western tribes; and with English encouragement they made war on the Ohio Indians to break up their trade with the French. The French in turn built forts to protect their trade and their Indian allies. By 1753 they had advanced to western Pennsylvania. That year Governor Robert Dinwiddie of Virginia, asserting the colony's claim to the Ohio country under its early charter, sent young George Washington to warn them to vacate. They refused and proceeded to build Fort Duquesne on the present site of Pittsburgh. Washington was sent back

78

the next year with a force to drive them out but was defeated. Thus the French and Indian War, which became a world war before it ended, began in the backwoods of Pennsylvania.

The story of General Edward Braddock's disastrous expedition against Fort Duquesne in 1755 has been often told. In the ambush that cost him his life and the defeat of his army were 72 Frenchmen, 146 Canadians, and 637 Indians. Probably Pontiac was there, for it is known that there were Ottawas among the warriors. The Indians then began to raid the exposed English settlements. "It is incredible," wrote a French captain, "what a quantity of scalps they bring us." They truly sensed that the advancing English frontier imposed a greater threat than the French fur trade.

The Caughnawagas were among the most active of the raiders from Canada, but their Iroquois brethren in New York were kept on the English side by Sir William Johnson. This remarkable man had come to the Mohawk Valley in 1738 as a youth of twenty-three. He started a trading house and prospered, building a great stone dwelling and living there in feudal magnificence. He treated the Indians fairly, and the Mohawks adopted him as a blood brother, moving their council fire to his grounds. A Mohawk girl, Molly Brant, his wife by Mohawk custom, became the mistress of his establishment and the mother of eight children. He led a combined force of Mohawk warriors and Yankee militia to take Lake George from the French—the only English victory in 1755—and later to aid in the capture of Fort Niagara.

The Europeans were equally active in trying to stir up Indian wars in the South. Governor Dinwiddie, at Washington's suggestion, incited the Cherokees to send a war party against the French-allied Shawnees of the Ohio country. "They will be of particular service— more than twice their number of white men," said the young officer. But he warned that "They are very humorsome, and their assistance is very necessary. One false step might not only lose us *that*, but even turn them against us."

The Cherokees made the condition that the English build forts in their country to protect their families while they were away. Governor James Glen of South Carolina accordingly built Fort Prince George and Fort Loudoun. But the Shawnee expedition was a failure, and the back-country Virginians murdered twenty-four of the warriors as they were returning home. The resentful Cherokees, encouraged by French agents, struck the war pole full force against the English. They burned the cabins and killed the settlers on the frontiers of Virginia and the Carolinas and massacred the garrison of Fort Loudoun. Then an English expedition marched into their country burning their towns, laying waste their fields, and killing great numbers of their people. They finally sued for peace, and the war ended in 1761.

French, English, and Cherokee agents tried to win the Creeks, but the great Confederacy, confident in its power and independence, remained neutral. Jean-Bernard Bossu went from New Orleans with a detachment of soldiers to Fort Toulouse in 1759. As he made his way up the Alabama, the Indians thronged the banks and offered him provisions—bread, roasted turkeys, broiled venison, pancakes baked with nut oil, deer's tongues, baskets of eggs of fowls and turtles. It was a beautiful country of prodigal abundance, happiness, and peace.

At Fort Toulouse he heard a chief make this speech: "Young men and warriors! Do not disregard the MASTER OF LIFE. The sky is blue—the sun is without spots—the weather is fair—the ground is white—everything is quiet on the face of the earth, and the blood of men ought not to be spilt on it. We must beg the MASTER OF LIFE to preserve it pure and spotless among the nations that surround us."

When the English made overtures to them during the English-Cherokee war, the whole Nation—Upper and Lower Towns—held a council, formulated their decision, and sent back this message: "The English are our friends and we love them dearly—we desire that goods may continue amongst us and your friendship as formerly. The Cherokees are what you called your greatest friends and we are sorry that you should be hurted by them. But [we] are resolved to have no hand in the war betwixt you—. It is our intent that our path shall not be spoiled, either to this place or to the Choctaws and Chickasaws. Some of the Cherokees may come to our towns; no doubt we shall have talks, if good, it's well, if bad, we shall give no ear to them. The day shall never come that the knot of friendship between us [i.e., the Creeks and the English] shall be loosed, it is not a slippery knot but tied very fast."

A few young hotbloods took it upon themselves to kill some of the English traders, but there was no general war. Probably Creek neutrality shielded the Choctaws and Chickasaws, for these two tribes remained relatively unaffected—their "path" was not "spoiled"—during the conflict.

By the familiar terms of the Treaty of Paris the French lost all their possessions on the continent. Canada and all east of the Mississippi except New Orleans went to England. Spain ceded Florida to England and received, as compensation from France, New Orleans and the trans-Mississippi half of Louisiana.

The Indians of the Ohio country were not happy with being passed from one empire to another. Jeffrey Amherst, the able English commander in chief during the latter part of the war, had tolerated them when he needed their help, but he regarded them as "more nearly allied to the Brute than to the Human Creation." Now with the English taking over the military posts, he saw no reason to conciliate this "execrable race. I am fully resolved whenever they give me an occasion to extirpate them root and branch."

Probably encouraged by the displaced French garrisons and incited by French traders, these Indians, with Pontiac as leader, formed a league to destroy the English. They won even the Senecas, the most western of the Six Nations, to their cause, and tribes as far west as Illinois and beyond. In 1763, the very year the Peace of Paris was signed, they captured all the western posts but Fort Pitt (Duquesne), Fort Niagara, and Detroit, massacred the garrisons, and ravaged the frontiers from New York to Virginia with fire and tomahawk. Johnson managed to hold all the Iroquois except the Senecas. Thus the Mohawk Valley escaped.

Johnson finally won back the Senecas. He held a great council of the hostiles at Fort Niagara and succeeded in making peace with most of them. Pontiac was present, but he and some of his die-hard western allies still held out. Johnson eventually won their submission and friendship at a council he called at Oswego. Then, in an attempt to fix the boundaries of the Iroquois against white advancement, he made a treaty with them at Fort Stanwix on the upper Mohawk in 1768. By ceding outlying portions of their range they received what was supposed to be permanent possession of their heartland.

But with the removal of the French menace the English colonists began everywhere to spill over the Indian boundaries. In New York they violated the Treaty of Fort Stanwix. Johnson tried to protect the Indians, but he died in 1774. The Creeks yielded to pressure from the Georgians and ceded a large tract on the upper Savannah in 1773. Settlers' stations, scattered cabins with a central fortified blockhouse in which the people could gather to fight off Indian raids, were springing up west of the Alleghenies. Watauga was established in the present Tennessee in 1769; by 1772 there were thirteen stations in that area. Daniel Boone made his celebrated hunting trip to Kentucky in 1769, coming back with tales of a beautiful bluegrass region cleared by nature and rich with game. The settlement, which began in 1774, was halted briefly when a league of western tribes led by the able Shawnee, Cornstalk, attacked the frontiers. But Lord Dunmore, the royal governor of Virginia, defeated the Indians, and the Shawnees were forced to the north of the Ohio.

The Indians of the Great Plains and the Spanish Southwest were relatively unaffected by the long contest between England and her French and Spanish adversaries. In 1763, Pierre Laclède and his teen-aged stepson, Auguste Chouteau, came up the Mississippi from New Orleans and founded St. Louis, which soon became the gateway to an expanding fur trade in Spain's newly acquired Louisiana country. But a new imperial rivalry developed on the Pacific.

Ever since 1564 the Spaniards had been returning from the Philippines by way of California, following the Japanese current to Cape Mendocino and skirting the coast to Acapulco. Along the way they had friendly contacts with the Indians, but made no attempt to settle the region. Then the Russians came in from the north. In 1728, Vitus Bering, sent out by Peter the Great, sailed from Kamchatka through the sea and strait that still bear his name, stopping at St. Lawrence Island on the way but failing to touch or—because of the fog—even to see the Alaska mainland. Starting again from Kamchatka in 1741 and striking east across the ocean, he reached the southeastern strip of Alaska. Then he turned back, skirting the coast and the Aleutian chain until his ship was driven ashore on an uninhabited island—his name is fixed on this also—of the Commander group, still belonging to Russia. Here were found the web-toed, five-foot-long sea otters, bearers of the most beautiful fur in the world. Bering and a number of his crew died there, but the survivors made their perilous journey back to Kamchatka. They carried nine hundred sea otter pelts, which brought eighty dollars apiece in the Chinese market.

The Russians set out for the new bonanza in anything that would float. The first ship brought back furs worth one million dollars; ten years later one cargo grossed nearly two and one-half million. They started at Bering Island, then moved east along the Aleutians, stripping each island as they passed. By the end of the French and Indian War they had fur-gathering posts on the Alaska Peninsula. It was a region of heavy rainfall and almost constant fog with no trees and no agriculture in a growing season of only 135 days. The Aleuts were a gentle people, who lived by hunting and fishing, searching the seas in little skin boats. They lived in underground shelters, and their women were skilled in basketry. The Russians treated them with unspeakable cruelty: they raped the women and held them as hostages until the men ransomed them with furs; they destroyed settlements and murdered people from sheer barbarity. It is estimated that the population when they came was 25,000; a count made in 1885 showed 3,892.

This Russian advance spurred the Spaniards to secure California. After preliminary explorations a typical Spanish colonizing expedition—soldiers, Franciscan missionaries, friendly Indians, horses, mules, and cattle—set out by land and sea from Lower California in 1769. They established a presidio and a mission at San Diego. The dedicated Fray Junipero Serra, who was the *presidente* of the Franciscans, preached to the Indians, gave them presents, and dedicated the mission on July 16. The military expedition went on north finding the Indians numerous and friendly. Some of its members looked down from a mountain height on San Francisco Bay, hidden by its encircling hills from two centuries of European exploration.

Thus the Europeans were advancing upon the natives from all sides when a new force appeared to influence their destiny.

CHAPTER FIVE

A NEW POWER RISES

In the American Revolution both sides worked to win the Indians, the imperial officials inciting them to attack the settlements, the revolting colonies urging them to remain neutral. Early in 1775, while Washington was trying to organize an army around Boston, the Continental Congress took steps to plan an Indian policy. Later in the summer a message was sent to the Iroquois informing them of the war, "as we are both on the same island," and advising them, "This is a family quarrel between us and old England . . . we desire you to remain at home, and not join on either side, but keep the hatchet buried deep." But only the Oneidas and Tuscaroras remained neutral; the other four tribes joined the British.

Sir John and Guy Johnson, son and son-in-law of Sir William,[1] espoused the Tory cause and went to Canada, and the Mohawks followed them there. The able Joseph Brant, a younger brother of Molly and a protégé of Sir William, became their leader. Most of the Mohawks still live in Canada. The town of Brantford, Ontario, with an important Iroquois reserve nearby, perpetuates the memory of this migration.

Similar overtures were made to the southern Indians in 1775. John Stuart, the British superintendent, had taken refuge in Florida. In September he was directed by General Gage at Boston to enlist Indians in the British army, and he sent a supply of ammunition to the Creeks and Cherokees. The American[2] commissioners advised the Creeks that

1 Molly Brant's predecessor was an indentured German girl. Johnson is said to have married her on her deathbed, thus legitimizing their son and two daughters. His son-in-law, Guy Johnson, is believed to have been his nephew.

84

the conflict was "like a dispute between a father and his child" in which they should have no concern. The Lower Towns in council decided on neutrality. Supremely confident of their power and influence, the headmen of all but the Euchees and Hitchitees drew up a message and sent it with ceremonial presents the following March urging the white men to make peace.

"We are now going to speak to our eldest brothers, the white people; we have heard all your talks to the red people and hope you will hear ours. We thought that all the English people were as one people but now we hear that they have a difference amongst themselves. It is our desire that they drop their disputes and not spoil one another; as all the red people are living in friendship with one another we desire that the white people will do the same. It is the custom with the red people when they send such a talk and these tokens to prevent any of our warriors from going to war and we hope that the white people will do the same and agree to our talk—We send this wing and tobacco as a token of friendship and desire that the beloved men [elder statesmen, hence government officials] will smoak the tobacco and look at the wing and agree to each others talk."

The Upper Towns rejected the Americans' message and asserted their loyalty to Stuart and the Great King. By the summer of 1778 they were raiding the outlying settlements, and all but two of the Lower Towns eventually joined them. Their attacks soon became so serious that they affected military movements in Georgia and the Carolinas.

Stuart hesitated to incite the Cherokees because there were many Loyalists in the back country of the Carolinas. Then in May, 1776, Cornstalk, with a delegation of Shawnees, Iroquois, Delawares, Ottawas, and Nantucas,[3] came to them with a war belt and a plan, probably British-inspired, to unite and fall upon the settlements from the rear while the king's troops would attack them from the coast. Some of the chiefs rejected the war belt, but an embittered element eagerly accepted it and struck the settlements. They had ample cause. Old Tassel, a leader of the peace group, summed it up in a letter to the governor of South Carolina:

"BROTHER: . . . We are a poor distressed people, that is in great trouble. . . . We have no place to hunt on. Your people have built

---

[2] Indians are also Americans. I have not limited the term to white Americans except to distinguish them from the nationals of other countries.

[3] Probably Nanticokes, a broken tribe from eastern Maryland that had removed to southern New York under the protection of the Iroquois.

85

houses within one day's walk of our towns. We don't want to quarrel with our elder brother; we therefore hope our elder brother will not take our lands from us, that the Great Man above gave us. He made you and he made us; we are all his children. . . . We are the first people that ever lived on this land; it is ours."[4]

Soon the Cherokees were in a general war against the Virginia, Carolina, and Georgia frontiers, with British agents supplying ammunition and encouragement. It brought punitive expeditions against them, more land losses, and the withdrawal of the more warlike faction to the Chickamauga region. Some refugees from the ravaged towns even fled to British protection in Florida. But the Cherokee raids, like the Creek, kept the militia immobilized and thus aided the British cause. In 1779 a new white settlement was established on the bend of the Cumberland in the Nashville area, and the Chickasaws, Cherokees, and Upper Creeks made repeated efforts to dislodge it.

Meanwhile, in the Northwest, Colonel Henry Hamilton, in command of the British post at Detroit, was encouraging the Indians to attack the frontier. (Paying a bounty for scalps, he was execrated by the Kentuckians as the "Ha'r Buyer.") In two campaigns in 1778 and 1779, George Rogers Clark with Kentucky militia crossed the Ohio, received the willing submission of the old French posts in Illinois, and captured Hamilton himself at Vincennes, Indiana. Later he came back and struck the prosperous Shawnee settlement in Ohio, killing many of the people. He destroyed their houses and a 500-acre field of corn almost matured, with beans running up the stalks and pumpkins planted between the rows. This and succeeding raids drove the Shawnees farther west into Indiana, and about four hundred families even removed to Spanish territory, settling above Cape Girardeau in Missouri. At the same time, the Americans, with their eyes on Detroit, made a treaty with the Delawares, who, crowded from their eastern homeland, had moved in the 1750s to the Ohio country.

The treaty was signed at Fort Pitt, September 17, 1778, the first treaty ever made by the United States with an Indian tribe. The Delawares agreed to let American troops pass through their country to attack the British posts on the Great Lakes; they would sell them corn, meat, horses, and other supplies, and their warriors would enlist in the

---

[4] Many excellent books have been written about different phases of Cherokee history. A convenient account in one volume is Grace Steele Woodward, *The Cherokees.*

army. Finally, should it "be conducive for the mutual interest of both parties to invite any other tribes who have been friends to join the present confederation and form a state whereof the Delaware Nation shall be the head and have a representative in Congress," this would be effected. No Indian state was ever formed, but the concept influenced Indian policy for more than a century thereafter.

The Americans did not march against Detroit, and the peace with the Delawares was short-lived. Moravian missionaries had begun working among these Indians while they still lived in the Wyoming Valley in eastern Pennsylvania and had later founded a new Delaware mission at Gnadenhütten in Ohio. In 1782, frontiersmen fell upon the unoffending Christian Indians of this settlement and murdered them. The Delawares then became the leaders among the hostile tribes of the Ohio country. Some of them soon began to settle near the Shawnees around Cape Girardeau.

The Wyoming Valley had long since become a thriving white settlement. In July, 1778, Major John Butler, with four hundred British soldiers and Tories and seven hundred Indians, mainly Senecas and Cayugas, invaded it. Most of the able-bodied men had gone to war, the few defenders were defeated, and a horrible massacre followed. The Cherry Valley in New York suffered a similar fate. The next year Washington sent General John Sullivan against the Iroquois. He fought a fierce battle with them and their Tory allies near Elmira, New York, and then marched through their territory. He found a thriving country with towns regularly laid out, good painted frame houses built with chimneys, broad and productive cornfields, and apple, pear, and peach orchards; he left it a smoking waste. The Revolution ended with the power of the great Iroquois Confederacy forever broken. Large segments of the tribes now live in Quebec and Ontario, and most of the remainder in separated, constricted reservations in New York.

By the Peace of Paris that closed the war in 1783, Spain won back Florida, and the boundaries of the new American republic were extended west to the Mississippi. To the diplomats at Paris the Indians went along with the land, but they had some ideas of their own, and again they were courted by three rivals. The United States sent out agents to establish peaceful relations with them—but with the ultimate purpose of acquiring their land. From Pensacola and Mobile, Spain intrigued with the still-powerful Southern tribes to unite them into a barrier state against the growing republic. In the North the British held a similar purpose of making all the Ohio country an Indian reserve; they delayed in surrendering their forts and encouraged the Indians to hold back the frontier.

In 1784 the Spaniards made treaties with the Chickasaws, Choctaws, and Creeks in which these tribes acknowledged themselves under Spanish protection and agreed to exclude all traders without a Spanish license. The Creeks at this time had a remarkable leader in Alexander McGillivray, the son of a Scotch trader and a half-blood Creek woman. He represented the still undivided Creek-Seminole Nation in transferring allegiance from England to Spain, and was paid a Spanish salary.

The next year American commissioners called a council at Hopewell in South Carolina. There on November 28 the Cherokees—outside the Spanish sphere of influence—made their first treaty with the United States. They acknowledged its sovereignty, and they gave up land previously seized and occupied by settlers, but the new boundary was strictly defined and the United States promised to restrain its citizens from further trespass. Finally, they might "send a deputy of their own choice, whenever they think fit to Congress." This, of course, before the adoption of the federal constitution, was equivalent to statehood.

The hopes of the Cherokees may be seen in the words of Nancy Ward, the influential "beloved woman" of the tribe. At the request of Old Tassel she spoke in council: "I have a pipe and a little tobacco to give to the commissioners to smoke in friendship. I have seen much trouble in the late war. I am now old, but hope yet to bear children who will grow up and people our Nation, and have no more disturbances. The talk I give you is from myself."

Little did she know that the weak Confederation Congress could not restrain the frontier. The Watauga settlers disregarded the new boundary, advancing and seizing lands in the very heart of the Cherokee country. Secretary of War Henry Knox informed Congress of unprovoked outrages amounting "to an actual though informal war" against the Indians. Congress did issue a proclamation warning the intruders, but was not strong enough to enforce it. Once the Cherokees attacked some surveyors and broke their compasses ("land-stealers") against a tree. At the same time, they were adopting the agricultural techniques of their white neighbors; but as early as 1785 a few of their people, mainly Chickamaugans, opposed to this progress began to drift to the unspoiled hunting grounds in the Spanish territory beyond the Mississippi and settle in Arkansas.

The Choctaws and Chickasaws had also been invited to the council at Hopewell. They decided to come, for Spain had not carried out its promises to supply them with trade goods. They arrived late and signed treaties in January similar to the Cherokee treaty except that they carried no promise of statehood. Commissioners were also appointed to deal with the Creeks at Galphinton in Georgia, but the Indians failed to appear. Asked to ratify a fraudulent land cession claimed by Georgia, an influential chief said, "Our lands are our life and breath; if we part with them we part with our blood." McGillivray then said that the Creeks had sought Spanish protection because of the encroachment of the Georgians, but if the United States would form an Indian state south of the Altamaha, he would be the first to take the oath of allegiance. Such a Creek state would have blocked the expansion of Georgia—latest and weakest of the thirteen—and in power, wealth, and population would not have compared unfavorably with some of the others.

The historian will remember that all the land back to the Mississippi was claimed by various states under the terms of their colonial charters; thus the Tennessee settlements were in North Carolina, and Kentucky was in Virginia. Then the states ceded their western territory to the central government, and Congress passed a series of laws providing for preliminary territorial governments and eventual statehood for the settlers. By the close of the 1780s the Watauga settlement had expanded and some of the stations had grown into villages, the Cumberland area was filling up rapidly, and there were more than 70,000 settlers in Kentucky. Throughout this region the log cabins in the clearings were being replaced by cultivated farms and substantial houses.

By the Northwest Ordinance of 1787, Congress provided for a more orderly development of the Ohio country: first, extinguish the Indian title; next, survey it in mile-square tracts; and then sell it to settlers. Congress chose General Arthur St. Clair as governor of the Northwest Territory with the additional duty of Indian superintendent —a two-fold responsibility of territorial governors from that time on. He was instructed to "ascertain who are the real head men and warriors of the several tribes, and who have the greatest influence among them; these men you will attach to the United States by every means in your power." Such "means," as everyone knew, were intoxication and bribery.

Congress had set out to make peace with these tribes immediately after the peace with England. Boundaries were to be fixed "convenient to the respective tribes, and commensurate to the public wants"—irreconcilable aims. Several treaties were made nominally freeing large sections of Ohio to white settlement, but the tribes did not recognize these cessions and for a time prevented the survey of the land. Meanwhile, squatters were making "tomahawk claims" along the Ohio River in defiance of both the Indians and the United States.

In 1787 an "Ohio Company" organized in Massachusetts bought a tract of land from Congress. The following spring it brought its colonists down the river and founded Marietta, the first legal white settlement in the state. Later in the same year, other colonists brought by a New Jersey land purchaser founded Cincinnati. These settlements were under constant Indian attack. They followed the typical pattern of log cabins in clearings grouped around a fortified blockhouse.

St. Clair arrived at Marietta shortly after its founding. There at Fort Harmer he called an Indian council, where he made a treaty—on January 9, 1789—confirming the former cessions. The Indians said the chiefs had signed without authority (no doubt St. Clair had followed his instructions in obtaining their consent) and refused to recognize it. But by 1790 the Northwest Territory had about 4,300 white inhabitants: probably 1,300 around Cincinnati, 1,000 at Marietta, and 2,000 in the old French villages farther west. St. Clair soon moved his capital to Cincinnati.

By this time the United States government had begun to function strongly under the federal constitution. George Washington was inaugurated as president at New York on April 30, 1789. He reappointed Henry Knox as secretary of war in his new cabinet. The President and the Secretary adopted an Indian policy that was as humane as possible, given its underlying purpose of extending the frontier and protecting it as it advanced. They had no wish to exterminate the Indians, but to assist them in acquiring economic techniques that would enable them to prosper within more restricted boundaries. In his first long report to the President on July 7, Knox said this would be difficult and would require deep knowledge of human nature and patient perseverance, but that it could be accomplished. He would give them domestic animals and farm implements and appoint agents and encourage missionaries to live among them and instruct them in more advanced agricultural methods.

Washington recommended this policy to Congress. Then in his annual message of 1791 he presented a carefully planned policy: impartial dispensation of justice, promotion of commerce under fair regulations, land purchases by orderly methods, training in civilization, and punishment of persons who infringed on Indian rights and violated treaties. Congress responded rather slowly with a series of trade and intercourse laws and provision for education and vocational training, but Washington's recommendations set the pattern of Indian policy throughout the subsequent history of the United States.[5] Meanwhile, something had to be done about the mutual outrages committed by whites and Indians on the frontiers.

Washington sent three military expeditions against the tribes that were raiding the Ohio settlements. In 1790, the first, under Josiah Harmer, was badly defeated and driven back by the warriors led by the able Miami chief Little Turtle. The next year Washington ordered St. Clair to take personal charge. The Governor marched one hundred miles north from Cincinnati, where on November 4, 1791, Little Turtle administered one of the most disastrous defeats in the history of United States Indian fighting. About nine hundred of St. Clair's men were killed and the rest fled in panic. The young Shawnee warrior Tecumseh especially distinguished himself in this battle.

The defeat was a crushing blow to Washington also. He turned to negotiation. First he invited the Iroquois leaders to Philadelphia, then the capital, and tried to induce them to use their good offices in restoring peace. They failed to respond. Then he sent three agents to confer with the hostiles. Two were killed and the third sought safety in Vincennes. Next, he invited Joseph Brant to Philadelphia. Brant said afterwards that Washington offered him a down payment of one thousand guineas and double the pension he was paid by the British and would give him a bonus of twenty thousand pounds if he should succeed in making peace. Pleading illness, he returned to Canada.

The Indians, for their part, held a jubilant council attended by delegations from the Southern tribes, the distant West, and Canada. They agreed that the Ohio River should be the boundary between the Indians and the American whites. The settlers already north of the river would be required to leave, but they might be given a little time to consider the order.

Washington meanwhile had put Major General Anthony Wayne in command of the United States forces in the Ohio country. While Wayne was drilling his army at Cincinnati, the President tried a peace

[5] An excellent account of the development of this policy is given in Francis Paul Prucha, *American Indian Policy in the Formative Years*.

commission to this council. As it was unsafe to venture into the Indian country, the commissioners went to Detroit, still held by the British, hoping to proceed from there; but the British commandant forbade them to go. They then entrusted their message to British agents, who made a negative presentation. A little later, Lord Dorchester, the governor general of Canada, in a formal address to the Indians, promised to help them expel the American settlers and maintain the Ohio boundary. To reinforce his threat an English column marched from Detroit into the Ohio country and built Fort Miami near the present Toledo.

At the same time, the Ohio tribes, especially the Shawnees, kept up their active contacts with the Southern Indians. For several years Cheeseekau, an older brother of Tecumseh, had been living among the Creeks and Cherokees and joining their raids on the Tennessee settlements. This remarkable family was closely bound to the Creeks, for the parents had belonged to the Shawnee element in the Confederacy before migrating to the Ohio country. Now in the spring following St. Clair's defeat, Cheeseekau sent for Tecumseh to join in an attack on the Cumberland, and he came with twenty or thirty warriors. The combined force of seven hundred Creeks, Cherokees, and Shawnees overpowered one station and threatened to wipe out the whole settlement, but in storming a station only four miles from Nashville, Cheeseekau was killed and the defenses held. Tecumseh, to avenge his brother's death, went to the Chickasaws and joined in their raids against the Tennessee settlers. Then he visited towns throughout the Creek-Seminole country making the pleasant contacts typical of Indian social relations. Soon he was called north by the Shawnee chief, Blue Jacket, to fight Wayne.[6]

Wayne, with three thousand men—regulars and mounted troops from Kentucky—left Cincinnati in the fall of 1793 and started north across Ohio. Shawnee scouts under Tecumseh watched his every move. Eighty miles north he fortified himself at a place he named Greenville and spent the winter there; then he resumed his march. Fourteen hundred Indian warriors under Blue Jacket collected before Fort Miami at a place since known as Fallen Timbers, where tree trunks uprooted by a tornado and a tangle of newer growth made an almost impenetrable thicket. In a desperate battle on August 20 the Indians were defeated. They fled to Fort Miami and found the gates

[6] A fine biography of Tecumseh is Glenn Tucker, *Tecumseh: Vision of Glory.*

closed! Their British friends were not willing to go so far as to start a war with the United States.

Wayne destroyed every Indian village he could find; then he built Fort Wayne in Indiana and retired for the winter to Greenville. There, in the spring, he called the Indians to a council attended by the leaders of twelve tribes and dictated a treaty in which they surrendered a strip of southeastern Indiana and all of Ohio except a tract in the northwest. Tecumseh refused to attend the council, and when the terms of the treaty were known, he announced that he would not recognize it; he withdrew to Indiana, and other uprooted Indians joined him there. White settlers flocked to Ohio, and it became a state in 1802.

Meanwhile, the Southern Indians were subjected to similar pressures. In his report to Washington in 1789, Knox had written: "The disgraceful violation of the Treaty of Hopewell with the Cherokees requires the serious consideration of Congress. If so direct and manifest contempt of the authority of the United States be suffered with impunity, it will be vain to attempt to extend the arm of government to the frontiers."

Washington thereupon called the Cherokees to a treaty council, which met in 1791 on the Holston River at the site of Knoxville. It was attended by forty chiefs, leaders of both the peace party and the hostiles of Chickamauga. A treaty was signed defining the boundaries (the Cherokees lost what had been seized in violation of the Treaty of Hopewell) and guaranteeing the tribe against future encroachments. It also provided that in order to lead the Cherokees "to a greater degree of civilization, and to become herdsmen and cultivators, instead of remaining in a state of hunters," the United States would furnish them "gratuitously" with "useful instruments of husbandry." (Such provisions were to be repeated many times in treaties with Indian tribes.)

In spite of the treaty, the border conflicts continued: white militia and volunteer units invading the Cherokee country, destroying towns (usually of the peace party), and killing the people; retaliatory raids by the Chickamaugans upon the settlements. The Chickamaugans continued to intrigue with the Spaniards at Pensacola. They were also in contact with the British at Detroit and the Indians of the Ohio country; some of their warriors had helped defeat St. Clair, joined in the exuberant council that followed, and fought Wayne at Fallen Timbers.

In 1790 the "Territory South of the Ohio" had been organized, with William Blount of North Carolina as governor. Two years later

Kentucky was cut off and admitted to statehood. Blount continued as territorial governor of Tennessee until it became a state in 1796. He was a land speculator—the Creeks called him Tuckemicco (Dirt King)— and correspondingly unsympathetic towards Indians.

Wayne's victory in the Northwest and a devastating foray of frontiersmen into the Chickamaugans' country induced even those recalcitrants to sue for peace. Blount called a council of the whole nation in the "Mother Town" of Tellico in the fall of 1794. Said Bloody Fellow, one of the Chickamauga leaders, "I want peace that we may . . . sleep in our houses, and rise in peace on both sides."

In the breathing spell that followed, the Cherokees entered into an era of progress that gave a distinct character to their history. Even during the wars they had made a good start. In the fall of 1796, Benjamin Hawkins, recently appointed agent to the southern Indians, visited their country. He reported fenced farms, orchards, plowed fields, sizable stocks of cattle and hogs, and comfortable dwellings. He saw some cotton and advised them to plant more, and he assembled the women and urged them to learn to spin. They promised to comply and asked for wheels and cards. He saw two women driving "10 very fat cattle" down to the white settlements for sale. At a home where he spent the night, he found the "hut . . . clean and neat" and was served "good bread," pork, potatoes, peanuts, and dried peaches. Everywhere he found the Cherokees eager for the extension of trade—they lacked markets for their farm produce—and the plows promised by the Treaty of Holston.

But that same fall a wild man appeared in Congress—young Andrew Jackson from newly admitted Tennessee—to denounce the Cherokees and the administration policy. "Some of the assertions of the Secretary of War are not founded on fact," he declared, and he was even ready to impeach the President. Nobody paid much attention to the uncouth Tennessean, but his attitude boded ill for the future.

During these same years, Washington was negotiating with the redoubtable Creek Confederacy, which was trying to hold back the frontier by raiding the Cumberland settlement and the tract being settled by Georgia under the fraudulent cession. The first year of his administration he appointed commissioners to treat, and he and Knox drew up secret instructions for their guidance. They were to demand the cessation of the Cumberland raids, to purchase the land claimed by Georgia, and to make "a solemn guarantee" by the United States of the Creeks' remaining territory. They were to grease the wheels of diplomacy by "gifts in goods, or money to some and if necessary, honorary military distinctions to others of the influential chiefs" and to McGillivray a commission higher than his Spanish commission and the "assurance of such pecuniary rewards . . . as you may think reasonable, consequent on the evidence of his future favorable conduct."

The commissioners sailed from New York with abundant presents and made their way up the Altamaha to Rock Landing on the Oconee, where McGillivray met them with two thousand chiefs and warriors. The power and solidarity of the assembled leaders was impressive as they carried out their ceremonials and received the white men with proud condescension. Presented with a draft treaty, they formally rejected it, broke camp, and returned home leaving the presents undistributed.

Washington decided to try once more. The following spring he sent Colonel Marinus Willett to visit McGillivray and invite the leading chiefs to New York where the Great Chief would sign with his own hand a treaty of peace "as strong as the hills and lasting as the rivers." Willett's report of his journey through the Creek country gives a vivid picture of an untouched people, rich and happy, living in security and peace. Populous towns welcomed him with speeches and ceremonials, entertained him with dancing, and feasted him on fish, venison, strawberries, and mulberries. Councils were called—one in the Lower, one in the Upper division of the Confederacy—and after deliberation it was decided to treat. Thirty of the chiefs, with McGillivray at the head, set out for New York. The delegation included the Seminoles, still a part of the Confederacy. As they passed through cities on their way— Richmond, Fredericksburg, Philadelphia—and finally at New York, they were received with a pageantry equal to their own. Then they settled down to the negotiations.

The Creeks acknowledged themselves within the limits and under the protection of the United States. They agreed to surrender the land claimed by Georgia, but there was a difference about the boundary. McGillivray warned the federal officials that he did not believe he could persuade his people to accept the one demanded, but it went into the treaty and the chiefs signed it. The United States guaranteed the Creeks' remaining territory and gave them permission to punish trespassers, and no United States citizen was to enter their country without a federal or state passport. The United States was to pay for the land cession with the goods still stored in Georgia, an annuity of $1,500 and gifts of livestock and farm implements. A secret treaty signed by Wash-

95

ington and Knox and McGillivray was uncovered many years later. It conferred upon McGillivray the rank of brigadier general with an annual salary of $1,200 and provided that six other leading chiefs, including one Seminole, should receive an annual stipend of $100.

Despite these bribes it appears that the chiefs were not purchased. It was probably the sight of the white man's power and wealth and the knowledge that the disputed land was already being settled that caused them to make the cession on the best terms they could. The Creeks, and this included McGillivray, held to a consistent "foreign" policy—to preserve their independence and their territorial integrity— and they had few scruples about making promises that seemed to further it. Immediately after the treaty of New York, McGillivray called on the Spanish governor and received a title and a "salary" of $3,500 from him. (He had the grace to reject subsequent payments from Knox.) Of the other bribed chiefs none was subservient, and at least one, Opothle Micco, was an uncompromising enemy of the United States, although as late as 1812 he was still receiving his "salary."

The Creeks accepted the land cession, but not the boundary McGillivray had questioned. Even as it stood, the Georgians disregarded it, killing the game and driving cattle and building houses on land unmistakably Creek. There were constant raids and counterraids along the border, with murders by Georgians and retaliatory murders by the Creeks. Then came the news of St. Clair's defeat in the Northwest, and Shawnees circulated through the country showing the scalps they had taken and inciting the Creeks to join in a general Indian war. Some of the towns did "take the war talk," but the Nation as a whole did not respond. The United States countered by a request for enlistments and an offer to pay a bounty for Shawnee emissaries or their scalps. The Creeks did not respond to this either. (If they had accepted, it might have ended Tecumseh's career.) Apparently some of their warriors fought against Wayne.

McGillivray died in 1793, but the Creeks retained their solidarity. This was impressively shown in a council with federal commissioners at Colerain on the St. Marys River in 1796. About four hundred chiefs, headmen, and warriors were present. Their intelligent understanding of the issues, their grave sense of responsibility, and their unity would have done credit to the deliberations of any great small nation in crisis. The commissioners—perhaps because Benjamin Hawkins was one of their number—made no attempt to exert undue influence, but they demanded the acceptance of the boundary as defined in the Treaty of New York. The Indians finally yielded though they said "it was like pulling out their hearts and throwing them away." They refused to make any further cession or accept the goods that had been brought for payment. "The land belongs to the Indians and they wish to keep it, . . . and hope the white people . . . will . . . keep their goods for other purposes." They were asked to permit the establishment of schools, but the suggestion was "received with so much dislike that it was postponed." They did accept two blacksmiths.

It was shortly after this that Hawkins was appointed as southern agent. After his visit to the Cherokees he went on to the Creek country and established his agency there. Eventually his duties were confined to the Creeks, and he served them with single-minded devotion until his death in 1816. He knew that white advance was inevitable, and he labored to prepare them to adjust to it. He held them at peace, he encouraged their economic progress in farming, homemaking, and commerce, and he tried—unwisely—to break down their communal life by undermining the towns and creating an artificial central government responsive to him. But it was evident by the end of the century that Creek power was declining. The Georgians intensified their encroachment, and they bore it with comparative meekness. In their frustration, some of the Alabamas and Coushattas even crossed the Mississippi to Spanish territory. They settled in Texas, where they still live on a reservation near Livingston.

In 1795, by the Treaty of San Lorenzo, Spain and the United States defined the Florida boundary. When surveyors came to run the line, the Creeks forced them to stop. Besides feeling the Indian horror of "cutting up" the earth, they apparently realized that an international division would separate the Seminoles from the Confederacy—as in fact it did.

The Spaniards remained undisturbed in the Southwest. Although the Indians there were not subjected to the intrigues of rival powers, the colonial administrators balanced the tribes against each other, always with the particular aim of enlisting them against the Apaches. The commander general of the interior provinces, first at Sonora, then at Chihuahua, regularly paid a bounty of twenty pesos for every Apache scalp or pair of ears. At first the same price was paid for live Apaches, but these captives usually escaped. In 1784 the order came to kill all except children seven years old or younger; older than that they were "implacable, cruel, and in no manner reducible." By this time the Apaches had taken to the mountains, where they were hunted down like coyotes. Still they managed to hide out and survive.

The Comanches had appeared on the New Mexican frontier about 1700. At first they harried the Spaniards and the Pueblos and fought the Apaches. The Spaniards encouraged their hostility to the Apaches and worked to win their friendship. In 1777 the able Juan Bautista de Anza became governor of New Mexico.[7] With great tact and consideration, supplemented by the inducement of trade and the cultivation of an influential native statesman named Ecueracapa, whom he built up as head chief, he managed to make peace with them. The culmination of his careful diplomacy came in a great council held at Pecos in 1786. The Comanches made a big hole in the ground and then refilled it "with various attendant ceremonies," meaning "they buried the war." With equal ceremony Anza bestowed upon Ecueracapa a staff "as an insignia of authority" and presented him with a uniform and a medal with the king's likeness. The Governor then opened a trade fair, marking off two lines, one for the Indians and one for the Spaniards, and filling the space between with Spanish goods. The Comanches traded more than six hundred buffalo robes, many loads of dried meat and tallow, fifteen horses, and three guns.

Anza also invited the Utes to the council and induced them and the Comanches, who had been fighting each other, to make peace. He incited the Comanches to kill Apaches, giving them a card to assist them in keeping their score. After the council, with some Spaniards, Pueblos, and Navahos, they went down the Río Grande as far as El Paso, killing Apaches on the way. When Anza reported to the commander general, the latter commended him for his accomplishments, especially this last—"Because one of the principal results we must seek from this is stimulating war upon the Apaches." He advised Anza to persuade the Comanches to settle down near the province and learn to farm. Anza did help one band to build a pueblo-type dwelling near the present Pueblo, Colorado, but they soon abandoned it.

Anza managed to install friendly chiefs with medals and ribbons among the Navahos also, and worked to set them against the Apaches of the Gila River region. In fact, one object of the Ute-Comanche peace was to alarm the Navahos and ensure that the Gilas would not take refuge with them. But the "old contacts of kinship" between the

[7] The fascinating story of his Indian policy is given in Alfred Barnaby Thomas, *Forgotten Frontiers.*

Navahos and Gilas proved hard to break. The Spanish officials even considered driving out the Navahos, thus depriving them of their herds, their woven goods, and their cultivated fields—an unconscious glimpse of their progress at that early date.

Anza also tried to reclaim the Hopis, still free a century after the Great Pueblo Revolt. In 1775 they numbered 7,494, grouped in seven pueblos set on three mesas; raised abundant crops of corn, beans, and chili and some cotton; and owned horses, cattle, and sheep. Fray Silvestre Velez de Escalante, the padre at Zuni, urged their reconquest and reconversion by a military expedition. He admitted that forcible conversion was disapproved by theologians and forbidden by royal decree, but that applied to people who had never been Christians or subjects and the Hopis were both (after the lapse of a century). Thus they were apostates and rebels. It would require a presidio to hold them, but it could be used for a base against the Apaches, who also might be reduced and Christianized.

The Spanish officials rejected his suggestion, fearing an attack on the Hopis would unite them with the Navahos and Apaches and bring on a general war, which the colony was too weak to withstand. Then in 1777 a terrible three-year drought began in the Hopis' country, and they left their pueblos and scattered through the hills seeking wild food. Now they might be won by missionaries and presents.

Anza accordingly visited them in 1779. He found not more than 798 people, the rest having died or gone to live with "heathen" tribes. They had planted extensively that year, but "what they call fields are sand hills," with no prospect of a harvest. Even their drinking water was scanty and stagnant. Anza talked with the headman, offering him a horse-load of supplies. He refused the gift, saying he had nothing to give in return, and "without such his customs would not allow it." Anza told him the priests would tell him about the Christian religion. Again he refused. Starving or prospering, they would remain free.

During this same time the Spaniards were advancing in California. In 1776 they founded a mission and presidio at San Francisco. In the following years a chain of missions and presidios was extended up the fertile coastal valleys from San Diego to the twenty-first and last, north of San Francisco, at Sonoma. Imposing buildings were constructed, olive groves and orchards were planted, and great herds of cattle, sheep, and horses were tended, all by Indian labor under the rule of the padres backed by the soldiery. The regime was benevolent, but every year the padres' carefully kept records showed more deaths than baptisms. Apparently the Indians could not endure the change in their way of life.

There was nothing benevolent about the way the Russians were advancing down the coast under a semiofficial corporation set up by the rulers. In 1787, Aleksandr Andreevich Baranov founded Archangel (now Sitka) on the island still called by his name. He brought along Aleutian slaves to take the sea otters, and he had two hundred Russian serfs, whom he treated with equal cruelty. He tried the same method on the neighboring Tlinget Indians, but they proved less submissive than the Aleuts; in 1802 they burned his fort. He defeated them in a battle following, but his rebuilt post was strongly fortified and guarded.

Other nations had discovered the fur trade. In 1792 there were twenty-one vessels under various flags plying the coast of the Northwest trading with the Indians. Most of these were American, owned by Boston merchants. They would spend two summers buying furs, spending the intervening winter in the Hawaiian Islands. After the second summer they would sail to China with their load, selling it for an immense profit (one hundred dollars for a sea otter pelt), and then return to Boston with Chinese products after two or three years' absence.

In 1792, Captain Robert Gray of Boston discovered the great river which he named for his ship, the *Columbia*. He sailed up the stream and anchored thirty miles above the mouth, thus forming the basis of an American claim. "The Indians," wrote young John Boit, fifth mate, "are very numerous, and appear'd very civill (not even offering to steal).... The Men ... are strait limb'd, fine looking fellows, and the women are very pretty." The river abounded in salmon and other fish, and the woods with moose and deer, "the skins of which were brought us in great plenty."

The Atlantic, the Gulf, now the Pacific. This completed the encirclement of the Indians from all the coasts. Soon these coasts would be connected from east to west across the interior.

CHAPTER SIX

THE NEW POWER ADVANCES

"We gave them forest-clad mountains and valleys full of game, and in return what did they give our warriors and our women? Rum and trinkets and a grave."—TECUMSEH TO SIR ISAAC BROCK, AUGUST 14, 1812.

The unexpected acquisition of Louisiana in 1803 was to white Americans what the discovery of the New World was to Western Europeans. The story has been often told of how President Jefferson sent Meriwether Lewis and William Clark to cross it and go on to the Pacific. They were to tell the Indians of his desire for peace between the tribes and his promise of trade goods to follow.

They left St. Louis with some forty men on May 14, 1804, and worked their way up the Missouri to the Mandan towns, where they spent the winter. (This country had all been penetrated by white men, first the French, then the British, from Canada.) Setting out again in the spring, the explorers employed the French Canadian, Toussaint Charbonneau, as guide and interpreter. His sixteen-year-old wife, Sacajawea, went along carrying her young baby on a cradleboard strapped to her back. She and the baby became the pets of the expedition, and her exploit has gone down in Western legend. When the party reached the Three Forks of the Missouri in western Montana, she was in familiar territory, for she was a Shoshoni girl captured in childhood by the Hidatsa Sioux and purchased by Charbonneau. She pointed out the right fork and the expedition soon reached her people.[1]

She danced for joy and eagerly sought out her family and friends. Meanwhile, the young chief, Cameahwait, ceremoniously started a council, and Sacajawea was called to interpret. Suddenly she recognized him as her brother. She ran to him, threw her blanket over their two heads, and embraced him with tears of joy. The explorers bought

[1] Her story is told in Trenholm and Carley, *The Shoshonis*.

horses from this friendly tribe, with which they crossed the mountains to the country of the Nez Percés.

They found these people camped at a camass meadow, for it was the time of the fall harvest of this product. The women dug up the bulbs with sharp curved sticks, piled them—perhaps twenty-five or thirty bushels at a time—on a bed of grass spread over hot coals in a fire pit, poured on water to produce steam, covered them with more grass and a layer of earth, and built a fire on top. After a day of cooking they were taken out and dried in the sun for permanent storage.

The Nez Percés had learned of the approach of the strange white men, had held a council, and decided to welcome them. They supplied them with camass and salmon and explained the course of the rivers by signs and a crude map. The party built dugout canoes, left their horses in the care of one of the chiefs, and floated down the Snake and the Columbia. A Nez Percé guide accompanied them as far as The Dalles making friends for them at the Indian villages along the way.[2]

The explorers noted the importance of the salmon runs in the economy of these river people. The Indians gathered at the falls and narrows of the streams, and as the great fish came up, the men caught them in nets or traps set in weirs. The women cleaned them and dried them on scaffolds, then pounded them into a powder between stones and packed the powder in baskets of grass matting lined with salmon skin.

The party went on down the river and spent the winter of 1805–1806 near its mouth. There they found the Chinook tribes, people of a distinctive linguistic stock, who lived on the lower Columbia and had already met coastal traders. The next spring the explorers began the return journey. They traded off their canoes at the mouth of the Walla Walla and went on to the Nez Percé country to reclaim their horses. With these they crossed the mountains and started down the Missouri tributaries.

Lewis, with three men, left the main party to explore the Marias River in northwestern Montana. He fell in with a band of Blackfeet, who were unimpressed with his peace message and attempted to steal the horses. In the encounter two Indians were killed. This fierce people had been trading with the Hudson's Bay Company and the Montreal-based North West Company at posts on the Saskatchewan. There they

[2] The history and life way of the Nez Percés including the Lewis and Clark visit is given in Francis Haines, *The Nez Percés*.

102

had acquired guns and had become a terror to the Shoshonis and other tribes armed only with bows and arrows. After their encounter with Lewis they became the unrelenting enemies of American travelers, although they continued to trade with the British.[3]

Except for the Blackfoot incident, Lewis and Clark found the Indians friendly and eager for the promised trade. It was not long in coming, for the explorers had found the mountain streams incredibly rich in beaver. At the Mandan towns John Colter, one of the best hunters of the party, received permission to join two young men from Illinois to go trapping up the Yellowstone. The others returned to St. Louis. Their favorable report inspired the Spanish-born fur trader Manuel Lisa to take two keelboats loaded with trade goods up the river the following spring. He built a fortified trading post and trapping center on the Yellowstone at the mouth of the Bighorn.

Other expeditions followed, establishing company posts, while "free trappers" worked the streams on their own. Thus the Indians became familiar with the "mountain man," a new breed of American pioneer. The Blackfeet were always hostile, and bands of the other tribes were not above killing isolated trappers and stealing their horses, traps, and caches of furs. But in spite of the danger, the lure of the wild life and the profit from a successful catch proved irresistible. There was cutthroat competition between rival American companies at St. Louis and between them and the British. The worst effect of this was the debauching of the Indians by whisky, which was the most effective product in the bid for their trade. The traders also brought the deadly smallpox. The Mandans were wiped out as a tribe in 1837; the few miserable survivors fled from their once flourishing towns, where the dead lay unburied, and took refuge with the Arikaras. Their descendants now live with the Sioux on the Fort Berthold Reservation in North Dakota.

Some of the mountain men were renegades; others were men of character and integrity with a lively interest in the beautiful savage land and the customs of its inhabitants. Most of them married Indian women, a good way of acquiring protection and a monopoly of the beaver catch of the tribe; some multiplied these advantages by taking wives all over the West. The actions of the more undisciplined among them were described in the complaint of Big Elk, the Omaha chief, to federal officials at St. Louis. "What would you think to see me take

[3] An excellent history of this tribe is John C. Ewers, *The Blackfeet*.

your women in the streets and violate them? The whites at our village take the women of the braves and violate them in open day—I myself have run to save them, and appease the injured."

A pleasanter aspect of these relationships was given by the famous mountain man Joe Meek, who married a pretty Shoshoni girl, Mountain Lamb (Umentucken). His pride in her and his indulgence is shown in this description: "She was the most beautiful Indian woman I ever saw, and when she was mounted on her dapple gray horse, which cost me three hundred dollars, she made a fine show. She wore a skirt of beautiful blue broadcloth, and a bodice and leggins of scarlet cloth of the finest make. Her hair was braided and fell over her shoulders, a scarlet silk handkerchief, tied on hood fashion, covered her head; and the finest embroidered moccasins her feet."

And of her horse: "His accoutrements were as fine as his rider's. The saddle, crupper, and bust girths cost one hundred and fifty dollars; the bridle fifty dollars, and the muck-a-moots fifty dollars more. All of these articles were ornamented with fine cut glass beads, porcupine quills, and hawk's bells, that tinkled at every step. Her blankets were of scarlet and blue, and of the finest quality."

Another famous mountain man, Jim Bridger, lost his Ute wife in childbirth. He brought up his infant daughter by shooting buffalo cows, it is said, for milk to supplement her diet, and when she was five years old he sent her to St. Louis, where she was placed in a convent. Later he married a Shoshoni woman. He finally returned to Missouri to live, taking her along and marrying her after the white man's law.[4]

In 1825, the St. Louis fur companies began to replace the permanent fortified trading post with the "rendezvous." Caravans of trade goods and supplies were sent overland to selected locations near the Continental Divide. There, in a carnival atmosphere of drinking and carousing, horse racing and gambling, reunions and storytelling, the trappers and Indians came with their beaver to exchange for supplies and luxuries.[5] At the first rendezvous $25,000 worth of furs was hauled back to St. Louis; two years later the take reached $500,000. This practice was continued until the decline of the beaver business about 1840.

If any of the traders, trappers, or explorers strayed too far south, they were captured by the Spaniards and imprisoned or finally ex-

[4] An easily available account of the mountain men's activities is found in Trenholm and Carley, *The Shoshonis.*

[5] Accounts of these picturesque meetings are given in Washington Irving, *The Adventures of Captain Bonneville, U.S.A.*, superbly edited by Edgeley W. Todd.

pelled. Then, in 1821, Mexico became independent, and traders were welcomed. The famous Santa Fe Trail connecting Independence, Missouri, and Santa Fe became an important highway of frontier traffic, and the South Plains tribes watched and sometimes raided the caravans.

The fur trade also extended to the Pacific Northwest, where British and American companies established posts and entered into active rivalry. The Indians of that region began to acquire hogs and cattle and chickens, to plant potatoes, and to appreciate the convenience of guns and iron kettles.

Meanwhile, as the Indians of the plains and mountains were experiencing this cutting edge of encroachment, the farming frontier on the other side of the continent was advancing inexorably against the tribes of the Ohio country and the still-powerful Indian nations of the South.

In a rapid succession of treaties during the opening years of the century, the Southern tribes ceded tract after tract as the settlers overran them, each time assured (and vainly hoping) that the new boundary would be permanent. These treaties regularly carried annuities to the tribes (the beginning of their public finance) and provided for increased assistance in their economic development.

At first President Jefferson, like his predecessors, advocated the policy of showing the Indians how to subsist on smaller areas. Then when he acquired Louisiana he began to see an alternative—their removal beyond the Mississippi. He suggested this to the Choctaws and Chickasaws without result. He had better success with the Cherokees, for the Chickamaugans still opposed the white man's "civilization." In 1809 they sent out an exploring party, and the migration began that year. Soon some 1,130 Cherokees, including the earlier settlers, were living in northwestern Arkansas.

The tribes of the Old Northwest were too disorganized to require this cautious encroachment. All the area west of the new state of Ohio had been organized as the Territory of Indiana, and William Henry Harrison had been appointed as governor. He established his capital at Vincennes and entered enthusiastically upon the dispossession of the Indians. He found an unexpected opponent in Tecumseh.

As statesman, orator, patriot, warrior, and as a chivalrous, generous, honorable human being, Tecumseh stands as one of the greatest Indians known to history. The Indians had always contended that a tribe was not bound by land cessions given by bribed individuals, but

Tecumseh developed the thesis that all the land belonged to all the Indians and that no tribe could sell a part of this common patrimony. He did not at first urge war on the whites, for he believed that if the Indians would unite in their primitive strength they could hold their heritage.

He was aided in his crusade by his brother, Tenskwatawa the Prophet, who through trances and supernatural revelations developed a native religion and propagated it with evangelistic fervor. His Indian Deity had told him that the white Americans "grew from the scum of the great water, when it was troubled by an evil spirit and the froth was driven into the woods by a strong east wind. They are numerous, but I hate them. They are unjust; they have taken away your lands, which were not made for them." But the Indians had transgressed by adopting white ways; hence, He had shut the game up in the ground to punish them. They should "throw away" all these corrupting influences—drunkenness, domestic animals, traders' products, even guns—and join in the songs and dances of the primitive revival. Supernatural forces would then sweep away the white men and restore the old conditions. (Later, when war came, the prohibition against guns was not universally observed.)

In 1808, the brothers built a "Prophet's Town" on Tippecanoe Creek in Indiana, where their converts lived in the purity of the old ways and practiced their rituals. Then the two leaders with several companions went around to the tribes of the Old Northwest, winning followers everywhere. The next year Tecumseh visited the Southern tribes, even the Florida Seminoles, where he made friendly contacts; the Osages in Missouri, who were interested but not aroused; and the Iroquois in New York, who rejected his message. While he was away, Governor Harrison called a few chiefs to Fort Wayne, "mellowed them"—his words—with alcohol, and got their signatures to a "treaty" ceding three million acres of land in Indiana, some of it belonging to tribes that had not even been present at the "council." When Tecumseh returned, he hotly condemned the fraud, and by the spring of 1810 he had one thousand warriors at the Prophet's Town training them to repel any attempt to settle the land. His plan for peace and unity had not been strong enough to hold.

In August, with three hundred followers in war paint, he went to see the Governor at Vincennes. The meeting was held under the trees with Harrison's soldiers and Tecumseh's warriors standing by. The Governor invited him to take a chair, "Your father requests you to take a seat by his side." "The Great Spirit is my father," he answered. "The earth is my mother—and on her bosom I will recline."[6] And he sat down on the ground. Later he spoke, presenting the Indian cause with such headlong eloquence that the interpreter was hard put to follow him. "Sell a country!" he exclaimed. "Why not sell the air, the clouds and the great sea, as well as the earth? Did not the Great Spirit make them all for the use of his children?" He even cited the United States as a precedent for his plan of Indian solidarity, "The States have set the example of forming a union among all the fires—why should they censure the Indians for following it?"

Harrison then spoke, saying the United States had always been fair to the Indians. Tecumseh sprang to his feet, crying, "It is false! He lies!" The Governor unsheathed his sword, several of his men aimed their guns, the warriors drew their tomahawks. A fight seemed imminent, but Harrison dismissed the council. The next morning Tecumseh apologized for his outburst, and the Governor visited the Indian camp. The two men sat down on a bench. Tecumseh kept crowding Harrison, and the latter kept moving over. When he reached the end, he protested. Tecumseh laughed and said that was what the white men were doing to the Indians.

Tecumseh then began another journey through the Northwest. In November he crossed into Canada from Detroit and addressed a council of many tribes at Fort Malden. He had now determined on war and hoped for British support, but the British, through both humanity and expediency, worked for peace. Harrison, believing, however, that they were inciting the Indians, wanted an excuse to attack the Prophet's Town. It came in July when the Potawatomis killed some white men in Illinois. Harrison asserted that the killers were followers of the Prophet and demanded that they be turned over to him. Tecumseh, now back home, called on the Governor and refused, but he said he was setting out on another journey and suggested a truce till his return.

This time he was gone for five months, visiting the Southern tribes, during which time a great comet flamed in the sky as a convincing portent. In his party were sixteen Shawnees, six Kickapoos, two Creeks, and six warriors of some tribe unknown to white Americans, probably Sioux from Minnesota. He first stopped with the Chickasaws—no record of this call survives—and then went on to the Choctaws, passing from town to town and winning many supporters. Finally, he addressed the chiefs and warriors at a great council, attended also—if one

[6] So translated in the artificial English of that day.

man's memory can be trusted—by the Chickasaws. The Choctaws' most influential chief, Pushmataha, urged continued friendship with the United States. The council was evenly divided, but the Choctaws had had enough of civil war. They left the final decision to a medicine man, who prudently divined the omens as supporting Pushmataha's argument.[7]

Tecumseh then went on to the Creek country. In these frustrating times the Creeks were trying to keep the peace and hold to their heritage. Sometime that year they formally agreed in council to inflict the death penalty on any chief who should agree to an unauthorized land cession. It would be interesting to know whether this was due to Tecumseh's influence. He reached the Upper division of the Confederacy about the middle of September and held councils in the main towns. The high point of his visit was a council in the leading town of Tuckabatchee.

Benjamin Hawkins had unsuspectingly called the chiefs there to consult them on tribal business, but the news that Tecumseh would be present had brought five thousand people from all parts of the country. He and his party marched into the square and seated themselves in silence. The agent, overconfident, finished his business and left; then before the assembled Indians Tecumseh urged his cause with his usual fiery eloquence. The chiefs tried to combat his influence, but he made many converts.

He left a relative, Seekabo, to instruct them in the religious part of his mission: the "Dance of the Lakes" and the use of magic red war clubs that would protect the Indians and drive the white men into quagmires. Then on December 15 came the first shock of one of the worst earthquakes on record. It was centered along the Mississippi, where great masses of the banks fell into the stream, two river towns in Missouri were destroyed, and the earth was thrown into great rolling waves that burst open in long fissures. The tremors were felt as far east as Savannah, and the shocks continued throughout the winter. When the Creeks' houses began to shake, they were sure Tecumseh had told them he would stamp his foot and the earth would tremble.

He had gone on to Florida, where he won the Seminoles. He visited the Lower Creeks in Georgia, then crossed Georgia to North Carolina and traveled the full length of Tennessee, trying with little

---

[7] A sentimentalized account of this council, based on the testimony of an eyewitness, may be found in H. B. Cushman, *History of the Choctaw, Chickasaw, and Natchez Indians*, now available in a new edition.

success to arouse the Cherokees. By December he was addressing the Delawares and Shawnees in Missouri and failing again with the Osages. He went on north to the Iowas and to the Sauk and Fox tribes, where Black Hawk was one of his most ardent supporters. Early in 1812 he was back with his brother in Indiana. It was an unhappy return.

As soon as Tecumseh was safely out of the way, Harrison had raised a force of 1,000 men and marched against the Prophet's Town, and on the night of November 6 he camped in front of the settlement. The Indians held an excited council. Tecumseh had told them to keep the peace, but some Winnebagos wanted to fight and the Prophet yielded. Some 450 Indians made the attack before dawn. In the battle Harrison lost 61 killed and 127 wounded; the Indians suffered fewer casualties, but they withdrew, and Harrison went on and burned the town. Thus Tecumseh found himself at war before he had effected his pan-Indian union. The tribes whose warriors had been killed began to fall on the settlements. Many settlers were killed, farms were abandoned throughout Indiana, and the country became dotted with blockhouses. One family was wiped out only five miles from Vincennes; others were killed within three miles of the regular army post of Fort Dearborn on the site of Chicago. None of this was in Tecumseh's plan.

Meanwhile, on June 18 the United States declared war against Great Britain. Both sides then sent agents throughout the Northwest to enlist Indian allies. Brigadier General William Hull, on his way to take command at Detroit, induced the Indians to hold a council at Fort Wayne. There several chiefs spoke in favor of joining the United States. Tecumseh argued passionately against it. "Here is a chance . . . such as will never occur again—for us Indians of North America to form ourselves into one great combination." Twice he broke peace pipes handed to him by a pro-American Wyandot (Huron) chief. (Later he smoked with the Wyandot; he wanted no hard feelings between Indians.) Then, gathering a large war party, he marched to Fort Malden and joined the British. He sent out his warriors to harass Hull, and they engaged in several skirmishes. Thus, it was an Indian, Tecumseh, who began the fighting in the War of 1812. Soon Major General Isaac Brock arrived with British reinforcements and Tecumseh helped materially in his capture of Detroit and Hull's entire army in August. At the same time, the Potawatomis captured Fort Dearborn and massacred the garrison.

Tecumseh's Southern converts were beginning their own kind of

109

warfare. The Creeks killed two Georgians and a family in Tennessee, and the Seminoles sent two scalps to the council of the Upper Creeks, inviting them to join the war. Hawkins demanded punishment, and the chiefs obediently killed eight men for the Georgia murders, three for the Tennessee family, and threatened the Seminoles, who were beyond their reach. At the same time, the frenzied dancing and incantations were going on in the towns. Hawkins was old and ailing, and the frontier hesitated to attack the still-formidable Confederacy.

In the fall Tecumseh again visited the Creeks, reporting the good news from the North and the promise of British support. He left bundles of red sticks, from which one was to be removed each day to set the time for a concerted attack. His overeager partisans then killed seven families of settlers at the mouth of the Ohio, and Hawkins threatened the Creeks with war if the killers were not punished. The chiefs dreaded the conflict with their own people, but they sent out enforcement parties, who battled with the hostiles and killed eight of them. It was April, 1813.

That same month Tecumseh returned to the North with 600 recruits from the Illinois tribes. He now had about 3,000 men. At one time or another warriors from thirty-two tribes fought under his command. But while he was away, the able Brock had been killed in battle and succeeded by the incompetent Colonel Henry Procter. In January a force of 850 Kentuckians advancing against Detroit had been annihilated on the River Raisin by the Indians under Procter, those not killed in battle being butchered after their surrender. When Tecumseh learned of it, he was equally angry at his Indians and at their incapable commander.

Harrison marched north to avenge this outrage and built Fort Meigs. Procter and Tecumseh besieged him there, and the warriors cut off some 800 Kentuckians on their way to reinforce him. Most of these soldiers were killed, but about 150 surrendered. The Indians took the prisoners to Procter's headquarters and started tomahawking and scalping them. An Indian rushed to the siege lines and told Tecumseh, who galloped to the camp and hurled himself upon the killers. The massacre stopped instantly. Then he went to Procter. "You are not fit to command," he raged. "Go and put on petticoats." Two days later, over Tecumseh's protests, Procter lifted the siege and returned to Fort Malden.

Apparently, the bundles of "broken days" left with the Creeks were set to run out in June. The nativists began by killing livestock and destroying articles of white manufacture throughout the Nation. They killed nine of the recent executioners of tribal law and destroyed Tuckabatchee, which had not joined the movement. It was in fact a civil war, with about half the Upper Towns and most of the Lower Towns remaining under Hawkins' influence. The white man's tortuous diplomacy had finally succeeded in dividing this people that had stood so long in the pride of its unity.

On August 30 the hostiles (now denominated as "Red Sticks") brought the United States into the war by falling on Fort Mims, a few miles above Mobile, where a number of frightened settlers had taken refuge. The commander, with criminal negligence, had failed to guard or even to close the gate, and the Indians rushed in and killed 107 soldiers, 160 civilians, and 100 Negro slaves. Only a handful escaped. But on September 10 came Perry's famous naval victory on Lake Erie, cutting off the British supply route from the east. Procter then abandoned the Detroit area and, with Tecumseh passionately protesting every step, started to retreat along the north shore of the lake. Harrison caught up with them, and Tecumseh was killed fiercely fighting with his Indian warriors in the Battle of the Thames on October 5. A monument with a Canadian flag flying above it now marks the place where his great design collapsed far from the homeland he had devoted his life to save.

Thus, with the Indians disorganized and leaderless and their British allies in retreat, the Americans soon regained control of the Northwest. Settlers flocked to the region, and there was the familiar pattern of land cessions from disunited tribes. Indiana became a state in 1816, and Illinois in 1818.

In the South that same winter of 1813–14, the white man's armies advanced against the Red Sticks from three directions: two invasions of Georgia militia and pro-Hawkins Creeks from the east; a federal army with a Choctaw contingent under Pushmataha up the Alabama River from the south; two Tennessee armies from the north, one of these under Andrew Jackson with six hundred Cherokee auxiliaries. This was another new experience for the Creeks. Their unpalisaded towns had seen no foreign invader since De Soto made his trail of death and rapine across their country nearly three centuries before. The Red Sticks fought desperately, strengthened by their incantations and relying for the most part on native weapons. Many were killed and several of their towns were burned—with houses "of a superior order for the dwelling of savages, and filled with valuable articles," said the

111

Georgia commander—but they drove back the invaders. Even Jackson had to retreat twice and reorganize his forces. Then he advanced the third time, and the final catastrophe came on March 27 at Horseshoe Bend on the Tallapoosa. There the warriors fought like demons until they were annihilated; only a few lying wounded in the piles of dead survived.

About one thousand of the Red Stick party fled to Florida with their families and joined the Seminoles. Among them was a young warrior named Osceola, said to have been one of the few survivors at Horseshoe Bend. Hawkins tried to induce them to return to their homes, but they sent back the defiant message, "We have lost our country and retreated to the sea side, where we will fight till we are all destroyed." From this time on they were the dominant party among the Seminoles.

In August, Jackson called the leading chiefs together to dictate a peace. All but possibly one belonged to the majority party that had fought for the United States throughout the war. They were made to sign a confession of war guilt and to cede two-thirds of their territory— an immense tract to the west of their heartland comprising about half of Alabama and a wide strip along the south to cut them off from the Seminoles. During the next forty years the federal treasury realized more than $11,250,000 from the sale of this ceded land to settlers. In 1962, the Creeks finally won a judicial decision—an award of $3,913,000 by the Indian Claims Commission which will be distributed among the descendants of those despoiled in 1814 as soon as these heirs can be determined.

Jackson went on with Pushmataha and his Choctaws to capture Pensacola and to win glory for the defense of New Orleans against the British. Then, with the war over, he headed commissions to make treaties with his other allies. This time he had no pretext of war guilt, but by intimidation, bribery, and pressure, and by their admiration for him as their brave and able war leader, he despoiled the Cherokees, Choctaws, and Chickasaws almost as effectively as he had despoiled the Creeks. He tried to persuade the Cherokees to exchange all their land for a western tract. About one-third of the tribe did remove to Arkansas, but the rest remained on their reduced holdings.

In 1818, Jackson invaded Florida, where British adventurers had been stirring up the Seminoles to raid across the boundary. He ousted the Spanish officials and executed two British subjects and two Red Stick leaders. When Spain protested, the American government demanded that she police the province adequately or sell it. Spain agreed to the sale and turned it over to American control in 1821. Settlers soon flocked there, and the Seminoles, now numbering about five thousand, were pushed into the swamps of the interior.[8]

Back from his Florida campaign, Jackson continued clearing Indian land for settlement. Louisiana had been admitted to statehood in 1812. Mississippi came in 1817 and Alabama in 1819. The next step was to clear Mississippi of Choctaws. In 1820 he finally persuaded them to exchange some of their land for a huge area in the West, which, after a modification in 1825, comprised the southern half of present Oklahoma. They had long hunted in that region, but to the disappointment of the federal officials they made no attempt to remove there.

Grievous as their land losses were to the Southern Indians, these were mainly peripheral areas, once valued hunting grounds, but now depleted of game by white intruders. The tribes still owned most of their heartlands, and they had taken the advice of their white well-wishers—learn "civilized" ways and prosper on a limited acreage—and they were determined to dig in and stay. The Cherokees were the leaders.

Along with their economic progress, they had begun to ask for schools. The Moravian Brethren came in 1801, and the Presbyterians opened a school a little later. Spectacular progress began when the American Board of Commissioners for Foreign Missions began its work there in 1817. Then the educational work of the missionaries was simplified when just at this time the Cherokee genius Sequoyah reduced the language to writing.

This remarkable Indian spoke—and of course wrote—no English, and he never came under missionary influence; but he knew that the white man had a system of conveying messages by making marks on paper.[9] He said, "I thought that would be like catching a wild animal and taming it." Working for years, finishing in Arkansas in 1821, he isolated eighty-six Cherokee syllables and assigned a character to each one. Thus the Indian simply memorized the characters; then he could read or write anything in the language. Almost immediately the whole tribe became literate, and the Western and Eastern divisions began to communicate with each other in writing. The great American Board missionary Samuel Austin Worcester went to Boston and had special

[8] The best account of this early period in Seminole history is given in Edwin C. McReynolds, *The Seminoles.*

[9] The standard biography of Sequoyah is Grant Foreman, *Sequoyah.*

type made for a printing press. In 1828 the tribe began to publish a newspaper with columns in English and Cherokee, and fullbloods in the most remote settlements became informed on current happenings. At the same time, Worcester—with the Board scrupulously paying the tribe for the use of the press—published books of the Bible, religious tracts, and hymn books in the Cherokee language. Meanwhile, mission schools multiplied, and adults in increasing numbers were joining Presbyterian, Methodist, or Baptist churches.

In 1808 the Cherokees had begun to formulate a legal code— necessarily written in English. Then step by step they developed a responsible government to take the place of the haphazard rise of chiefs. In 1828 they elected delegates to a constitutional convention, which created a government with a principal chief, a bicameral council, and a system of courts with orderly procedures and jury trial; and they participated freely in the election that followed. John Ross was chosen as principal chief. One-eighth Cherokee by blood, but all Cherokee in feeling, he had the complete confidence of the fullbloods, who elected him repeatedly to that office until his death in 1866. Their government functioned smoothly and effectively, financed by council appropriations of the $6,000 annuity paid by the United States under various treaties. They laid out a capital (named New Echota), erected public buildings, and began to publish their newspaper there. They were a united people, safe, they thought, from further land cessions by bribed or intimidated chiefs.

As soon as the American Board began its mission among the Cherokees, the Choctaws petitioned for one in their country. The first station, named for the pathetic John Eliot, was established in 1818. The next year a demonstration farm and school was started there, and the warriors in council appropriated their annuities and donated $1,800 and eighty cows and calves for its support. This tribe had no Sequoyah, but the missionaries reduced its language to writing, and while the children were receiving the conventional schooling in English, the adults were reading religious works in their own tongue. Soon after, missionaries working with the Chickasaws used the same written language for that tribe.

Only the Creeks were a dispirited and divided people, sunk in apathy, drunkenness, and economic stagnation. Their old way of life had failed. Then slowly, and under Cherokee influence, they began to summon their ancient unity and even to adopt some of the hated white ways as a measure of survival. In 1822 they gave reluctant consent to the establishment of two mission schools—a Methodist and a Baptist—but they sternly forbade the conversion of adults. Two years later in a council at rebuilt Tuckabatchee they adopted a solemn declaration of policy, which was probably reduced to writing by mission-trained Cherokees.

It began with a nostalgic reference to their past greatness and admitted the calamitous results of their division and war. "Our fathers never spent a thought on what was to be their end, or what was to become of their offspring," but now they could support themselves only by agriculture and civilization, and they resolved to acquire these skills and remain in their ancestral homes. "This is the land of our fathers; we love it . . . and on no account whatever will we consent to sell one foot of [it], neither by exchange or otherwise. This talk is not only to last during the life of the present chiefs, but to their descendants after them. . . . We recommend that our laws may be kept in writing, in order that our chiefs may keep in mind what laws have been passed. We are Creeks; we have a great many chiefs and head men but, be they ever so great, they must all abide by the laws. We have guns and ropes: and if any of our people should break these laws, those guns and ropes are to be their end. These laws are not made for any person in particular, but for all." They would live in peace with the United States, but "We were here before there was the face of a white man seen on this island," and "We earnestly admonish our white brethren . . . to treat us with tenderness and justice."

Later that same year they were asked to make another land cession. They held a council and firmly refused. But the leading chief of the Lower Towns, the half-blood William McIntosh, had for some time been advocating emigration to the West. He was probably attracted by the possibilities of this unspoiled region, but also—as he revealed in a letter to John Ross—he was receptive to bribery. Now the federal commissioners held a private conference with him and a few of his adherents and drew up a "treaty" exchanging all the Creek land in Georgia and much of Alabama—not hunting grounds but settled heartland—for a tract in Oklahoma. McIntosh was to receive $25,000 for his residence in the ceded area. Opothle Yahola, the spokesman of the council, officially warned him of the fatal consequence should he "sign that paper," but the commissioners promised protection, and it was duly signed. The Creeks then called a council which pronounced a death sentence against the signatories, and an official posse carried it out. They issued a formal statement reassuring the Georgians, ex-

115

plaining that this was a legal execution (as indeed it was) and resolving to "die at the corners of their fences . . . rather than . . . abandon the land of their forefathers."

When President John Quincy Adams learned of the fraud, he decided to negotiate a new treaty. The Creeks managed to save their Alabama land, but feelings ran so high in Georgia that they had no choice but to make the cession there. The United States undertook to finance the emigration of those who chose to remove. At a general council they took leave of their former opponents with mutual expressions of friendship and good will. (The Creeks were always more inclined to unity than to factionalism.) In 1828, about 1,300 were brought by steamship to the new location. Others followed, until they numbered more than 2,000. In general, they represented a prosperous mixed-blood element in the tribe, and after some pioneering hardships they began to prosper. The rest of the displaced Creeks joined their brethren in Alabama. An English traveler saw them "wandering about like bees whose hive has been destroyed." Their agent distributed clothing and food, but many died. Georgia was at last cleared of the Creeks. It had been slightly less than a century since that strong and confident people had welcomed Oglethorpe to set up a trading post for their convenience.

But in spite of some migrations to the West, the four great Southern tribes as a whole remained in their homeland. They had shown that they could make the adaptations necessary for survival in the surrounding white society. Why could they not remain there?

CHAPTER SEVEN

AN "INDIAN TERRITORY" IS ESTABLISHED

Andrew Jackson was elected president in 1828. It was clear to the frontier that, whatever his professions of benevolence, he would remove the Indians to the West by force. Even before his inauguration, Georgia and Mississippi passed laws extending their jurisdiction over the Indians within their borders, and Alabama followed before the year was over. Georgia and Alabama invited their citizens to plunder the Indians at will by making it illegal for an Indian to testify in court against a white man; Mississippi did not go so far, but the bias of the local courts achieved the same result. Jackson immediately informed the Indians, officially and through secret envoys, that the federal government was helpless to interfere with state laws; their only remedy was to remove. When Congress convened, he recommended removal legislation, and it was enacted on May 28, 1830.[1]

The peaceable Choctaws were the first to yield. In 1830, Mississippi abolished their government, imposing fine and imprisonment upon any Indian attempting to hold office in the tribe. They then agreed to cede all their homeland and remove to Oklahoma, and they received the guarantee that "no Territory or State shall ever have a right to pass laws for the government of the Choctaw Nation . . . and that no part of the land granted them shall ever be embraced in any Territory or State; but the U.S. shall forever secure said Choctaw

---

[1] The standard work on the removal of the five southern tribes is Grant Foreman, *Indian Removal*. Separate accounts of the removal of the Cherokees, Creeks, and Seminoles and of their development in the West may be found in the tribal histories previously cited; and of the Choctaws in Angie Debo, *The Rise and Fall of the Choctaw Republic*. A full-length history of the Chickasaws by Arrell M. Gibson will be published in 1971 by the University of Oklahoma Press.

Nation from, and against all laws except such as . . . may be enacted in their own National Councils, not inconsistent" with federal authority.

The treaty also gave every head of a family the option of remaining, selecting an individual farm ("allotment"), and becoming a citizen of the state. More than one third decided to stay, but the federal agent refused to register their selections, and white settlers took possession. Many of them, landless and penniless, eventually joined their brethren in the West. A few remained in poverty and degradation in Mississippi. In 1918 they began to receive some belated services from the federal government, but they are still an isolated group subject to racial discrimination. The Choctaws emerged from this experience determined to accept no more individual land holdings.

The main body of the tribe removed during 1830–33. Many died from the hardships of the migration and the settlement of a wild frontier—and from plain heartbreak. One observer noticed that many of them reached out and touched the trunks of the trees before they turned away on their journey. One gathering point was near a mission station, and the young son of a missionary never forgot the wailing of the women as they sat in groups with their children, their heads covered with blankets, their bodies swaying, and their cries rising and falling in unison, while the men stood silent and sad. This went on day and night until their departure.[2]

The Creeks came next. In the fall of 1829 they held a full council and voted to remain and submit to the state laws. This proved impossible; in 1831 the Lower Creek chief furnished the administration a list of fifteen hundred intruders laying out farms in that area. Washington's answer: removal. The Creeks then signed a treaty the following spring, surrendering all their land in Alabama. Like the Choctaw treaty, it carried the guarantee of autonomy in the West and the provision that individual Creeks might stay and select allotments. Land-grabbers then flooded the country and obtained contracts of sale. Their methods are significant, for the identical techniques were repeated many times when Indians tried to hold land by individual title: misrepresentation, the Indian not knowing what he was signing; the use of intoxicants; the misuse of notary seals on blank instruments, to be filled in at the swindler's convenience; outright forgery and a specialized kind, the bribing of some subservient Indian to impersonate the owner and sign in his place; and rigged probate procedure in the state courts corrupted by the general dishonesty.

2 Cushman, *History*, 114–15.

These "purchasers" drove the Indians from their homes, took over their crops, and stole their livestock. The Indians wandered over the country, starving and demoralized, but still set against removal. About 2,500 joined the Cherokees, not realizing that that tribe would be next. Small parties finally enrolled for emigration and, after suffering terrible losses on the journey, joined their people in Oklahoma. By the summer of 1835, Opothle Yahola was preparing to set out with the main body of Upper Creeks. Then some of the towns were driven to desperate acts of hostility, stealing food, burning houses, and killing settlers. The secretary of war immediately ordered the removal of the whole tribe as a military measure and the governor of Alabama issued a proclamation that all Creeks who should not aid in quelling the "uprising" would be treated as enemies. Once again the Nation was plunged into civil war. Opothle Yahola with 1,806 warriors joined the military command and did most of the fighting against the "hostiles." Before the summer of 1836 was over, their resistance was broken. The men were placed in irons and with their wailing women and children— a total of 2,495 people—were transported to Oklahoma and, literally naked, without weapons or cooking utensils, were dumped there to live or die. Opothle Yahola and large detachments of his party came voluntarily shortly thereafter.

The next year 543 Creeks were hunted out by the military from among the Cherokees and dragged to their new home. Some remained with the Cherokees, only to be removed with that tribe, with whom they still live in the Oklahoma Ozarks. About 800 fled to the Chickasaws, and when that tribe was removed, they joined their own people in Oklahoma. Of the few remaining in Alabama, several were hanged for participating in the "uprising," and others were reduced to slavery. Later, some of these latter unfortunates were found and ransomed by the emerging Creek Nation in the West, but others remained in bondage.

A century later Creeks in Oklahoma, entirely unfamiliar with the written record, remembered incidents of the journey that fit exactly into the scholarly accounts by historians. One woman recalled the story related "many years ago" by her grandmother. The military collected the people and brought them to "a crudely built stockade." There "was the awful silence that showed the heartaches and sorrow at being taken from the homes and even separation from loved ones . . . but times became more horrible after the real journey was begun. Many fell by the wayside, too faint with hunger or too weak to keep up with the rest. . . . A crude bed was quickly prepared for these sick and weary people. Only a bowl of water was left within the reach, thus they were left to suffer and die alone. The little children piteously cried day after day. . . . They were once happy children. . . .

"There were several men carrying reeds with eagle feathers attached to the end. These men continually circled around the wagon trains or during the night around the camps. . . . Their purpose was to encourage the Indians not to be heavy hearted nor to think of the homes that had been left."

Some of these informants told how "my grandfather died" or that "Some of the dead were placed between two logs and quickly covered by shrubs." One elderly man gave circumstantial details of the six-day crossing of an Arkansas swamp, hunting knolls for sleeping places at night. "My father even told of the time that he once had the luck to find a bone which was the large shoulder blade of some large animal and this he used for a rest for his head." Another heard the story from an old woman of a contingent taken by steamboat up the Mississippi. Carrying "a small bundle of her belongings . . . she began a sad song which was later taken up by the others . . . 'I have no more land. I am driven away from home, driven up the red waters, let us all go, let us all die together. . . .'"

When the Creeks were finally collected and enumerated, it was found that they had lost 45 per cent of their population.

The Cherokees were the next victims. They fought for their homeland with all the resources of their new learning. Among their leaders were Chief John Ross and the families of two remarkable fullblood brothers—Walking-on-the-mountain-tops, known as The Ridge (*Major* Ridge after serving with Jackson in the Red Stick War), and Oowatie—both married to mixed-blood women. Their sons were able and well educated: John Ridge and his cousin, Buck (the Male Deer) Oowatie (renamed Elias Boudinot), in an American Board school in Connecticut, where they married white girls; and Stand Oowatie (Watie) in a mission school in Tennessee. Elias Boudinot became the editor of the tribal newspaper, and his brilliant editorials strengthened the people to stand together.

The very year the paper was launched, gold was discovered in the Cherokee country in Georgia, and ten thousand intruders began laying out mining claims. The dispossessed Indians, having no recourse in the state courts, abandoned their cabins and farms and withdrew to other parts of their country. Then in December, 1830, Georgia followed the passage of Jackson's Removal Act by a series of savage laws against the Cherokees: forbidding their judicial officials to hold court or their council to meet except to ratify land cessions, forbidding them to mine their own gold, authorizing a survey of their land and its disposal by lottery to Georgians, and creating the Georgia Guard to enforce state law in their country. Legislation against the missionaries required white men living among the Indians to swear allegiance to the state under pain of four years' imprisonment for noncompliance.

The Georgia Guard was composed of ruffians, who terrorized the Cherokees—putting them in chains, tying them to trees and whipping them, throwing them into filthy jails. In communications to the Georgia officials, the President encouraged their anti-Cherokee policy; to the Indians he argued that he was powerless to prevent the operation of state law. The Cherokee council, meeting in defiance of the prohibition, then authorized Chief Ross to employ counsel and test this contention in the courts. The Nation had no income, for the President had stopped the annuities on the ground that the tribal government was extinct; but through private donations and the generosity of the attorney, the case was carried to the United States Supreme Court.

To come under the court's jurisdiction, the Nation had to qualify as a "foreign state." In the *Cherokee Nation* v. *Georgia* decision on March 5, 1831, the court, though expressing great sympathy for the Cherokees, rejected this contention and refused to assume jurisdiction. But its definition of the status of the tribe became a constitutional landmark. It was "a distinct political society . . . capable of managing its own affairs and governing itself"; and such societies were "domestic dependent nations," whose "relation to the United States resembles that of a ward to his guardian."

The opportunity to test the repressive laws came to the Cherokees later that year when Worcester and another American Board missionary, Elizur Butler, refused to take the oath of allegiance to the state. They were arrested with great brutality by the Georgia Guard, convicted, and sent to prison. (In after times Worcester used to joke wryly about his skill as a cabinetmaker acquired in the penitentiary.) This time there was no question of the Supreme Court's jurisdiction, and in the *Worcester* v. *Georgia* decision in February, 1832, the Cherokees won a complete victory. Said the court:

"The Cherokee Nation, then, is a distinct community, occupying its own territory, with boundaries accurately described, and which the citizens of Georgia have no right to enter, but with the assent of the

121

Cherokees themselves, or in conformity with treaties and with the acts of congress. The whole intercourse between the United States and this nation is, by our constitution and laws, vested in the government of the United States." And the law under which Worcester was convicted "is consequently void, and the judgment a nullity."

The joy of the Cherokees was beyond imagining. Their homes, their government, their peaceful progress—all seemed restored. Boudinot, in Boston on tribal business, wrote to his brother of the "glorious news. . . . It creates a new era on the Indian question." Truly it did promise more than a Cherokee deliverance. It had come too late to save the Choctaws, but it would have protected the Creeks and the other southern tribes.

John Ridge, in Washington with other Cherokee leaders at the hearing, expressed equal joy, but more caution, "the Chicken Snake Andrew Jackson has time to crawl and hide."[3] He was right. Whether or not the President used the words ascribed to him—"John Marshall has made his decision; now let him enforce it"—he ignored the court ruling and advised the Georgia officials to continue their persecution of the Cherokees.

Later that same year the state held its land lottery. The elegant plantation houses and extensive fields of the wealthy mixed-bloods fell to the holders of lucky numbers. Among the dispossessed was John Ross, who with his ailing wife, Quatie, and their children moved into a one-room cabin across the border in Tennessee. The mission properties with their school buildings, residences, and demonstration farms also fell to the winners, as did the public and private buildings at New Echota. Throughout the country fullbloods were evicted from their cabins and fields and robbed of their livestock.

A few Cherokees yielded to this pressure and began to emigrate, joining the "Old Settlers" in the West, who by this time had been pushed from Arkansas to Oklahoma. The governor then released the two imprisoned missionaries, and they joined the Western division of the tribe. Boudinot had begun to see emigration as inevitable, but when he cautiously approached the subject in the tribal newspaper, Chief Ross forced his resignation. In his valedictory issue, August 11, 1832, he wrote, "I cannot tell [my beloved country and people] that we will be reinstated in our rights when I have no such hope." The publication was continued under a less able editor until it succumbed

[3] The letters of the Ridge-Watie-Boudinot family from 1832 to 1872 have been published in Edward Everett Dale and Gaston Litton, *Cherokee Cavaliers.*

in 1834. Attempts to revive it failed when the next year the Georgia Guard confiscated the press and type.

By 1834 the unity of the Nation began to break up, an overwhelming majority still holding out under Ross's leadership, and a small "Treaty Party" led by the Ridges, Boudinot, and Stand Watie. Grace Steele Woodward has uncovered proof of secret collaboration between this latter group and the federal and state officials, and it is certain that their property was withdrawn from the lottery wheel, but nobody has found any evidence of bribery. Apparently they had decided upon what was best for their people and were willing to bypass the democratic process for their supposed benefit. Then as feelings mounted, the difference of opinion between the parties erupted into hatred.

Finally, Ross also saw removal as inevitable. He proposed selling the land for twenty million dollars, and he made overtures to Mexico for the purchase of a refuge there. He may have had his eyes on Texas, for as early as the winter of 1819–20 sixty families of Arkansas Cherokees under a chief known as The Bowl had established a settlement in that province. But the federal officials scornfully refused to treat with Ross. They knew where they could get the land cheaper. They wrote a treaty with the Ridge-Boudinot-Watie party and presented it in October, 1835, to a full council of the Nation, meeting—with their capital lost—at Red Clay on the Tennessee line. John Howard Payne, planning to write a Cherokee history, had come to interview Ross in his meager cabin. He saw the fullbloods when they stopped to greet the Chief as they walked past on their way to the council ground. They carried tin cups and bed rolls, wore turbans and hunting shirts belted with sashes, and conducted themselves with deep seriousness. The council unanimously rejected the treaty and authorized Ross to head a delegation to go to Washington and negotiate for more favorable terms.

To prevent his going, twenty-five members of the Georgia Guard crossed into Tennessee, arrested Ross and Payne, and threw them into a Georgia jail. There, chained near them, they found the son of the speaker of the council, and hanging overhead was the decomposing body of a Cherokee executed some time before. They were kept there for thirteen days. No charges were ever brought against them.

Ross finally managed to reach Washington. While he was there, the federal officials called another council to meet at New Echota to sign the rejected treaty. Only the Ridge-Boudinot-Watie family and a handful of their followers attended and registered their consent.

People of good will throughout the United States protested the ratification of this malodorous pact, but it received Senate approval. By its terms the Cherokees sold their land for five million dollars—much of which became an endowment for schools and other public purposes—and agreed to remove within three years.

A few small bands, including the "Treaty Party," left at once, but the majority held out. Three of them—named Aitooweyah, The Stud, and Knock Down—wrote to Ross in Washington: "We the great mass of the people think only of the love we have to our land . . . where we were brought up . . . for we say to you that our father who sits in Heaven gave it to us. . . . to let it go it will be like throwing away . . . [our] mother that gave . . . [us] birth. . . ."

In its maturity Georgia, more than any other state, has made historical restitution for its frontier excesses against the Indians. Its Historical Commission has restored many Cherokee landmarks, especially the newspaper plant and other buildings at New Echota; in 1962 its legislature formally repealed the oppressive laws of 1830, with the admission that these "must now be read with humility and sadness"; and, most important of all, its scholarly writers present the damaging facts with complete objectivity.[4]

None of this helped the Cherokees at the time. Their treatment had aroused so much public indignation that they hoped to obtain a new treaty permitting them to remain in Tennessee. But in the summer of 1838, General Winfield Scott (who was sickened by his assignment) was sent with 7,000 soldiers to remove them forcibly. They were rounded up in stockades and taken in detachments to the West. So many died that Ross finally got permission for them to manage their own removal. Even then, the loss of life was appalling: The first detachment of 858 was reduced to 744; the second of 858 was reduced to 654; the third, of 950, was more fortunate, with six births and only 38 deaths; the next, of 1,250, was reduced to 1,033—and so on. Grant Foreman estimated that of 18,000 who went West following 1835, about 4,000 died in the stockades or on the journey.

An army private who served during the removal recalled the experience in after years: "I saw the helpless Cherokees arrested and dragged from their homes, and driven by bayonet into the stockades. And in the chill of a drizzling rain on an October morning I saw them

---

[4] Typical of these is the publication by the University of Georgia Press of one of the finest books ever written of early Cherokee history, Henry Thompson Malone, *Cherokees of the Old South*.

loaded like cattle or sheep into wagons and started toward the west.[5]

". . . Chief Ross led in prayer and when the bugle sounded and the wagons started rolling many of the children . . . waved their little hands good-bye to their mountain homes."

The same private was with the Ross contingent when it camped in a storm of sleet and snow. Here the frail Quatie gave her blanket to a sick child. The child recovered, but the Indian woman contracted pneumonia and died. "I was on guard duty the night Mrs. Ross died," he remembered. "When relieved at midnight I did not retire, but remained around the wagon [where Quatie lay] out of sympathy for Chief Ross and at daylight was detailed . . . to assist in the burial. . . . Her uncoffined body was buried in a shallow grave . . . and the sorrowing cavalcade moved on."

Several hundred Cherokees hid out and escaped capture, living in the mountains of North Carolina and subsisting on wild products. Finally, a white man they could trust bought some land for them with money allowed by the government for their confiscated property, and they were permitted to remain there. They now number about 4,500, mostly fullbloods, living in a beautiful and picturesque region, making their living by farming and tourism—selling their crafts and recreating their history in the famous drama *Unto These Hills*.

Unlike the Cherokees, the Chickasaws left their native land without resistance. They were educating their children, building churches, and farming by Mississippi frontier standards, but they were confronted with the same argument that the federal government could not prevent the extension of state control. In a series of treaties beginning in 1832 they received more favorable terms than any other tribe. They removed to Oklahoma during the winter of 1837–38, paying the Choctaws for the right to settle on the land of that tribe.

The Seminoles suffered the most of all. Tricked into a removal treaty, they refused to go, and the ensuing Seminole War was the most costly to the United States in lives and money of any Indian war in its history. Under Osceola and other chiefs they hid out in the Everglades, and the army and navy with bloodhound trackers tried to hunt them down. A few were dragged out from time to time and taken to Oklahoma in chains. One of them, Wild Cat, described their condition, "transported to a cold climate, naked, without game to hunt, or fields to plant, or huts to cover our poor little children; they are crying like

---

[5] A wagon was provided for each twenty *évacués*, to carry the baggage, the small children, and the weak and ailing.

wolves, hungry, cold, and destitute." Such hardships added to the war and the removal reduced their population by nearly 40 per cent. By a census made in 1859 the number in the West was 2,254.[6]

Osceola was captured under a flag of truce and put in prison, where he died. George Catlin, the painter of Indian portraits, visited him there and wrote a moving account of his death. Osceola directed his two wives and his children to bring his magnificent war outfit. Then sitting up in bed, he dressed and painted himself carefully and bade farewell to the officers and to his family. Lying back down, he drew his scalping knife from his belt, grasped it in his right hand, and calmly died.[7]

The government finally gave up and let the remaining Seminoles stay in Florida. Many years later some of them accepted reservations and federal services. They now number about seven hundred. About four hundred recalcitrants, the non-Creek Mikasukis, held out, insisting that they were still at war with the United States. A hardy and healthy people, they lived in unwalled palm-thatched "chickees" set in trackless swamps. They hunted and fished; raised small patches of sugar cane, potatoes, pumpkins, squash, and corn; dressed in vari-colored clothing made of narrow strips of cloth sewn together; and made a little money by selling frogs' legs and garfish, guiding sportsmen, and even wrestling alligators for spectators. But draining projects were encroaching on their refuge, and the Association on American Indian Affairs, with the support of concerned Floridians and a dedicated federal agent, brought about a three-cornered compact, concluded in 1962. The tribe resumed relations with the United States (after 127 years); the state gave them title to the 235,000 watery acres where they live; and the Indian Bureau assumed responsibility for schools and other services. They adopted a constitution, borrowed federal money for tribal development, and are making good progress in education and the tourist business.

The removal of the five great Southern tribes and its continuing aftermath were paralleled in the North by events less spectacular but no less relentless. A few tribes escaped. Elaborate plans were made to remove the Iroquois, first to Arkansas, then to Wisconsin, finally to

[6] Their hardships in the West are described in Grant Foreman, *The Five Civilized Tribes* and in McReynolds' tribal history previously cited.

[7] The most easily accessible place to find this account and Catlin's portraits of the Chief is in Harold McCracken, *George Catlin and the Old Frontier*.

Kansas. Some of the Oneidas did accept a reservation in Wisconsin, where they still live; and a fraudulent treaty with the others was even ratified by the Senate, but the New York Quakers defended them vigorously and Jackson allowed them to remain. The history of the tribes of the Old Northwest is a dreary record of encroachment and a more or less voluntary removal to the West.[8] The Sauks resisted, in the Black Hawk War of 1832, but without being able to stay the inevitable expulsion from their homeland.

Soon the white frontier crossed the Mississippi, crowding these tribes still farther west. Missouri became a state in 1821 and its Indians were removed to Kansas: tribes that had migrated from the Old Northwest were settled in the eastern portion, and the Osages received a great tract along the southern border in their former hunting range. As Arkansas became settled, not only were the Western Cherokees pushed into Oklahoma, but the remnants of the indigenous Quapaw tribe after much wandering finally acquired a small reservation there northeast of the Cherokees. Thus Arkansas was clear of Indians when it was admitted to statehood in 1836. Iowa became a state ten years later, and all the Indians of that area were successively removed to the west of the Missouri except that after years of drifting back the Foxes (Mesquakies) with state consent bought with their own money a small acreage there, where they still live.

Thus by the end of the 1830s many displaced tribes were living west of the Iowa-Missouri-Arkansas line on tracts of land guaranteed (as always) to them in perpetual ownership. A few indigenous tribes had also signed treaties, ceded land, and received guarantees of the remainder. This Indian-owned land added up to some tracts in Nebraska and a solid block of reservations along the eastern and much of the southern boundary of Kansas, while the five great Southern tribes owned all of Oklahoma except the Panhandle and a small tract in the northeast corner belonging to the Quapaws and some Senecas (possibly never belonging to the Iroquois Confederacy) and associated Shawnees brought there from Ohio in 1832. This whole region became known as the Indian Territory, although it never had a territorial government. Eventually, as white settlement advanced into Kansas and Nebraska, the term was restricted to the Oklahoma portion.

The Southern tribes held their land under patented titles—exactly the same title that protects any white landholder. Their settlements were concentrated in the eastern half of their country, while the South

[8] Their separate histories can be found in Wright, *Guide*.

127

Plains tribes still ranged over the west. To distinguish them from the buffalo-hunters, they became known as the Five Civilized Tribes. In preparation for their coming the United States had established Fort Gibson in 1824, and expeditions went out from this base to establish friendly relations with the Plains Indians. As the frontier of the Civilized Tribes expanded, other posts were established farther to the west. In 1855 the United States leased a large tract in the southwest— thereafter known as the Leased District—from the Choctaws and Chickasaws to be used as a permanent home for any Plains tribes that might be induced to settle there.

Except for the buffeted Seminoles the Civilized Tribes soon conquered their wild frontier and prospered. The land was tribally owned, and every citizen was protected in his occupancy. Under this system the mixed-bloods laid out great plantations worked by Negro slaves and built beautiful houses filled with furniture brought up the rivers from "the States." Only the Creeks at first practiced their communal agriculture, but soon they, too, moved out to individual farms and the "town" became only a local unit of government and a community meeting place. Thus throughout the country the fullbloods farmed and lived in the same manner as the frontier white people of their day.

In their governmental development the Cherokees were at first torn by feuds growing out of the removal. In 1839 the anti-treaty party met somewhere and laid secret plans, and in one day assassinated Major Ridge, John Ridge, and Elias Boudinot. Stand Watie also was marked for death, but escaped. Frequent murders continued for a time until the factions finally united.[9] Then the Cherokees laid out a capital (named Tahlequah, i.e., Tellico), revived their newspaper, and resumed their orderly progress.

The Choctaws and Chickasaws adopted similar constitutions and governed themselves effectively under their borrowed Anglo-American procedures. The Creeks wrote a short constitution of their own design. In general, the Lower Creeks had settled on the Arkansas, the Upper on the Canadian. Each "District" had its local chief and council, and midway between the two was a meeting place for conducting tribal affairs. The councils had both legislative and judicial functions, and the councilmen reported the laws back to the towns. Elections were held by the voters lining up behind their candidates. With their long

[9] A fascinating account of one of these murder trials in a Cherokee court was written by John Howard Payne, *Indian Justice*.

experience of solidarity the Creeks carried no trace of the removal factions to their new land.

The Cherokees, Choctaws, and Chickasaws as soon as possible, the Creeks more slowly, established comprehensive school systems administered by their own officials and supported by their annuities. There were one-room neighborhood schools for the common branches and boarding schools in imposing brick buildings for higher learning. The first three tribes, with the help of their missionaries, reorganized their churches as soon as they arrived. The embittered Creeks at first forbade Christian services, but this ban was relaxed by 1845. Every settlement of the four tribes soon had its Presbyterian, Methodist, or Baptist church, usually with a native pastor conducting services in the local language. Naturally a devout people, they had found in Christianity a steadying influence to compensate them for the disruption of their ancient ways. There was still much crime, and drunkenness was a demoralizing influence, but their society was as law-abiding as the pioneer white communities surrounding them.

The Seminoles were long without a stable foothold in the West. The United States tried vainly to settle them among the Creeks, then finally in 1856 made a treaty purchasing some land for them from the Creeks and providing them a school fund. Now with a home of their own they began to settle there and were taking steps to organize a tribal government and a school system when their progress was interrupted by the Civil War.

Others besides the Five Civilized Tribes found a refuge in Oklahoma. Bands of Shawnees, Delawares, and other fragments of tribes from the Old Northwest drifted there and established prosperous settlements with the informal consent of the owners, instead of joining their people on the Kansas reservations. Still others came from Texas.

Through the years there had been accessions to The Bowl's colony from the Arkansas Cherokees. There in east Texas they had laid out farms, raised livestock, built comfortable houses, and wore clothing spun and woven by the women from their own cotton; and through Sequoyah's invention they had become literate in the native language. Associated with them were some Delawares, Shawnees, Kickapoos, and migrant bands from the Southern tribes. When the white Americans in Texas began their War of Independence from Mexico in 1835, they first sought the friendship of these Indians, recognizing their "just claims" to their land under Spanish or Mexican grants and guaranteeing their "peaceable enjoyment" of it. President Sam Houston, always sympathetic towards Indians, tried to carry out these pledges. He did manage to set aside the small reservation where the Alabamas and Coushattas still live, but he failed with the others. In 1839 his successor went against The Bowl, killing that chief and a large number of his warriors in battle, and drove the rest across the Red River into the Indian Territory. That was a bad year for another band of bitter, hopeless évacués to join the Cherokees, but Sequoyah sent them a letter urging them to come and they took his advice. At the same time, bands of their Shawnee, Delaware, and Kickapoo associates fled to the Indian Territory, while about eighty Kickapoos crossed the Río Grande into Mexico.

When Texas entered the American Union in 1845, unlike other states it retained its public domain; hence, the federal government could not reserve even the usually unstable tracts of land for the Indians there. As the white frontier advanced, the peaceable Caddos and related tribes were crowded out of their homeland, and there were constant raids and reprisals between the settlers and the Kiowas and Comanches of the Plains.[10] Finally, in 1846 through the good offices of federal officials and leaders of the Civilized Tribes, a peace treaty was made with the Caddos and their relatives; the Tonkawas, a small indigenous tribe unrelated to any other; and the Southern or Penateka band of Comanches, who lived in the belt of timber adjoining the Plains. Eight years later, after repeated urging by the federal officials, the state legislature set aside two reservations far out on the frontier for these tribes.

Both groups settled down gratefully. They built houses, fenced their fields, raised corn and vegetables, and sent their children to school. But the Indian-hating Texans, with real grievances against the Plains raiders, found it easier to murder the peaceable than to fight the hostile. They fired on a sleeping camp, killing or wounding men, women, and children; they invaded one of the reserves, threatening to wipe it out but fading away before a company of infantry; and then large mobs began organizing for a massacre. Robert S. Neighbors, himself a Texan who had fought in the War of Independence, was the federal agent. Starting out on August 1, 1859, he brought the Indians—1,430 Caddos and associates, 380 Penatekas—with a military escort to the Leased District, traveling 170 miles on foot through the heat and

[10] An excellent history of Texas-Comanche relations is Rupert Norval Richardson, *The Comanche Barrier to South Plains Settlement.*

Apache family group in front of wickiup.
"The Apaches have few friends. There seems no settled policy, but a general policy
to kill them wherever found."
U.S. Signal Corps photograph

Joseph Brant, by George Romney.
The town of Brantford, Ontario, perpetuates the Mohawks' migration to Canada.

COURTESY SMITHSONIAN OFFICE OF ANTHROPOLOGY,
BUREAU OF AMERICAN ETHNOLOGY COLLECTION

Little Turtle, who defeated Harmar and St. Clair, 1790 and 1791.
COURTESY OHIO HISTORICAL SOCIETY

Tecumseh. Portrait preserved in the family of George Rogers
Clark and William Clark.

*He believed that if the Indians would unite, they could hold
their heritage.*

Tenskwatawa, brother of Tecumseh, while living with the Shawnee
band in Kansas. Portrait by George Catlin, 1830.

*He preached that the white Americans "grew from the scum of the
great water."*

Opothle Yahola.

A young warrior sent to warn McIntosh of the fatal consequence should he "sign that paper."

COURTESY BUREAU OF AMERICAN ETHNOLOGY

Osceola, by George Catlin, 1838.
Catlin wrote a moving account of his death.
COURTESY NATIONAL COLLECTION OF FINE ARTS,
SMITHSONIAN INSTITUTION

137

Rabbit Skin Leggings, sole survivor of the Flathead–Nez Percé delegation to St. Louis, painted in Sioux costume by George Catlin on the
return trip in 1832.

No Horns on His Head, another member of the Flathead–Nez Percé
delegation, also painted in Sioux costume by George Catlin in 1832.

Tilaukait, Cayuse leader of the Whitman massacre, painted by Paul
Kane shortly before the tragedy.

Tamahas, Cayuse leader of the Whitman massacre, by Paul Kane.
They had grievances, some real, some imaginary.

Sequoyah, inventor of the Cherokee syllabary.
"I thought that would be like catching a wild animal and taming it."
COURTESY LIBRARY OF CONGRESS

John Ross, by John Neagle, 1846
The Cherokee factions finally united and they resumed their orderly progress.

COURTESY PHILBROOK ART CENTER, TULSA

Stand Watie.
He was a man of character and integrity.

Oktarharsars Harjo, or Sands.

"He thought the old U.S. was alive yet and the old treaty was good."

COURTESY BUREAU OF AMERICAN ETHNOLOGY

145

A Navaho woman and her baby in a cradleboard at Bosque Redondo.
Always they begged to return to their homeland.
COURTESY MUSEUM OF NEW MEXICO COLLECTIONS

leaving their household goods and farm equipment behind them. They settled there on the Washita with the indigenous Wichitas, and the Wichita Agency and Fort Cobb were established for their protection and guidance. Except for the Tonkawas they still live in that area, commonly classed together as the "Wichitas and affiliated tribes." (Incidentally, Neighbors was murdered when he returned to Texas.)

At the same time, first Missourians from across the border, then settlers coming into Kansas, began to invade the Kansas reservations, stealing the Indians' livestock, cutting down their timber, and murdering their people with impunity.[11] In 1853, Congress authorized the President to negotiate with the tribes of Kansas and Nebraska to extinguish their land titles, and the following January, Stephen A. Douglas introduced his Kansas-Nebraska Bill for the formation of territorial governments there. Even before this bill became law, the commissioner of Indian affairs obtained land cessions from eleven tribes in Kansas and three in southeastern Nebraska cutting their holdings from eighteen million to one and one-third million acres. Seven of these tribes were induced to take allotments, only to be dispossessed by the methods used in Alabama against the Creeks. At the outbreak of the Civil War the Indians that had been "permanently" settled in Kansas twenty years before were homeless or in process of becoming so. The Delawares even petitioned the government for a home in the Rocky Mountains. They knew the country: members of their scattered bands had migrated to the Pacific Northwest, where they were employed by the Hudson's Bay Company; others had served as guides to American mountain men and explorers. In 1857 two hundred Wyandots, dispossessed in Kansas, came to northeastern Indian Territory and settled with the Senecas.

Land-grabbers were also looking with covetous eyes at the property of the Five Civilized Tribes. In 1857, Robert J. Walker, the territorial governor of Kansas, urged that they be removed to the western, and supposedly worthless, half of the Indian Territory, and that the eastern half be made into a state. "The Indian treaties will constitute no obstacle," he said, "any more than precisely similar treaties did in Kansas." And in the presidential campaign of 1860, William H. Seward publicly advocated that "Indian Territory south of Kansas must be vacated by the Indian."

---

[11] Their experiences are presented as accurately as in any formal history in the fictionalized biography of Chief Journeycake of the Delawares by Argye M. Briggs, *Both Banks of the River*.

Also, bills were introduced in Congress providing for United States citizenship and allotments of individual farms to the Indians, opening the remaining land to white settlement, and establishing a territorial—and ultimately a state—government for the whole population. Then when Major Elias Rector of Arkansas became southern superintendent in 1857, he filled his reports with glowing descriptions of the potential wealth of their country and the advantage to them of admitting thrifty whites to settle there and influence them in civilization. Two years later the commissioner of Indian affairs made them a formal proposition to allot their land.

The Indians were not deceived by these benevolent pretensions. They knew what happened to an Indian and his land when the tribe was liquidated so that he stood alone in an alien society, and they joined as a unit against it. Their treaty guarantees were so specific, their determination so strong, and their achievements so impressive that the good faith of the United States was not ready to crumble before the greed of the exploiter.

In their western refuge they were undisturbed by white intruders. The admixture of white blood from an earlier period was not an alien influence. Each tribe had a resident United States agent, whose duties were nominal. The military posts once established in their country for their protection were progressively abandoned except for three on their western frontier. A few missionaries, who still worked among them, were completely identified with native interests. They had an active commerce with the outside world, carried on mainly by their own citizens, usually mixed-bloods. Graduates of their boarding schools often went to "the States" for further education, returning to become leaders of their people.

They had begun very early to call intertribal councils. Among themselves they made compacts regulating such matters as the requisition of criminals and intertribal naturalization. The fragmented tribes from the East came to request their aid and advice and to gain security from their power and stability. At a council held at Tahlequah, eleven tribes from the Old Northwest were represented, and among the Shawnee delegates was the son of Tecumseh. It was at a council called by the Creeks that the Caddoan tribes and the Penateka Comanches enlisted their help in making peace with the Texans. The Osages and the buffalo hunters of the Plains also attended, exchanging symbols of peace and friendship, impressed as no white man ever impressed them by the advantages of a settled life.

148

Said Chitto Harjo of this period in their history: "I had made my home here with my people, and I was living well out here with my people. We were all prospering. We had a great deal of property here, all over this country. We had come here and taken possession of it under our treaty. We had laws that were living laws, and I was living here under the laws. . . . I was living here in peace and plenty with my people and we were happy."

But while the Indians were prospering on this sheltered island, white settlement was sweeping like a tidal wave over the mountains to the Pacific.

CHAPTER EIGHT

HISTORY REPEATS ITSELF

The Pacific Northwest came first. The famous Oregon Trail became the highway to this region. Starting from Independence, Missouri, it followed the valley of the Platte and North Platte, crossed the Continental Divide by the South Pass in southwestern Wyoming, and reached its destination by way of southern Idaho. The territory of the United States reached only to the Continental Divide, but a treaty made with England in 1818 gave the two countries joint occupancy of the region beyond. The first impulse to settle it came in response to an urgent invitation from the Indians. The story has been often told.

From the Hudson's Bay posts the Indians learned of the white man's "power" of literacy and had been told something of Christian beliefs. Some Caughnawagas or Hurons from the St. Lawrence, previously employed by the company, had settled with the Flatheads and told them of Catholic practices. In 1825, Sir George Simpson, company administrator, held a council on trading business with the chiefs of the Spokanes, Flatheads, and Kutenais (neighbors of the Flatheads) and was greatly impressed when they asked him to send someone to teach them the white man's religion and ways. That was not done, but he did take two eleven-year-old sons of chiefs to be educated in an Anglican mission school at the Red River settlement in Canada. One of the boys died; the other, known as Spokane Garry, returned, the only literate Indian in the Northwest. His tribe flocked to hear him read the Bible, and they set up a school, where he taught the new "medicine."

The Nez Percés and Flatheads decided to go in search of the same accomplishments. They probably decided on St. Louis instead of the

Red River because of their memory of Lewis and Clark. A delegation accordingly set out on the two-thousand-mile journey. Four of them reached their destination in the fall of 1831 and were warmly welcomed by Clark. Nobody in St. Louis could speak their languages, but they managed to indicate that they wanted religious instruction. Only a lone Nez Percé survived the long trip home, and he was killed shortly afterward in a war with the Blackfeet.

Meanwhile, the story of their quest had been circulated in religious journals, where it stirred up great enthusiasm, but not much money. In 1833 the Nez Percés crossed the mountains to the traders' rendezvous, but no teacher came. The next year Jason Lee, a Methodist, appeared, but he went on to the fertile Willamette Valley near the coast, already being settled by white people, retired Hudson's Bay employees and others coming by sea. Finally, in 1835, Samuel Parker and Marcus Whitman of the American Board came up with the traders' wagon train. When they saw the eagerness of the Nez Percés, they decided that Whitman should return with the train to bring back permanent workers, while Parker should go on with the Indians to survey the field. Whitman was a physician, an able, energetic man, who had the respect of the rough mountain men and freighters.

The Nez Percés joyfully escorted Parker over great stretches of the Northwest, where with the aid of interpreters he conducted religious services. One of his escorts, a leading warrior later baptized as Joseph, was an interested listener. Parker then returned by way of Hawaii, where the American Board had a mission. In the next year, five missionaries came up with the caravan to the rendezvous. Whitman brought his new wife, Narcissa, a beautiful, sensitive young woman with a glorious singing voice. The others were Henry H. Spalding and his wife, Eliza, and William E. Gray. Spalding was sincere, but emotionally unstable; Mrs. Spalding, plain, levelheaded, and capable. Gray, a young recruit who had joined at the last minute, had no serious qualifications for mission work. The Nez Percé women joyfully embraced and kissed the two missionary wives, the first white women to cross the continent.

At the earnest solicitation of the Cayuses, the Whitmans settled with that tribe. These people, belonging to the small Waiilatpuan stock, had separated recently from the kindred Molalas of west and southwest Oregon. The site chosen for the mission was on the Walla Walla River in southeast Washington. It was named Waiilatpu. The Spaldings settled among the Nez Percés at Lapwai near the present

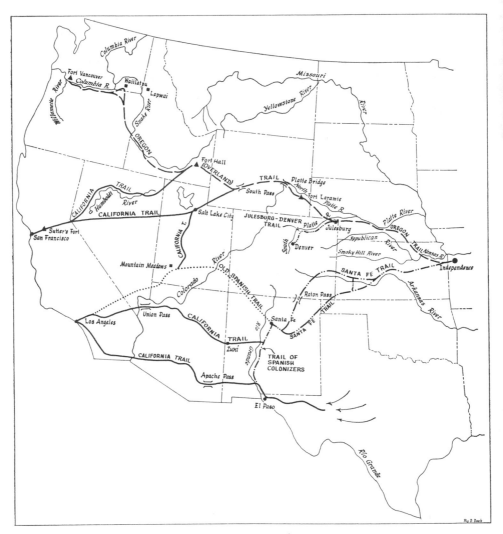

Western Trails

Lewiston, Idaho. More than one hundred miles of untouched Indian country separated the two stations.

Spalding directed the willing Nez Percés in cutting timber and building a combined dwelling and school. Mrs. Spalding began at once to teach the children. A gifted linguist, she learned the Shahaptian language and reduced it to writing, teaching at first from handmade copies. Two hundred pupils flocked to her school, deftly copying the words and teaching them to their families at home. Soon hundreds of

Nez Percés could read and write a little in their own language and a few were acquiring English. After two years the Hawaiian mission gave the station a printing press, and Spalding printed a dozen books, including parts of the Bible, in the native tongue. With some initial help from the Hudson's Bay posts he soon had the men raising cattle, sheep, hogs, and chickens and—using hoes as their only tools—planting grain and garden vegetables. He set up a water-powered mill and began to grind their wheat into a coarse flour. At the same time, he preached to them. Among his first converts were Joseph and a village chief who received the baptismal name of Timothy.

The Whitman mission also started out well. In 1838, eight more missionaries came, the women staying with Narcissa while Whitman and Spalding helped the men locate. Two couples settled among the receptive Spokanes. But dissensions, in which one of the newcomers and Spalding were the most active, developed.[1] Also, Catholic priests were traveling to the Hudson's Bay posts and making converts. At the same time, the American Board became short of funds. In 1842, the Spaldings were recalled and the Whitmans were instructed to join the Spokane work, thus abandoning the two stations. Whitman went back to the East to protest. By this time the Cayuses had become hostile, and after her husband left, Mrs. Whitman had to seek safety at another mission. Whitman reported to the Board, which had already rescinded its action. His return the next year was marked by an event celebrated in Oregon history, but ominous for the Indians.

In 1840, Joe Meek and a party of mountain men had brought three wagons up the trail, the first wheeled vehicles to cross the mountains. This opening pointed the way to a mighty movement. In 1843, a great train of one thousand immigrants starting out from Independence was glad to receive Whitman's guidance. From that time on, a constant stream of settlers came up the trail. They came with exhausted teams and depleted provisions. The mills at the two missions supplied them with flour, and the Indians sold them horses, meat, salmon, camass, and grain and vegetables from their little cultivated plots. (Even yet it is common to speak of a western horse as a "cayuse.") In exchange they received cattle, clothes, and tools. The Nez Percés had to travel some distance to meet the immigrants, but the trail crossed the Cayuse

[1] The details may be found in Alvin M. Josephy, Jr., *The Nez Percé Indians and the Opening of the Northwest*. This scholarly volume gives a circumstantial, day-by-day narrative of events from the coming of the white man until the final subjugation of the Nez Percés in 1877, and presents the various Indian leaders as distinct personalities.

153

country, a branch passing the mission. The Cayuses valued the trade, but they were annoyed when the travelers killed the game, fished out the streams, grazed their cattle and horses on the pasture ground, and even stole the Indians' horses. Also, the white men brought smallpox, measles, and scarlet fever.

The Nez Percé mission, off the trail, continued to prosper, probably reaching its height in 1844 and 1845. But Tom Hill, a Delaware from Kansas, who had been a hunter with Kit Carson, Joe Meek, and other mountain men, had married a Nez Percé girl and was becoming influential in the tribe. Devoted to the native religion and customs, he argued that all the missionaries should be killed, and he could relate enough of his own tribe's experience with white men to reinforce his argument. Then Mrs. Spalding became ill and Spalding had to take over her teaching duties. It is probably not a coincidence that from this time the mission declined.[2] The school, which had once enrolled 234 pupils, was closed in 1846 because the children ceased to attend. The Indians broke all the windows in the building, tore the shingles off the roof, and pulled down the mission fences for firewood.

The winter of 1846–47 was especially severe, killing the Indians' cattle and much of the wild game, and they suffered greatly from cold and hunger. It was followed by a late salmon run. Then a severe measles epidemic broke out among the Cayuses. Whitman worked day and night to save them, but he could not overcome their treatment of a steam bath followed by a plunge in cold water. The disease attacked the mission family also, but with them it was not fatal. A half-blood Maine Indian named Joe Lewis coming by with a wagon train that summer had made himself so unpopular that he was put off at the mission. He told the Cayuses that Whitman was poisoning the sick Indians so he could take their land and pointed to the recovery of the physician's white patients as proof.

The catastrophe came on November 29, 1847. As usual, the mission, located on the busy trail, was full of white people—volunteer workers, hired hands, immigrants, and children. Among the last were the half-Indian daughters of Joe Meek and Jim Bridger, seven orphaned immigrant children adopted by the Whitmans, and the Spaldings' oldest daughter. The Indians struck without warning, kill-

[2] A more favorable picture of Spalding as a teacher is given in Robert H. Ruby and John A. Brown, *Half-Sun on the Columbia.* This fine biography of Chief Moses, of a Salish-speaking tribe of the middle Columbia, gives the whole background of Indian and pioneer history in Washington.

ing the Whitmans, killing or wounding all the other men (eleven were killed, a few wounded escaped), and taking the women and children prisoners. Three of the little girls, including the daughters of the mountain men, were ill at the time with measles and died from exposure. Three of the older ones were taken as wives, but they and the other captives, fifty-one in all, were eventually ransomed by the Hudson's Bay Company.

Meanwhile, one of the wounded men reached Lapwai, where some of the Nez Percé hotheads were ready for another massacre. Spalding was away at the time, but Mrs. Spalding courageously collected the mission group and appealed to the head chief for protection. Although he was unfriendly to the mission, he formed a cordon of guards around them and brought them to a place of safety. The hostiles then pillaged the property.

The first outsider to hear of the Waiilatpu tragedy was Father Brouillet, a Catholic missionary. He went there and helped the captive survivors bury the dead and read the burial service, with the Indians standing by painted and armed. On his way back he met Spalding, who was coming to visit his daughter. The priest's warning saved his life. He made the terrible journey in a driving storm to Lapwai expecting to find his own family wiped out. He never recovered from the shock of this experience, and his garbled accounts have found their way into print to plague historians.

Many of the Nez Percés were distressed over the destruction of the mission. It was thirteen years before they received any more religious guidance. And the Cayuses found that killing the missionaries did not bring the expected deliverance. The year before the massacre, Great Britain and the United States had fixed the present boundary of the Northwest. A military expedition of the regular army and volunteers from the Willamette region went against the Cayuses. The Indians fled to the mountains, and after two years of wandering, five of the guilty leaders gave themselves up to be hanged in order to purchase peace. Asked why he had surrendered, one of them reportedly said, "Did not your missionaries teach us that Christ died to save his people? So we did it to save our people."

History has dealt harshly with this tribe and its leaders. The attractive qualities of the Whitmans and their tragic fate have obscured the Cayuses' grievances, some real, some imaginary but no less real to them. Probably also they sensed what is apparent in the Whitmans' letters: that Whitman was patriotically stirred by the "manifest destiny" of his expanding country; and that Mrs. Whitman, for all her dedication, could establish rapport only with people of her own culture. Selflessly, through the labor of their hands and the drudgery of their days, they served the Indians, but their true commitment was to the alien society that was engulfing them.

In the spring of 1849—less than two years after the Whitman massacre—a territorial government was established over the Oregon country. In 1853 it was divided by an east-west line into the territories of Oregon and Washington. Joel Palmer, superintendent of Indian affairs for Oregon,[3] and Isaac I. Stevens, territorial governor of Washington, soon made treaties with the small tribes west of the Cascades, assigning them to reservations with the usual provisions for annuities and educational training, and clearing the land in that rapidly settling area; then they prepared to meet the relatively untouched Indians of the interior. Chief Kamiakim of the Yakimas traveled through the country trying to unite all the tribes to resist, and they apparently met in council in the Grande Ronde Valley and marked the whole region into definite boundaries. The white men then called *their* council in May, 1855, in the Walla Walla Valley not far from the ruined Waiilatpu Mission.

The Nez Percés, numbering about twenty-five hundred, came in first. A diary kept by a young officer with the military escort describes their arrival "on horseback in one long line. They were almost entirely naked, gaudily painted and decorated with their wild trappings . . . [sitting] upon their fine animals as if they were centaurs."[4] Their horses, too, were brightly painted, with beads and fringes hanging from the bridles, and eagle feathers fluttering from the manes and tails. About a mile off, they halted while the chiefs rode forward to greet Stevens and his party. Then the rest raced in, clashing their shields, beating their drums, and singing, and formed a circle around them. After the chiefs smoked the peace pipe with Stevens, they all went to their camping ground. Two days later three hundred Cayuses arrived "whooping and singing." Finally, eight tribes, numbering about five thousand including some women and children, were present.

Throughout the council the Nez Percés had Christian prayers in their lodges every morning and evening and services several times on Sunday. The same officer saw two of the chiefs—probably Joseph and Timothy—officiating at one of these Sunday services, using the Ten

[3] In this instance the office was separate from that of governor.
[4] His account is given in Haines, *The Nez Percés*.

Commandments as the text. "Every thing was conducted with the greatest propriety, and the singing, in which they all joined, had an exceedingly musical effect." He found an "odd mixture" of native and borrowed elements in their practices—"an equal love for fighting and devotion—the wildest Indian traits with a strictness in some religious rites." After this service "we rode through the Cayuse camp, but saw no evidence of Sunday there. The young warriors were lounging about their lodges, preparing their arms or taking care of their horses, to be ready for the evening races."

Stevens proposed settling all the tribes on two reservations with the Nez Percés and the Yakimas. The Nez Percés and their neighbors objected violently. He accordingly negotiated three treaties. The first was with the Nez Percés. (Their literate members had kept notes throughout the conference.) They ceded some of their outer grazing land in central Idaho and southeastern Washington for $200,000 in goods and the government's promise to operate schools, blacksmith and other shops, two mills, and a hospital, and to keep all white people but Indian Office employees off their reservation. The other tribes were formed into two groups for the treaty making. They were not co-operative.

A Cayuse leader called Young Chief said: "I wonder if the ground is listening to what is said? . . . The ground says, It is the Great Spirit that placed me here. . . . The Great Spirit directs me, Feed the Indians well. The grass says the same thing, Feed the horses and cattle. . . . The ground says, The Great Spirit has placed me here to produce all that grows on me, trees and fruit." Said Chief Owhi of the Yakimas,[5] "Shall I give the land which is part of my body and leave myself poor and destitute? . . . I cannot say so."

But as usual, the unity that Kamiakim had built did not hold. The tribes Stevens grouped with the Yakimas, many of which were not present at the council, were represented as ceding nearly ten million acres in Washington east of the Cascades, retaining only a small "Yakima Reservation." The Walla Wallas, Cayuses, and Umatillas ceded large areas in southeastern Washington and northeastern Oregon and agreed to remove to a "Umatilla Reservation" in Oregon. These treaties also carried promises of goods and "civilizing" agencies. But the tribes left the council in a hostile mood; soon the whole country was aflame in what is known as the Yakima War.

Stevens had told the Indians that they would not be required to

[5] The diarist mistakenly classes him as a Umatilla.

157

vacate the ceded land "till our chief the President and his council sees this paper and says it is good, and we build the houses, the mills and the blacksmith shop," a delay of two or three years, he assured them. (Actually it would be four years before ratification by the Senate, and much longer before any of the promised payment was made.) But within twelve days Stevens and Palmer published notices that the area was open to settlement. Land hunters rushed in, and miners criss-crossed it on their way to new gold strikes in Canada and the Colville region on the upper Columbia. The Indians began killing the prospectors, and the army attempted to punish them. The Nez Percés, feeling bound by their treaty obligation, went against their friends and former allies, and a number under Joseph and Timothy enlisted in the army. Becoming disillusioned, some of their warriors eventually joined the hostiles. Several battles were fought, a number of which the Indians won. The military managed to capture and shoot or hang several war leaders, in some instances after inviting them in for peace talks. The Indians were finally defeated in two battles near the present Spokane in 1858.

The Klamaths, Modocs, and Molalas of southwest Oregon and northern California were affected by these same events. They visited the Willamette and lower Columbia settlements to trade. John C. Frémont passed through their country twice. In 1846 a new immigrant trail branched off from the Oregon Trail in Idaho, crossed the Modoc land, and entered the Willamette Valley from the south. The Indians had been friendly to the explorers, but now there were the usual incidents and reprisals. When the Cayuses destroyed the Whitman mission, their Molala relatives stirred up the neighboring tribes to attack the Willamette settlements while many of the men were away hunting out the Cayuses, but the settlers struck first.

By this time the international boundary had disappeared, for the same year in which the United States acquired the Pacific Northwest marked the beginning of the war with Mexico, which brought the acquisition of the Spanish Southwest. A few days before the Treaty of Guadalupe Hidalgo was signed on February 2, 1848, gold was discovered in California, and the fabulous rush of 1849 followed. One influx of miners came up the Willamette to northern California, and a lawless element among them abused the Indians so outrageously that in 1853 the Indians rose against them in what became known as the Rogue River War.

In later years General George Crook described the conditions that

158

he observed as a young lieutenant around the rough mining town of Yreka: "It was of no unfrequent occurrence for an Indian to be shot down in cold blood, or a squaw to be raped by some brute. Such a thing as a white man being punished for outraging an Indian was unheard of. . . . The consequence was that there was scarcely ever a time that there was not one or more wars with the Indians somewhere on the Pacific coast.

". . . The trouble with the army was that the Indians would confide in us as friends, and we had to witness this unjust treatment of them without the power to help them. Then when they were pushed beyond endurance and would go on the war path we had to fight when our sympathies were with the Indians."[6]

In 1855 the Rogue River War became merged with the Yakima War. With the ending of that war, peace of a sort came to the whole Northwest, with the Indians broken and defeated and in process of being assigned to reservations. One of the Modoc chiefs said in after years: "I thought if we killed all the white men we saw, that no more would come. We killed all we could; but they came more and more like new grass in the spring. I looked around and saw that many of our young men were dead and could not come back to fight. My heart was sick. My people were few. I threw down my gun. I said, 'I will not fight again.' "

While the gold rush from the Oregon settlements was invading northern California, other gold seekers were coming from the eastern United States. They followed the Oregon Trail through the South Pass, then turned southwest, crossing the Great Basin through Utah and Nevada to the Sacramento area. That was not the first crossing of this arid land. As early as 1776 the Spaniards had opened a trail along the southern edge. It curved north from Santa Fe into Colorado and crossed Utah, the toe of Nevada, and the Mohave Desert in California to their coastal settlements. It was convenient for the Spanish, and later Mexican, slave business. The stronger and more active Utes of the southern region raided the feeble, impoverished desert dwellers and carried off the women and girls to the markets at either end of the trail. In 1826–27 the mountain man Jedediah Smith followed this trail to San Diego and then returned west-east across the central area to Great Salt Lake. In 1833, Joseph Reddeford Walker, equipped with Mexican passports, struck west in search of beaver from Great Salt Lake to the

---

[6] His experiences in the Rogue River and Yakima wars may be found in General George Crook, *His Autobiography*.

Humboldt River. He followed that stream to its sink and then crossed more desert and the Sierra Nevada wall to the lush land of giant redwoods, fish and game, and mission settlements. His route became the trail of the gold seekers.

The forlorn primitives of this meager land were terrified at their first sight of white men. Timoak, a desert Shoshoni, later told of his fear when he encountered three of the bearded "dog face people." The educated Paiute woman, Sarah Winnemucca, recalled that in childhood she screamed, "Oh, Mother, the owls!" and that all night long she lay awake thinking of their "big white eyes" staring from their hairy faces. Their unreasoning fear was followed, alas, by more accurate knowledge. Some of them pilfered the beaver traps set by the Walker party, the trappers then killed several inoffensive Indians, and finally Walker fired into their bands. When his route became the California Trail, such incidents multiplied—lawless travelers shooting Indians for sport, Indians plundering wagon trains.

Other gold seekers' trails were the result of the Mormon colonization. Brigham Young had planned to establish his theocratic empire in Mexican territory, but in less than a year after his first colonists reached Great Salt Lake in 1847, they were within the boundaries of the United States. As these thrifty people brought the land under control, it became convenient for the California trains to turn south and buy supplies from them and then cut across the Basin on a parallel trail south of the Humboldt. Soon, as the Mormon settlements advanced south to the Old Spanish Trail, some California travelers turned down to that route.

The Territory of Utah, also including Nevada and western Colorado, was organized in 1850, and Young was appointed as governor. He scarcely needed this federal authority, for his orders on matters religious, economic, and political went down through the hierarchy to every obedient member of the colony. His Indian policy, like everything else, was clearly designed and executed. He and the missionaries he sent out labored to make friends with the natives, convert them, induce them to make peace with each other, and train them in "civilization." They did not make many converts, but in other ways they had fair success. Young made peace between the Shoshonis and Utes after a long period of hostility by calling them to a council at Salt Lake City. Chief Walkara ("Walker") led some Basin Utes against the Mormons in what is known as the Walker War, but it was soon ended by prompt military action and Young's diplomacy.

So serious a conflict of authority developed between Governor Young and outsiders appointed to other territorial offices that President Buchanan sent a military force under Albert Sidney Johnston to bring the Mormon empire under federal control. The expedition fizzled out without firing a shot, and Young yielded his office—if not his actual power—to a Buchanan-appointed successor; but feeling ran high for a time. The Mormons had been driven from too many places before finding their desert refuge; this time they intended to stay. Their missionaries had established stations along the Old Spanish Trail to train the Paiutes in agriculture and peace. Now they taught their pupils to hate the "Mericats" (Americans).

While the army was approaching from the north and the feelings of the beleaguered Mormons were mounting to frenzy, a large California-bound party passing south through their settlements openly boasted of their part in driving them from Missouri and Illinois and taunted them with the destruction now on the way. When the emigrants, numbering about 140 men, women, and children and driving a large cattle herd, reached the Mountain Meadows in southern Utah, the local militia, with the help of the Indians, killed all but eighteen small children believed to be too young to remember, stripped the bodies, plundered the wagons, and took the cattle herd. Young did not learn of the plot until too late to stop it, but his orders prevented a repetition. The next train was escorted through with no loss of life, but lost its herd of 480 cattle.[7] When the excitement died down, the Mormons found that it had been easier to stir up the Indians than to quiet them. The Paiutes settled down to routine depredations, but an unreckoned damage had been done to their progress in "civilization."

While the Paiutes in the southern desert were helping the Mormons, Chief Washakie of the Shoshonis offered twelve hundred warriors to the federal army. Johnston advised him to take his people to the buffalo country and stay out of trouble, and they did remain neutral. Two years later their wilder allies, the Bannocks, started a general war against the travelers on the trails, and Washakie could not restrain his warriors from joining them. In less than half a century since the Shoshonis had helped Lewis and Clark, they had seen that first precarious journey to the Pacific swell into a continuous stream—first bound for Oregon, then to the Mormon colony, and, greatest of all, to

---

[7] An account that combines intellectual objectivity with humane insight by a scholar who is also a Mormon is Juanita Brooks, *The Mountain Meadows Massacre.*

California. All passed through their country before branching to the separate destinations. They had suffered greatly from the destruction of their game and the depletion of their grazing areas. Washakie knew all this, but seeing the futility of resistance, he sought the best terms he could.

In 1860 the Basin Shoshonis and Paiutes joined the war, and for a time all travel through the area was disrupted. Soon national attention was focused on the Civil War. Finally a column of California and Nevada volunteers under Brigadier General Patrick E. Connor arrived to protect the trails, and on January 29, 1863, he inflicted a crushing defeat on the Shoshonis on Bear River near the Idaho-Utah line. It was followed by peace treaties with all the hostile tribes, in which they agreed to permit travel on the trails and the construction of a railroad and were to receive annuities in goods and food.

To the south of this region came the extension of American control over New Mexico, also organized in 1850 as a territory comprising the present New Mexico, Arizona, and southern Colorado. The small settled area around Santa Fe and the Pueblos was surrounded by untamed raiders. On the west were the Navahos; on the north, the Utes and Jicarilla Apaches; on the east, the Mescalero Apaches. On the southwest were many Apache tribes—White Mountains, Coyoteros, Aravaipas, and others—and south of *them* were the wildest of all Apaches, the Chiricahuas and several closely related tribes that occupied the mountain fastnesses of southeastern Arizona and the rugged Sierra Madre of Mexico; and the Mimbreños and Warm Springs (sometimes one tribe, sometimes two), closely intermarried with the Chiricahuas, living on the other side of the line in present New Mexico. (Many of these were classed together as the Gilas.) Still farther west were the Tonto Apaches, mixed tribes of the rugged Tonto Basin; and beyond *them* were Yuman tribes, including the misnamed Apache-Mohaves (Yavapais) and Apache-Yumas (Tulkepaias). Too remote for the government's concern were the peaceable, agricultural Pimas, Papagos, and other tribes of western Arizona.

The Mexicans had continued the Spanish custom of enslaving Apache women and children and paying a bounty for scalps. These buffeted people were at first inclined to welcome the "Anglos" as enemies of the Mexicans, but this cordial relationship could not last. Many American frontiersmen were as savage and cruel as Apaches, without the latter's saving code of honor. Soon there were atrocities on both sides and the building up of grievances with retaliation on the innocent. Then the government established military posts, trying to hold the hostiles in check but often "punishing" the wrong Indians.

After two administrations too brief to be effective, the able David Meriwether served as territorial governor through 1853–57. As he analyzed the situation, "I had heard on my arrival in the territory that the Indians were not the aggressors, but I well knew that when the Indians and the whites once commenced fighting, the Indians would never make peace until whipped, and, therefore necessity compelled me to whip them." His whole term was filled with raids, military pursuits, and battles in which the Indians as often as not were victorious. He succeeded in making peace treaties with some of the raiding tribes, but none of these was ratified by the Senate, leaving the Indians to wonder why his promises were not carried out. He was most successful with the Southern Utes and the Jicarilla Apaches.[8]

Conditions grew steadily worse in the years following Meriwether's administration. More Anglos came in to work the mines or establish ranches, and incidents multiplied. The white men made their greatest mistake when they stirred up the Chiricahuas and their friends.

One day the able Mangas Coloradas, chief of the Mimbreños, made a friendly visit to some gold miners at Palos Altos in southwestern New Mexico. They tied him up and whipped him unmercifully. Understandably, he went on the war path. Then some Apache band—probably from the Pinal Mountains—captured a twelve-year-old half-Irish, half-Mexican boy, later known as Mickey Free. Cochise, the chief of the Chiricahuas, had always been friendly to the Anglos; he regularly sold wood to the stage station at the gateway to the tortuous Apache Pass that wound through his mountains. Now a detail of cavalry was sent to demand the stolen boy. With some of his warriors he came unsuspecting to the station to explain that he knew nothing about the captive. The rash young officer in command then seized the Indians, intending to hold them as hostages for the return of the boy. Cochise and three of his men cut a hole in the tent where they were held and escaped. Then he captured some of the stage people and tried without result to exchange prisoners. The dispute ended with Cochise killing his captives and the military hanging theirs. Then Cochise joined Mangas Coloradas in a war that brought swift-striking

---

[8] David Meriwether, *My Life in the Mountains and on the Plains* is a fascinating story of western adventure from about 1811 to the narrator's experiences as governor of New Mexico.

Apache death to hundreds of people and devastated a large part of Arizona. (Mickey Free grew up as an Apache and became a well-known interpreter.)

The southern routes to California across New Mexico and Arizona carried almost as much traffic as the great northern thoroughfares. The gold seekers of 1849 were followed by the covered wagons of emigrants and droves of sheep and cattle to feed the new settlements. From Santa Fe they struck west, crossing the Continental Divide east of the Zuni pueblos, or they turned south to join a great stream of travel that, washing across Texas, funneled through El Paso and continued on a southern route through Apache Pass. The trail ahead was bloody with Apache depredations, but farther on were the Pimas and their neighbors selling the travelers produce from their irrigated fields.

To the California Indians this influx of white Americans was an unmitigated calamity. There, besides the docile Mission Indians, were untamed tribes of the back country. These had at first been friendly to the Spaniards, but dissatisfied Indians from the missions had run away and joined them and they became hostile. The Spanish settlers were never very numerous. A few established great sprawling haciendas, where they lived in feudal magnificence—superb horsemen, with scattered herds of longhorn cattle. There the Mission Indians with their acquired skills found employment, and the "wild" Indians became adept at stealing the livestock and escaping into the mountains, where they lived precariously, hunted out by avenging *vaqueros*.

In theory, under Spanish policy the friars were to train the Indians at the missions until they should be able to take over the lands and herds and be served by secular priests. After Mexican independence the new government tried to carry out this policy. Their padres opposed it, and the Indians failed to claim their rights. Then the United States came in, and the land became public domain. A few feeble attempts to set aside reservations for the Indians were largely defeated because of California opposition. Finally, in the early 1900s the government purchased some small homesites for them. There are now 117 such tracts varying in size from less than forty acres up to three large enough to show on a map. The ownership is inextricably tangled and most of the land is worthless.

California was admitted to statehood in 1850. It began with a savage anti-Indian policy. Early statutes legalized the indenture of children and adults, authorizing any justice of the peace to sell their services to the highest bidder, and deprived them of all recourse by making their testimony inadmissible in court. Thus Indians were taken into virtual slavery, especially women for the use of the miners. In 1854 a California newspaper stated: "Abducting Indian children has become quite a common practice. Nearly all of the children belonging to some of the Indian tribes in the northern part of the state have been stolen. They are taken to the southern part of the state and there sold." (This, it should be noted, was during the Rogue River War.) The census of 1890 enumerated 17,000 descendants of an aboriginal population estimated at 150,000.[9]

Thus the history of the Atlantic tribes was repeated two centuries later on the Pacific, with the embattled hinterlands of each—South and Old Northwest, Western mountains and deserts—completing the parallel. Between the two areas the Great Plains represented to the white man only a dreary waste to be crossed to the wealth beyond. There the Indians hunted the buffalo, gloried in their horse herds, held their ceremonials, and won renown in individual exploits. They resented the damage to their hunting—the Oregon Trail, in fact, cut a barren strip through the buffalo range, separating the animals permanently into a northern and a southern herd—and there were some isolated acts of violence by the lawless of both races; but, considering the magnitude of the traffic, such incidents were few. In 1858 gold was discovered in Colorado, there was a rush to the new diggings, and the city of Denver sprang up there. Some of this travel followed a new trail striking west up the Kansas River and its Smoky Hill or Republican branches. The main route left the Oregon Trail at the South Platte and followed that stream to Denver.

The government tried to protect the travelers by establishing military posts and holding treaty councils with the Indians. In 1849, Fort Laramie, a former fur-trading post on the Oregon Trail in eastern Wyoming, was purchased and garrisoned. Two years later a great council of the northern tribes was held on nearby Horse Creek, eight to twelve thousand Indians camped in a forest of tipis in the valley. The Sioux were there in all their glory; Washakie came with his Shoshonis; and there were Crows from the upper Yellowstone, and Cheyennes and Arapahos from the Central Plains. Many of them had never met before except in battle. Some good promises were made, but Cut Nose of the Arapahos was too optimistic when he said: "I will go home

[9] The best brief history of the California Indians is a pamphlet entitled *Indians of California* by the American Friends Service Committee. Glimpses of what was happening are seen in Kroeber, *Ishi*.

satisfied. I will sleep sound, and not have to watch my horses in the night, or be afraid for my women and children. We have to live on these streams and in the hills, and I would be glad if the whites would pick out a place for themselves and not come into our grounds."[10]

Two years later a similar council was held with some of the Comanche bands and their Kiowa allies at Fort Atkinson near the present Dodge City, Kansas. They agreed to refrain from molesting travelers on the Santa Fe Trail in return for an annuity of $18,000 in goods. These Indians were usually at peace with the United States, but to their mind the United States did not include Texas.

That was the year that Stevens went out to assume his duties as governor of Washington. On the way, through the good offices of a Blackfoot woman married to a trader, he made the first friendly contact ever made by an American official with the chiefs and warriors of that hostile tribe. Then at the Walla Walla council he learned how the tribes he met there suffered from Blackfoot attacks when they went across the mountains to hunt. Accordingly, as soon as the council closed he took a delegation of Nez Percés, Flatheads, and others back to meet the Blackfeet. There a treaty was signed with them, defining their boundary and admitting western tribes to hunt outside it; permitting the United States to establish roads and military posts; and providing an annuity and civilization fund.

The Blackfeet, with plenty of buffalo, were not enthusiastic about "civilization." Still, the next year, Lame Bull, head chief of the Piegan tribe of Blackfeet, said to a Presbyterian missionary, "When we catch a wild animal on the prairie & attempt to tame him we sometimes find it very hard. . . . But almost any animal can be tamed by kindness and perseverance. We have been running wild on the prairie and now we want the white sons and daughters of our Great Father to come to our country and tame us."[11]

The missionary, however, did not remain. And as for the military posts established to protect the Plains highways, it is apparent that they stirred up more trouble than they prevented. Too many young West Pointers yearned for action, and once they started something, their superiors felt obliged to back them up. The Grattan affair illustrates the whole sequence.

In 1854 near Fort Laramie, a Sioux killed a decrepit cow lagging

[10] One of the best accounts of this council is in Trenholm and Carley, *The Shoshonis.*
[11] Quoted in Ewers, *The Blackfeet,* 222–23.

behind a train. The chief, Bear That Scatters, tried to make reparation, but the owner demanded more money. Brash young Lieutenant J. L. Grattan then marched with thirty men to the Sioux camp to arrest the cow murderer. During the futile parley the soldiers suddenly fired, fatally wounding the Chief; and the Sioux thereupon annihilated the whole force. Brigadier General William S. Harney was then ordered to march from Fort Leavenworth in eastern Kansas to punish the "hostiles." Meanwhile, five of the Chief's friends avenged his death by killing three innocent men on a mail wagon. The next year, Harney reached the Sioux country and attacked a camp, killing eighty-six Indians, then marched on to Fort Laramie and demanded the surrender of the five. The chiefs appealed to them to give themselves up for the good of their people, and they rode in, dressed in their war finery and singing their death songs, expecting to be hanged. (Hanging was a terrible fate for an Indian, shutting him out forever from a warrior's hereafter.) Harney did, indeed, intend to hang them, but the Indian agent intervened. They were kept for some months at Fort Leavenworth, living in almost complete freedom, then were pardoned by President Pierce. One of them was a young warrior named Spotted Tail. He was so impressed by the numbers and power of the white men as he observed them in Kansas that in later years he exerted his influence as a peace chief.[12]

And so it went. Then came the Civil War, bringing more complications into Indian-white relations. Its first effects were felt by the settled, prospering tribes of the Indian Territory.

[12] Many accounts of this affair have been written. Probably the best is in George E. Hyde, *Spotted Tail's Folk*.

THE INDIAN TERRITORY JOINS
THE WHITE MAN'S WAR

As Chitto Harjo saw it:

"What took place in 1861? . . . I tell you that in 1861 . . . my white fathers rose in arms against each other. . . . At that time Abraham Lincoln was president of the United States and our Great Father. He was in Washington and I was away off down here. . . . In that war the Indians had not any part. It was not their war at all."

But the Indian Territory tribes could not maintain this neutral position. A few of their leading men owned plantations worked by Negro slaves, and ardently supported the South;[1] but, in general, the Indians allied themselves with the Confederacy because it was the only chance they saw. With Arkansas on the east, Texas on the south, and vast unsettled areas of Texas and Kansas on the west and north, they were entirely cut off from the United States.

Like the states in the larger conflict, the tribes were influenced by their location. The Choctaws in the southeastern corner, in the angle formed by Arkansas and Texas, voluntarily joined the South and never wavered seriously in their support. The Chickasaws, to the west of the Choctaws and farther away from these influences, had a strong Union minority, but their government remained stanchly Southern. The three tribes north of the Canadian and Arkansas rivers had a position analogous to that of the border states. The Cherokees, on the northeast, touched secessionist Arkansas; a corner of divided Missouri; and Kansas, admitted to statehood in January, 1861, ardently Union, but convulsed with frontier violence. The Creeks and Seminoles, to the west

[1] This was not uniformly true. John Ross and Opothle Yahola owned many slaves, but, as we shall see, they opposed the Southern alliance.

of the Cherokees, touched no white settlement. All three of these tribes had civil wars of their own.

Everything the Indians saw and heard indicated that the United States had abandoned them. Superintendent Rector at Fort Smith and the agents to the tribes were secessionists and used all their influence to bring the Indians to their side. When new agents were appointed by the federal government, they stayed in Kansas, and the Indians were unable to contact them. Early in the war the federal garrisons evacuated the military posts in the Territory, just ahead of invading Texans, and retreated across Kansas to Fort Leavenworth. Even the annuities, the financial support of the tribal governments and schools, were withheld lest they should fall into Confederate hands. At the same time, delegations and communications from Arkansas and Texas urged the tribes, sometimes with threats, to join the South.

Their argument was that the Union had been divided, leaving the Indians in the Southern part; therefore, the new government would take the place of the one with which they had been formerly connected. And so far as the Indians could see, this was true. Moreover, they had reason to fear the Lincoln administration, for they remembered Seward's words during the campaign. The wonder is that they did not unanimously cast their lot with the South. But they were Indians, and, Indian-like, the conservative fullblood element among the Creeks and Cherokees and probably a majority of the fullblood Seminole tribe refused to change. They had made treaties with the United States, and that was that.

Because of his greater understanding of the situation, Chief John Ross became the leader in the struggle for neutrality. In October, before the fateful presidential election of 1860, he advised the Cherokee council: "Our duty is to stand by our rights, allow no interference in our internal affairs from any source, comply with all our engagements, and rely upon [the] Union for justice and protection." During the following winter and spring, while Southern states one after another were seceding, he wrote to all the tribes advising neutrality. Superintendent Rector, the governor of Arkansas, who was the superintendent's cousin, and other prominent citizens of the state tried to move him without result. To one of them he wrote, "I am—the Cherokees are—your friends and the friends of your people but we do not wish to be brought into the feuds between yourselves and your Northern Brethren. Our wish is for peace. Peace at home and Peace among you."

But the Choctaws were willing to accept the dissolution of the

169

Union as an accomplished fact. On February 17, even before the seceded states meeting at Montgomery had formed the Confederate government, the council authorized the principal chief to appoint delegates to any intertribal council that might be called to determine their relations with the United States "so long as such Government is in existence, otherwise to urge a renewal of such relations with such Confederacy as may be framed among the Southern States." The chief was also authorized to communicate to the Southern governors the Choctaws' regret over the "present unhappy political disagreement" between the sections, but the assurance that if the Union should be dissolved, their "natural affections, education, institutions, and interests" would bind them to the South. The Chickasaws joined them in similar pronouncements.

A number of intertribal meetings were held during the early months of 1861. At some of these, neutral sentiments prevailed; at others, visiting Texans were gratified by the Southern sympathy they found there. On March 5 the Confederate government commissioned Albert Pike of Arkansas to negotiate treaties with the Indians. He called a council to meet at North Fork Town in the Creek Nation. On the way he stopped in the Cherokee country to confer with John Ross, but was unable to shake his neutrality. He went on then to the council. There, under his leadership, a constitution was adopted creating an Indian confederacy, the "United Nations of the Indian Territory," which should legislate through a "Grand Council" of member tribes to resist the "invading forces of Abolition under Abraham Lincoln." Then the Creeks on July 10 and the Choctaws and Chickasaws on July 12 signed treaties with the Confederate government which were more favorable than any the Indians had ever made with the United States. The Confederates assumed all the financial obligations of the old treaties, made explicit guarantees against territorial government and allotment, and gave the tribes the privilege of sending delegates to Congress.

Pike then went on to the Seminole council house accompanied by some of the Creek leaders. There, on August 1, he signed a treaty with some of the chiefs, though others refused. In all of these negotiations Superintendent Rector and the former federal agents, now holding their positions under the Confederate government, took a leading part.

With a large mounted escort of Creeks and Seminoles, Pike proceeded to the Wichita Agency. Matthew Leeper, once the Union but now the Confederate agent, had made efficient preparations. Besides representatives from the Leased District reservations—the Wichitas and Caddos and their relatives, and the Penateka Comanches—there were present 140 chiefs and headmen from the four most important bands of the Plains Comanches, and the chiefs of the Kickapoos. Pike made two treaties, both signed on August 12, one with the reservation tribes, the other with the Plains Comanches. Both treaties explicitly included Texas in the peace, and both promised livestock, agricultural implements, and training in farming.

The Kiowas and their Apache subtribe had defiantly stayed away from the council, and the Kickapoos refused to subscribe to any peace that included the Texans. But Pike was hopeful that he could eventually persuade all the South Plains Indians to accept reservations in the Leased District and cease their raiding. The Comanches, he said, "seemed very anxious to be allowed to settle on lands of their own, and to live in peace."

Throughout all his conferences with the Indians, Pike posed as their protector against the predatory designs of the United States. But in his report to President Jefferson Davis he defended his favorable treaties with a lyrical description of the fertility, mineral resources, and beauty of the Indians' country and with the argument that the "concessions" made to them "are really far more for *our* benefit than for *theirs*; and that it is *we* . . . who are interested to have this country . . . opened to settlement and made into a State." Truly the Indians, whether "civilized" or "wild," had no guile to match such duplicity.

Meanwhile, Brigadier General Ben McCulloch, a former Texas Ranger, had been given command of the Confederate military district embracing the Indian Territory. He wrote to Ross from Fort Smith demanding the right to organize Southern sympathizers among the Indians into military companies. Ross replied on June 17: "Our country and institutions are our own. However small the one or humble the other, they are as sacred and valuable to us as are those of your own populous and wealthy State to yourself and your people. We have done nothing to bring about the conflict in which you are engaged with your own people, and I am unwilling that my people shall become its victims.

"I am determined to do no act that shall furnish any pretext to either of the contending parties to overrun our country and destroy our rights. . . . The Cherokee people and government have given every assurance in their power of their sympathy and friendship for the people of Arkansas and other Confederate States unless it be in voluntarily assuming an attitude of hostility toward the government of the United States. . . . That I cannot advise them to do."

But Stand Watie, Ross's old enemy from Removal Treaty days, organized a regiment with himself at the head, and McCulloch accepted it for the Confederate service on the very day that the Choctaws and Chickasaws signed their treaty with Pike. Then on August 10 came the Confederate victory over the Union forces at Wilson's Creek in southwest Missouri. This brought Confederate arms ominously close to the Cherokees. Even more ominous was the fact that Watie's regiment had crossed the line and fought there on the Confederate side. The prospect of a Cherokee civil war was fearfully apparent. Ross's neutral position was clearly untenable.

He called a mass meeting to discuss the situation, and on August 21 four thousand men assembled at Tahlequah. On the eve of this meeting some intimate friends asked him whether a Confederate alliance would be permanent. He answered: "We are in the situation of a man standing alone upon a low naked spot of ground, with the water rising all around him. . . . The tide carries by him, in its mad course, a drifting log. . . . By refusing it he is a doomed man. By seizing hold of it he has a chance for his life. He can but perish in the effort, and he may be able to keep his head above water until rescued or drift to where he can help himself."

At the meeting he advised the alliance, stressing the need for unity: "Union is strength, dissension is weakness, misery and ruin! In time of war, if war must come, fight together. As Brothers live; as Brothers die!" The meeting voted to join the Confederates, but left the details to the Chief. He wrote to Pike, who came back to confer with him, and the treaty was signed on October 7. It carried the same favorable provisions as the treaties made with the other four tribes. Especially notable was the fact that under these treaties a Choctaw-Chickasaw, a Creek-Seminole, and a Cherokee delegate sat in the Confederate Congress throughout the war—a prospect held out to the Indians ever since the Delaware treaty in 1778, but never implemented by the United States.

In response to communications from Ross, representatives of the Osages from southern Kansas and the Senecas, Shawnees, and Quapaws from the northeast corner of the Indian Territory also came to confer with Pike, and they also signed treaties. The Osages promised to furnish five hundred warriors to the Confederate army. Recruiting was already under way among the Five Civilized Tribes. There was a

Choctaw-Chickasaw regiment (later three regiments), a Creek regiment and a Creek-Seminole battalion (later the battalion became a second regiment), and for the Cherokees, Stand Watie's regiment and a newly formed regiment of fullbloods under a Ross adherent, John Drew.

But Ross's desperate attempt to prevent an Indian civil war was doomed to fail. The division became apparent first among the Creeks. The Confederate treaty had been regularly negotiated and ratified by their government, but a fullblood group from the Canadian District refused to accept it. On August 5 they met in council, deposed the chief, and installed the second chief (an office corresponding to vice president), Oktarharsars Harjo, usually called Sands by white men. Sands later summarized Pike's reasoning: "That man told Indian that the Union people would come and take away property and take away land—. . . Tell them there ain't no U.S.—ain't any more Treaty—all be dead—Tell them as there is no more U.S. no more Treaty that the Creeks had better make new Treaty with the South . . . Mr. Pike makes the half breeds believe what he says and the half breeds makes some of the full blood Indians believe what he says . . . [but] as for himself[2] he dont believe him yet. Then he thought the old U.S. was alive yet and the [old] treaty was good. Wont go against the U.S. himself."

The trusted Opothle Yahola became the recognized leader of the Union faction.[3] On August 15 he and Sands wrote to President Lincoln to request the protection promised by the Removal Treaty. "Now I write to the President our Great Father who removed us to our present homes, & made a treaty, and you said that in our new homes we should be defended from all interference from any person and that no white people in the whole world should ever molest us . . . and should we be injured by anybody you would come with your soldiers & punish them. but now the wolf has come. men who are strangers tread our soil. our children are frightened & the mothers cannot sleep for fear."

It was easier to write this letter than to get it out of the country, controlled as it was by Confederates. On the extreme western frontier of their settlements the Union Creeks called a great council, attended by sympathizers from all the Civilized Tribes but the Choctaw, by the settlements of broken tribes from the Old Northwest, and by several

[2] The interpreter put Sands's words in the third person.

[3] Some writers, reasoning from Cherokee history, have assumed that this division originated in a feud growing out of the McIntosh treaty, but this is not true. The causes and the lines of separation were new.

bands of Plains Indians. The Shawnee, Thomas Wildcat Alford, a great-grandson of Tecumseh, heard the story told and retold in his childhood. Years later he wrote of the feeling of the scattered bands living on the Creek frontier: "This is no fight of ours. It is between the whites—no good comes to us from war—let them fight their own fight."[4]

The council sent Micco Hutke, a Creek, and Bob Deer and Joe Ellis, Shawnees, with the letter and an oral message on a far western route to the Shawnee Agency near Kansas City. Again they repeated the arguments of the Confederate agents—"But we doubted their statements and promises and went to talk with the Agent and Superend [Superintendent] which our father has always kept among us. but they were both gone." They earnestly asked that a federal official be sent to meet them some place in Kansas. Sands, Micco Hutke, Bob Deer, and a few Seminoles and Chickasaws finally managed to make their way through the bandit-infested Kansas border, and on November 4 they found a Creek agent. This was their first official contact with the United States since their country was abandoned early in the war.

During all this lonely time they had looked to John Ross as their leader. They could hardly believe it when he advised them to join the Confederacy. Opothle Yahola sent back word that he wanted only to remain at peace and not make war on anybody. His followers prepared stores of food, rounded up their livestock, loaded their wagons with the family possessions, and gathered at a great camp on their southwestern frontier.[5] Here they intended to wait out the war. They were joined by about half of the Seminoles; a number of Chickasaws; some Kickapoos, Shawnees, Delawares, and Comanches (probably Penatekas); and a considerable body of Negroes, their own slaves and runaways from the Confederate party. The Creek chiefs who had made the Confederate alliance suggested to Ross that an attack be made on the camp. Ross rejected with horror an action that would involve the Creeks in civil war. Colonel Douglas H. Cooper, former federal agent to the Choctaws and Chickasaws, was in command of the Confederate forces in the Indian Territory. He restrained his too eager Creek allies and tried without success to arrange a conference with Opothle Yahola to heal the division in the tribe. But the Union Creeks apparently

[4] Alford's book, *Civilization*, is a revealing account of his people's experiences in the Indian Territory.

[5] These locations are of only local importance. For any Oklahoman who may be interested I have made a careful identification in "The Location of the Battle of Round Mountains," *Chronicles of Oklahoma*, Vol. XLI (Spring, 1963), 71–104.

realized the danger of an attack, for at the meeting with their agent in Kansas on November 4, Sands asked for a relief expedition. Through his interpreter, he explained that "The way he left his country his people was in an elbow surrounded by secessions," but he had 3,350 warriors ready to join the force.

Cooper, unaware of the impotence of the federal forces in Kansas, was afraid of that very thing. With his Choctaw-Chickasaw and Creek-Seminole troops and a detachment of Texas cavalry, he advanced to the camp and found it deserted. The long cavalcade of Union Creeks—warriors, families, baggage, livestock—had made "a large trail" to the northwest. He thought they were on their way to Kansas. Actually they were circling the settlements, west, north, east, to join Union sympathizers among the Cherokees with whom they were in communication. Even John Ross, with his uncanny understanding of the full-blood mind, did not suspect that his own party had had second thoughts about the Confederate alliance—that they "complained because they were compelled to dig up the hatchet and fight their Great Father, after they had agreed to remain neutral."

What Opothle Yahola planned to do after effecting the junction will never be known. Cooper caught up with him, and an indecisive battle was fought east of the present Stillwater, Oklahoma, on November 19. The Union Creeks continued their orderly exodus and entered the Cherokee Nation. Cooper reached them again on December 8 and was reinforced—as he supposed—by Drew's Cherokees, but almost the entire regiment deserted and joined the Union Creeks. The battle fought the next day on Bird Creek north of Tulsa was indecisive, but the defection of the Cherokees was so alarming that Cooper retreated to Fort Gibson.

The Union Indians established a stronghold on Hominy Creek northwest of Tulsa. Here they were attacked on December 26 by a white force from Arkansas. They were posted on a rugged timbered hill, and it required desperate hand-to-hand fighting to dislodge them, but they were finally routed. They abandoned their wagons with their food, bedding, and clothing, and their herds of livestock—about 800 or 900 cattle, 250 ponies, and 190 sheep—and fled on foot through a blizzard to Kansas. The men tried to cover the flight of the women and children, but many froze to death and their bodies were devoured by wolves. Children were born and died on the naked snow.

"At that battle," so the chief of the Seminole contingent reported it, "we lost a great many of our law men, and capable men to do business, and a great many of our young men, and women and children. We left them in cold blood by the wayside. At that battle we lost everything we possessed, everything to take care of our women and children with, and all that we had."

The fugitives slowly collected in east-central Kansas. The Military Department of Kansas furnished them some supplies, and Congress appropriated the unpaid annuities for their support, but this relief was inadequate and was not well administered. At the first count there were 3,168 Creeks, 53 Creek slaves, 38 free Creek Negroes, 777 Seminoles, and a few Cherokees, Chickasaws, and others. An army surgeon who visited the place in February found them lying on the frozen ground with only a few scraps of cloth for shelter. More than one hundred frozen limbs had to be amputated. Among the dying was the daughter of Opothle Yahola. The old leader himself was ill, though he was not to die until the following year. On a switch above him was stretched a blanket so narrow that it failed by two feet to reach the ground. Once he had been a very rich man in slaves and cattle. Now he and all alike were destitute.

More fugitives kept arriving, but many died on the way. By April there were 7,600 in the camp. The men were anxious to enlist in the Union army and recover their country. After much confusion they were finally organized under white officers as the First Regiment of Indian Home Guards. As Chitto Harjo related it, using his favorite first person:

"I left my laws and my government, I left my people and my country and my home . . . in order to stand by my treaties . . . and I arrived in Kansas. It was terrible hard times with me then. . . . Then I got a weapon in my hands, . . . for I raised my hand and called God to witness that I was ready to die in the cause that was right and to help my father defend his treaties. All this time the fire was going on and the war and the battles were going on."

Meanwhile, in the Indian Territory, Drew's men were reinstated and with Stand Watie's regiment and the Choctaw-Chickasaw regiment fought on the Confederate side at Pea Ridge, Arkansas, in March. This Confederate defeat opened the way for a Union invasion of the Cherokee country from Kansas. The expedition, white soldiers and Home Guards, set out in June, and about fifteen hundred refugees went along, hoping to return to their homes. On the way down they were opposed by a Missouri battalion and Stand Watie's Cherokees, but the Home Guards were constantly augmented by Cherokee enlistments, including most of Drew's regiment. John Ross refused to defect, saying the Nation was honor bound to the Confederate alliance, and was taken prisoner. The expeditionary force captured Fort Gibson, then abruptly returned to Kansas, with the refugees streaming along for another dismal year. Their numbers were augmented by one thousand Cherokees, for their country was now torn by civil war.

These events in the settled part of the Indian Territory had a striking parallel on the western prairies. The exodus of Opothle Yahola was matched by a similar exodus of Shawnees, Delawares, Kickapoos, and other broken tribes on the frontier and by the Wichitas from the Leased District, who had become disillusioned by Confederate neglect. They settled in southwestern Kansas, hunted buffalo, and remained relatively undisturbed. They were encouraged by Kansans to raid the Indian Territory—Confederate country, hence subject to plunder. The Kickapoos, always a warlike people resistant to "civilization," were especially active in this patriotic business, driving back herds of cattle which were acquired by prominent Kansans and sold on army and refugee contracts.

The military expedition of 1862 to the eastern Indian Territory was also matched by a less orthodox expedition to the west. In October of that same year, a war party of Shawnees, Delawares, and Kickapoos, incited by Union officials in Kansas, swept down to the Wichita Agency. The Texas garrison had been withdrawn from Fort Cobb, leaving the Tonkawas to protect the place. Leeper escaped, but the raiders killed his employees and the white traders, seized the records, and burned the buildings. Then they almost annihilated the Tonkawas, hated for their adherence to Texas and accused—whether rightly or wrongly is not known—of practicing cannibalism. (The descendants of the surviving Tonkawas—57 by the last count—now live in Oklahoma.) The invaders returned to Kansas with many captured ponies and delivered to the Union officials $1,200 in Confederate currency, the Pike treaty, and other papers, all carefully wrapped in a Confederate flag.

Shortly after this raid about six hundred Kickapoos set out to join their relatives in Mexico, and an equal number followed two years later. Both times they made a wide circle around the Texas settlements. Even so, they were discovered and attacked, but they beat off their attackers, hating Texans more than ever. They settled near Nacimiento in Coahuila, where the Mexican government gave them a tract of land, welcoming them as a protecting shield against the raiding Kiowas and Comanches.

Thus the Confederate overtures failed to enlist the western tribes. In the east the Union forces finally reoccupied Fort Gibson, but the Confederates occupied the surrounding area. At the same time, some of the Creeks who had been serving in the Southern army slipped through the lines and joined the Federals. The whole Creek-Cherokee country was desolated by guerrilla warfare, with the partisans of both sides killing each other on sight. The notorious Quantrill Band also came down from raiding in Kansas, and added to the killing, burning, and plundering.

After the capture of Ross, the Confederate party declared his office vacant and elected Watie as principal chief. Ross's supporters held a council and repudiated this action, also abrogating the Confederate treaty. Ross was eventually paroled and waited out the war in Philadelphia and Washington, representing the Cherokees at the capital, while an acting chief carried on the local administration. Thus the Cherokees, like the Creeks and Seminoles, had rival governments, each claiming legality. They functioned smoothly, with the men in the army meeting to transact the public business, just as in earlier times chiefs and warriors in council made decisions for the tribe. Typical is a letter, dated May 29, 1863, from an officer in Watie's regiment to his wife: "It looks singular Thus to be legislating in Camps. Our Council House is a large Sybley tent or was until we were run out of it by lice."[6]

Skirmishes took place between the beleaguered Federals at Fort Gibson and the surrounding Confederates. Then on July 17, 1863, at Honey Springs, south of the present Muskogee, the Confederates were defeated in the greatest battle of the war in the Indian Territory. Like Gettysburg and the fall of Vicksburg, which occurred the same month and marked the turning point in the larger conflict, it was decisive in the Indian warfare. The families of the Southern party among the Creeks, Cherokees, and Seminoles[7] then became refugees, fleeing in great numbers to the untouched Choctaw-Chickasaw country and north Texas.

[6] This and other letters in Dale and Litton, *Cherokee Cavaliers*, give an intimate picture of the war as seen by the Ridge-Boudinot-Watie family.

[7] No study has been made of the Seminole refugees. McReynolds' history of the tribe virtually closes with the settlement in the Indian Territory before the war.

In the 1930s, elderly people recalled this experience of their child-hood. Said a Creek woman: "Men folks were fixing up the wagons while the women folks were getting the quilts ready, gathering pots and other cooking utensils, and loading up the wagons." She remem-bered that her father placed her and another child on top of a pack on a loaded horse, and that at the end of the journey they built a camp on the Red River, making crude bark houses "arranged along a street-like clearing . . . and in the center of the street was dug a long ditch, . . . and this was done to build a fire in it and cooking was done over the fire."

They were never reduced to the helpless destitution of their rela-tives in the North. The Choctaws and Chickasaws "were always willing to give us a part of anything they had," and charitable Texans con-tributed supplies. The Confederate army commissariat furnished rations, and the soldiers were given furloughs to build shelters and plant crops for their families. The Richmond government not only paid the annuities, but advanced loans to the tribes. Even so, there was much suffering among the refugees. The number of Cherokees was about 6,000; of Creeks, 6,500.

In 1864, the Northern refugees were brought to the Indian Terri-tory, where they huddled around Fort Gibson. Congress gave them inadequate support, and much of it went into the pockets of dishonest contractors. They could not leave the protection of the fort to raise food, for their country was still ravaged by Confederate guerrillas. Stand Watie, commissioned a brigadier general in May, 1864, was the most active of these partisan commanders. In June that year he cap-tured a steamboat coming up the Arkansas with food and clothing for the soldiers and refugees at the fort. In September he joined a Con-federate force that captured a supply train of three hundred loaded wagons coming from Kansas with goods valued at $1,500,000. Mrs. Watie in Texas had been spinning, weaving, and sewing to make clothing for her men in the army. Now she wrote to her husband, "I thought I would send you some clothes, but I hear that you have done better."

In spite of the ruthless quality of the war he waged, Watie was a man of character and integrity. In a letter to his wife he expressed his reaction to a Quantrill raid: "Quantrell crossed the Arkansas river near the Creek Agency and killed eight men (Creeks) one of them shot a little boy and killed him. I have always been opposed to killing women and children although our enemies have done it." In another letter he said, "I am not a murderer." Mrs. Watie trusted her husband, but still

179

she worried: "be a good man as you always have been," she wrote him once. She was more concerned about their son, Saladin, who at barely fifteen had become a captain in his father's regiment. Upon learning that he and his young cousin had killed a prisoner, she wrote, "tell my boys to always show mercy as they expect to find God merciful to them. I do hate to hear such things. I find myself almost dead some times thinking about it. I am afraid Saladin never will value human life as he ought."

After Honey Springs the Federal commander at Fort Gibson made sorties into the Choctaw Nation offering amnesty, and some of the Choctaws made a cautious attempt to return to the Union. But, as one of their leaders expressed it, "We dont wish to be divided like other Nations if we can be saved any other way. As we all come out together and we should all like to come in together." Nothing came of these overtures, and the Choctaws remained with the Confederacy until it collapsed.

The Grand Council had met under Confederate auspices throughout the war. Now it invited tribes from Kansas and the Plains to join in a general meeting in the Leased District. There, on May 26, 1865, fourteen tribes made a compact declaring that "An Indian shall not spill another Indian's blood" and pledging themselves to maintain the integrity of the Indian Territory as the future home of their race. On that very day E. Kirby-Smith surrendered all the Confederate forces west of the Mississippi. Three of the tribes, tenacious of their independent position as allies of the Confederacy, surrendered separately through their chiefs: the Choctaws on June 19, the Cherokees—by Stand Watie—on June 23, and the Chickasaws on July 14. Then the Grand Council invited the Union Indians to meet with them at the Choctaw capital the first week in September.

They had dire need of unity in making a peace with the United States. Kansans were clamoring for their land as a home for their own tribes, or for white settlement, or both. Railroad promoters were scheming for grants. Secretary of the Interior James Harlan argued that the Indians, by their "perfidious conduct" in "making unprovoked war upon us" in "flagrant violation of treaties which had been observed by us with scrupulous good faith," had given him a clear slate; and the recently appointed commissioner of Indian affairs, Dennis N. Cooley, was in ardent sympathy with the exploiters. They rejected the invitation to meet the Indians in council at the Choctaw capital and summoned them to the alien atmosphere of Fort Smith. A Kansan wrote gleefully from Wyandotte, near Kansas City, to his congressman, "White men from here and Kansas City will go along. Treaties will be made and railroad grants fixed up and things done generally . . . & we should have a hand in it."

The council convened on September 8, with Cooley presiding. The Union leaders came first, innocently assuming that the purpose of the meeting was to unite the factions. Then in fulsome and pious language Cooley informed them that they had "rightfully forfeited" all their annuities and lands, but that the President was "willing to hear his erring children in extenuation of their great crime" and make new treaties with them. He read the list of culprit tribes, and they listened in consternation. They answered by the story of their loyalty and their sufferings. Even the three small tribes in the northeast corner had their individual tragedies. Speaking for them was Isaac Warrior, chief of the Senecas.

He told how they had been brought by their agent to the meeting with Pike at Tahlequah "and when we got there we found ourselves surrounded." They held a private council, "and they all said it's pretty hard, and we don't know what to do. . . . We have treaty stipulations with the United States to protect us, and now none of them are here." They signed the treaty under pressure, then went to Kansas in search of their "Grand Father," found a federal agent, "and told him all we had done. . . . Not one of our men, of these three tribes . . . went south; . . . we didn't do anything to our Grand Father, didn't even scratch him; and . . . our young men went into the army and helped our Grand Father to fight. . . . Then we always thought . . . when we ran away we did nothing, and always consider the land we have as ours yet, and we want to stand there yet."

At no time in the council did the officials ever admit the justice of the Indians' defense. John Ross, old and ill, arrived late. The commissioners feared his diplomatic skill, so different from the groping trust of the fullbloods. Cooley wired to Harlan, and Harlan said to "depose" him from his office as principal chief. Cooley then denounced him in a public tirade as the "emissary of the States in rebellion," who had induced his people to join the Confederacy.

The Confederate leaders came in a body from their meeting at the Choctaw capital. When they arrived, all the tribes except the feud-torn Cherokees composed their differences and presented a united front to the officials. The council finally ended with some preliminary statements, leaving definitive treaties to be negotiated at Washington the following year.

There were at that time 19,000 refugees clustered around Fort Gibson, still in Kansas, or scattered through the Choctaw and Chickasaw nations. As soon as the tribal factions made their own peace at Fort Smith (no thanks to the federal officials), the refugees began to return to the desolate waste of weed-grown fields, burned orchards, and blackened chimneys standing to mark their former homesites. Their horses, hogs, and cattle were virtually all gone—it is estimated that 300,000 cattle had been driven out by white Kansans and their willing Indian helpers—and wolves, panthers, and bears had increased enormously. But neighbors and even families that had been separated were reunited in settlements throughout the country, where—as a Creek woman recalled it in 1937—"those Indians that had been parted came together again and made peace among themselves." By the following March the Creek agent reported that all were "farming to the best of their ability according to their teams and other means." Sometimes, as another elderly woman remembered it, "one hoe had to do for the whole settlement." But in spite of such difficulties they had become self-supporting.

The definitive treaties of 1866 varied in severity according to the bargaining strength of the tribe. The Choctaws and Chickasaws, united in Southern sentiment, received the best terms. The Cherokees were divided, but they had John Ross; he managed to save something for them. The Creeks and Seminoles, who had suffered more for their loyalty to the Union than any white population, were even required to subscribe to a confession of war guilt.

Upon the whole, the Indians obtained better terms than had been threatened at Fort Smith. They ceded the western half of their country as a home for other Indians. Most of this area was beyond their settlements, but the entire Seminole tribe was displaced and removed to a new location. Their annuities were restored, and payment was provided for their ceded land. They agreed to the construction of one north-south and one east-west railroad across their country. They escaped the dreaded territorial government, but provisions were made for an intertribal council that, as Cooley predicted, "will doubtless lead to that result." The Cherokees, Creeks, and Seminoles were required to give their freed slaves citizenship and property rights. The Choctaws and Chickasaws might adopt their freedmen and receive payment for the ceded land; otherwise the United States would re-move the Negroes and use the money for their benefit. Both tribes requested their removal; but the United States ignored the obligation, and the freedmen remained in the country with no legal status. Finally, after twenty years, the Choctaws adopted them; but the Chickasaws held out for the rest of their tribal history.

A few days after the last treaty was signed, Congress gave fran-chises with grants of public land to the projected railroads: one from Missouri to the Pacific would receive alternate sections in a forty-mile strip along the right of way; the other from Kansas to Texas was prom-ised a twenty-mile strip. The Indian Territory was, of course, not public land, but the railroads were invited to intrigue to make it so. For the first, the United States undertook to extinguish the Indians' title "as rapidly as may be consistent with public policy and [their] welfare, . . . and only by their voluntary cession"; for the second, there was a greater promise, "whenever the Indian title shall be extinguished by treaty or otherwise." The real forces at work behind the Reconstruction treaties are apparent in these grants.

But the treaties, punitive as they were, permitted the Indians to re-establish themselves under their own institutions. They had surpris-ing powers of recovery. As young Saladin Watie, helping his family gain a new economic foothold, wrote in 1867: "and better than all mama has grown to be stout and healthy. She steps about like some young sixteen year old girl."

Meanwhile, other Indians throughout the United States had be-come affected, though in less degree, by the white man's war.

CHAPTER TEN

THE WHITE MAN'S WAR
AFFECTS THE FRONTIERS

Outside the Indian Territory it was the Indians on the frontiers of white advancement who were affected by the Civil War. There was no consistent pattern. As the military forces were withdrawn for fighting the great battles in the East, the Indians in some places had a breathing space; in others they seized the opportunity of going on the war path; in still others they were the victims of local Indian-haters while public attention was fixed on the larger conflict. In 1861 the white frontiers were in the North, on the Great Plains, and in the Southwest. The most unexpected event was the Sioux uprising in Minnesota.

The Santee Sioux had remained there when their relatives migrated to the buffalo plains. By 1862 the government had acquired all their land except a strip 10 miles wide and 150 miles long along the south side of the Minnesota River. Their affairs were administered at two agencies, an Upper and a Lower; and there was an unfortified army post, Fort Ridgely, across the river outside the reservation about 15 miles below the Lower Agency. In payment for their many land cessions they were receiving annuities in goods, food, and cash. Most of the cash went into the hands of traders clustered around the agencies from whom they had purchased goods on credit. For their living they depended largely on these annuities and an annual hunting trip to the buffalo plains. A few were learning to farm, sending their children to school, and attending mission churches.

They had grievances stretching back through the familiar pattern of frontier encroachment and rigged treaties. Now they suspected that the traders' debts were inflated. When they left the reservation to hunt through the lakes and swamps of their former domain, they found the

184

game depleted. From New Ulm, a town just below the southern end of their reservation, settlers were spreading out into their remaining land. (On April 3, 1861, thirty-two of these intruders sent a petition to President Lincoln asking protection in their illegal occupation.)

As bad luck would have it, the money for their 1862 annuity was delayed. The supplies were stored in the agency warehouses, but their agent, a recent political appointee, refused to distribute them until he could do it all in one operation. July passed—the time for their buffalo hunt—and still they waited. As their hunger increased, so did their anger. Finally, on August 8 the bands of the Upper Agency stormed the warehouse and compelled the distribution. The Lower Agency bands continued without buffalo meat or annuities. Then the traders cut off the credit. Still, neither the settlers, nor least of all the Indians, expected an uprising. It began with an incident so trivial as to be ludicrous except for the tragic outcome.

On Sunday, August 17, about twenty young men from the Lower Agency bands, returning from an unsuccessful hunt in the "Big Woods" near the Mississippi, were passing through the settlements. One found a nest of eggs belonging to some farmer's vagrant hen and began to gather them. Another cautioned him against taking property belonging to a white man. A quarrel arose—"I'm not afraid of any white man"— and four of them set out to prove their manhood. Coming to a house where some families had gathered for Sunday visiting, they killed three men and two women. Then they rode rapidly to their reservation and reported the murders. A council was hurriedly called at the home of Little Crow, an influential chief who had been showing some interest in "civilization."

They debated all night. Two chiefs, Wabasha and Wacouta, spoke for peace. (They were to remain at peace throughout the war.) Little Crow also spoke for peace. "The Whitemen," he said, "are like the locusts, when they fly so thick that the whole sky is a snowstorm. . . . We are only little herds of buffaloes left scattered." But others argued that no matter what they did, they would be punished; therefore they should strike first. Probably they knew that most of the able-bodied men in the settlements were away somewhere fighting on distant battlefields. The council decided on war, and Little Crow, to retain his prestige, became the leader of the hostiles.

Early Monday morning they struck the unsuspecting families grouped around the agency, killing twenty-three men and capturing ten women. Then they fell to looting the buildings, thus giving the rest of the people a chance to run to the river. There an unsung hero, the operator of a small ferry, crossed back and forth, carrying a load at each trip until the Indians noticed what was happening and shot him. By that time most of the fugitives were across and on their way to Fort Ridgely.

While this was happening at the agency, other parties of Sioux were fanning out twenty and thirty miles from their reservation surprising the people in their houses and fields. Some of the women they killed; others they held as captives, subjecting them to mass rape. The children they killed or captured according to the impulse of the moment. Of the men, they spared a few who had been their friends, but in general they killed friend and foe alike. The death toll on that first day ran into the hundreds. Nobody had time even to seize a gun. Many of the settlers, in fact, were Germans, who probably did not own one.

The first fugitives from the agency reached Fort Ridgely in midmorning. The commander, with more courage than judgment, set out with forty-seven men to put down the uprising. At the ferry he ran into an ambush. The men sought cover in the thickets, and when night came only twenty-three survivors found their way back to the fort. One of the Indians was killed there at the ferry, the only casualty that first day of what must have seemed to them a very satisfactory war.

Meanwhile, Little Crow had dispatched a message to enlist the bands at the Upper Agency. They debated long in council and decided to remain neutral, a decision that greatly limited the scope of the uprising. They did loot the traders' stores, killing one man and mortally wounding another; but a small group of Christian Indians herded the whites into a brick warehouse and guarded them, then escorted them— sixty-two men, women, and children—to safety three days' journey distant. At the same time many young hotbloods rode south to join the war.

On Tuesday the hostiles continued their raiding and killing, bringing to more distant settlements the first knowledge of the outbreak. Thus they lost their chance to take Fort Ridgely, almost bare of defenders and crowded with refugees. Before the day was over, reinforcements began to arrive there. Among them were the driver and guards of the coach on the way to the agency with the delayed annuity. (If only it had come two days earlier!) Little Crow invested the fort on Wednesday. On Friday, when eight hundred of his ranging warriors had collected, they made a determined attack, creeping up under cover, charging from the open prairie. They lost probably one hundred killed or wounded, but they failed to take the fort. They had their eyes on the rich lower valley stretching on to St. Paul and the Mississippi, and they knew that this was the key to its defense. As one of them said in later years, "But the defenders of the fort were very brave and kept the door shut." Failing there, Little Crow decided to bypass it and go down the valley to New Ulm. It was unfortified, and its population of about nine hundred was swelled by many refugees. The Indians attacked on Saturday. There was desperate fighting from house to house, and most of the town was reduced to ashes, but a small area in the center held. The door was indeed shut. The Indians went back to their homes and took their families and captives to a safe place near the Upper Agency.

Meanwhile, the governor was raising militia to defend the state. He gave the command to Henry Sibley, a former fur trader, who had served as the first governor when Minnesota was admitted to statehood in 1858. Sibley spent most of his time in camp or advancing so slowly that he avoided any encounter with the Indians, while they continued their raids. Even now there is no way of knowing how many of the settlers were killed. One conservative modern estimate is five hundred. Thousands more fled from their homes. An area embracing twenty-three counties in southwestern Minnesota was completely depopulated; many years passed before it was resettled.

The Indians won several battles with units of the state forces. Then Sibley, with 1,619 men, started a slow advance toward the place near the Upper Agency where the Indians, hostile and non-hostile, were living in a great camp with their families. Little Crow laid a skillful ambush, hiding his warriors in the tall grass on both sides of the line of march, expecting to cut the strung-out column to pieces; but a foraging party unexpectedly came upon some of the hidden Indians. Then the battle started—on September 22—and the Indians were defeated. They went back to their camp, took down their tipis, packed their belongings, and prepared to leave. They debated what to do with the prisoners. Some were for killing them, but Wabasha took them under his protection. Little Crow and most of the hostiles then set out for the Plains, and Sibley came and "rescued" the captives. They numbered 269, mostly women and children, a tragic group showing the marks of their terrible ordeal.

Sibley had been slow in war, but he became swift in vengeance. He scouted through the country and collected about two thousand Indians—a few hostiles, but mainly of the peace party—and sorted out about four hundred suspects. Then he set up an extra-legal court of his own, using the captives as witnesses. It worked fast, running the accused through in five minutes each. Even clear evidence that the suspect had aided whites was disregarded. The "trials" ended with 306 sentenced to hang for murder, rape, or taking part in a battle, and 16 given prison terms for robbery. These were taken in chains to a prison stockade down the valley from New Ulm at Mankato. The remaining 1,700, mostly women and children, were taken to Fort Snelling near St. Paul. As they passed through the towns, the soldiers guarding them had a hard time holding off the people, who came out with pitchforks, even scissors in the hands of women, anything they could lay their hands on, raging to tear them to pieces.

One Minnesotan kept his balance. The Episcopal bishop, the Right Reverend Henry Whipple, made a personal appeal to President Lincoln, showing that the Indians had ample cause for hostility. The President then ruled that those condemned to die merely for fighting in a battle should be treated as prisoners of war. This left thirty-eight to be hanged for murder or rape. (Even here, there was at least one case of mistaken identity.) A special scaffold was constructed so that all the traps would drop by cutting one rope. On December 26 the condemned were brought in and placed. The surrounding crowd became silent as they sang their death songs. Then the rope was cut, and the bodies fell.

The "prisoners of war" remained for a time at Mankato. They gave no trouble, and most of them became Christians before the winter was over. They were then placed in the camp for Confederate prisoners at Rock Island, Illinois. There they were given much liberty, and many worked at unskilled labor in the community. The other captives were kept for a time in a stockade at Fort Snelling. Finally, with the Upper Agency bands they were settled on a reservation in northeastern Nebraska, and the Rock Island prisoners joined them there. They had a hard time at first, but they became Christians and farmers, to the disgust of their proud relatives of the buffalo range. They still live there. By a recent count they numbered 1,372.

Thus the Sioux Reservation was wiped off the map of Minnesota. A few individuals who had given conspicuous service to the whites were permitted with their families to remain in the state. About 582 of their descendants still live there in scattered settlements.

In the spring following the outbreak, a military expedition of more than six thousand men went into North Dakota in pursuit of the hostiles but failed to catch them. Some joined their untamed brethren near the Black Hills, showing their plunder, boasting of their victories, and trying to stir up a general war. Others with Little Crow went into Canada, remembering the promises made to them when they fought under Tecumseh, promises long since outlawed by the white man's peace. In the summer they slipped past the searching armies and entered Minnesota again, killing about thirty people and camping one night within sight of St. Paul. This time Little Crow was shot from ambush while picking berries. Another chief was captured later and hanged at Fort Snelling. This ended the most disastrous Indian uprising white Americans had experienced since the attacks of Opechancanough and Philip on the Virginia and Massachusetts frontiers two centuries before.[1]

It had repercussions throughout the Plains. Settlers on the exposed frontiers of Iowa, northeastern Kansas, and southeastern Nebraska were thrown into a panic, expecting all the great Sioux tribes to sweep down upon them. The governors sent frantic appeals to Washington, and the government returned Volunteer units from Southern battlefields to strengthen the military garrisons on the trails. In the judgment of Hyde, "It was undoubtedly the coming of these troops that brought on the war with the plains tribes in 1864."[2]

It could hardly have been a coincidence that Indian depredations on the trails showed a marked decrease as soon as the soldiers were withdrawn at the beginning of the Civil War. Throughout the whole vast Plains region, with its thousands of peerless mounted warriors, were only four military posts with skeleton garrisons: on the Arkansas at Fort Larned in Kansas were 39 infantrymen, and farther up the river at Fort Lyon in Colorado were 33; on the Platte at Fort Kearny in Nebraska were 125 cavalrymen, and far up the North Platte at Fort Laramie were 90 infantrymen. Surely the Indians could have taken these posts and stopped all the travel if they had been hostile.

There was much to tempt them: great freight trains of ox- or mule-drawn wagons loaded with supplies for the mines in Colorado and new mines in western Montana or even for the West Coast; regular mail and stage lines; and emigrant trains, never stopped by the war. On the Platte trails were stations ten or twelve miles apart supplied by ranches,

[1] A detailed account of this uprising may be found in Ralph K. Andrist, *The Long Death*. The author, himself a Minnesotan, has made a careful study of incidents and individuals involved.

[2] George E. Hyde, *Red Cloud's Folk*, 102.

and at almost every ranch was a store and "pilgrim quarters" where travelers could sleep. In the fall of 1861, a telegraph line following the Platte route was linked at Salt Lake City with one coming from California, and a branch went up the South Platte to Denver.

The Sioux tribes lived on the Northern Plains from the Platte through the Dakotas to the upper Missouri. The Horse Creek Treaty of 1851 had defined the Cheyenne and Arapaho range as the area between the North Platte and Arkansas rivers stretching from the mountains into western Kansas and Nebraska. But both tribes were already forming Northern and Southern divisions, with the Northern living between the North Platte and the Yellowstone. Each tribe continued to think of itself as one people—they still do—but the Northern bands became allied with the Sioux, and the Southern with the Kiowas and Comanches. All these mutually friendly tribes hunted in each other's range at will. The Sioux satisfied their love for glory by raiding the Crows to the northwest and the Pawnees in Nebraska, and the Cheyennes and Arapahos sent their war parties against the Utes in western Colorado.

With the approach of the Civil War, pressures of which they were unaware were building up against the Cheyennes and Arapahos. According to the Horse Creek Treaty, rip-roaring, fast-growing Denver and all the Colorado mining camps, to say nothing of the ranches spreading out along the trails, were squatting on their land. Federal agents therefore called them in council at Fort Lyon (briefly known as Fort Wise) and persuaded a few peace chiefs—Black Kettle, White Antelope, and other Cheyennes, Little Raven and some other Arapahos —to sign a treaty on February 18, 1861, accepting a small reservation in southeastern Colorado. Ten days later Congress provided a territorial government for Colorado, and the next year John Evans came out to serve as governor. He spent much time vainly trying to induce the other chiefs to sign the treaty, but even the signers repudiated it. At a later council Little Raven said, "The Cheyennes signed it first, then I; but we did not know what it was. That is one reason why I want an interpreter, so that I can know what I sign." They never settled on the reservation.

In May, 1862, it was learned that the Confederates were planning to come up from the Indian Territory and capture Fort Larned and Fort Lyon. It will be remembered that the invasion came the other way, but the uneasiness remained. Then in August the terrible events in Minnesota brought fear to the Plains country and the return of the

Volunteer units to defend it. Most of these citizen soldiers had the callous frontier attitude towards Indians. One example among many: Lieutenant Eugene F. Ware has told that Kansas troops at Camp Cottonwood on the lower Platte lobbed shells during artillery practice into a perfectly friendly Sioux camp simply for the fun of it.

Such incidents made the Sioux ready to listen when the Santees came to incite them. But Colonel William O. Collins, in command at Fort Laramie, was a capable and level-headed officer, and he managed to keep the peace. The Cheyennes and Arapahos were not so fortunate. Colonel Jesse H. Leavenworth at Fort Larned also kept his balance; but Major General Samuel R. Curtis, who commanded the department comprising Kansas and Colorado, believed that the way to keep Indians in their proper place was to "punish" them, and Colonel John Chivington, the commander of the District of Colorado, was a ruthless Indian-hater with political ambitions. Still, for more than a year after the Minnesota uprising, Evans continued to promote the Fort Lyon Treaty and to report that all was quiet on the Plains. Early in 1863 a Cheyenne-Arapaho delegation, including Black Kettle, White Antelope, and a Cheyenne chief named Lean Bear, was taken to Washington to see the Great Father's power and benevolence. Then in November, Evans began to send frantic reports to Curtis and to Washington of a great conspiracy of all the Plains tribes to launch a full-scale war in the spring. Some writers have thought that loosely circulating rumors had thrown him into a panic. Berthrong believes that having failed to clear the Cheyennes and Arapahos from eastern Colorado by persuasion, he deliberately stirred up a war to drive them out.[3] This interpretation does, in fact, make all the Governor's actions consistent.

Ironically, the provocative incident was never proved against the Indians. On April 7, 1864, Chivington reported to Curtis that the Cheyennes had driven off 175 work cattle from a ranch on the Smoky Hill stage route. Later, when events erupted into a national scandal, a thorough investigation was made, and no evidence of the theft was ever presented. The oxen probably stampeded or strayed, and some of them were later found and picked up by the Indians.

Detachments of the Colorado Volunteers immediately took the field. It is evident that they were under Chivington's orders to kill every Cheyenne they found and take no prisoners and that their officers were

[3] Full accounts of this war may be found in Donald J. Berthrong, The Southern Cheyennes, and George Bird Grinnell, The Fighting Cheyennes.

spoiling for a fight. They attacked four unsuspecting villages, killing or driving off the people and destroying their tipis and supplies, and they had a running fight with a small war party on its way north to raid the Crows. Their reports are interspersed with accounts of Cheyenne raids, which add up to picking up four stray mules, stealing some property from a ranch, and running off some horses from a stage station. None of the villages attacked had taken part in these depredations or was aware that a war was in progress.

These events had taken place near the Platte or the long Central Plains rivers that formed the headwaters of the Kansas. A detachment of Chivington's command under the trigger-happy Lieutenant George S. Eayre wandered far from his district to stir up the Indians along the Arkansas. On May 26 they found a large band—250 lodges—under the peace chiefs, Lean Bear and Black Kettle, about fifty miles from Fort Larned. Lean Bear, wearing the medal and carrying the papers he had been given in Washington, rode out with some other chiefs to tell the soldiers that they were friendly. Eayre gave a sharp command and the troops fired, killing Lean Bear and another chief. A fight started, but Black Kettle rode up and called off the warriors. This enabled the troops to retreat to Fort Larned, chased by some vengeful Indians that Black Kettle could not restrain. Then these warriors raided the trail between Fort Larned and Fort Riley on the Kansas.

Major T. I. McKenney, a confidential staff officer sent by Curtis to investigate conditions, made this appraisal on June 15: "I think if great caution is not exercised on our part, there will be a bloody war. It should be our policy to try and conciliate them, guard our mails and trains well to prevent theft, and stop these scouting parties that are roaming over the country, who do not know one tribe from another and who will kill anything in the shape of an Indian. It will require only a few more murders on the part of our troops to unite all these warlike tribes."

The following day Governor Evans issued a circular inviting the friendly Indians to camp near the posts while the troops pursued the hostiles. The well-known trader William Bent carried this message to an Arapaho band under the friendly Left Hand near Fort Larned. They tried to hold a council with the commander at the post, a drunken incompetent who treated them with contempt. Then the Kiowas, under the noted chief Satank, ran off the horse herd, including Eayre's mounts, leaving the cavalry on foot. The next day Left Hand and his warriors approached with a white flag, intending to offer their help in recovering the animals, and the commander ordered his soldiers to fire. Nobody was hit, but the Arapahos were not friendly any more. They began to raid up the Arkansas toward Fort Lyon.

In the middle of July all the Southern Cheyennes and Arapahos moved up to the Solomon and Smoky Hill in western Kansas and with some of their Sioux friends began the war in earnest. And a terrible war it was. They struck the trails at widely separated points, killing tele-graph operators, station keepers, and ranchers. During three weeks in August, at least fifty people were killed on the Platte route alone. Soon all travel ceased: the California mail went by way of Panama; Denver was near famine. Curtis himself took the field, but the troops failed to find the hostile camps. There the Indians were happily decking them-selves out in finery from the captured trains and holding continuous scalp dances as the warriors returned from their forays.

To the south the Kiowas with their Apache subtribe and the Comanches were raiding the Santa Fe Trail, though the travel there was not entirely stopped. On August 11, Governor Evans issued a proclamation virtually declaring an open season on Indians. The War Department authorized him to raise a regiment of men enlisted for one hundred days. It became the Third Colorado Cavalry.

Soon some of the Cheyenne peace chiefs became tired of the war. Using the literacy of George Bent, William Bent's half-Cheyenne son, who was living with his mother's people, they sent a letter to their agent at Fort Lyon and to Major Edward W. Wynkoop, the com-mander of the post, offering peace. It was dated August 19 and signed, "Black Kettle and Other Chiefs." Wynkoop, a capable and humane officer, saw a chance to narrow the scope of the war. Using the letter bearers as guides, he set out with 130 men to the camp on the Smoky Hill. Here he was confronted by six to eight hundred warriors, but he held his ground, managed to talk with some of the chiefs, and waited while they met in council. They were not all agreed to stop the war, but they surrendered four children they had taken as prisoners, and seven chiefs, including Black Kettle and White Antelope, went back with the officer to consult with the Governor.

A conference was held at Camp Weld near Denver. Evans told the chiefs that his offer of June 16 still held. Chivington said he would fight them "until they lay down their arms and submit to military authority," and advised them to go to Major Wynkoop "when they get ready to do that." Later both men explained that their statements meant that the army would impose terms after the submission of the entire tribes. The Indians, of course, did not understand this technicality. They thought they had made peace. They led their people to the vicinity of Fort Lyon under the protection of Wynkoop. The hostile warriors remained out in their camps, but the raids tapered off and traffic began moving again on the trails. Even so, the army might have been justified in attacking the hostiles. Unfortunately, the ones who had surrendered were easier to catch.

If Chivington was to use his hundred days' men, he had to attack soon. He complained to Curtis about Wynkoop's conciliatory policy and Curtis replaced him with Major Scott J. Anthony. Anthony encouraged the Indians to remain near the post, in order—there is no doubt of this—to have them available for a massacre. About forty miles northeast, on Sand Creek, a wide, almost dry watercourse, there were about one hundred lodges of two hundred men and five hundred women and children, ten lodges being Arapahos under Left Hand, the others Cheyennes under Black Kettle, White Antelope, and other peace chiefs. About six hundred Arapahos under Little Raven were camped on the Arkansas sixty-five miles below the post.

Chivington marched to Fort Lyon, reaching it on November 28. There Anthony joined him with 125 men of the garrison, saying, "I believe the Indians will be properly punished." Chivington now had 700 or 750 men, his Third Regiment and some units of the First Colorado Cavalry. They marched all night and reached the camp at dawn on November 29. Some of the women saw them, but Black Kettle said there was no danger. He ran a large American flag and a white flag up on a lodge pole in front of his tipi and he and his wife and White Antelope took their position under it. Then the soldiers fired, while others cut off the horse herd.[4]

Some of the young boys managed to make away with a few horses. The rest of the Indians fled. Some ran into the sand hills, where most of them were pursued and killed by the troops. The main body ran up the dry stream bed and hid in pits they dug in the sandy banks, and the soldiers followed, shooting into the pits. Such of the warriors as had been able to snatch up weapons fought desperately, killing nine and wounding thirty-eight of their assailants. White Antelope refused to flee. He stood in front of the lodge singing his death song,

[4] The inside story of this massacre and of the events that followed it is told in George E. Hyde, *Life of George Bent*. Hyde has organized the writings of this articulate half blood into a connected narrative to make one of the most interesting books ever written about Indian history.

Nothing lives long
Except the earth and the mountains

until the soldiers cut him down.

Black Kettle and his wife followed the others up the stream bed. The woman was shot down; the Chief turned and looked at her and, thinking her dead, ran on. "We, of course, took no prisoners," wrote Anthony. Terrible things happened: a lieutenant killed and scalped three women and five children who had surrendered and were screaming for mercy; a little girl was shot down as she came out of a sand pit with a white flag on a stick; mothers and babes in arms were killed together. The pursuit continued for about five miles. Then the soldiers turned back to the camp, stopping on the way to mutilate the bodies in manners too horrible to relate. Finally, they plundered the tipis and divided up the horse herd.

Chivington and Anthony next marched down the Arkansas to do the same to Little Raven's Arapahos, but word must have reached these Indians, for the soldiers found only deserted camps. Then Chivington and his hundred days' men returned to Denver, where they exhibited more than one hundred scalps and were lauded as heroes. But the facts began to come out, and investigations were made. There was plenty of testimony, some from officers and men of the First Colorado who had been sickened by what they saw. Chivington could not be court-martialed because he had left the service, but neither he nor Evans ever attained their political ambitions in Colorado.

How many Indians were killed? They counted the missing: Left Hand and 46 Arapahos, only four survivors; 137 Cheyennes—28 men, the others women and children. Among the dead Cheyennes were eight leading chiefs besides White Antelope. As soon as the soldiers left, the survivors, about half of them wounded, came out of the pits and started upstream. Black Kettle went back for his wife's body and found her still alive, although the soldiers had shot her eight more times as she lay on the sand. He put her on his back and joined the feeble retreat. Then some of the boys came with the few ponies they had saved, and they placed the wounded on these. They stopped for the night in a ravine. It was bitterly cold, and they had run out of their lodges thinly clad. There was no wood, but those who were able gathered grass and made fires, moved the wounded close, and covered them with grass to keep them from freezing.

Before daylight they started towards the Smoky Hill camp, forty

195

or fifty miles away. Soon they began to meet mounted Indians bringing horses, cooked meat, and blankets. Some of the young men who
had got away with horses had ridden to the camp and reported. With
this help the fugitives made the rest of the journey in greater comfort.
When they reached the camp there was great wailing, for nearly
everyone there had friends and relatives among those killed.

They held an angry council and decided to send war pipes to a
Sioux camp on the Solomon and to a band of Northern Arapahos who
had come south that year and camped on the Republican. Both groups
accepted. It was a truism of army men that Indians would not go to
war in the winter, but this was different. In late December the three
tribes gathered in a great camp of about 800 lodges—150 of Oglala
Sioux, 250 of Brulé Sioux, 80 of Northern Arapahos, the rest Cheyennes. This meant about 1,600 warriors, among the greatest mounted
fighting men the world has ever seen.

About one thousand picked warriors set out for Julesburg, an
important supply depot on the South Platte Trail in northeastern
Colorado, with Fort Rankin, a stockaded army post, nearby. They
traveled in form, with the Sioux chiefs leading and carrying the war
pipes, soldier societies policing the flanks to prevent premature charges,
women, closely guarded by warriors, with extra ponies to bring back
the plunder. They struck on the morning of January 7. The garrison
sallied out to attack, but was driven back with severe losses. Then in
plain sight of the troops, the Indians loaded their ponies with captured
goods. When they reached their camp, the mourning that had continued since Sand Creek changed to dancing and feasting.

They advanced their camp, held another council, and decided to
make a great raid on the trail and then move on to the north. Here
Black Kettle, with eighty lodges of his people, left the group and
turned south. The main camp headed north, the war parties fanning
out—Cheyennes to the west, Arapahos in the center, Sioux to the east.
The camp and the war parties all reached the trail the same day,
January 28, and in a few hours they wrecked seventy-five miles of it.
The camp remained on the South Platte six days while the warriors
ranged, looting and burning ranches and stations, destroying the telegraph line, rounding up horses and cattle (1,500 cattle in one haul, 500
in another), capturing trains (22 wagons in one), and killing more
people than Chivington had killed on Sand Creek.

On February 2 they broke camp and moved on to the North
Platte. They had some skirmishes with troops and took some cavalry

horses and mules. Then they went on and joined their Oglala Sioux and Northern Cheyenne and Arapaho relatives in the "Powder River Country," a huge unspoiled area in northeastern Wyoming and southeastern Montana traversed by the Powder, Tongue, Rosebud, and Bighorn tributaries of the Yellowstone. They had traveled four hundred miles in the dead of winter with their women and children, their loads of plunder, and their vast herds of captured livestock.

The stories they told of the wrongs they had suffered and the gratifying revenge they had inflicted stirred their warlike relatives to emulation. After a pleasant spring of hunting and resting, and fattening their ponies on the new grass, they all held a council and decided to raid the great overland trail on the Platte and North Platte. Small parties struck at widely separated places from eastern Nebraska to the South Pass. Then in July they massed their strength—three thousand warriors—for a big raid on a point at the present site of Casper, Wyoming, where a bridge had been built across the river and a military post established nearby to protect it. Among the leaders were Red Cloud of the Oglala Sioux and Roman Nose of the Northern Cheyennes. Their raid had no important strategic result, but was satisfying by Indian standards of glory. They wiped out a small military train of dismounted cavalry traveling in wagons that was approaching the post and drove back a party from the garrison that attempted to escort it in.

Soon after the Platte Bridge fight, three army columns—1,500, 1,000, and 600 troopers—started out to encircle and destroy the Powder River camps. General Connor, fresh from his victories over the Bannocks and Shoshonis, was in command. He instructed his subordinates not to "receive overtures of peace or submission," but to "kill every male Indian over twelve years of age." It did not work out that way. The Indians harried the columns, captured horses, and slipped away unharmed. Connor did burn one Arapaho village and capture the pony herd, and he built a post on the Powder River before his inglorious retreat. It had been a happy summer for the Indians. They had no premonition of the great drive of frontier advancement released by the ending of the Civil War.

Meanwhile, Black Kettle's people, who had turned south the previous fall, found the Kiowas, Kiowa-Apaches, and Comanches in snug winter camps in northwestern Indian Territory. They were received with great friendliness and sympathy. Their Cheyenne relatives had supplied their most pressing needs after Sand Creek; but now their hosts gave them horses and lodges, even calling the most destitute into the center of the camp circle and presenting them with lodges just as they stood, furnished with beds, cooking vessels, riding equipment—everything. These tribes also had a story to tell. They had made their camps that winter on the Canadian in the Texas Panhandle, and during the same November as the Sand Creek massacre, Kit Carson had attacked them with 350 New Mexico Volunteers and 75 Ute and Jicarilla Apache allies. They chased him back, but withdrew to the new location.

Black Kettle's people tried to enlist them in the same kind of war against the Santa Fe and Smoky Hill trails as was then devastating the Platte roads, but they preferred to wait till spring. Colonel Leavenworth, then serving in a civilian capacity as their agent, sent out runners urging them to keep the peace. The army still wanted to "punish" them, but William Bent and Kit Carson warned against the disaster that would result. Through most of 1865 war policy versus peace policy was fiercely debated between the War and Interior departments at Washington. Finally the government decided to try peace.

In October, near the present site of Wichita, Kansas, councils were held and treaties were made with Black Kettle's and Little Raven's Cheyennes and Arapahos. In contrast to the Reconstruction treaties forced on the Creeks and Seminoles, it was the United States that made the confession of war guilt—"the gross and wanton outrage" of Chivington—and provision was made for indemnity to the widows and orphans of the massacre. Another treaty was made with the Kiowas, Kiowa-Apaches, and six of the nine bands of Comanches. All the tribes promised to refrain from raiding, and tentative reservations were assigned to them. Thus, in what would turn out to be a brief truce, the Indian war ended on the South Plains.

The Civil War also had repercussions in New Mexico and Arizona. In the summer of 1861, while Texas forces were capturing the military posts in the Indian Territory, another Texas expedition advanced from El Paso up the Río Grande behind retreating Federal garrisons. Then the following spring they were turned back at Glorieta Pass east of Santa Fe. Meanwhile, a California Column of Volunteers was advancing under Brigadier General James H. Carleton. On July 28 they established Fort Bowie at Apache Pass, but they reached the Río Grande too late even to see the retreating Confederates.

Carleton then became military commander of New Mexico and launched an active campaign against the Indians, beginning with the Mescaleros, using Kit Carson, who was serving as a colonel in the territorial militia, to spearhead the attack. Army units invested their mountains from all sides. Many were hunted down and killed, a few slipped away and joined the Gilas, but some were captured. Carleton placed the captives on the Pecos on a forty-mile-square tract of semi-arid land with a grove of cottonwoods known as the Bosque Redondo, and he built Fort Sumner there to control them. By March, 1863, over four hundred had been collected. They went to work with characteristic Apache energy, laying out irrigation ditches and planting crops. They might have succeeded with intelligent planning, honest administration, and good luck. They had none of these things.

Obviously, they needed food and clothing at first, but Congress made scant provision, and dishonest contractors kept much of that. Carleton forbade them to leave the reservation to hunt or even to go out and make mescal,[5] a food so important in their diet that it gave them their tribal name. Their first crop supplied them with some food, but it was the only one they ever raised. After that came insects, hail, floods, drought—something every year. Then came the Navahos. With the outbreak of the Civil War, Fort Defiance in their country had been evacuated, and they started raiding. Carleton sent Carson to round them up and bring them to the Bosque. They still remember the bitterness of that "Long Walk." By the spring of 1864 they numbered 8,474. They made no attempt to co-operate with their jailers; always they begged to return to their beloved desert homeland, lying protected by their gods within its four cornering sacred mountains.

Carleton never considered that the two tribes he dumped together were mutually hostile. Even had they been friends, the land could not support nine thousand people. In 1865 he had to cut their scanty rations. The Mescaleros held secret councils. Then on the night of November 3, they vanished. Even to this day no white man knows where they spent the following years. No doubt they raided; with so many wild Apaches and white outlaws about, it was hard to pin down the raids. Finally, on May 29, 1873, an executive order set aside a reservation for them in their own mountains. They had many troubles after that, but they still live there and have recently launched ambitious plans for economic improvement.[6]

The Navahos obtained a treaty in 1868 permitting them to return

[5] Mescal is made by steam cooking the huge fleshy bulb of the Agave (century plant). Some writers and even dictionaries have confused it with the hallucinatory peyote. The two plants and their uses are unrelated.

[6] The history of the tribe is found in C. L. Sonnichsen, *The Mescalero Apaches.*

home. The government gave each man, woman, and child three sheep or goats to start their herds, and they promised not to raid any more. This promise was kept; and since nobody wanted their desert, they were not disturbed. They made a frugal living by tending their sheep, raising food on every patch of irrigable land, and selling their startlingly beautiful blankets and silver and turquoise jewelry. They maintained their pride and dignity, cherished their own customs, and held themselves apart. In recent years they have entered upon a great creative drive similar to that of the Cherokees in the early nineteenth century.

Carleton was not able to capture other Indian raiders. Gold mining was developing rapidly in Arizona during the Civil War years, and it became a separate territory in 1863. The whole area west of the Río Grande was red with atrocities and counteratrocities between miners and Apaches. The California Volunteers did lure Mangas Coloradas in to make peace, where—to quote General Nelson A. Miles—he was "foully murdered." (The official euphemism was "shot while attempting to escape.") As we have seen, Carleton even sent Kit Carson against the Kiowas and Comanches. If he planned to pen them up with the others on the Bosque Redondo, he failed in that, too.

Then came the end of the Civil War, and the released energy of the white man was directed to the still unoccupied areas of the West. To the young returned soldier and his family, this meant the extension of the farming frontier. To the "robber barons" of that unrestrained capitalistic era, it meant creative building or exploitation. To the adventurer it meant excitement and a wild freedom. All the pressures previously felt by the Western Indians were intensified. These pressures were directed also against the stable tribes in their Indian Territory refuge.

CHAPTER ELEVEN

RECONSTRUCTION IN
THE INDIAN TERRITORY

The immediate problem of the Five Civilized Tribes was physical restoration. The Creeks had lost 24 per cent of their population, the Cherokees and Seminoles probably about the same. Thus it was a fragmented people that returned from refugee camps, Northern or Southern, to rebuild their ravaged country. South of the Arkansas-Canadian dividing line, the loss in life and property was not so great, but it was serious enough to justify the bitter words of the Choctaw chief to the council: "This was the second time in our history that the bright future prospect for the Choctaws . . . have been impeded and paralyzed by direct and indirect acts of the Government of the United States," the direct act being the removal from the "ancient and much loved homes in Mississippi," and the indirect, "their own unfortunate intestine war," in which the Choctaws had become involved.

But all the tribes made a rapid recovery. The mixed bloods, no longer slaveowners, employed hired labor, and they acquired extensive land holdings, ran many range cattle, and again built big houses filled with expensive furniture.[1] The fullbloods practiced a subsistence agriculture and lived in comfort, except that they sometimes suffered in a bad crop year. Their way of life is plainly seen in the Creek court records.[2]

When a man or woman died, the estate, no matter how small, was partitioned through the tribal courts. The judge and two disinterested

[1] Ellsworth Collings, *The Old Home Ranch* is an excellent account of the economic techniques and family and social life of this class. It was on this ranch that Will Rogers was born and grew to manhood.

[2] The Creeks may be taken as typical. I have used them because of my own investigations in this field. See Debo, *The Road to Disappearance*.

neighbors rounded up the livestock, counted the fruit trees, listed the fields, buildings, and fence rails, and made an inventory of the farm equipment and every dish and article of furniture in the house. Here it can be seen that the average Creek fullblood owned a wagon, a plow or two, possibly some other farm machinery, a saddle, some harness, a hoe, some axes, and other implements of the white man's manufacture. He used horses or oxen to pull his plow. He cultivated from six to twenty acres of land, raising corn, a little cotton, and possibly some wheat. The family owned from six to twenty horses, mostly ponies; from six or eight to fifty cattle, running on the range, but branded and known; ten to twenty hogs, running almost wild, but irregularly penned and fed; a few chickens about the yard; and possibly ten or fifteen turkeys that had been domesticated by placing the eggs of the wild fowl under barnyard hens. They lived in a log cabin furnished with bedsteads, tables, benches, and cupboards made of rough lumber by the man, while the wife made the clothing from home-grown cotton and used cooking utensils and dishes bought from the trader. Close to the house were a smokehouse, a hen house, and other outbuildings. Nearby was a garden plot, and almost every family owned an extensive orchard of apple and peach trees and a few cherries.

As soon as their annuities were restored by the treaties of 1866, all the tribes reopened their schools. Except for some attempt by the Southern Cherokees to maintain schools in the refugee camps, the children had been without any schooling for five years, and many of the buildings had been burned or had fallen into disrepair. Before the winter of 1866–67 was over, the neighborhood schools began to function, and, soon after, the boarding schools were reopened. All the tribes believed fervently in education as their only defense against the white aggression that threatened them.

The Indian Territory had lost its protected isolation. A major influence came with the railroads built under the 1866 franchises. The north-south grant was acquired by the Missouri, Kansas, and Texas, universally known as the "Katy." It reached the northern border on June 6, 1870, and crossed the Red River into Texas the day before Christmas in 1872. The east-west grant was acquired by the Atlantic and Pacific. It crossed the Missouri border into the northeastern corner and built thirty-three miles southwest to a junction with the Katy.

The construction crews were lawless and disorderly, and underworld characters flocked to the temporary terminals for pickings in gambling, murder, and vice. As the construction moved on, ambitious little towns sprang up at the stations, populated by boosters chafing at the restricted opportunity for white enterprise. Even passengers on the trains were carried away by the sight of the Indians' holdings. One of them, temporarily detained at the new station of Muskogee, subscribed to a newspaper published by the Creeks with this characteristic remark: "I want to keep the run of things in this Territory. If the government is going to get possession of this land I want to know it. I want to get hold of some."

More subtle but more influential were the railroad promoters. Neither of the roads had been constructed for legitimate traffic, but for speculation in the Indians' land. The Katy had issued fourteen million dollars in bonds to finance the building, securing them by a mortgage on the railroad property and the contingent land grant. As it happened, it traversed important coal deposits; thus the validation of the grant would have wiped out this debt. (One cannot accuse the builders of designing this—the road followed the obvious route, the main north-south trail across the Territory—but the discovery of the coal put an unexpected premium on their greed.) The Atlantic and Pacific had issued bonds of more than one million dollars on the road and one-half million on the land along its short stretch of track. These bonds had dropped to about five cents on the dollar, and the company brought suit against the government in the Court of Claims to compel the validation of the grant so it could continue with the construction. During the whole time, the officials and bondholders of both roads worked on Congress to break down the Indian regime.

Thus the fifty thousand Indians of the Five Civilized Tribes fought to hold their heritage against the onrushing force of "manifest destiny" and the sinister power of intrigue in high places. They owned their land and governed themselves under guarantees as strong as the faith of a nation could make them, but bills for breaking these pledges were introduced in every session of Congress. To oppose such schemes they kept delegations in Washington: educated mixed bloods skilled in diplomacy, versed in law and governmental procedure; and earnest fullbloods, appealing in their trust to the public conscience. Thus they managed to hold back the tide for almost a generation.

In this they were completely unified. In other respects also they recovered from the division of the war. Only with the Cherokees were there traces of the feud that had persisted since the removal, and even in this tribe the two factions, after a few years of disorder, resolved their differences through constitutional procedures. (John Ross died

203

in less than two weeks after the Cherokee treaty of 1866 was signed; Stand Watie lived only until 1871.) The Choctaw, Chickasaw, and Seminole governments functioned as smoothly as those of the surrounding states. The Creeks had constitutional difficulties, but from causes unrelated to the war. Their experiences are illustrative of full-blood conservatism and the intrigues of Kansans, who hoped that by upsetting the stability of this one tribe they might undermine the whole.

Soon after they returned from the Fort Smith council—on November 5, 1865—the Union and Confederate leaders and the headmen of the towns met in their own country to heal their division. There the chief of the Southern faction surrendered his office, and Sands was recognized as principal chief of the united nation. After this came the return of the refugees and the negotiation of the Reconstruction Treaty. Through 1867 they spent many days in council to form a permanent government. They began in February by adopting a solemn declaration that "those who were North during the late war, were not to be called Northern peop[le] and those who were South, were not to be Southern people; in short there was to be no North and no South among the Muscogee[3] people but peace and friendship." In this spirit they drafted, and after many councils adopted, a new constitution on the Anglo-American model such as had long been effectively used by the Cherokees, Choctaws, and Chickasaws.

When it came to putting it into practice, however, the conservatives objected to the procedure. On voting, for example, "I had never been used to making a chief with papers spread before me," one of them said. This practice would permit "stealing of votes." Lining up behind the candidates "is the only way in which it will be done satisfactorily—and right in the sight of God." At the first election, those who voted "on papers" chose their officials. The others "formed ourselves in rank on the prairie west side of the Council House and the whole prairie was full. We elected our Chief by the majority." Thus the Creeks had two governments elected by different methods.

Matters came to a crisis in 1871. Their agent, Franklin S. Lyon,[4]

[3] The Creeks often used this designation. Now "Muskogee Nation" became the official name of the tribe.

[4] Lyon was a Baptist appointee under the new policy initiated by President Grant of assigning the agencies to religious denominations. He had been serving as president of a small college and was chosen without his knowledge or solicitation. He immediately left his snug job to accept what seemed to him a call to greater service. Many historians have written of this system of denominational

managed by patient negotiations to bring about a settlement. But just at that time the Katy Railroad was building across the Nation, and emissaries from Kansas came into the country, insinuated themselves into the confidence of the fullbloods, and persuaded them to renew their opposition to the constitutional government. It has never been determined who paid these agitators, but Senator Samuel C. Pomeroy of Kansas, himself a railroad promoter, forwarded their complaints to the Indian Office, charging that a "rebel ring" had seized control of the tribal government. The Indian Office sent a special investigator who listed every office holder from the principal chief down to the light-horse (tribal police) privates and ascertained the Civil War affiliation of each one. His findings vindicated the constitutionally elected government and showed that the division in the tribe was not a continuation of wartime differences. Pomeroy did manage, however, to bring about Lyon's dismissal. The next agent, in his turn, made peace between the factions, but the Kansans stirred up further disorders. By 1877, Daniel C. Finn of Coffeyville had become their instrument. The state legislature had just passed a resolution expressing great interest in the welfare of the Indians and calling for beneficent action in the form of territorial government, allotment, and the opening of their country to white settlement; and Senator John J. Ingalls was sponsoring it in Congress. The relationship between Finn and Ingalls is shown in a letter Finn wrote from Coffeyville to the Senator: "I will return to Muskogee in a few Days and anything I can do for Your [interest] or the interest of Kansas will be performed."

In 1882, the disaffection of the conservatives reached the proportions of a civil war. A permanent peace was made the following year—by that time the land-grabbers had adopted other tactics[5]—and the dissenters came under the constitution and learned to express themselves through its processes. But the Creeks had had sixteen years of civil disorder, originating in a premature adoption of alien institutions, and continued by the machinations of those who intrigued to dispossess them. Even through the worst of the disturbances, however, their "international" policy—their relations with the United States and with

appointments, but apparently it was actually practiced only at the beginning. Certainly Lyon's appointment was the only one the Baptists ever made to the Creek Agency or to its successor, the Union Agency to the Five Tribes. All subsequent appointments were strictly political, except that the choice was narrowed to deserving Baptists.

[5]See *infra*, pp. 296-97.

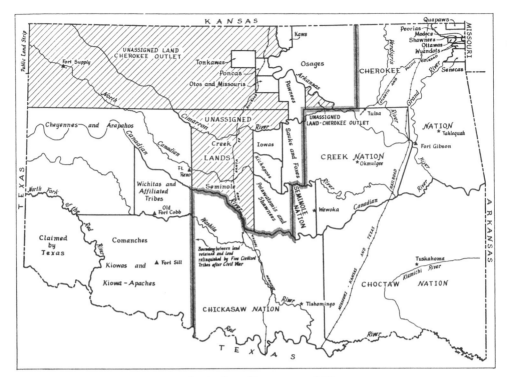

The Indian Territory, 1888

other tribes—was unified. Members of the two factions worked together on Washington delegations and in intertribal conferences.

The Indian Territory was rapidly becoming the home of many diverse tribes as the government carried out the removal policy envisioned by the land cessions of the Reconstruction treaties. To the tribes on Kansas reservations, it was a refuge from exploitation; to distant tribes from the North, it was a land of exile at the end of a journey as sad as the weary trek of the Southern tribes in the 1830s; to the hunting tribes of the Plains, it was a diminished portion of a once great range.

The process of dispossessing the tribes settled in Kansas from the Old Northwest had continued throughout the Civil War. Now Delawares, Iowas, Sauks and perhaps some Foxes, Potawatomis, Shawnees, Peorias (united Illinois tribes), and Ottawas found homes in the Indian Territory. They had lost much—houses, cultivated fields, herds of livestock—but once more they prospered. The conservative, warlike

Kickapoos were more rebellious, but eventually they, too, settled on a reservation there. A few Potawatomis and Kickapoos still live in Kansas, and two little reservations—the Iowa and the Sauk and Fox—overlap the Kansas-Nebraska border, but except for those enclaves, Kansas was cleared of Indians.

Only one detailed study of the liquidation of the Kansas reservations has ever been made—that of the Kickapoos[6]—but the forces that operated against them are typical of those that despoiled the others. This tribe was one of the victims of the treaties made when the Kansas-Nebraska Bill was pending in 1854. Their treaty provided for the cession of most of their reservation and the voluntary allotment of the remainder. The ceded portion was immediately opened to white settlement, and intruders constantly encroached on their diminished holdings.

The Kickapoos had no intention of accepting the allotment provisions of their treaty. Dividing the land was exactly like cutting up their mother—they meant this literally—and destroying what the Great Spirit had given them. But their agent working hand in glove with the Indian Office contrived to bring it about. Among the railroad companies springing up in Kansas like sunflowers, with declared destinations to distant points but immediate land schemes, was the Atchison and Pike's Peak, with Senator Pomeroy as president. In 1862, the agent drew up a treaty providing an allotment to each member of the tribe and the sale of their remaining land—nearly 125,000 acres—to the railroad company at $1.25 an acre. (It represented them as saying that they wanted a railroad because it would increase the value of their land and that the Pike's Peak possessed advantages over all other companies.) The chiefs refused even to call a council to consider it, but the agent visited the people in their homes and obtained some signatures of "chiefs and headmen." One of these was a legitimate chief; among the others were a ten-year-old boy, the child's mother, and some men of no influence in the tribe. It carried the date of 1862, and was duly submitted to the Senate and ratified in May of the following year.

Its provisions somehow had been kept secret, but with its ratification a storm broke. All the disappointed land speculators and railroad promoters in Kansas—and possibly some good citizens—were outraged at the favoritism shown Pomeroy's company. There was an investigation, but the treaty stood. The historian will remember that Pomeroy was very influential with the Radical Republican faction in the Senate

[6] A. M. Gibson, *The Kickapoos*.

at this time. One incident is significant. During the investigation, the Kickapoo chiefs had testified that their agent had made no attempt to prevent systematic lumbering operations on their land by timber thieves. Once they found twenty-five or thirty teams at one time hauling away logs, and again they discovered two acres of logs ready for hauling; but when they notified the agent, he failed to act. Now that Senator Pomeroy was interested in the timber, he wrote a peremptory letter to the Indian Office ordering the stealing stopped, and the commissioner obeyed with alacrity.

The allotments were all completed by February, 1865, and the company began selling its land to settlers the following summer. Not many Kickapoos accepted allotments, but a few did; before the year was over, one of the "paper chiefs" sold his allotment to Pomeroy. Most of them abandoned their reservation in disgust. About 50 went out on the Plains to hunt buffalo; more than 150 joined their relatives in Mexico. By 1867 most of them had returned to their holdings, now shrunk to a tract five miles square.

The Kickapoos in Mexico had settled down industriously, as was their wont, at their primitive farming and hunting. They had another source of income. Texans had expelled them from their prospering settlement in 1839 and without provocation had attacked their two migrating bands during the Civil War. This meant that they were "at war with Texas." They raided across the Río Grande, bringing back cattle and horses, for which conniving Mexicans supplied a ready market. Texas appealed to the government for protection, and in 1870 federal commissioners began trying without success to persuade the tribe to come to the Indian Territory. Then in 1873, a military force under Colonel Ranald S. Mackenzie was sent to bring them in forcibly. He watched through spies until he learned that the men had gone out on a hunt; then he invaded Mexico and attacked the undefended villages. The troopers killed a number of the Indians and captured forty women and children, fired the lodges and destroyed the stores of food, and beat a hasty retreat to Texas before the hunters returned. They took the captives to Fort Gibson and held them as hostages to compel the removal of the tribe.

This proved to be the argument that persuaded 317 of the Kickapoos to come in. They refused to traverse the settled part of Texas, crossing the Río Grande above the Pecos and entering the Indian Territory from the west. Their families were restored to them, and they selected a tract of rich river bottom and timber between the North

Canadian and the Deep Fork as their reservation. By the early spring of 1874 their women were clearing patches of ground and planting their corn, squash, beans, and pumpkins. Before the summer was over, they were living—in the words of their agent—in an "elegant and substantially built little village of bark houses." These lodges, in their centuries-old pattern, were made of poles bent to form an oval about sixteen feet long, twelve feet wide, and ten feet high, thickly covered with bark mats held in place with strips of bark and rawhide. They raised a bountiful crop that year, and their men found good hunting.

The Indian Office continued its efforts to bring the rest of the Kickapoos from Mexico, now relying only on persuasion. Two bands of 115 and 30 did come in 1875, using the same roundabout route. The others, numbering about 350, remained in Mexico. United States troops and Texas Rangers deployed along the Río Grande stopped their plundering, and, like their Indian Territory relatives, they settled down to their old pursuits of subsistence farming and hunting. They all continued their intercourse with each other. In 1878, 40 of them came from Kansas to the Indian Territory reservation.

The Indian Office, mindful of its duty to "civilize" them, tried to establish schools, and they indignantly refused; it supplied them with livestock and farm implements, and they ate the animals and allowed the machinery to rust; it tried to break down the influence of their chiefs, and they continued under their primitive government. Any suggestion of change was met by the threat that they would return to Mexico. They also rejected missionary efforts until one Quaker woman, Miss Elizabeth Test, with the kind of patience and understanding that seems restricted to Quakers, eventually won their friendship. The women welcomed her help in their sewing and cooking, the sick came to her for medicine, and finally, in 1890, she persuaded the first nine children to enroll in her school. Thus the Kickapoos at long last began to adopt the practices of their more progressive neighbors.

While the Kickapoos and other peoples of the Old Northwest were finding homes in the Indian Territory, tribes formerly living on the Missouri River and its western tributaries were also settling there. Squatters in great numbers were intruding on the Osage Reservation in southern Kansas, until, in 1870, Congress passed a law acquiring the land for them. The Indian Office and the Osage agent, now under a reform administration, managed to get good terms for the Indians and to persuade them to accept; and they exchanged their lost Kansas holdings for a tract of rolling hills and rich grass west of the Cherokees. The money from the forced sale of their Kansas land was invested for their benefit so that they became a wealthy tribe. They followed the same kind of progress made by the Five Civilized Tribes, adopting a written constitution and entering actively into intertribal affairs.[7] In 1872, Congress began a series of acts acquiring the land of their relatives, the small Kaw or Kansa tribe, and this buffeted people bought a tract of land from the Osages, where they slowly recovered from the losses of their Kansas experience.

Nebraska was admitted to statehood in 1867. It had been settled by white people more slowly than Kansas, having only 30,000 people at the outbreak of the Civil War. Also, it had fewer Indian reservations. Thus it never adopted the ruthless Indian policy of its neighbor state.

The Pawnees, always friendly to the United States, had gradually ceded all their land except a reservation thirty miles long and ten miles wide along the Loup River. There they were constantly raided by the Sioux. In 1872, they voluntarily ceded this tract and removed to the Indian Territory. They first clustered around their agency and its school and hospital; then they began gradually to spread out, to farm and raise livestock. The Otos and Missouris, united to form one small tribe living on a reservation in the rich valley of the Big Blue on the Kansas-Nebraska line, were so crowded by intruding settlers that they gladly removed to the Indian Territory on a tract adjoining the Pawnees. In 1956, they were awarded more than one million dollars in a suit they brought before the Indian Claims Commission for land they had occupied under aboriginal title in Iowa, Kansas, and Missouri.

The removal of the peaceable Poncas from northeastern Nebraska was a tragic instance of bureaucratic blundering and insensitivity. Their reservation had been specifically guaranteed to them by treaty in 1865. Later the government deeded it to the Sioux and in subsequent years worked without success on the Brulé Sioux to occupy it. In 1876, Congress authorized the Interior Department to remove the Poncas to the Indian Territory to make way for the Brulés. The Poncas were not consulted; they first learned of the plan when an agent of the Indian Office came to them the following January to carry it out. They said they would rather die than to leave their homes. Their frantic protests to the government officials were ignored, and a detachment of twenty-five soldiers was sent to force their removal.

[7] John Joseph Mathews, *Wah'Kon-Tah* relates their reservation experience. *The Osages*, previously cited, gives the whole history of the tribe from the Osage point of view.

Thus, through persuasion and the threat of coercion, they started out, 681 persons led by their chief, Standing Bear. By this time it was summer, and their journey in the heat was a two months' disaster, with torrential rains, swollen rivers, and even a tornado. A number died on the way. No preparation had been made to receive them, and they continued to die, constantly begging for permission to return home. Standing Bear had lost a married daughter on the journey. When his little son died, he refused to bury him in the alien land. With one old wagon drawn by worn-out horses carrying the body of the child, the Chief and thirty of his people started out on foot in a blizzard early in 1879 for the old Ponca burial ground. They reached the reservation of their friends and close relatives, the Omahas, in eastern Nebraska, where they received sympathy and asylum. Then the secretary of the interior ordered their arrest, and General Crook was directed to take them back to the Indian Territory. Crook's sympathy was all with the Indians, but he took them into custody.

Much public indignation had been aroused in Nebraska by the treatment of this small, inoffensive tribe. T. H. Tibbles, an Omaha newspaperman, became their champion, and public-spirited Nebraskans raised money to employ counsel and apply for the Chief's release on a writ of habeas corpus. The case was tried in the Federal District Court at Omaha. The government argued that Indians were not "persons" within the meaning of the Constitution and thus were not eligible for the writ. The trial was a dramatic occasion in a courtroom crowded with white sympathizers of the Poncas. Standing Bear spoke in his own defense with an eloquence that moved his hearers—including the presiding judge and General Crook—to tears. When he ended, the audience rose to its feet and cheered, and when the judge adjourned the court, all crowded around to shake his hand.

A few days later the judge filed a decision that became a landmark in Indian law, holding that an Indian is a person and is entitled to the same constitutional protection as a white man. The friends of the Indians hoped to carry the case to the Supreme Court for a final ruling, but the government shrank from appealing the decision. Standing Bear and his followers were released, and they went on to their old home and buried the boy with tribal honors.

After an investigation at the order of President Hayes, Congress made an appropriation early in 1881 to compensate the Poncas for their losses and to establish them in their new home. Provision was also made for them to return, if they wished, to their Nebraska reservation.

(The Brulés had never settled there.) By this time, however, they were becoming adjusted to life in the Indian Territory. In the summer following Standing Bear's trial there had been twenty-six deaths and only sixteen births among them. Now in 1880, for the first time, their population showed a slight gain. Their chief, White Eagle, testified that winter before the investigating commission. He told of their former troubles, "but from last spring up to this time we have not had sickness. We had made a turn in our course; turned over a new leaf, and we think now . . . that we'll have better times. . . . For five winters I've been looking for some one to help me, and now the sickness is going away. . . . I said to my agent, . . . I will dwell in this land."

Thus most of the Poncas established themselves in the Indian Territory. Standing Bear remained in Nebraska, and 170 of his people joined him. Their descendants still live in the two locations: 441 in Nebraska by a recent estimate; 926 in Oklahoma.

This removal of reservation tribes from Kansas and Nebraska to the Indian Territory was paralleled by an attempt to restrict the range of the hunting tribes of the Central and South Plains and settle them on reservations there. The treaties made with them in 1865 were makeshifts. Both Black Kettle and Little Raven had said at the time that they doubted the wisdom of committing the Cheyennes and Arapahos while most of their people were still in the North, and the commissioners told them that only the bands that signed would be bound and that the others might accept it later. It gave them a reservation in southern Kansas and northern Indian Territory; then the Senate amended it by eliminating the Kansas portion. That same fall of 1865, the bands began to leave their northern retreat and move back to their old range. All through 1866, Major Wynkoop, now serving as their agent, labored with little success to gain the consent of the new arrivals to the treaty and to persuade the whole tribes to accept the Senate amendment. The Kiowas and Comanches had agreed by their treaty to accept a reservation east of the boundary of New Mexico embracing a huge area in Texas and the Indian Territory. This location was clearly untenable. The federal government owned no land in Texas, and hardly a Texan since Sam Houston had been willing to admit that Indians had a right to live anywhere.

Most of all, these Indians had no intention of changing their way of life. They had been annoyed by incidents on the trails and driven to war by military blundering, but they did not realize that the white advance that had overwhelmed so many Indians was closing in on them, too. In the development following the Civil War their land was the new frontier.

First came the railroads, with their construction crews, maintenance operations, and stations, paralleled by great grants of public land, inviting extensive advertising and development. The construction of the Kansas Pacific striking west from Kansas City to Denver began immediately after the war; during 1867 it was building up the Smoky Hill through the choice Cheyenne-Arapaho hunting range. At the same time, the Union Pacific from Omaha, Nebraska, was building up the Platte, then cutting west to effect a junction with the California-based Central Pacific near Ogden, Utah, in 1869, thus completing the first transcontinental route. By 1870 the Atchison, Topeka, and Santa Fe had reached Emporia, Kansas, and during 1871 the construction was following the Santa Fe Trail up the Arkansas.

Not only along the railroads, but up all the river valleys the farming frontier was advancing across the Plains. The Homestead Act, passed in 1862, meant opportunity to the landless family to stake out a 160-acre tract and gain an economic foothold. In Texas, with no Homestead Act, the cattle frontier of open range and large-scale land purchase also worked its way up the Plains.

Another business was the buffalo killing. The Indians themselves had always sold dressed hides or even raw hides to the traders, but it had made no noticeable diminution in the great herds. They had complained about the wide belts of destruction along the trails, but unspoiled hunting areas remained. The buffalo furnished the main food supply for the railway construction crews. William F. ("Buffalo Bill") Cody, who was engaged to supply the laborers on the Kansas Pacific with meat, killed 4,280 in one year and a half, with no prospect of running short. In 1868, a train on the Kansas Pacific ran 120 miles through one mighty herd. It took General Sheridan three days to ride through another.

There had been some killing by hide hunters during the Civil War, but the business boomed when the war ended. Even so, an estimated fifteen million remained on the Plains in 1870. The destruction through the following decade is almost beyond belief. The one firm of Rath and Wright shipped out more than two hundred thousand hides from Dodge City, Kansas, the first season after the Santa Fe Railroad reached that place in 1872, and it was Wright's opinion that other dealers handled at least an equal amount. In the single year 1873, it is estimated that five million of the beasts were slain. By 1875 the

213

Southern herd was dwindling; by 1878 it was virtually annihilated. The Northern herd was about finished by 1883. The whole country stank from the rotting flesh, and soon the prairie was littered with bones.

This, at least, was business, but other men killed wantonly for sport. Passengers on the trains shot from the windows into the massed herds, killing many and wounding more, and letting them lie where they fell. In 1868, the Kansas Pacific began selling excursion tickets to this kind of slaughter.

No white person could understand the anger and despair of the Indians as they watched the source of their whole economic life—food, lodging, bedding, tools, household utensils—and even the basis of their religion, disappear. And while they resented the killing, they looked for deeper causes. Surely some offended spiritual forces had trapped the buffalo underground, and they engaged in desperate ceremonies to bring them back.

With these developments undermining their existence, no treaties could hold the Indians at peace. It required a decade of Indian wars to subdue the proud people of the Central and South Plains and settle them with the other tribes that were filling the Indian Territory. At the same time, a strong unifying influence was developing there through the intertribal council provided by the Reconstruction treaties.

CHAPTER TWELVE

HUNTERS OF THE PLAINS
SETTLE IN THE INDIAN TERRITORY

The first encroachment noticed by the Indians was the threat to the unspoiled hunting ground on the Kansas tributaries. When the Southern Cheyennes and Arapahos returned from the North in the fall of 1865, they found a new stage line in operation on the Smoky Hill route to Denver—a precursor, if they had known it, of the coming railroad. Still the whole area remained at peace through 1866. General Sherman, now the commanding officer of the division, made a personal inspection that summer and concluded, "God only knows when, and I do not see how, we can make a decent excuse for an Indian war," and he made cynical reference to the local hunger for army contracts. It was his idea to take over the main central area of traffic and railroad building between the Platte and the Arkansas and to establish the Indians north and south of those rivers.

Obviously, it would be difficult, even with patience and understanding, to persuade the Indians to vacate this wide corridor. But Major General Winfield Scott Hancock, the department commander, thought all the Plains Indians needed a lesson; the exemplary punishment of one tribe would intimidate them all. He selected the Cheyennes, as they would "appear to be as deserving of chastisement as any other." They seemed to justify his judgment in early 1867: they ran off the horses of a party of buffalo hunters, compelled a rancher to cook them a meal, and stole forty horses and mules from a wagon train. Sherman approved Hancock's plan, with this comment: "Our troops must get among them, and kill enough of them to inspire fear, and then must conduct the remainder to places where Indian agents can and will reside among them, and be responsible for their conduct."

215

Hancock assembled about 1,400 men at Fort Larned. He was not free to start a war, but he might provoke the Indians to do it. On the Pawnee Fork of the Arkansas about forty-five miles west of the post was an encampment of three hundred lodges: Cheyennes under Bull Bear, with the noted Northern Cheyenne warrior, Roman Nose; and a southern band of Oglala Sioux, usually friendly to the white man. Wynkoop persuaded Bull Bear and the other headmen to come to the post to meet Hancock. The General treated them with studied arrogance and announced that he would march to their camp for the conference. They protested, telling him that their women and children, remembering Sand Creek, would run away. Wynkoop also remonstrated with him, but he set out for the camp.

The Indians were convinced that he planned an attack. Roman Nose wanted to ride out and kill him. "This officer is spoiling for a fight," he said. "I will kill him in front of his own men and give them something to fight about." Bull Bear and the other leaders dissuaded him, saying their women and children would be the first victims. The warriors all formed in battle array in front of the advancing column, outnumbered more than four to one but prepared to defend their families. With bows strung, quivers full, rifles and revolvers at hand, they sat their ponies and awaited the orders of their chiefs. Hancock formed his troops; the cavalry came into line at a gallop with drawn sabers, and the artillery unlimbered. Then Wynkoop rode forward to meet the Indians and brought their leaders back to confer with Hancock. Roman Nose, bearing a flag of truce, was their spokesman.

Hancock abruptly broke off the conference and ordered the march resumed. But the women and children had used the pause to pack their ponies hastily and flee, leaving their lodges standing, with their household possessions and food stores. Hancock was sure that this flight proved their treachery. Roman Nose answered, "Are not women and children more timid than men? The Cheyenne warriors are not afraid, but have you never heard of Sand Creek? Your soldiers look just like those who butchered the women and children there."

Hancock tried to guard the village, but the warriors also slipped away during the night. Now the General *knew* they were hostile; whether or not they had actually committed depredations was not "of much importance, for I am satisfied that the Indian village was a nest of conspirators." The Indians, for their part, believed that he had intended to surround their camp and murder their families. When, in spite of Wynkoop's protests, he burned their lodges, they were doubly convinced. Now Hancock had his war.

He sent Major General George A. Custer, then serving as lieutenant colonel with the Seventh Cavalry, to pursue the fugitives. Custer wore out his horses and men, but never found them. Other expeditions were equally unsuccessful. Hancock's command in four months of active campaigning killed four Indians. Two were friendly Cheyennes from Black Kettle's camp south of the Arkansas; the others were two Sioux killed in a fight in which a lieutenant and ten men bearing dispatches to Custer were wiped out.

There were other military casualties, but civilians paid a much higher toll. Every station on the Smoky Hill Road for 170 miles was attacked; a number were burned and the keepers killed. Railway construction, working up the Smoky Hill and the Platte, was halted. Soldiers in the military posts or detailed to protect the stations were in a state of siege. The Cheyennes even learned to disable a railroad. Years later, one Porcupine told the story to George Bird Grinnell.[1]

Hancock's destruction of their village "had made us poor. We were feeling angry." Traveling north, they came to the Union Pacific Railroad, reaching it below the end of construction at the Platte forks. It was running trains to this temporary terminal. "It was the first train of cars that any of us had seen. We looked at it from a high ridge. Far off it was very small, but it kept coming and growing larger all the time, puffing out smoke and steam." They watched it pass and disappear in the distance. Then they rode down "to look at the ground . . . to see what sort of trail it made." Now they had a closer view of the trains and their purpose; "we could see white people going up and down" on the track in "wagons."

"Not long after this, as we talked of our troubles, we said among ourselves: 'Now the white people have taken all we had and have made us poor and we ought to do something. In these big wagons . . . there must be things that are valuable—perhaps clothing.'" They decided to try throwing them off "the iron they run on." They "got a big stick" and tied it to the rails. Then they watched. They saw "a small thing coming with something on it that moved up and down." This was a handcar with men pumping it, a crew of five on a maintenance job. When it "struck the stick, it jumped high into the air." The men were thrown off; they jumped to their feet and started running, "but were

[1] In *The Fighting Cheyennes*, 263–68.

soon overtaken and killed." (The Indians were mistaken about one of the victims; he recovered consciousness and escaped, living the rest of his life without a scalp.)

Encouraged by this success, the Indians pulled out the spikes and bent up one of the rails. When the next train reached the bent rail, the engine jumped the track and the cars piled up. Only one of the crew survived, and they killed him. Then they plundered the cars. They found bolts of muslin and calico; they tied the ends of these to their ponies' tails and raced over the prairie with the lengths of cloth unrolling behind. It was all great fun. Then they loaded their ponies with sacks of flour, sugar, coffee, and articles of clothing, everything they could carry, and moved off towards the Republican River. Soon another train came and stopped at the wreck. Many soldiers got out, but they did not try to follow the Cheyennes. What could they do? They were on foot, and pursuit would have been futile.

At the same time, as will be seen in the next chapter, the Indians of the North Plains had been even more successful. It was apparent that the military policy had failed, and a commission was appointed to try peace. The prominence of its personnel indicates the seriousness of the situation: General Sherman and other distinguished military men; Commissioner of Indian Affairs Nathaniel G. Taylor, notable for his humane principles, and other federal officials; and the chairman of the Indian Affairs Committee of the Senate. They met first with the Northern tribes,[2] then they came to the tribes of the Central and South Plains. The place chosen was on Medicine Lodge Creek in southern Kansas. Sherman was unable to be present, but the other commissioners arrived at Fort Larned, the starting place, in October, 1867. They were accompanied by reporters representing the leading newspapers in the United States. (Among them was young Henry M. Stanley, destined to fame as an African explorer.) Governor Samuel J. Crawford and Senator Edmund G. Ross of Kansas joined them there, vigilant to see that no land in their state should be assigned to Indians. The agents to the tribes, and a number of Indian chiefs and warriors, including Little Raven of the Arapahos and Satanta of the Kiowas, were on hand to guide them to the council ground.[3]

There was a military escort under young Major Joel H. Elliott and a long train of wagons loaded with food and presents. On the first day

[2] See *infra*, chapter 13.
[3] Much has been written about this famous council. The most convenient, organized account is Douglas C. Jones, *The Treaty of Medicine Lodge.*

out, a large herd of buffalo was sighted, and newspapermen, extra wagon drivers, soldiers, including Major Elliott—all rode out to join in the shooting. Some of them dismounted to cut out the tongues of the animals they killed; a few cut steaks from the humps; others left the carcasses lying untouched as they rode on to kill more. Satanta was furious. "Has the white man become a child that he should slay and not eat?" he asked the commissioners. They ordered the slaughter stopped. No more buffalo were killed except for food.

More than five thousand Indians were present at this great council. The only ones who failed to come were the Quahadi Comanches, wildest of all the Comanche bands, who lived on the High Plains ("Staked Plains") of the Texas Panhandle. There were many interpreters—old Indian hands and educated half-bloods like George Bent and his brother, Charles. Even in translation the recorded speeches of the tribal leaders are eloquent statements of their point of view.

Ten Bears, of the Comanches, began with the usual expressions of Indian courtesy: "My heart is filled with joy when I see you here, as the brooks fill with water when the snows melt in the spring; and I feel glad as the ponies do when the fresh grass starts in the beginning of the year." Then he went on to justify the wars, especially the ceaseless conflict with the Texans. "There has been trouble on the line between us, and my young men have danced the war dance. But it was not begun by us. It was you who sent out the first soldier and we who sent out the second. . . . The blue-dressed soldiers and the Utes[4] came from the night when it was dark and still, and for campfires they lit our lodges.

"So it was in Texas. They made sorrow come in our camps and we went out like the buffalo when the cows are attacked. When we found them we killed them, and their scalps hang in our lodges. . . . The white women cried and our women laughed."

He knew what he wanted. It was exactly what he could not have. "I was born on the prairie where the wind blew free and there was nothing to break the light of the sun. . . . I want no blood upon my land to stain the grass. I want it clear and pure, and I want it so that all who go through among my people may find peace when they come in and leave it when they go out."

Satanta was even more specific. "I love the land and the buffalo and will not part with it. . . . I want the children raised as I was. I have heard that you want to settle us on a reservation near the [Wichita]

[4] Apparently referring to Carson's attack in 1864.

mountains. I don't want to settle. I love to roam over the prairies. There I feel free and happy, but when I settle down I feel pale and die. A long time ago this land belonged to our fathers; but when I go up the [Arkansas] river I see camps of soldiers on its banks. These soldiers cut down my timber; they kill my buffalo; and when I see that it feels as if my heart would burst with sorrow." As to the "civilizing" influences offered by the commissioners, "This building of homes for us is all nonsense. We don't want you to build any for us. Look at the Penatekas! Formerly they were powerful, but now they are weak and poor. I want all my land, even from the Arkansas south to Red River. My country is small enough already. If you build us houses the land will be smaller. . . . Time enough to build us houses when the buffalo are all gone. . . . This trusting to agents for food I don't believe in."

The Cheyennes came late to the council, arriving with a dramatic display of horsemanship and the firing of guns. They had not heard the speeches of the others, but they said exactly the same thing. The commissioners told them that the buffalo would soon be gone, and in order to survive they must "change the road" followed by their fathers. "Before all the good lands are taken by whites we wish to set aside a part of them for your exclusive use. . . . You can go there and be fed and clothed."

The Indians were unconvinced. Why, then, did they sign the treaties? These set aside reservations for them in the Indian Territory, made the usual provision for schools and agricultural training, and promised annuities in food and clothing during the transition years. The very things the Indians specifically said they did not want! But the Kiowas and Comanches refused to sign until the treaty was amended to permit free hunting through all the land south of the Arkansas, and the Cheyennes and Arapahos had to be assured orally that they could continue to hunt through their old range between the Arkansas and the Platte. Also, they were impressed by the good will shown by the commissioners and by the great loads of gifts they carried away on their ponies. Freedom, peace, and gifts—not bad, as they saw it.

Their feeling may be seen in a personal expression by the aging Satank of the Kiowas. He had not spoken during the council, but as his people broke camp and prepared to leave, he came alone to bid farewell to the commissioners. As he stood there, holding the reins of his well-groomed pony, he spoke with such eloquence that even the most cynical of the reporters were moved.[5]

"I come to say that the Kiowas and Comanches have made you a peace, and they intend to stick to it. . . . We have warred against the white man, but never because it gave us pleasure. . . . In the far distant past there was no suspicion among us. The world seemed large enough for both. . . . But its broad plains seem now to contract, and the white man grows jealous of his red brother. He once came to trade; he now comes to fight. . . . We thank the Great Spirit that all these wrongs are now to cease, and the old days of peace and friendship to come again. You come as friends. You have patiently heard our many complaints. . . . You have not tried as many do, to get our lands for nothing. You have not withdrawn a single gift. . . . For your sakes the green grass shall not be stained with the blood of the whites. . . . I am old and will soon join my fathers, but those who come after me will remember this day."

It did not work out that way. The United States had officially accepted the blame for the war of 1864–65; the peace commission—and Sherman read and signed its report—came to the same conclusion regarding Hancock's action and the war of 1867; but now the cause was deeper. The Indians had promised to stay away from the trails and settlements, but the frontier did not remain static. They saw their hunting area shrink as it advanced. The homesteader with his plow and his sod house and his dreams of a tamed and developed land was the final enemy, and they sensed it. They held no war council and organized no great concerted raids, but during the following summer bands of hostiles struck several settlers' families in western Kansas, killing the men, raping and killing the women, carrying off the children, plundering and burning the houses, and driving away the livestock. At the same time there were sporadic raids on the trails. General Philip H. Sheridan had been appointed as commander of the department, but he had no more success than his predecessors. Sherman, in frustration, said that "fifty Indians could checkmate three thousand troops."

Finally, Major George A. Forsyth was authorized to enlist fifty old-time frontiersmen as "scouts" to fight the Indians in their own way. The ensuing Beecher Island fight in northeastern Colorado has become famous in western lore. The scouts dug in on an island in a wide, sandy stream bed, and although six of them were killed and fifteen, including Forsyth, seriously wounded, they held off the Indians for nine days

[5] This speech is sometimes attributed to Satanta, an error due to the similarity of names and the difficulty of rendering Kiowa sounds into English spelling.

until help arrived. Roman Nose was killed in leading a charge against the island. He wore a special war bonnet with a long train of black and red eagle feathers that was supposed to make him invulnerable, but he had unwittingly violated a certain taboo connected with its use, and this breach, the Cheyennes fervently believed, was the cause of his death.

Foiled again in its summer campaign, the army decided to strike the Indians in their winter camps. In furtherance of Sherman's plan to draw them away from the Kansas settlements, old Fort Cobb was chosen as the place for issuing the treaty annuities. The Wichitas and their relatives and the Penateka Comanches were still living on their reservation in the vicinity. Colonel William B. Hazen was detailed to act as agent for whatever friendly Indians might assemble there—in the words of Sherman's endorsement on a communication, "friendly Indians who will be left at the close of the War, a residue which he [i.e., Sherman] hopes will be small."

The Cheyennes and Arapahos, with bands of Kiowas and Comanches, were encamped on the upper Washita seventy-five miles above Fort Cobb, in the western edge of the Indian Territory. Black Kettle and some other chiefs went down and called on Hazen. "I have always done my best to keep my young men quiet," said Black Kettle, "but some will not listen, and, since the fighting began, I have not been able to keep them all at home. But we all want peace, and I would be glad to move all my people down this way. I could then keep them all quietly near camp." This was an accurate statement. Black Kettle had worked for peace, not because he was subservient to the white man, but because he believed it was the only way to save his people; but war parties *had* gone out from his camp the two previous summers.[6]

Hazen could only tell the chiefs that Sheridan was in the field and that any peace must be made with him. The troops had marched south from Fort Larned and built Camp Supply in northwestern Indian Territory. From that place Custer, with his Seventh Cavalry, set out for the Washita encampment. At dawn of a bitterly cold day on November 27 he surprised Black Kettle's village, which was at the upper end of a long line of camps. Black Kettle and his wife were killed, as were an uncounted number of other Indians, and fifty-three women and children were taken prisoner. Other women and children fled down the valley to the lower camps, with their men holding off the

[6] George Bent tells of joining in raids on the Santa Fe Trail, although he was married to Black Kettle's favorite niece and lived in the chief's family.

pursuers; and warriors from below swarmed up to meet the soldiers. A detachment under Major Elliott was caught between the two parties and was annihilated. Custer burned the village, rounded up and shot the horse herd, and retreated hastily to Camp Supply.

The destruction of Black Kettle's village was a tragic incident, but it was not another Sand Creek. A war party, whether from his band or another, had just returned to his camp from a raid in Kansas. On the other hand, if Hazen had been able to offer him protection at Fort Cobb, these blithe spirits would have been forced to disassociate themselves from his peace party.

After this "Battle of the Washita" the Indians fled to the Red River region. Two weeks later Sheridan marched from Camp Supply to Fort Cobb. On the way the Kiowa chiefs, Satanta and Lone Wolf, came to make peace. Sheridan treacherously put them under arrest and sent word to the Kiowas by Satanta's son that he would hang the two unless the tribe would come in to Fort Cobb. These acts brought them in, but one wonders why Black Kettle had been refused when he offered to take the same action voluntarily.

In January, Sheridan established Fort Sill in the Kiowa-Comanche-Apache Reservation, and it then became the base of operations against the hostiles. Custer went out on a peace mission to the Cheyennes, invited their chiefs to his camp, seized three of them, and prepared a tree and ropes to hang them unless the tribe would carry out his demands. They surrendered two white women captives and agreed to come in to the post. Custer kept the hostages; two were later killed by their guards while in captivity.

(Just at this time there was a change in the army command. When Grant became president on March 4, Sherman succeeded him as commanding general of the army, and Sheridan succeeded Sherman as commander of the division embracing the Plains.)

When the Cheyennes came in, one band broke away and went back to their old haunts on the Republican and began raiding. After the usual futile pursuit, the army, for once, surprised them on July 11, 1869, at Summit Springs in northeastern Colorado and defeated them in a desperate battle. Some of the survivors joined their relatives in the North, but most of them filtered down to the Indian Territory.

Thus, five years after the outbreak of the Plains War in 1864, the Cheyennes were finally settled on a reservation, and their women and children captured in the Battle of the Washita were returned to them. The Arapahos, always more peaceable than their allies, settled there with them. A patient Quaker agent tried to guide them into the new order.[7] It was hard going, but they remained at peace until a general war broke out in 1874–75. The other three tribes continued to raid in Texas, and some young Cheyenne warriors slipped away and joined them.

Meanwhile, a strong unifying influence was being felt among all the Indian Territory tribes. In 1870 the United States convened the first session of the council authorized by the Reconstruction treaties with the Five Civilized Tribes. Unlike councils called voluntarily by the tribes, this one was official—the government paid the expenses and Central Superintendent Enoch Hoag, supervisor of all the Indian Territory agencies, presided—but the Indians had their own ideas about the agenda, uniting throughout to defend their institutions. Because it held its meetings at Okmulgee, the Creek capital, it is usually known as the Okmulgee Council. Fourteen tribes, including recent arrivals from Kansas, attended the first session. Although speaking through many interpreters, the delegates fell into the smooth parliamentary practice typical of Indian meetings. Resolutions were adopted expressing "friendship and kind feelings" for the troubled Plains tribes, and a delegation was appointed to invite them to the Council. Committees prepared detailed statistics of educational and agricultural conditions in the various tribes. A memorial to the President of the United States was drawn up citing the guarantees of the treaties and protesting against the threat of territorial bills and railroad grants.

After a draft by a committee and much work on the floor, a constitution was adopted providing a federal government with an elected governor and General Assembly and a system of courts. It would go into effect when ratified by tribes constituting two thirds of the population of the Territory. The Indians never had an untrammeled opportunity to act on it. The administration advised Congress to amend it to retain a veto on laws passed by the Assembly and to make the governor and judges presidential appointees. Harlan, who was then in the Senate, used it to further his own plan of a territorial government controlled by white men.

The delegates from the Council met the Plains tribes at the Wichita Agency the following April. The Wichitas and their associates and the Cheyennes and Arapahos agreed to attend the next meeting,

[7] A fascinating account of these difficulties is in John H. Seger, *Early Days among the Cheyenne and Arapahoe Indians.*

but the other three tribes refused. Satanta protested that "the time has not come yet." Within a month, with one hundred Kiowa, Kiowa-Apache, and Comanche warriors, he made a raid into Texas. Satank, now disillusioned—his favorite son had been killed on a Texas raid—was with the party. Another prominent Kiowa leader was Mamanti (Sky Walker), famous in medicine as in battle. They barely missed bringing back the most important scalp ever taken in Indian wars.

William Tecumseh Sherman, four-star general of the army, successor only to Washington and Grant, had set out from New Orleans on a tour of inspection. Traveling in an army ambulance with three officers and an escort of only fifteen cavalrymen, he was approaching Fort Richardson in north Texas. It was a bright May day and all seemed peaceful. The Indians were concealed in a patch of scrub oak overlooking the trail. In later years, with the hindsight of tradition, they told the story. The preceding night an owl had hooted, and Mamanti had interpreted the message: "Tomorrow two parties of Tehannas [Texans] will pass this way. The first will be a small party. . . . But it must not be attacked. The medicine forbids. Later in the day another party will come. This one may be attacked. This one will be successful."

Owl message or not, it is true that one hundred painted warriors watched Sherman's party pass and that Mamanti held them in check. Two or three hours later ten mule-drawn wagons loaded with corn for a military post came into view. The galloping horde swooped down. In the short, swift battle seven of the twelve teamsters were killed; five ran to the timber and escaped. The Indians plundered the train and made off with forty-one mules. They lost three of their own warriors in the raid.

During the night a wounded teamster reached Fort Richardson with the story. Sherman ordered Mackenzie, the post commander, to proceed to the place and then pursue the Indians, while he went on to Fort Sill. There, besides inspecting that post, he visited the nearby Kiowa-Comanche-Apache Agency and told Lawrie Tatum, the Quaker agent, of the attack on the wagon train. Soon after he returned to the post, Satanta and other Kiowa chiefs came to the agency, and Tatum, hoping to find out which tribe was guilty, started to question them. He had better success than he expected.

Satanta rose impressively from his seat on the floor and answered: "Yes, I led that raid. I have heard that you have stolen a large portion of our annuity goods and given them to the Texans.[8] . . . Some years

[8] Probably some of their annuities had been diverted to reimburse the victims of their depredations.

ago we were taken by the hair and pulled close to the Texans where we have to fight. . . . When Gen Custer was here two or three years ago, he arrested me & kept me in confinement several days. But arresting Indian is plaid [played] out now & is never to be repeated."[9] And he went on to boast of the raid and began to name the participants—Satank, Eagle Heart, Big Tree. . . .

Tatum told the Kiowas that there was a big soldier chief from Washington at the post and that they should talk to him. Meanwhile, he sent a swift message to Sherman. Sherman concealed all the soldiers in strategic places and confronted the chiefs. Satanta repeated his defiant account of the raid, Sherman gave a sharp command, and the soldiers appeared with leveled carbines. The General then told them that they must return the mules and that he would take the leaders to Texas for trial. There were some tense moments when it looked as though the Indians would kill Sherman and precipitate a massacre, but the General's nerve held. Satanta, Satank, and Big Tree were arrested, and the other Kiowas broke and fled. (Eagle Heart escaped. Apparently the white men did not know about Mamanti.)[10]

Sherman then left to visit the Okmulgee Council. Soon Mackenzie arrived at the post, having failed to find the raiders, and learned of the arrest of the leaders. He placed the chiefs, manacled hand and foot, in wagons followed by a cavalry escort and started for Texas. Satank began to sing the death song of his warrior society, the Ko-eet-senko. Speaking in Comanche, the lingua franca of the South Plains, he said to George Washington, the chief of the Caddos: "Take this message to my people. Tell them I died beside the road." Satanta also entrusted a message to the Caddo: "Tell the Kiowas to bring back the mules, and don't raid any more. Do as the agent tells them." The wagons moved on and Satank resumed his death song:

O sun you remain forever, but we Ko-eet-senko must die,
O earth you remain forever, but we Ko-eet-senko must die.

The soldiers were unaware of what was happening, but "Caddo George," riding beside the wagons, knew. "See that tree?" said Satank. "When I reach that tree I will be dead." He slipped the handcuffs over his slender Indian hands, severely lacerating them, and, producing a knife he had hidden, wounded a guard, seized the man's carbine, and

9 As Tatum set down the interpreter's words.
10 The whole dramatic story is told in W. S. Nye, *Carbine and Lance*.

226

attempted to fire it. Before he could succeed, he was shot by the soldiers. Word was sent to the Kiowas that they might claim the body, but they were in flight; thus he was buried in the post cemetery.

Sherman, meanwhile, was on his way to the Okmulgee Council. This 1871 session was held in June, and twenty-two tribes were represented, including the Wichitas and their relatives and the Cheyennes and Arapahos. The newcomers were received ceremonially by old Indian customs, and Sands was selected to give the address of welcome. The Plains chiefs came in all the proud splendor of paint and feathers and beaded buckskin, profoundly disturbed over the encircling menace of the white man's settlements and seeking guidance from friendly Indians to an untried way of life. The Five Civilized Tribes counseled them from their own dark history to accept peace and agriculture as their only hope of survival.

But when Sherman was called on to speak, he showed them how precarious was the future they were striving to build. He told them bluntly that their land was better than Kansas or Nebraska; it could feed and clothe six million people. The implication was clear that it should be developed by white men. Several Indians rose to defend their tenure, and he warned them that white Americans were just but earnest, and when anything stood in their way they brushed it aside.

The contrast between their objectives and his was shown by the Cheyennes and Arapahos. They were touched by their cordial reception. Their spokesman said they had heard that their red brethren had adopted the ways of the white men and lived in warm, dry houses, had schools for their children, and raised corn, cattle, and hogs for their support. They had come to inquire into the truth of this. His people had been born on the Great Plains where the buffalo and elk had afforded them abundance of food; but the white men had invaded these plains, built railroads over them, and placed their cities and farms there, and had driven the game away so that they had no means of support. He told of Sand Creek and of Custer's destruction of Black Kettle's village. These fearful scenes haunted his thoughts sleeping and waking, and he wanted no more trouble with soldiers. Now they had seen the progress of their red brethren, and if they could have a reservation in the Indian Territory safe from the encroachments and depredations of white people, and if their civilized brethren would admit them to their great council fire, they would go back and advise their people to learn their way of life.

This was the spirit of progress that Sherman was so avid to wipe out. No white man could have brought such influence to bear upon the "wild" tribes.

The next month—July 5, 1871—Satanta and Big Tree were brought to trial in Jacksboro, Texas, near Fort Richardson. The courtroom was packed with angry Texans, but all legal safeguards were observed. A cowboy jury brought in a verdict of guilty, and the two were sentenced to death by hanging. Satanta made a dramatic appeal for clemency, claiming he had always been a friend of the white man. He promised, "If you will let me go, I will withdraw my warriors from Tehanna. . . . But if you kill me, it will be a spark on the Prairie—make big fire—burn heap."

There was too much truth for comfort in this last threat. Central Superintendent Hoag, Agent Tatum, and the trial judge all appealed to the governor, and the governor commuted the sentences to life imprisonment. The two chiefs were delivered to the penitentiary at Huntsville on August 2.

For a time the Indians were relatively quiet. But Mackenzie started out on the Staked Plains to "punish" them, and the Quahadi Comanches ran off 70 of his mounts and escaped unharmed. The Kiowas delivered the 41 mules to Tatum and asked continually for the release of their chiefs. Then, failing to get action, they made a series of rapid raids in the spring: they made off with 127 army mules near Camp Supply; they captured an army ordinance train in Texas, killing seventeen teamsters; and they raided the home of a Texas family, killing the parents and one child and taking three children captive. They killed a lone white man here and there—the son of Satank killed eighteen men to avenge his father's death.

The Okmulgee Council, meeting in June, devoted much time to these events and appointed a delegation to accompany Superintendent Hoag to meet the hostile tribes. At the meeting held near the Wichita Agency the following month, the relations were cordial, but the Kiowas laid down conditions for calling off the war: the release of their chiefs and the extension of their reservation to include all the land between the Platte and the Río Grande. This conference, however, paved the way for a trip to Washington by several chiefs, including Ten Bears of the Comanches and Lone Wolf, successor to Satank and Satanta, of the Kiowas. Satanta and Big Tree were brought up from prison to an affecting meeting at St. Louis with their friends. Then the delegation went on to Washington, where the Kiowas were encouraged to win the release of their chiefs by good behavior.

In September, Mackenzie marched to the Staked Plains, where for the first time he defeated the redoubtable Quahadis in battle and returned to Texas with about 120 captive women and children. The Quahadis then joined the other Comanches on their reservation, and a strange quiet descended upon the Texas frontier.

The Okmulgee Council convened the following year in May. It welcomed the good news from the Plains and sent a memorial to the president requesting the release of Satanta and Big Tree. The next month the Comanche captives were brought back to a joyful reunion with their people and a story of good treatment at the hands of the military. (They had to be moved by stealth around Jacksboro to prevent the citizens from murdering them.) Their happy husbands and fathers embraced the officer in charge, and many said they would never again fight the army. But the Indian Office had a hard time persuading the governor of Texas to release the Kiowa chiefs. Finally, to the disgust of Tatum and Sherman, he brought them to Fort Sill.

The Indians all pleaded for them. The hostiles made good promises. Tribes like the Caddos and Penatekas, which had not joined in the raiding, added their entreaties. Satanta's aged father stepped out unexpectedly from the throng of spectators and spoke so earnestly that his words scarcely needed interpretation. "I want you to pity me and give up my son. The Indians love their children as much as the white people do theirs. . . . Never again will we raid upon Texas." Satanta promised everything.

The governor finally yielded and released them. It was understood that they were on parole and would be returned to prison if the Indians should violate the peace. One condition, added apparently as an afterthought, was that the Comanches surrender five unidentified young warriors to be punished for some unspecified raid. This demand brought about the South Plains War of 1874–75.

The Comanches simply would not give up their young men to suffer an unknown fate. They moved out on the plains, and raiding parties set out for Texas and Mexico. Kicking Bird, the Black Kettle of the Kiowas, told the agency schoolteacher that the demand for the five "has set all this country on fire." He was hopeless about the outcome. He thought it would take the white man "two or three, maybe four years" to "destroy us all." Then the world would "turn to water, or burn up. It is our mother, and cannot live when the Indians all are dead." He managed to persuade about three-fourths of the Kiowas to camp near Fort Sill and remain at peace, but Mamanti and Lone Wolf joined the hostiles. The Cheyennes and Arapahos also went to war.

There were the usual incitements. Wild young men thirsting for military glory would break away from the restraint of the chiefs and go on raids. Then if one was killed, revenge became a sacred duty. But underlying such incidents were fundamental grievances.

By this time the buffalo herds were noticeably dwindling, and the Indians watched the slaughter in helpless rage. It is significant that the first organized battle of the war was an attack on June 27 by all five tribes on Adobe Walls, a settlement of buffalo hunters in the Texas Panhandle. The hunters, sheltered inside the buildings, were able with their long-range buffalo guns to pick off the circling warriors, and the attack was a failure.

Another cause was the intrusion of white people on the reservations. Much has been written about the Indians' raids on the settlements, but no study has ever been made of equivalent raids by white men on the Indians. Buffalo hunters operated there, timber thieves cut down the trees and hauled away the wood, and horse thieves from Kansas and Texas stole hundreds of the Indians' ponies and sold them to willing confederates—the "good citizens" of their respective states. Nobody ever counted the Indians killed on their own land by these marauders, but if any of *them* were killed, it was charged to "Indian atrocities."[11]

There was an even more ominous intrusion. The government sent in surveying parties to block the land out in township, section, and quarter-section squares, with no possible object except for the convenience of future white homesteaders. Even Commissioner of Indian Affairs Edward P. Smith announced in his *Annual Report* for 1874 that not all the land ceded by the Five Civilized Tribes only eight years before for the settlement of other Indians would be required for them and that he planned to concentrate them in one area and make a large amount available for whites.

The Indians sensed this threat. Said Kicking Bird: "This country

[11] See, for example, Zoe A. Tilghman, *Marshal of the Last Frontier*, 93 ff., for Bill Tilghman's unashamed account of hunting buffalo on the Cheyenne and Arapaho Reservation, his pride in a stolen Indian horse, and his killing of Indians in self-defense. Equally casual references to white intrusion may be seen in Nye, *Carbine and Lance*, 140, 147, 296. See also Berthrong, *The Southern Cheyennes*, 381–83, and Hyde, *Life of George Bent*, 355. For mention of organized pony stealing from the Cheyennes and Arapahos, see Oliver Nelson, *The Cowman's Southwest*, *passim*.

was given by Washington to his red children. I now see white men in it, making lines, setting up sticks and stones with marks on them. We do not know what it means, but we are afraid it is not for our good." The Cheyennes and Arapahos watched the surveyors at work. Then they pulled up a stake and examined it carefully. Their Kiowa friend, Mamanti, told them: "It is white man's medicine. They do not kill the buffalo, they seem harmless. But they make this medicine over all the land. It is bad medicine. It will take the land away from us, just as they have already taken our hunting grounds." The Indians thereupon wiped out the surveying party. Another surveyor was killed near the Wichita Agency, still another on the Red River. These deaths were chalked up as Indian "outrages."

The Okmulgee Council that year, deeply concerned over the renewal of Plains hostility, voted to hold an extra session at the Wichita Agency in September. The session was never held; that same September, Sheridan made final plans to surround the hostiles on the Staked Plains. In the winter campaign that followed, columns of troops converged on them from all directions. There were some skirmishes, but mainly it was the burning of camps and supplies, the capture and killing of pony herds, and constant pursuit that gave the Indians no rest. Runners were sent out from the friendly camps to induce them to surrender, and first in small bands, then in larger numbers, they began to come in, the last ones being the Quahadis, who came to Fort Sill in June. They were disarmed, their ponies were shot or sold at auction for their benefit, and their leaders were placed in irons. Of these last, nine Comanches, twenty-six Kiowas—including Mamanti and Lone Wolf—thirty-three Cheyennes, and two Arapahos were placed in the custody of Lieutenant Richard H. Pratt and taken to the military prison of Fort Marion at St. Augustine, Florida. The Lieutenant won their affection and respect, and some of the younger ones became the nucleus of his famous Indian school at Carlisle, Pennsylvania. In 1878 the Florida prisoners were released and allowed to return to their people.[12]

Satanta and Big Tree were sent back to the Texas penitentiary. Big Tree was eventually freed, but Satanta was kept in prison until he committed suicide by throwing himself from a balcony. After many years of effort by his son, then by his grandson, to obtain his body from the Texas authorities, the grandson, James Auchiah, a leading Okla-

[12] For a Cheyenne warrior's account of this experience, see Cohoe, *A Cheyenne Sketchbook.*

homa artist, was finally successful in 1963. He brought the Chief's bones back and buried them with the old Kiowa ceremonials in the post cemetery beside the grave of Satank.

The winter campaign of 1874–75 ended the wars on the Central and South Plains. All five of the former hostile tribes participated in the Okmulgee Council the following summer, as did also the recently arrived Kickapoos. Altogether, thirty tribes were represented. Again they wrote a constitution for "a purely Indian government," but Commissioner Smith reported that they had failed and advised Congress to establish a government dominated by Washington. Thirteen territorial bills were introduced during the following session of Congress, but the appropriation for the Okmulgee Council was discontinued, and it never met again. It had not failed; it had only succeeded too well in welding an Indian nationality and defending Indian rights.

Meanwhile, the wars on the Central and South Plains were paralleled by similar events in the North.

CHAPTER THIRTEEN

NORTH PLAINS AND NORTHWEST TRIBES FIGHT FOR THEIR HOMELANDS

After the dismal failure of the army's attempt to "punish" them in 1865, the Sioux and Northern Cheyennes and Arapahos of the Powder River country continued their old untroubled life. But their turn was coming next. The gold diggings of western Montana were difficult to reach by working up the Missouri to Fort Benton, or by cutting across the mountains from Fort Hall on the Overland Trail in eastern Idaho. In 1862, John M. Bozeman found a better route, leaving the trail just west of Fort Laramie and passing northwest through the heart of the Powder River country. A few prospectors, at risk of life and scalp, managed to slip through, but the Indians knew too much about trails. They were determined to keep their land whole.

In 1866, commissioners lured them down to Fort Laramie to gain their consent to the passage. While they were negotiating, a long column of troops with a large wagon train came in sight. One of the chiefs asked the commanding officer, Colonel Henry B. Carrington, where he was going. Carrington said he was on his way to the Powder River country to build forts to protect the new road. This news broke up the council. "Great Father sends us presents and wants new road," said one, "but white chief goes with soldiers to steal road before Indian can say yes or no." And they took down their tipis and set out for home. Spotted Tail and a few other chiefs of Brulé and Oglala bands that were then living south of the Platte did sign the treaty. Spotted Tail, like Black Kettle and Kicking Bird, was convinced that war would bring disaster, and he was trying to save what he could. The treaty with these few signatures was solemnly ratified by the Senate.

These southern bands returned to their hunting grounds on the rivers that formed the Kansas, only to become involved, as we saw in the preceding chapter, in the Cheyenne war. Carrington went into the Powder River country and built three military posts on the Bozeman Trail: Fort Reno, near Connor's old post; Fort Phil Kearny, on another branch of the Powder; and Fort C. F. Smith, on the Bighorn. But they protected no traffic, for the garrisons were in a state of siege. Carrington reported that in the first five weeks 33 travelers had been killed on the new road—with the Indians capturing such prizes as the bell mare and 174 mules from one train—and that 70 head of government mules had been run off from Fort Phil Kearny alone. The most successful raid occurred on December 21 of that year against this garrison.

The Indians used their familiar stratagem: select certain warriors to attack and then retreat to decoy the soldiers into an ambush. The maneuver was usually disrupted by some glory-seeking young brave dashing out of hiding too soon, but this time it worked without a hitch. A wagon train was sent out from the post to bring in wood. The Indians attacked, and the woodcutters corralled their wagons and stood them off. Carrington sent a force to their relief under the command of Captain William J. Fetterman, a brash young officer given to boasting that with eighty men he could ride through the whole Sioux Nation. Ironically, he had exactly that number in his detachment. Carrington gave him explicit orders not to pursue the attackers. He deliberately disobeyed; after relieving the wood haulers, he galloped joyfully after the retreating Indians. They sprung their trap and annihilated the whole command.

Said Sherman, "We must act with vindictive earnestness against the Sioux, even to their extermination, men, women, and children." But, as we have seen in the preceding chapter, Congress created a peace commission instead. The commission made two futile attempts to hold a council with the Indians in the fall (1867); then the next spring it induced them to come in to Fort Laramie and sign a treaty. They were given a reservation comprising the western half of South Dakota and extending slightly into North Dakota; and the Powder River country—the whole huge area between the North Platte and the Yellowstone and extending west to the Bighorn Mountains—was defined as "unceded Indian territory" from which white persons would be excluded. The government agreed to close the Bozeman Trail and abandon the forts. Red Cloud, the great war leader of the hostile Sioux, withheld his signature until he saw the posts actually evacuated by the garrisons and burned by the rejoicing warriors. Although Indians had often won battles or even campaigns against white soldiers, this is probably the only time they ever won a war against the United States and dictated the peace terms. One provision was slipped in permitting the construction of rail and wagon roads and "other works of utility and necessity" within the territory, but the Indians failed to notice it.

Agencies were established within the reservation: three on the Missouri on its eastern edge, Standing Rock in the north, Cheyenne River and Crow Creek farther down; and the Spotted Tail and Red Cloud agencies in the southwestern corner—actually found to be in Nebraska when the state boundary was surveyed. Some of the Indians settled around the agencies. Most of them remained in the "unceded" land until they began to see an advantage in visiting the agencies sporadically for presents, or perhaps in making their winter camps there. Some irreconcilables under the Sioux leaders, Sitting Bull and Gall, never deigned to approach them.

Meanwhile, the Territory of Montana had been established in 1864, and that of Wyoming in 1868. The usual outcry was made against leaving a large tract of Indian land within the territorial borders, and armed bands of prospectors and would-be settlers began to invade it. Also, the Northern Pacific Railroad was advancing from the east. By 1873 it had reached Bismarck, North Dakota, and surveyors were at work ahead of the line, following the Indian side of the Yellowstone in Montana. Soldiers were sent along to protect the surveying crews, and military posts were established to encircle the entire area. Among the latter were Fort Abraham Lincoln, across the Missouri from Bismarck, and Camp Robinson and Camp Sheridan near the Red Cloud and Spotted Tail agencies, respectively. A few years earlier Fort Rice had been built on the Missouri above the Standing Rock Agency, as had Fort Ellis near the Montana gold fields.

In the "unceded" land there were minor clashes between the Indians and white invaders, whether survey parties or intruding civilians, and even within the reservation the Indians were in virtual control of the agencies; but peace of a sort continued for eight years following the treaty of 1868. Meanwhile, there came an action that started the great war.

In the spring of 1874 an expedition was sent out under Custer to explore the Black Hills. This area was within the reservation, a place beloved of the Sioux, not only for its abundant game and as a convenient source of lodge poles, but sacred in their religion and tradition.

235

For years, rumors had been floating through the white settlements that it was rich in gold, and there is no doubt that the true purpose of the expedition was to explore its economic resources. Custer and his men were accompanied by scientists, newspaper reporters, and a party of gold seekers—1,200 men with 110 wagons. Even before the company returned, a courier was sent out with the report of "gold at the roots of the grass," and when the newspaper men got their stories in, the rush began in earnest. At first the troops removed some of the trespassers and turned them over to the courts, where they were promptly released to turn around and go back. Others were not even arrested. The Sioux were furious; they called Custer "the Chief of all the thieves," and his trail "the Thieves' Trail."

In 1875 the government sent commissioners to negotiate with the Sioux, ready to lease the mining rights for $400,000 a year or to buy the Hills for $6,000,000. When they attempted to hold a council near the Red Cloud Agency, they were surrounded by 7,000 mounted, circling warriors, and only the authority of the chiefs enabled them to escape to Camp Robinson. Then the Sioux held their own council and rejected the offer. The commissioners had hoped to buy the "unceded" land also, but that was clearly impossible.

As soon as the negotiation failed, the white invaders went in openly and laid out towns, organized local governments, and demanded that troops protect them from the Indians. Although the Indians had the law on their side, it seemed easier to displace them than the intruders. In November, President Grant held a council with the secretary of war, the secretary and assistant secretary of the interior, and the commissioner of Indian affairs in which it was decided to notify all the Indians in the "unceded" land to come in to the agencies by January 31 or be driven in as "hostiles." This would be a good way to obtain the Powder River country as well as the Black Hills, for even if the Indians had wished—as they probably did not wish—it would be impossible for them to comply with the ultimatum.

The order reached the agencies late in December, when the winter of that savage climate had already closed down. Runners were sent out to the various camps. Some received the message after the deadline; others never received it at all. In any case, they could not take down their tipis, load their possessions on horses, and bring their women and children through blizzards and snow drifts to set up their camps on the wind-swept plains near the agencies. Even the soldiers assigned to "punish" them for their noncompliance were unable to move from their posts until spring. But the government now had its cause for war. Converging columns were to march west from Fort Lincoln, east from Fort Ellis, and north from the North Platte to invade the "unceded" land.

Brigadier General Crook, brought up from fighting the Apaches in Arizona, was the first in the field. On March 1 he started from the North Platte on a scouting expedition up the Bozeman Trail. Even at that date, a month nearer spring than the deadline set for the Indians, he ran into a blizzard so severe that the thermometer froze (mercury freezes at –38° F.), and several of his men were disabled by frostbites. The column destroyed a Sioux-Cheyenne camp on the Powder River and ingloriously returned.

In May the army began to prepare for its three-pronged campaign. By this time many of the Indians that had wintered at the agencies had joined their nonreservation comrades in their good buffalo country. Blithely unworried, they held their annual sun dance in a great camp on the Rosebud. There, Sitting Bull vowed a "red blanket" to the supernatural powers. A friend cut fifty pieces of skin from each of his arms; then he danced with his eyes fixed on the sun until he fell unconscious. In this state he had a vision of soldiers falling into his camp. Soon afterward, the camp moved off to the Little Bighorn branch of the Bighorn.

Meanwhile, Crook, with about 1,300 men, including Shoshoni and Crow auxiliaries always eager to fight the Sioux, was advancing again up the Bozeman Trail. A war party of about 1,000 to 1,500 Sioux and Cheyennes intercepted him on the Rosebud on June 17, and a fierce battle was fought. It ended in a draw, but Crook retreated to a base camp, where he was immobilized the rest of the summer. Crook was the greatest Indian fighter the United States ever had, but he had been stopped.

At the same time, Colonel John Gibbon, with 450 men, mainly infantry, was coming down the Yellowstone from Fort Ellis, and Major General Alfred Terry, with the glory-seeking Custer and his favorite Seventh Cavalry, was marching from Fort Lincoln. A supply base had been established on the Yellowstone at the mouth of the Bighorn by a steamboat coming up from the Missouri, and there the two columns met as planned. Terry was in over-all command. He sent out a scouting party and decided that the Indians were probably on the Little Bighorn. He accordingly moved with Gibbon up the Bighorn toward their camp and sent Custer to circle the stream and strike them from above. The army's whole strategy was designed to keep the Indians from escaping. Nobody realized the seriousness of the war. Custer had even boasted that with his one regiment he could defeat the whole Sioux Nation. He had about 31 officers and 585 enlisted men, besides Arikara and a few Crow scouts.

Custer drove his men relentlessly, clearly hoping to defeat the Indians before Terry could encounter them. On June 25 he came in sight of an immense camp, located as expected on the Little Bighorn. The number of Sioux, Cheyenne, and Arapaho warriors has been variously estimated, but with their women and children they probably formed the largest concentration of Indians ever assembled at one place within the area of the United States. They were camped in five or more great tribal circles with every tipi in its appointed place.

All their great war leaders were there—Gall, Sitting Bull, and many others whose names have gone into the histories. They had spent the night before in their usual social dancing. As a leading Cheyenne expressed it later, "It seemed that peace and happiness were prevailing all over the world." They were rich in everything that constituted Plains wealth—lodges, stored food, clothing, and horses. (The first discovery of the camp by Custer's scouts was the sight of a vast pony herd covering the distant prairie like a blanket.)

Custer, still determined to keep the Indians from running away, divided his regiment. Thinking that they might leave the village for the sanctuary of the Bighorn Mountains, he sent Captain Fred Benteen with about 125 troopers to cross the head of the stream and scout through the hills on the west while the rest of the command went down the river toward the encampment. He left 130 men to guard the pack train with the ammunition and ordered Major Marcus A. Reno, with 112 troopers and 29 scouts, to strike near the head of the camp while he, with 225 men, rode parallel to the stream to strike below.

Reno's force was badly mauled. He retreated to a hill, and Benteen, having found no Indians, arrived in time to save him from annihilation. Later the pack train came up, and the combined force fought off the Indian attacks. The main excitement for the Indians was farther down the stream, where, as all the world knows, they wiped out Custer and his men. Only Indians were left to tell the story. "I tell no lies about dead men," said Sitting Bull in later years. "Those men who came with 'Long Hair'[1] were as good men as ever fought." Said a

---

[1] As it happened, Custer had his long golden locks clipped short at the time of the battle.

Cheyenne warrior, "I have been in many hard fights, but I never saw such brave men."

The Indians could have destroyed the men on the hill, and done the same to Terry moving up the stream to their camp, and to Crook, licking his wounds after the battle eight days before on the Rosebud. But now it was time for other activities. That night they held funeral rites for their warrior dead, which the beleaguered soldiers mistook for a victory celebration. The next morning they renewed their attacks on the hill while the women packed. Then in the afternoon they evacuated their camp with clocklike precision, each band moving as a unit, with tipis packed, goods loaded, women and children riding, mounted warriors guarding the line, great pony herds driven along, and set out for the Bighorn Mountains. They left rich tipis enshrining the bodies of their slain warriors lying on burial scaffolds, dressed in their finest clothes, and around them was a circle of dead horses ready to serve their riders in the spirit land.

Terry reached the deserted encampment and the ghastly piles of Custer's dead on June 27. He relieved the remnant of the regiment still dug in on the hill; there the casualties were forty or fifty killed, fifty wounded. His men buried the dead, improvised litters for the wounded, and struggled back down the valley to the steamboat. Bearing the wounded, and with its derrick and jack staff draped in black and its flag at half mast, it reached Bismarck and Fort Lincoln on July 5. Then the news went out to the world over the telegraph wires. At about the same time a courier, traveling west while the steamer was heading east, sent the same message from Helena, Montana. The Indians at Fort Lincoln did not need to be told. Long before then they knew, but they did not confide the reason for their excitement. And in the distant Indian Territory the Pawnees told their agent that Custer was dead ten days before the white men knew. Apparently the Indian telegraph was smoke signals.

The date July 5, 1876, was a bad time for such news to reach white Americans. With a "world's fair" at Philadelphia and observances throughout the country, a proud and confident people was celebrating one hundred years of progress and expansion under its "manifest destiny," all culminating in an emotional climax on July 4. Then the nation was plunged into mourning.

In August, Crook and Terry set out with reinforcements to hunt the hostiles, and Colonel Nelson A. Miles invaded the country from the Yellowstone. They failed, except for two insignificant skirmishes, to find any to fight. As the Indians saw it, they had won their war and it was over. They held an exultant victory celebration in the Bighorn Mountains. Then they scattered in separate bands over their hunting grounds. There was much dancing and feasting in their camps. It was probably the happiest summer of their lives; they had no premonition that it would be their last happy summer.

Also in August, commissioners came to the Indians who had remained at the agencies with the demand that they surrender the Black Hills and their "unceded" Powder River country and remove to the Indian Territory. To the latter demand one of the chiefs replied, "My grandfathers and relations have lived here always. There is no blood on this paper; we are not at war with you; and therefore when you speak of a strange land, a land where we were not brought up, a land far away, my chiefs and soldiers are very much displeased." But Spotted Tail finally went with a delegation to inspect the country, although he warned that he would keep his eyes and ears and mouth shut on the journey. Late that fall they held a council with the Creek leaders near Okmulgee. The Creeks would have welcomed them as fellow Indians, and they probably sensed also that filling up the country with Indians was the best way to keep it from the whites.

The Sioux enjoyed the visit, but they refused to consider removal. They received unexpected support. Kansans and Texans cried out in angry terror against bringing these bloody-handed "murderers" of Custer to the Indian Territory. They may have had some apprehension, though the Creeks, who would have been much closer neighbors, were not afraid. The strongest motive—at least of the Kansans—was the intent to keep the land vacant for their own purposes. They persuaded Congress to forbid the removal. But the land cessions were forced upon the Sioux. In succeeding years one mine in the Black Hills—the Homestake at Lead, South Dakota—accounted for $715,000,000 in bullion. Recently the Sioux had their day in court and won a judgment in the Indian Claims Commission for the illegal seizure of the Black Hills in 1876.

The army followed up its disastrous summer by a winter invasion of the Powder River country similar to the campaign that had reduced the South Plains tribes two years before. Crook, Miles, and Mackenzie converged on the area, fought a number of battles with the Indians, destroyed their winter camps, and harassed them until their position was untenable. Sitting Bull and Gall, with about four hundred lodges,

240

crossed into Canada. The other Sioux surrendered and settled around the agencies on their reservation.

The Arapahos surrendered at Camp Robinson, where they lived for a year as unhappy prisoners of war, reduced from a proud, rich tribe of 2,000 to a miserable 938, of whom only 198 were warriors. Then, although the Shoshonis had long been hostile to the three Powder River tribes, Washakie took pity on their homeless condition and gave them a temporary refuge.

Washington conveniently accepted the settlement as permanent, even dividing the Shoshonis' money with the visitors. Washakie protested in 1891: "At the time the Arapahos came to this Res. we did not tell them they could come here and stay nor did we give them any land. They and the Sioux had been fighting the soldiers and got whipped; they came up here and we have allowed them to live here since, thinking they would not hurt the land by living on it, we do not think that this would give them any right to the land."

Finally, in 1927, Congress gave the Shoshonis permission to bring their case to the Court of Claims, and they were eventually paid $6,364,677.91, the appraised value of half of their land. The two tribes still live there on the Wind River Reservation in Wyoming. They are no longer enemies, but they still hold themselves apart.

The surrendered Cheyennes were taken to the Indian Territory to settle with their Southern relatives. Soon they began to die. One of them explained it this way: "I have been sick a great deal of the time since I have been down here—homesick and heartsick and sick in every way. I have been thinking of my native country and the good home I had up there where I was never hungry, but when I wanted anything to eat could go out and hunt buffalo. It makes me feel sick when I think about that, and I cannot help thinking about that."

They constantly begged to return home. Finally, in September, 1878, they warned their agent that they were leaving and started back under their chief, Dull Knife (his Sioux name; the Cheyennes called him Morning Star), with their war leader, Little Wolf, directing the journey. They numbered 353, with only 60 or 70 fighting men, and they traveled more than 400 miles through an open country, with soldiers attacking them from all sides. They beat off one attack after another, stole horses when necessary, and killed cattle for food. As Little Wolf told it: "We tried to avoid the settlements as much as possible. . . . We did not want to be seen or known of. I often harangued my young men, telling them not to kill citizens, but to let them alone. . . . I know they

241

killed some citizens, but I think not many. They did not tell me much of what they did, because they knew I would not like it." They did kill a few lone men and some isolated western Kansas settlers, but they left no such trail of rapine as frontier headlines reported.

After they crossed the North Platte, they thought they were in their own country, safe from pursuit. They divided into two bands, Little Wolf going on north, Dull Knife turning northwest towards Camp Robinson.

Dull Knife thought he would be permitted to settle at the Red Cloud Agency, not knowing that it had been moved that year to Pine Ridge, sixty miles northeast. He told his followers, "Now we have again reached our own ground, and from this time forth we will no more fight or harm white people." Meeting soldiers from Camp Robinson, they gave up their horses and arms and were brought in to the post. By then it was October 25, and the snow was deep on the ground. They were comfortably housed in a large barracks and supplied with fuel and food while Washington decided what to do with them. Then in midwinter, with the thermometer ranging from zero to forty degrees below, they were told that they would be returned to the Indian Territory. Said Dull Knife, "No, I am here on my own ground, and I will never go back. You may kill me here; but you cannot make me go back." When the commandant saw that they could not be persuaded, he posted guards around the building and cut off their rations, their fuel, and finally their water. He tried to induce the women and children to come outside and receive care, but the band refused to be separated. They suffered terribly from hunger and cold, most of all from thirst. Still Dull Knife told the commandant, "The only way to get us there is to come in here with clubs and knock us on the head and drag us out and take us down there dead."

They finally concluded, "It is true that we must die, but we will not die shut up here like dogs; we will die on the prairies; we will die fighting." On the afternoon of January 9 they put on their best clothes and painted their faces, then kissed each other for the last time. They produced five guns they had managed to secrete when they were disarmed; also, it seems, eleven pistols and some ammunition. After sunset a young man, armed, placed himself at each window; then they knocked out the sashes and shot at the guards as the people poured through, 149 in all. The ground was covered with snow, and the moon was full. The soldiers rushed out of their barracks and began to fire at the fleeing figures. The fugitives first ran to the nearby White River

George Bent and his wife Magpie.
The writings of this articulate half-blood give the inside story of the Sand Creek massacre and the events that followed.

COURTESY GEORGE E. HYDE

Cherokee capitol built in 1869 to replace the one destroyed in the
Civil War.

*The immediate problem of the Five Civilized Tribes was physical
restoration.*

Potawatomi girls of the Indian Territory in the 1880's. Photograph by
W. S. Prettyman.

To the tribes on Kansas reservations it was a refuge from exploitation.

Satanta.
"This building of houses for us is all nonsense."
COURTESY BUREAU OF AMERICAN ETHNOLOGY

Satank.

"We have warred against the white man, but never because it gave us pleasure."

COURTESY BUREAU OF AMERICAN ETHNOLOGY

Chief Joseph, photographed by F. J. Haynes, Bismarck, Dakota Territory, November, 1877.

"From where the sun now stands I will fight no more forever."

COURTESY SMITHSONIAN INSTITUTION, OFFICE OF ANTHROPOLOGY

248

Sitting Bull.
He had a vision of soldiers falling into his camp.
COURTESY BUREAU OF AMERICAN ETHNOLOGY

Little Wolf (standing) and Dull Knife. Photograph believed to be by
William H. Jackson prior to 1877.

*They traveled more than four hundred miles through an open country,
with soldiers attacking them from all sides.*

Geronimo.
"You have never caught me shooting."
COURTESY NATIONAL ARCHIVES

Young Apache prisoners of war at Fort Sill. On the left, Ramona, daughter of Chihuahua and wife of Asa Daklugie, son of Juh; right, Eva, sixteen-year-old daughter of Geronimo.

Still they died, and still they begged to go home.

From *Geronimo's Story of His Life*, by S. M. Barrett

Comanche girls, settled in southwestern Oklahoma after the South
Plains wars. Right, Mary Parker, daughter of Quanah Parker.
They were expected to conform to an alien pattern.

Chitto Harjo, Creek fullblood.
He gave his own interpretation of Indian history.
COURTESY R. S. CATE COLLECTION, MUSKOGEE, OKLAHOMA

Old Jason Betzinez, once one of Geronimo's band, greeting members of the Oklahoma Historical Society, May 3, 1958.

Young Indians in boarding schools were brainwashed of all traces of Indianness. A few "entered the mainstream of American life."

Photograph by Edith Greenwood

AUTHOR'S COLLECTION

Pleasant Porter.
"This is an important question—one of life or death."
FROM DEPARTMENT OF THE INTERIOR *Annual Report*

256

Niganithat, or He Who Flies First, member of a Kickapoo delegation
to Washington, April, 1895.
"They were removed as cumberers of the ground."
COURTESY BUREAU OF AMERICAN ETHNOLOGY

Okmulgee Council delegates posed in front of the Creeks' log capitol. The Council succeeded too well in welding an Indian nationality and defending Indian rights.

COURTESY OKLAHOMA HISTORICAL SOCIETY

and threw themselves down to drink, while five young warriors with the guns stayed behind to cover the flight and fought till all were shot down. The others straggled up the valley and into the hills, too weak from hunger to run fast and falling in great numbers before the soldiers' guns.

Wagons went out from the post to pick up the wounded; they brought in 65 that night. In the morning more wagons brought in the frozen corpses. All that day and in the days following, the soldiers hunted the Indians out of the hills. Some had found strong positions and defended themselves with their pistols, but most of them were killed. Dull Knife, his wife, son, daughter-in-law, and grandchild hid in a hole in the rocks and were not found. Then they set out for Pine Ridge, eating their moccasins and such roots as they could find, reaching the place after eighteen days' wandering.

The day after the outbreak, the commandant went into the prison and asked the captives, "Now, will you go south?" A girl badly wounded in the foot managed to stand by supporting herself against the wall. She answered, "No, we will not go back; we will die rather. You have killed most of us, why do you not go ahead and finish the work?"

Of the 149 Cheyennes, 64 were killed, 78 were captured, most of them wounded, and 7 were never found, probably dying in the hills. But even in their last desperate flight, they were still the "fighting Cheyennes"; with all the odds against them, they killed 11 soldiers and wounded 9.

Little Wolf's band was equally steadfast, but more fortunate. They spent the winter in the sand hills of western Nebraska, undiscovered by white men, and found plenty of deer and antelope. In March they started for the Powder River country and were found by an army officer whom they knew and trusted. He took them to Miles at Fort Keogh, a new post at the mouth of the Tongue River, on the Yellowstone. Miles invited the men to enlist in the army as scouts, and they accepted. They gave good service in hunting out small bands of hostiles that still ranged the country.

So much public sympathy had been aroused by the heroism and sufferings of the Northern Cheyennes that a reservation was set apart for them on the Tongue and Rosebud rivers. Even the hunting was good for a few more years. Dull Knife died there in 1883; Little Wolf lived on for nearly thirty years longer. Their names are revered by present-day Northern Cheyennes, a sturdy people still preserving their tribal unity. They exchange visits with their Southern relatives, but they pronounce even the name of Oklahoma with marked distaste.

Conquered tribes from the Pacific Northwest were also unhappy in the Indian Territory. First came the Modocs from their war in the lava beds of northern California.

Continued conflicts in this area after the Rogue River War led to a treaty in 1864 by which the related Klamaths and Modocs and some fragmented tribes surrendered much of their land and received a reservation in southern Oregon. This, the commissioner who nego-tiated it hoped, would be a refuge, "strictly an *Indian* settlement," guarded against "the contamination of white association." But the Modocs were not happy with the Klamaths, and in 1870 a band under a leader known to whites as Captain Jack went back to their old home. The army tried to force their return to the reservation, and they retreated to the lava beds south of Tule Lake, a jumble of fissures, caves, pits, and ridges from which it was impossible to dig them out. Finally, in April, 1873, Captain Jack and other leaders were induced to meet a peace commission of four members headed by Brigadier General E. R. S. Canby.

Many times, at other places and in other wars, Indians had been invited by the military to talk peace, only to be seized and imprisoned or even hanged; and in several instances, unarmed white envoys went safely into hostile camps. This time it was the Indians who plotted treachery. They murdered Canby and another commissioner; the others barely escaped.

Sherman responded with his favorite word, *extermination.* An army of 1,000 regulars, 78 Indian scouts, and a company of Oregon Volunteers surrounded the place, trying to dislodge about 165 Indians of whom about 50 were fighting men, who picked the soldiers off at will from hidden positions. But the Modocs finally became tired of the war and surrendered on June 1, 1874. The army held a court-martial and hanged Captain Jack and three others for the murder of the com-missioners. The Modocs were then brought to the Indian Territory. The Okmulgee Council sent them a message of "sympathy and brother-ly feelings" and arranged a ceremonial reception for their delegates. They settled down, a peaceable, industrious band, always longing for their old homeland. Finally, in 1909, they were allowed to return to the Klamath Reservation. A few chose to remain, and about 40 of their descendants still live in Oklahoma.

Other northwestern Indians sent to the Indian Territory were the

Nez Percés. The encroaching white men soon violated the treaty of 1855. They found gold near Lapwai, and the mining town of Lewiston sprang up there. Settlers spread out over the country, tearing down the Indians' fences, stealing their livestock, and murdering Indians with impunity. In 1863 the chiefs were called in council and a fraudulent treaty never accepted by the Indians was drawn up and ratified by the Senate. It restricted the reservation to a small area east of Lewiston around Lapwai.

In the territory claimed to be ceded was the Wallowa country west of the Snake Canyon, a huge tract with salmon-filled rivers, camass meadows, and plentiful game. Its nutritious grass made it a stockman's paradise, and the Nez Percés were capable stockmen, rich in horses and cattle and in money from the sale of livestock. The chief of the Wallowa band was Joseph, Christian convert, leader of progress, and friend of the white men in peace and war for thirty years. Now he tore up his treasured New Testament, done with the white man and all his ways.

Before his death in 1871 he said to the elder of his two sons, also known as Joseph: "My son, my body is returning to my mother earth and my spirit is going very soon to see the Great Spirit Chief. When I am gone, think of your country. . . . Always remember that your father never sold his country. . . . A few more years and the white man will be all around you. They have their eyes on this land. My son, never forget my dying words. This country holds your father's body. Never sell the bones of your father and mother."

As Young Joseph told it in later years, "I buried him in that beautiful valley of the winding rivers. I love that land more than all the rest of the world." He was at that time about thirty-one years old. Able and intelligent, attractive in personality, and incorruptible in character, he was destined to appear in history as one of the great Indians of all time. He had barely succeeded his father as chief when the Wallowa country was opened to homesteaders. The Nez Percés remained there, and friction developed.

At this time some of them were coming under the influence of a nativist "prophet" named Smohalla, from a small Shahaptian tribe living on the Columbia.[2] He inveighed against the economic precepts being instilled by the agent at Lapwai. "You ask me to plough the ground," he protested. "Shall I take a knife and tear my mother's bosom? You ask me to dig for stone. Shall I dig under her skin for her

[2] For Smohalla's beginnings, see Ruby and Brown, *Half-Sun.*

261

bones? You ask me to cut the grass and make hay and sell it and be rich like white men. But dare I cut off my mother's hair?" Among his ardent followers was Toohoolhoolzote, chief of a band living in the rugged land east of the Snake.

The Nez Percés, as usual, tried to keep the peace, and Joseph and his brother, Ollicut, presented their case so logically that they convinced the Indian agent at Lapwai and Major General Oliver Otis Howard, commander of the Department of the Columbia, that the so-called cession was invalid. But the administration at Washington decided to enforce it, and the agent and the general easily adjusted their consciences and ordered all the Nez Percé bands to remove to Lapwai. By the fall of 1876 the tense situation was aggravated by the Sioux war. Although usually a man of humanitarian feelings, Howard had become obsessed by the fear that Joseph would unite all the tribes of the Northwest for another Little Bighorn.

Joseph knew that the Lapwai tract was too small for his people's livestock, but he persuaded them to submit; he never regarded this yielding to coercion as a violation of his father's dying behest. Then in May, 1877, Howard overruled his plea that this was not the season to move animals and ordered the Indians to come in within thirty days or be driven in by force. Joseph sent his men to comb the hills. They rounded up all the horses and cattle they found, and with what personal possessions they could bring from their lodges, they assembled at Hell's Canyon on the turbulent Snake, swollen from the spring rains. They made rafts to ferry their people, and strong young men on the best horses swam along and towed them across with ropes. The rafts were often swept far down the stream, but thanks to the Indians' expert horsemanship, no human lives were lost. Next they drove their herds into the current. The strongest animals made it, but hundreds of brood mares and fresh cows with their young colts and calves were lost. Then the band crossed the flooded Salmon River Canyon and camped a few miles from the reservation, where they were joined by other nonreservation bands. Here they rested and relaxed, putting off the evil hour as long as they could. They still had about ten days before the deadline.

One day two youths, spurred on by an angry taunt from camp, rode off and killed several men who had committed outrages against their people. Their actions started a war party of about twenty, who found some whisky and killed fourteen or fifteen men, mistreated women and children, and plundered houses—the sum total of all

Nez Percé atrocities of the war. Joseph and Ollicut were away from camp butchering some of their cattle for meat; none of the Wallowa band had taken part in the raid, but the whole encampment scattered, fearing punishment. Howard chose to think that his big war had begun and started after them. One of his commands, for no reason in particular, struck an unsuspecting village on the reservation, a band under the well-known leader, Looking Glass, which owned cultivated and fenced fields and herds of horses and cattle, even milch cows. Understandably, his people joined the nonreservation bands. In the ensuing fights and pursuits through their rugged homeland, the "hostiles," still making futile overtures for peace, outgeneraled and defeated Howard's forces. Then they began their epic 1,300-mile retreat through the mountains of Idaho, Wyoming, and Montana.

The story has been often told. Looking Glass was in command, Joseph had the responsibility of moving the camp, and Ollicut fought with the warriors. They beat off their attackers, buried their dead, made litters for their wounded, and traveled on. They did not even scalp the enemy dead, though Howard permitted Bannock scouts with his army to disinter and mutilate the Nez Percé bodies. They attempted to pass through the country peaceably, *buying* supplies from the settlements in western Montana and paying for them with coins and currency. Then, after being struck by army units and Volunteers hurrying to intercept them, they killed as potential enemies the few white men they met.

They first sought refuge with the Crows, friends of many hunting trips to the buffalo country, but the Crows, at peace with the whites, refused them sanctuary. Then they started for Canada, but they made the usual Indian mistake of regarding wars as local. They had far outdistanced their enemy, Howard, so they slowed down to give their hunters time to kill buffalo and their weak and wounded a chance to recuperate. On September 29, a bare thirty miles from the border, Miles, coming up from Fort Keogh, attacked them unprepared. There were several days of fighting in a cold gale with driving snow. Then on October 4, Howard reached the battleground. He offered terms of surrender, the return of the Indians to Lapwai. The few surviving chiefs, surrounded and hopeless, held their last war council. Joseph urged surrender, and his argument carried. His words to the council became the message transmitted to the waiting officers. The interpreter, a reservation Nez Percé with Howard, wept as he delivered it.

"Tell General Howard I know his heart. . . . I am tired of fighting.

Our chiefs are killed. Looking Glass is dead. Toohoolhoolzote is dead. . . . He who led on the young men[3] is dead. It is cold and we have no blankets. The little children are freezing to death. My people, some of them, have run away to the hills. . . . I want to have time to look for my children and see how many I can find. Maybe I shall find them among the dead. Hear me, my chiefs. I am tired; my heart is sick and sad. From where the sun now stands I will fight no more forever."

Two hours later Joseph rode up and delivered his rifle to Howard. Then the others straggled in—87 men, 184 women, and 147 children. About half of the men and many of the women were wounded. They surrendered 1,100 horses, 100 saddles, and more than 100 guns. Over the indignant protests of Howard and Miles, Sherman and the War Department, still fearing a general uprising, ordered them taken first to Fort Leavenworth and then settled in the Indian Territory. On the way, at Bismarck, they received a sympathetic reception rare in Indian wars. In their new home they were given a start of 100 cattle, and their agent wrote in 1880, "The Nez Perces appear to be natural herders, and show more judgment in the management of their stock than any Indians I ever saw." Their herds increased, and they began to prosper, but they continued to pine for their mountains—and to die. Finally, so much public sympathy was aroused in their behalf that a special act of Congress provided for their return to the Northwest in 1885. About half of them were settled with their people at Lapwai; Joseph and the others were dumped with some unrelated Columbia River tribes on the Colville Reservation in Washington.

Joseph never gave up the hope of returning to the Wallowa country. In 1892 he began trying to persuade the government to permit him to remove to the Umatilla Reservation with his Cayuse friends just across the Blue Mountains from his lost homeland. In 1899 and again in 1900 he was allowed to visit the Wallowa, even to stand with tears in his eyes at his father's grave. He found the country occupied by white settlers, but he was willing to live there on any terms. He tried to buy a tract of land, but the settlers refused to let him return. He died on the Colville in 1904.[4]

The fear of a general Indian war in the Northwest did not end with the removal of the nonreservation Nez Percés. The next year it was the Bannocks that started it, the very same Bannocks who had

[3] Ollicut.
[4] Joseph's last years in the deadly monotony of reservation life are given in Ruby and Brown, *Half-Sun.*

enlisted with Howard. Following the wars of 1859–63 they had been assigned to a reservation around Fort Hall, with the privilege of hunting buffalo and harvesting the roots on Camas Prairie in western Idaho. But the buffalo were gone, Congress failed to provide the rations promised by the treaty, and the Bannocks were literally starving. When the time came to gather the camass, they found the settlers' hogs rooting up the bulbs and 2,500 cattle grazing there. They started killing the settlers and tried to arouse the Washington and Oregon Indians, but only the Paiutes and some Western Shoshonis joined them. The army should have known by this time that unrelated tribes never united in a general war. Howard defeated the hostiles before the year was over. Crook visited them and reported: "The encroachments upon the Camas prairies was the cause of the trouble. . . . This root is their main source of food supply. I do not wonder . . . that when these Indians see their wives and children starving, and their last source of supplies cut off, they go to war. And then we are sent out to kill them."

In 1879—the year after the Bannock War—a "Ute Uprising" proved very profitable to Colorado, admitted three years before to statehood. By this time settlers and prospectors were entering the "Western Slope" beyond the Continental Divide. About 3,500 Utes lived there in six loosely organized bands. Ouray, their most influential chief, conceded the necessity of cutting down their holdings and cultivating their reduced acreage after the white man's manner; but the Coloradans were determined to drive them completely out of the state. The governor had been elected on a "Utes Must Go" platform, and Senator Henry M. Teller became the leader of the land-grabbers. This made the Indians uneasy.

Two bands on the White River in the northwest had always been peaceable, but their aging chief, Douglas, and a young firebrand named Jack advocated fighting for their homeland. Their agent, Nathan Meeker, was an elderly eccentric. The Utes were fine horsemen and raised cattle; but to force them into intensive farming, Meeker plowed up their winter pasture and warned them that the government would take away their reservation if they would not cultivate it. That was exactly what they feared, and they became so hostile that he called for troops. Now they were convinced that they would be driven away. Jack fought off the soldiers, while Douglas and about twenty followers killed Meeker and his employees and captured the women and children at the agency. This gave the Coloradans their needed atrocity. Friendly

265

and hostile alike, the Utes were driven to barren lands in Utah, where they still live on the Uintah and Ouray Reservation. Only the Southern Utes were allowed to remain in a narrow strip along the southwestern edge of the state.

Nobody mentioned moving the Bannocks or the Utes to the Indian Territory. In the session of 1878–79, a Texas member of Congress introduced an amendment to the Indian Appropriation Bill providing "That no Indians living . . . outside the Indian Territory shall be moved into said Territory." Some members were no doubt sincerely influenced by humanitarian motives, citing the sufferings of the Poncas and Nez Percés, but Kansans, Missourians, and Arkansans expressed naked greed. The Indians, said a member from Kansas City, "stand as a Chinese wall around the most fertile and beautiful land in our whole country"; he would bring in no more Indians and open it to white settlement. But the act as finally passed narrowed the restriction to the Apaches and other Indians of New Mexico and Arizona. It became law February 17, 1879. Even so, the only Indians settled in the Indian Territory after that date were a few stray refugees. And the Apaches of the Southwest were still to be reckoned with.

CHAPTER FOURTEEN

THE APACHES MAKE
THEIR LAST STAND

The subjugation of the Apaches of the Southwest was the last of the Indian wars. All the errors and crimes of two and one-half centuries of the Anglo-American frontier and all the difficulties of a primitive people to adjust to a new order were intensified there. When Carleton and his California Volunteers headed home after the Civil War, the regular army took over. The random policy of those first years is illustrated by the report of an "Interesting scout among the White Mountain Apaches in the summer of 1869" by Lieutenant Colonel John Green.

As Green was planning to set out from his camp on the Gila, a Coyotero chief named Pin-dah-kiss, or Miguel, came to him asking for a reservation and protection. He carried a letter from Carleton and the commander at Fort Wingate, New Mexico, stating that he had always been at peace with the whites. Green sent a Captain Barry with fifty mounted men to accompany him to his village to investigate. "Believing that many of these Indians, if not all, had been guilty of marauding, I instructed Captain Barry, if possible, to exterminate the whole village, but gave no positive orders; he was to be governed by circumstances."

As soon as Barry left, Green moved up the White River and destroyed the corn he found there. "At least one hundred acres of fine corn, just in silk, were destroyed, and it took the command nearly three days to do it. I was astonished, and could hardly believe that the Apache Indians could and would cultivate the soil to such an extent; and when we consider their very rude implements, and the labor it requires to dig the *acequias* for irrigation, one cannot help but wonder at their success. Their fields compare very favorably with those of their more civilized brethren."

Barry, meanwhile, was approaching Miguel's village. White flags were flying from every wickiup and prominent point, and men, women, and children came out to meet the soldiers, cutting corn for their horses and showing such delight that the officers felt it would have been murder to kill them. They found no evidence that the band had been hostile. Barry told Miguel that he was in Arizona, outside Fort Wingate jurisdiction; he accordingly advised him to take his request for a reservation to Camp McDowell, a post halfway across the territory, established four years before by the California Volunteers, and gave him a letter to the commander there.

Green concluded, "The Apaches have few friends, and, I believe, no agent. Even the officers, when applied to by them for information, cannot tell them what to do. There seems no settled policy, but a general policy to kill them wherever found. I am also a believer in that, if we go in for extermination," but in his opinion, if Miguel's band had a reservation and a fort to protect them, others would join them, and they would form a nucleus of civilization and would also help the army against the hostiles.

So far as known, Miguel never managed to follow Barry's complicated directions. But some irregular attempts were made to settle the defeated and peaceably inclined Apaches around the military posts springing up through the two territories. The Camp Grant incident is typical of the diverse forces at work.

Camp Grant was at the confluence of the San Pedro River and Aravaipa Creek, home of the Aravaipas. These people were accused of raiding and greater than usual Apache atrocities. In 1863 a company of California Volunteers from the post attacked a rancheria at the head of their canyon and killed fifty-eight of its seventy people. Other such invasions drove them to desperation. In February, 1871, five hungry, ragged old women came down to the post from their mountain hide-outs bearing a flag of truce. The commander, Lieutenant Royal Emerson Whitman, received them kindly and promised them sanctuary. Soon five hundred under Eskiminzin and other chiefs collected there, saying that this place had always been their home before they were driven away by the soldiers and that they wanted to plant crops along the creek. Whitman employed them to cut and bring in hay and arranged with the neighboring ranchers to give them work at field-hand rates for the approaching barley harvest. It seemed to him that he had found the solution to the Apaches' problems.

He kept close tab on his Indians to see that they did not commit depredations, but there were some Apache raids south of the Gila, with six Anglos killed and some livestock driven off. The turbulent citizens of the little adobe village of Tucson decided to take revenge on Indians they could catch. They enlisted some Papagos (a familiar practice—five years before they had raised money by popular subscription to pay Papagos and other Indians one hundred dollars for each Apache scalp) and set out—7 Anglos, 48 Spanish Americans, and 92 Papagos. At dawn on April 30 they surprised the sleeping Aravaipas when most of the men were away and started killing them, the Papagos clubbing them to death, the white men shooting those who tried to escape. They murdered about 125 people—all but perhaps 8 being women and children—and captured 27 children, who were turned over to the Papagos to be sold as slaves in Sonora. Not one of the assailants was even wounded.

When Whitman learned what had happened, he went to the ravaged camp, where the ground was strewn with mutilated bodies. Not a living Indian was in sight; all the survivors, some sorely wounded, had fled to the mountains. He took a party with spades and shovels to bury the dead, and sent messengers to persuade the fugitives that the army was not guilty. They began to straggle in, with "expressions of grief, too wild and terrible," he said, "to be described." Eskiminzin carried a small daughter in his arms, the only member of his family to survive. He had been clubbed into insensibility, and when he revived he found her hiding under some loose hay.

The Indians trusted Whitman. Their faith in him probably saved many Arizonans from Apache vengeance. But he was reviled in the local press, and the vicious slanders circulated against him even found their way into reputable books.[1] At the same time, President Grant told the governor that if the participants in the massacre were not brought to trial, he would put the territory under martial law. A trial was accordingly held, and the jury after nineteen minutes' "deliberation" acquitted the one hundred-odd defendants. But it did put the record straight, for the testimony revealed the flimsy quality of the "evidence" that connected the Aravaipas with the depredations and justified the attack on their camp.

[1] For a scholarly evaluation of the sources, see Dan L. Thrapp, *The Conquest of Apacheria.*

Similar influences were at work with the Warm Springs–Mimbreños bands. In 1869, army officers and Indian Office employees held conferences with Loco and Victorio, successors to Mangas Coloradas, and found them anxious to settle in their old home, plant their crops, and remain at peace. Within the next two years about 1,200 collected there, where they received some irregular supplies of food and blankets. Then the miners and settlers organized for a repetition of the Camp Grant massacre, and the Indians learned of the plot and fled to the mountains.

In that same year (1871) the government for the first time formulated a definite Apache policy. Congress appropriated seventy thousand dollars "to collect the Apache Indians of Arizona and New Mexico upon reservations . . . and to promote peace and civilization among them"; and the well-known humanitarian Vincent Colyer, of the newly created Board of Indian Commissioners, was sent to hold conferences with them. At the same time, General[2] Crook, with his pre-Civil War experience in the Indian wars of the Northwest, was placed in command of the Department of Arizona. He had barely started on his campaign when he learned, to his disgust, of Colyer's mission. Said the too confident General, "if this entire Indian question be left to me . . . I have not the slightest doubt of my ability to conquer a lasting peace with this Apache race in a comparatively short space of time." But he waited impatiently while Colyer held councils with the various bands, settling them near the military posts in their home areas. Then, sure that they would resume their raiding, he again made extensive preparations to hunt them down, only to be even more disgusted the next year to learn that General Howard was being sent on another peace mission.

Military men and westerners were repelled by Howard's ostentatious piety; but Indians, less reticent than white men in expressing their religious feelings, liked and trusted him.[3] He continued Colyer's work by a more formal location of reservations. The related White Mountains and Coyoteros, the best farmers and most peaceable of Apaches, were guaranteed their homeland around Fort Apache, a new post on the White River. (Thus Miguel finally found the reservation he sought.) Between this and the Gila was another extensive reservation named San Carlos, and the pathetic Aravaipa survivors were removed

[2] Brevet rank; he was serving as lieutenant colonel. He was promoted to brigadier general October 29, 1873.

[3] His treatment of the Nez Percés four years later was not typical; the Sioux War had warped his judgment.

there from Camp Grant. A third reservation was laid out near Camp Verde, east of the wild new mining town of Prescott. Eventually, after some shuffling, the Tonto Apaches and the non-Apache Yavapais and Tulkepaias were settled there.

Howard also went unarmed into Cochise's stronghold and made peace with that redoubtable chief, confirming the Chiricahuas in their native mountains. Geronimo, an emerging war leader in a related band, was included in this settlement. Many years later he remembered it with gratitude. "This treaty lasted until long after General Howard had left our country. He always kept his word with us and treated us as brothers . . . and even to this day [the Indians] frequently talk of the happy times" following the peace he made with them.[4] Their Warm Springs relatives were not so fortunate; they continued to wander in the mountains until their homeland was finally set apart for them in 1874, with nearby Fort McRae to protect them.

Thus the pattern was nicely fixed: reservations under the protection of military posts, where the Indians would be fed and guided into habits of industry by civilian agents and where the military would assist the agents to keep order and operate in the field against those who stayed out and continued raiding. It could have succeeded if it had been consistently followed.

Crook worked energetically, outfitting expeditions to converge upon the hostiles' sanctuary in the unmapped mountains and canyons of the Tonto Basin. His columns traveled light, using mule pack trains so efficiently organized that his methods were still followed during World War II by the army in Southeast Asia and New Guinea. Convinced that even the most rugged of white soldiers could never find the hidden rancherias, he went to the reservations and enlisted Apaches as scouts. They had no compunction against fighting their own people. As old Jason Betzinez of Geronimo's band told it in later years, "They were as happy as bird dogs turned loose in a field full of quail."[5]

Crook sent out word by spies and captured Indians that all bands away from the reservations would be regarded as hostiles. He issued these instructions to his columns: accept the surrender of all who submit; hunt down the others until all are killed or captured; avoid

[4] S. M. Barrett, *Geronimo's Story of His Life* was dictated by Geronimo when he was a prisoner of war at Fort Sill. It contains some errors due to faulty interpretation or the imagination of the editor (references to scalping, for example, never an Apache practice), but it is true to the Apache spirit.

[5] In *I Fought with Geronimo*, a fascinating firsthand picture of Apache life. Betzinez lived until 1960.

killing women and children, and do not abuse prisoners; enlist prisoners as scouts, if possible, the wilder the better, because the wild ones will know the nature and retreats of those still out; and never abandon a trail, but follow the enemy on foot if the horses play out.

The campaign began November 15, 1872. The winter that followed appears in the army reports as a succession of hardships, individual exploits, fights, pursuits, and the destruction of rancherias. By early spring hostile bands began to come in to the posts to surrender. Crook said, "Had it not been for their barbarities, one would have been moved to pity by their appearance. They were emaciated, clothes torn in tatters, some of their legs not thicker than my arm."[6] In April the Yavapai Cha-lipun came in with over three hundred, saying that he had never been afraid of white Americans, but now he had to fight his own people as well. Crook assured him that if the band would settle down, he would be the best friend they ever had, and the Indians found that he could be trusted to keep his promise. Cha-lipun and his Yavapais settled on the Verde Reservation. Another band came in under the Tonto Apache, Delshay, who "said he had one hundred and twenty-five warriors last fall, . . . but now he had only twenty left. He said they used to have no difficulty in eluding the troops, but now the very rocks had gotten soft, they couldn't put their foot anywhere without leaving an impression by which we could follow . . . ." (So much for tracking by Apache scouts.)

Crook commended his troops for having "finally closed an Indian war that has been waged since the time of Cortez." His optimism was as badly misplaced as his history. A few hostiles remained in the Tonto Basin, and before the year 1873 was over, others had joined them there. Delshay became dissatisfied—nobody ever figured out why— and with about forty other malcontents he left the Verde Reservation and fled to his mountains. Some surrendered Tontos on the San Carlos Reservation, incited by an unprincipled agent, killed an army officer and also slipped back to their rugged retreat. Soon Arizona had a fresh epidemic of Apache atrocities. The number engaged in the depredations was not large, but it did not require many Apaches to make bloody marks on the map.

Early in 1874, Crook again sent his troops to comb the Tonto Basin and the surrounding mountains. When the hostiles from San Carlos tried to surrender, he demanded the heads of the three leaders of the outbreak, and he offered the Tontos a bounty for Delshay's head.

[6] Crook's own account of these wars is in *Autobiography*.

His loyal scouts joined in the work and gave him good measure—seven San Carlos heads and two of Delshay. Of the latter he said, "Being satisfied that both parties were earnest in their beliefs, and the bringing in of an extra head was not amiss, I paid both."

After this second campaign a few wild Apaches hid in the Basin and dashed out on sporadic raids to steal livestock or kill some un-protected white man. Army details searched them out, killing a few at a time. Most of this fighting was done by the Apache scouts. Al Sieber, beginning his famous career as chief of scouts, was in virtual command of this auxiliary force.[7]

Crook's seven Apache heads were neatly arranged in a row on the parade ground when John P. Clum came as Indian agent to San Carlos. He lacked three weeks of being twenty-three years old when he arrived that year (1874), but he was honorable, able, and efficient; and he had all of Crook's single-minded confidence that he could manage all the Apaches by himself if only the wicked rival service (in Crook's belief, the civilian "Indian ring"; in Clum's, the army) would keep out of it. He liked the Indians and treated them fairly, and they reciprocated.

Actually, in spite of their contempt for each other, good men in the two services followed an almost identical policy on the reserva-tions. They set up crude but effective courts with the leading chiefs as a council of judges, and they enrolled and trained the warriors—*scouts* in army parlance, *police* in agency terminology—to enforce order on the reservations and assist in campaigns against the hostiles. They called the Indians in for a regular count, not only to ensure against their straying, but to give them an alibi when falsely accused of raiding. They encouraged industry by buying supplies from them and hiring them for necessary labor around the agency or the post. They made a clear distinction between friendly and hostile Indians, and they found the loyalty of these wild people, once they had entered government service, a strange and moving thing.

But too many army officers thought of Indians only as vermin to be exterminated, and too many agents were political spoilsmen using the reservation supplies for large-scale grafting. At the same time, turbulent frontiersmen, who cried out against Apache depredations, blocked any constructive settlement; wars brought soldiers and fat army contracts—two million dollars annually to Arizona economy— and ration-consuming Indians were equally profitable.

Moreover, as soon as the Indians were settled, the Indian Office

[7] Dan L. Thrapp, *Al Sieber* is the definitive biography of this famous scout.

273

adopted the cruel and stupid policy of concentrating all of them at San Carlos. Economy in administration was the official explanation, but land hunger certainly had its influence, for the vacated reservations were restored to the public domain. (To gratify mining interests, large tracts were at the same time cut from the combined San Carlos–Fort Apache Reservation and towns sprang up there.) The result was disastrous; whenever a contingent of these scarcely tamed people was removed from its own locality, some always slipped away and became hostile. Thus there were eleven more years of Apache wars, with the most arduous military campaigns in American history, the death of hundreds of Arizona and New Mexico civilians and an unreckoned number of Mexicans, and destruction beyond reckoning to the Apaches.

The Verde Reservation with almost 1,500 Indians was the first to be abolished—early in 1875. Although they protested against leaving the area where they had always lived and which had been guaranteed to them "forever," they set out on the 180-mile journey. But the Tonto Apaches and their long-time Yavapai and Tulkepaia enemies were thrown into too close proximity on the route, and they got into a fight. For a time it looked as though they would cancel each other out and stop the troubles of that particular contingent, but Al Sieber jumped in and stopped them.[8] Only five or perhaps seven were killed and ten wounded. The caravan moved on over the almost impassable mountains and rivers to San Carlos. They were welcomed by Clum, who hardly noticed that almost one hundred had slipped away to their old haunts.

Soon afterward, Crook was transferred to his unsuccessful campaign against the Sioux and Cheyennes on the North Plains. In Arizona, Clum entered into such a feud with the army officer at Fort Apache that he was instructed to transfer the Indians of that reservation to San Carlos. Next came the Chiricahuas and their relatives.

Cochise had loyally kept his agreement with Howard, and when he died in 1874 he admonished his sons to observe it. But probably the peace did not stop the raiding in Mexico. Juh,[9] the leader of a wild band in the Sierra Madre, had relatives on the American side of the boundary and sometimes visited there. Geronimo had married a girl of his band, and the couple had become the parents of three children;

[8] A lively account of this fight is in Thrapp, *Al Sieber*.
[9] It is impossible to render this explosive syllable in English characters. Among the variants are *Whoa* and *Hoo*.

then the Mexicans had murdered his whole family during a supposed trading truce. Geronimo married other wives—he usually had two at a time during his later years—but he never forgot how he felt when he returned to his empty dwelling and saw the playthings of his children and the robes and skins his young wife had decorated, and he never relaxed his hatred of Mexicans.

In 1876, two white men sold some whisky to three or four Chiricahuas. The Indians became drunk and killed the whisky dealers and another white man. The Indian Office then ordered Clum to remove the whole tribe to San Carlos. He went into the mountains with fifty-four of his Coyotero and Aravaipa police to collect them. Cochise's sons agreed to remove, but Geronimo and Juh hastily broke camp and fled. Clum returned with 325 good Chiricahuas, only about one third of their number. The wilder two thirds were with Juh in Mexico or hiding out in their mountains on the American side. Within two months, twenty murders of white men and the theft of at least one hundred horses were charged to their account in raids north of the border.

The next spring it was learned that Geronimo and his band had joined their relatives on the Warm Springs Reservation. Clum was sent to arrest them and bring them to San Carlos to be tried in the civil courts for murder and robbery. He hid his trusty Apache police in the agency buildings and called Geronimo in for a conference. Then the police swarmed out and surrounded Geronimo and six of his followers. This was the only time the elusive raider was actually "captured," and even then by a ruse. He spoke truth when he taunted the military in after years, "You have never caught me shooting."

On orders from Washington, Clum then removed all the Warm Springs Indians. Victorio did not resist, though aged members of his band insisted as late as 1960, "That was *our* country. The government didn't give it to us. It had always been our home. And we had been peaceable. We were not to blame for what Geronimo did." Clum returned to San Carlos with 343 of Victorio's people and 110 of Geronimo's. He reminded Washington that he had consolidated five agencies, increasing his charges from eight hundred to five thousand Indians; now if the Department would increase his salary and equip two more companies of Indian police, "I will volunteer to take care of all the Apaches in Arizona—and the troops can be removed."

Washington ignored his overconfident offer, and he resigned in a huff. Geronimo and the other shackled leaders were released. (Their guilt, even if true, could not have been proved; Apaches did not leave living witnesses.) Weak or corrupt agents were placed in charge at San Carlos. Mutually hostile tribes were crowded together on the arid flats along the Gila, where even Apaches could not make a living, and there was the influence of their untamed brethren happily raiding from their mountain hideouts. Victorio with 310 followers left in September. In Arizona, New Mexico, and even in west Texas, the hidden terror struck from the mountains, killing settlers, herders, prospectors, and trail drivers and making off with plunder, while the army wore itself out in futile pursuit. On October 14, 1880, Victorio was killed in a battle with Mexican troops in Chihuahua, but the aged and rheumatic Warm Springs warrior Nana, with fifteen survivors, made a lightning raid into New Mexico, where he was joined by about twenty Mescalero recruits. In six weeks they killed thirty to fifty people, captured hundreds of horses, and eluded one thousand soldiers and hundreds of civilians before they returned to their Mexican refuge.[10]

Geronimo also left the reservation and joined Juh in Mexico. Later they came in with their followers and apparently refrained from raiding. But in the deadly tedium of reservation life during this time of mismanagement, the Indians turned, as Indians do, to the teachings of a prophet. Late in August, 1881, the commandant at Fort Apache attempted to arrest him. His followers attacked the troops and even the scouts defected and joined them. The prophet and about eighteen other Indians and seven soldiers were killed. Troops in great numbers were then rushed to the reservation, and Juh, Geronimo, and Cochise's son, Naiche, convinced that they were all to be annihilated, fled with seventy-four of their people to Mexico.[11] Most of the Warm Springs band remained on the reservation under the peaceably inclined Loco. Then in April, Geronimo came up from Mexico and forced them at gun point to leave with him.[12] With that, all were committed to the old life of raiding. From their mountain sanctuary they made lightning forays across the border, and nobody knew where they would strike.

Crook was reassigned to his old command in September. He cleaned up affairs at the agency and allowed the Indians to move to locations of their own choice on the two reservations. Then in April,

[10] Thrapp, *Apacheria* gives the details of the fighting.

[11] For the Indians' justification, also accepted by Crook, see *ibid.*, 225–28.

[12] Young Jason Betzinez and his family were among those taken away. His book describes the incident and the months of outlawry that followed.

1883, with 193 Apache scouts, 45 cavalrymen, and 2 pack trains, he started out against the hostiles. With the permission of the Mexican government he penetrated to their camp in the Sierra Madre. Dismayed at the invasion of their stronghold, they agreed to return to the reservation. Nana, Loco, and a leader named Bonito, with all the people they could conveniently collect—49 warriors and 273 women and children—came back with him. Other bands came in later, and young Lieutenant Britton Davis met them at the border to protect them on their way to the reservation from angry Arizonans. They were by no means a beaten people; Davis marveled at their physical perfection as they sped uphill and down with their tireless, effortless stride. Juh had died in Mexico, but Geronimo came with fifteen or sixteen warriors and about seventy women and children. Driving 350 head of stock cattle he had taken from the Mexicans, he was prepared to settle down and make it pay. (In our day the San Carlos Apaches have one of the most extensive ranching enterprises in the world.) He was deeply aggrieved when Crook had the cattle sold and the money turned over to the Mexican government to be given to the owners.[13]

The hostiles settled in a beautiful mountain region on the Fort Apache Reservation, and Davis was placed in charge. To maintain order, he enlisted a company of their warriors as scouts, with Chatto, a former hostile leader—"one of the finest men, red or white, I have ever met"—as first sergeant. Crook was able to report in 1884 that "for the first time in the history of that fierce people, every member of the Apache tribe is at peace." But he and Davis knew how precarious was their hold on their wild charges.

The Indians were forbidden to make *tizwin*, a native beer made by fermenting sprouted corn, because it invariably led to disorder and violence. They insisted that all the white soldiers had their drink; why make special rules for them? A young troublemaker named Ka-ya-ten-nae held a *tizwin* drink with his followers. Davis had him arrested by his loyal scouts and sent to the army prison at Alcatraz. There he was given much liberty, and after eighteen months he returned, able to read and write a little, and willing to co-operate with the military. But at the time, the Indians knew only that he had been carried away to an unknown punishment. Geronimo, in particular, became convinced that his turn was coming next. The soldiers would point out the leaders by

[13] Britton Davis, *The Truth about Geronimo* is a firsthand account of these events.

name, "Which is Geronimo? Which is Naiche?" Then some private with rough humor would draw his hand across his throat, and another would be heard to say that they "ought to be hung."

On the morning of May 15 the chiefs told Davis that they had engaged in a *tizwin* drink the night before and asked him what he proposed to do about it. Obviously he could not arrest them all; he told them he would ask Crook, and he sent a message in the army way "through channels." But one of the "channels" was closed by too much of the white man's *tizwin* in the usually shrewd mind of Al Sieber, and the message was pigeonholed. Crook and Davis always believed that if the General had received it, he could have prevented the outbreak. The Indians waited two days. Rumors began to circulate through the camp: Geronimo would certainly be hanged; the whole band would be arrested and taken away somewhere. Finally on May 17, Geronimo, Naiche, old Nana, Mangas Coloradas' son Mangus, and a leader named Chihuahua left with all their people they could persuade to join them—34 men, 8 well-grown boys, and 92 women and children—and headed for Mexico. The rest of the 500-odd hostiles that Crook had brought up the year before loyally remained on the reservation.

The war that followed, in which the American army was pitted against a handful of men and boys encumbered by more than twice their number of women and children, is an epic of the Southwest. Finally, in January, 1886, army officers with a force composed only of Apache scouts again penetrated the Sierra Madre and captured their camp. The hostiles melted into the brush, but Geronimo and Naiche sent a woman to arrange a conference. Remembering Clum and the shackles, Geronimo insisted that the commander, Lieutenant Marion B. Maus, come unarmed, and the hostile warriors, rifles ready, seated themselves in a circle around him. Geronimo promised to collect his people and meet Crook near the border in "two moons." He delivered to Maus one of his wives and his four-year-old daughter, one of Naiche's wives, the aged Nana, and five other members of his band. Maus took these captives back with him to Fort Bowie.

Geronimo announced his approach by a signal smoke, and the conference with Crook was held on March 25–27 at the Canyon de los Embudos. Geronimo chose the setting—a brushy elevation with ravines leading down to safe retreats—and his hidden warriors had their rifles trained on the group. As always, the hostiles were in superb physical condition and well mounted, warmly clothed, and armed with the newest weapons, all at Mexican or American expense.

Crook, always honorable in dealing with Indians, had every word recorded. Geronimo spoke in great agitation, with sweat rolling down his face. "I want to talk first of the causes which led me to leave the reservation. . . . I was behaving well. I hadn't killed a horse or man, American or Indian . . . and I learned from the American and Apache soldiers . . . that the Americans were going to arrest me and hang me, and so I left. . . . I was praying to the light and to the darkness, to God and to the sun, to let me live quietly there with my family. . . . I never do wrong without a cause. . . . Every day I am thinking, how am I to talk to you to make you believe what I say."

He asked to return to the reservation; but Crook, remembering Ka-ya-ten-nae, who was present in his new character at the conference, said that the men, with such members of their families as might choose to accompany them, must first spend not more than two years as prisoners of war. The hostiles accepted these terms, and the General left Maus to bring them to Fort Bowie while he hastened ahead to telegraph the good news to Washington. But the Indians traveled apart, ready to vanish into the canyons. The second night, almost at the border, they were met by a renegade American who sold them some pulque and told them that they were to be hanged as soon as they should reach Arizona. (He was probably in the pay of army contractors, dealers in stolen livestock, or others interested in prolonging the Apache wars.)[14] Geronimo and Naiche, with sixteen men, thirteen women, and six children, slipped away and headed into the mountains. Crook informed Washington; Sheridan, Sherman's successor as supreme commander, blamed him in an angry telegram; Crook asked to be relieved; and Sheridan ordered Miles to replace him. The surrendered hostiles at Fort Bowie were put on the train to be sent to Fort Marion, Florida.

Miles arrived at Fort Bowie on April 12. He had five thousand men under his command. Scornful of Crook's reliance on Apache scouts and pack trains, he tried the pursuit with cavalry. Then he dismounted his troopers. All without result; their hardships reached the limit of human endurance against an enemy that melted away unharmed. During all this time the four hundred-odd members of their tribes, many of whom had served as scouts, remained at peace, making a start in farming, accumulating livestock, and cutting hay to sell to the army;

[14] This is the conclusion of Thrapp in *Apacheria*, 345–47. Geronimo, to the end of his life, believed that Crook had indeed planned to hang him. See Barrett, *Geronimo's Story*, 136–39.

279

but they were hated by white Arizonans and disliked by the other tribes on the reservation.

Miles could at least catch *them*, and they might even help him to catch the hostiles. Early in July he persuaded two of them, Kieta and Martine, to make contact with Geronimo. At the same time, he suggested to Sheridan that the whole band be removed from Arizona. Sheridan agreed and so did the secretaries of war and the interior (in accord for once) and President Cleveland. Miles suggested their resettlement in the Indian Territory, but Washington explained that that had been forbidden by Congress. Late in August, when they came unsuspecting to Fort Apache for their weekly count, they were surrounded by troops and were soon on their way as prisoners to the railroad at Holbrook to be shipped to Fort Marion.

Meanwhile, Lieutenant Charles B. Gatewood, who was known and trusted by the Apaches, crossed the border with Kieta and Martine and an interpreter and located the hostiles. At the risk of their lives the two scouts went in to the camp and persuaded Geronimo to confer with Gatewood. (Strange how the army officers could trust their lives to this wild warrior's primitive code.) The Indians were tense and serious, and several times they withdrew for private conferences, but they finally agreed to surrender. They set out the next day, the Indians, armed and vigilant, with Lieutenant Gatewood; and an army column, previously kept in the background, paralleled their march to protect them from Mexican or American forces. On September 3, Miles met them at the border.

The General, mindful of Crook's mistake, made every effort to win Geronimo's confidence. He laid out three separate pebbles to represent the separated bands, and moving the three together he assured him that within five days families and friends would all be united in Florida. He also described a mythical reservation, a pleasant land of wood and water, where they would be settled in peace and prosperity. Geronimo accepted these terms and his surrendered band started to Fort Bowie. But the night before they reached the post, three men, three women, and a child escaped. Two separate columns went far down into Mexico—each traveling two thousand miles in pursuit—but they never came in sight of them.

The number of prisoners sent to Florida totaled 509. Geronimo and Naiche and their last holdouts were sent to rigorous confinement in Fort Pickens at Pensacola; the others, including Kieta and Martine, were sent to Fort Marion. Then two years later these bands were reunited at Mount Vernon Barracks in Alabama. Meanwhile, their children and young adults were placed in school at Carlisle. Whether in the rude huts crowded together within these posts or in sanitary Carlisle, they died—119, or almost one fourth, the first three years. "Homesickness, change of climate, and the dreary monotony of empty lives," diagnosed General Crook, who was sent to report on their condition. Geronimo saw nothing ahead but ultimate extinction. "We are vanishing from the earth," he observed some years later, "yet I cannot think we are useless or Usen would not have created us." He found a chance to save one wife and her two children. She was a Mescalero, and he managed to have her included with five Mescalero families caught in the Fort Apache roundup which were sorted out and sent back to their reservation in 1889.

Crook died in 1890, vainly trying to influence Congress to modify its prohibition against settling Apaches in the Indian Territory. But the government had already opened the land to homesteaders, and the Indian reservations were in the process of liquidation.[15] In 1894 the Apaches were brought there, but only as prisoners to Fort Sill. They were a bedraggled-looking lot, now numbering 296 plus about 45 at Carlisle. They were placed in the custody of Lieutenant Hugh Lenox Scott, who became sincerely interested in their welfare.

Forty-odd Apaches remained at Mount Vernon Barracks, victims of a separate tragedy. Eskiminzin and his band had prospered at San Carlos. Lieutenant Davis described them as living in 1883 like a colony of prosperous Spanish-American farmers, with adobe houses, fenced fields, modern farming implements, and good horses and cattle. At Eskiminzin's home he was served an appetizing meal on a well-set table covered by a clean white cloth; then the Chief took him in his buggy to Tucson, where a merchant told the young officer that the credit of the band was good for four or five thousand dollars.

But the reservation line was changed, and these Indians, finding themselves outside, lost their improved farms to white settlers. They moved and started up again. Then Eskiminzin's daughter was married to an Aravaipa known to white men as the Apache Kid. In a series of incidents following a *tizwin* drink, he was driven to outlawry, a lone raider, never captured.[16] An unverified suspicion that Eskiminzin aided him caused Miles to take the whole band away as prisoners.

[15] See Crook, *Autobiography*, 289-300; *infra*, pp. 296-98 and Chap. 16.
[16] The whole story, culminating in prejudged trials and rigged verdicts, is given in Thrapp, *Al Sieber*, 320-41.

Scott tried to obtain their repatriation, but Miles declared they would never be released while he lived. He had picked up a story somewhere —no evidence was ever presented—charging Eskiminzin with the fiendish torture of a white man when he was in the mountains as a hostile many years before. But the General finally yielded and allowed the band to be sent back to San Carlos. As soon as they began to recognize familiar landmarks, they ran far ahead of the baggage wagons with tears of joy streaming down their faces. They became the most industrious and progressive people on the reservation.

The Fort Sill prisoners were never returned to their homeland. Under Scott's direction they built neat, permanent houses over the military reservation, accumulated a fine herd of cattle, raised feed and baled hay to sell to the garrison, and tended gardens for their food and the sale of the surplus.[17] Still they died, and still they begged to go home.

Because Geronimo's fame had traveled far, he was exhibited at expositions, where he did a good business selling souvenirs. He even rode in Theodore Roosevelt's inaugural parade. ("I wanted to give the people a good show," said the irrepressible Teddy.) There he made his final appeal to the President: "Great Father, other Indians have homes where they can live and be happy. I and my people have no home. . . . Let me die in my own country."

But he died a prisoner in 1909. Several of the other leaders died at Fort Sill: old Nana, still unreconciled, in 1896; Chihuahua, an earnest Christian, in 1901; Mangus, also in 1901; Loco, a loyal scout, in 1905. In 1913 the prisoners were finally released. By that time they numbered only 261. Most of them belonged to a generation born since the wars, but public feeling in Arizona was still too strong to permit their return there. They were given the choice of remaining in Oklahoma or joining the Mescaleros. About one third remained, and farms were purchased for them from the Kiowas and Comanches. They still live in that area, where the town of Apache perpetuates their name. Among those who joined the Mescaleros were: Naiche, a gifted native artist, a courteous gentleman, and an active Christian; Kieta and Martine, strangely unembittered by Miles's treachery; Ka-ya-ten-nae, known as a mild and quiet Indian; and Chatto, resenting his captivity but cherishing the memory of Crook. Of Geronimo's

[17] Their life as prisoners at Fort Sill is described in Hugh Lenox Scott, *Some Memories of a Soldier.*

children, only the two Mescaleros survived to perpetuate his family. His son, Robert Geronimo, lived until 1966.

The uncaught Apaches that remained in the mountains of Mexico and Arizona raided from time to time, killing and stealing and then vanishing. In 1913, Pancho Villa told Scott, then a major general in command on the border, that he knew where they were. But Miles's "capture" of Geronimo and Naiche and their little band in 1886 may be said to mark the end of the Indian wars. From that time, on lands set apart—i.e., "reserved"—for their occupancy, the Indians were committed to learning a new way of life.

CHAPTER FIFTEEN

NOW THE RESERVATIONS

With the end of the Indian wars the pattern of reservations was set throughout the United States. To Indians like the Iroquois, the Pueblos, or the Papagos, still holding at least a portion of their native homelands; to the Five Civilized Tribes and others, who had found a refuge in the Indian Territory; and even to the Navahos, undisturbed on their desert, the reservation was the base of their economy, their self-government, and their cultural institutions. To recently "pacified" tribes like the Sioux or the Cheyennes, who had lost their livelihood, their wild independence, and their glory, reservation life was frustrating and deadly dull.[1]

The self-sufficiency of their former life way appears in the description of a Crow encampment visited by young Lieutenant Scott in 1877, during the mop-up following the winter campaign against the Sioux and Cheyennes and Arapahos. He found the Crows "rich in everything an Indian required to make him happy. They wore wonderful dresses of the primitive style, buckskin ornamented with beads, porcupine quills, and ermine. . . .

"The camp was full of meat drying everywhere. Everybody was carefree and joyous . . . . All the life of a nation was going on there before our eyes. Here the head chiefs were receiving ambassadors from another tribe. Following the sound of drums, one would come upon a great gathering for a war-dance, heralding an expedition to fight the Sioux. Or one came to a lodge where a medicine man was

[1] This aspect of reservation life may be seen in George E. Hyde, *A Sioux Chronicle*; Seger, *Early Days among the Cheyenne and Arapahoe Indians*; and Ruby and Brown, *Half-Sun*.

doctoring a patient to the sound of a drum and rattle. Elsewhere a large crowd surrounded a game of ring and spear, on which members of the tribe were betting everything they owned; the loser lost without dispute or quiver of an eyelid. In another place a crowd was witnessing a horse race with twenty-five horses starting off at the first trial. . . .

"I was completely fascinated with the life in that great village of skin lodges, the color, the jollity, the good-will and kindness encountered everywhere. . . . I would pick out our camp, unsaddle, put my rifle belt of ammunition on it, with field-glasses, and go visiting all around the village, without seeing my property for hours in the midst of that camp of more than three thousand wild Indians. . . . My rifle, ammunition, and field-glasses would have been a fortune for a Crow, but I never lost so much as a cartridge." He described the great lodge of the head chief, Iron Bull, with its dark, cool shade of thick tanned skins contrasting with the stifling heat of the army tents. "Beds of buffalo robes were all around the wall, and the floor was swept clean as the palm of one's hand."

These Indians owned more than fourteen thousand horses, from two horses to five hundred at each lodge. They "ran buffalo once a week with savage ceremony," and any tribesman who disturbed the herds "on an off day" or failed to observe the rules of the hunt was severely punished by the soldier societies. Scott and Captain Benteen once rode to "the top of a high peak that overlooked the country for twenty miles . . . and everywhere we looked the prairie was full of buffalo. Benteen thought that we could see at least three hundred thousand buffalo in one view."

Scott rode with some of the Northern Cheyenne scouts who had surrendered to Miles after helping to destroy Custer the year before. "They were all keen, athletic young men, tall and lean and brave, and I admired them as real specimens of manhood more than any body of men I have ever seen before or since. They were perfectly adapted to their environment, and knew just what to do in every emergency and when to do it, without any confusion or lost motion. Their poise and dignity were superb; no royal person ever had more assured manners. I watched their every movement and learned lessons from them that later saved my life many times on the prairie."[2]

In the enforced peace of the reservation they were, in the words of Gordon Macgregor, "warriors without weapons." The native Indian was not lazy. He was accustomed to intense physical exertion in pro-

[2] Quoted by permission from Scott, *Some Memories of a Soldier.*

curing food, whether in stalking game, killing the buffalo, or seeking wild products. Soon after the Apache prisoners came to Fort Sill, they asked Scott's permission to gather some mesquite beans, which they had not tasted since their old days of freedom. They were subject to regular hours of labor under military supervision, and the nearest grove was forty-five miles away, but Scott allowed them to go during the weekend. They started after work Saturday noon, traveling on foot with a few horses to carry supplies and bring back the beans. They trotted the ninety miles, gathered three hundred bushels of beans, and were ready for work at seven o'clock Monday morning.

With their old resources gone, they were to be fed until they could be guided into self-support through agriculture. But the farm pattern of the white American had been fixed east of the Mississippi, and these techniques were not adapted to the semiarid reservations. If the warrior tentatively bent his proud back to this unaccustomed labor, he saw his crops destroyed by grasshoppers, drought, or the vagaries of western rivers. Geronimo was more practical than his white "civilizers" in choosing the range-cattle industry. (Even the way he proposed to get his start was not unknown in the cow country.) But it was impossible to keep white cattlemen off the reservations. Since the Indians were usually hungry, even starving, on insufficient rations, a temporary expedient was to require the intruders to pay rent in beef—an informal leasing system that prevented the Indians from learning to use their own range.

In other than economic techniques, they were expected to conform to an alien pattern, and there was to be no nonsense about imposing it. George E. Ellis, a well-known Massachusetts clergyman and author, expressed this a little more bluntly, perhaps, than others in his history of Indian affairs published in 1882:

"We have a full right, by our own best wisdom, and then even by compulsion, to dictate terms and conditions to them; to use constraint and force; to say what we intend to do, and what they must and shall do. . . . This rightful power of ours will relieve us from conforming to, or even consulting to any troublesome extent, the views and inclinations of Indians whom we are to manage. . . . The Indian must be made to feel he is in the grasp of a superior."

These "civilizers" came up against the Indian's unyielding spirit— "he is formed out of rock," said Senator Ingalls. The Senator concluded that "all these efforts [to effect a change] are valueless unless they are based upon force supplemented by force and continued by force."

286

There were different kinds of force. The army had set out to "punish" the tribes; civilian administrators could cut off the rations. This enforced obedience did incalculable harm to the Indian spirit. The effect is apparent even today when the energy and self-confidence of relatively untouched tribes like the Navahos on their desert or the Mikasukis in their swamps is contrasted with the demoralization of those subjected to the most overhead control. It is evident also in the paternalism—the "Father knows best" attitude—still lingering in the minds of some well-intentioned Bureau officials. The conscientious agent who tried to help a half-tamed people adjust to a new life way truly had a perplexing task. It was easier to enforce orders than to encourage self-direction; thus to break down the authority of the chiefs and reduce all to the level of submissive subjects. From Jamestown on, too many white well-wishers had uncritically assumed that everything Indian was wrong.

There was, for example, the determination to dissolve the plural marriages, regardless of what this would mean to the discarded wives and children. An "ex post facto law," was the characterization of the clear-headed Scott; he reasoned that if new plural marriages were forbidden, the custom would die out harmlessly with the older generation. "Breaking up of families," said the indignant Chief Moses. Chief Quanah Parker of the Quahadi Comanches, the last band to surrender in the South Plains War of 1874–75, explained it thus:

"A long time ago I lived free among the buffalo on the Staked Plains and had as many wives as I wanted, according to the laws of my people. I used to go to war in Texas and Mexico. You wanted me to stop fighting and sent messages all the time: 'You stop, Quanah. You come here. You sit down, Quanah.' You did not say anything then, 'How many wives you got, Quanah.' Now I come and sit down as you want. You talk about wives; which one I throw away? You pick him? You little girl, you go 'way; you got no papa—you pick him? You little fellow, you go 'way; you got no papa—you pick him?"[3]

The "civilizers" were equally insensitive in their determination to "educate" the Indian children by changing them into white people. In 1885 the federal superintendent of Indian schools, referring to his task of making the Indian "a member of a new social order," envisioned it thus: "To do this we must recreate him, make him a new personality." Therefore, remove the children from the demoralizing influence of their families to the boarding school, the more distant the better. They

[3] *Ibid.*

287

were taken from their grieving parents and kept for years, punished for speaking their own language, and brainwashed of all traces of Indianness. Many died (children died at home, too, but this was different); a few "entered the mainstream of American life";[4] most returned suspended in vacancy, separate from both cultures.

In their raids on the settlements the Indians if sufficiently angered killed whole families, but in kindlier moods they adopted the children and reared them as their own. Frontier history is full of stories of captured children who were never found or who grew up as Indians changed past recovery. The mother of Quanah Parker, for example, was a child captive who became a Comanche in all but blood; and her subsequent recapture and the failure of her sorrowing white family to reclaim her spirit is an epic of the Southwest. No other tragedy of frontier life brought such anguish, no other phase of Indian warfare aroused such hatred as this capture of children.

White men, in raiding Indian villages, also killed the children if sufficiently angered, and in kindlier moods they also spared them. Placing them in a distant school was an extension of this humane impulse. It never occurred to the educators that the practice of both races was exactly parallel. They never understood the desperation of the bereaved parents. Even the Apache prisoners crowded within stockades found ways to hide some of their children from the Carlisle kidnapers. (This alien acculturalization was, of course, very different from the eagerness with which the Indians of the Five Tribes requested schools in their country and established educational systems of their own as a means of defending—not destroying—their nationality, and from the way in which even the "wild" tribes of the Territory consciously set out to follow their example.)

Throughout the history of the white man in the New World, individual travelers had observed and recorded Indian customs and culture. This interest became official when the Bureau of American Ethnology was founded in 1879, and that organization began immediately to conduct scientific studies and to publish its findings in many volumes. But for half a century this government agency might as well have been located on another planet so far as its influence on Indian policy was concerned. Why study Indian ways while in process of blotting them out?

In their despair, the pacified tribes turned in the Indian manner to

[4] Jason Betzinez, for example, and Dr. Charles A. Eastman of the Minnesota Sioux.

288

a prophet promising the return of the old order. This time it was a Paiute named Wovoka living in the remote Nevada desert. He had worked for a settler and learned something of Christianity by hearing the Bible reading and family prayers in the home. In 1888, during an eclipse of the sun, he "died for a time" and talked with God, who told him to return and teach love and peace. "Do no harm to anyone. Do right always. Do not tell lies. When your friends die, you must not cry. You must not fight."

He and his followers became convinced that he was the Indian Messiah. Christ had come to earth once, and the white people had killed him; now he had come to the Indians. God gave him a certain sacred paint and new words to sing with the Paiute dances, and if these were used in faith, the old ways and the dead Indians would return. The cult and its accompanying ceremonies, known to the whites as the "ghost dance," spread first to the Shoshonis and Bannocks, then to the Crows and across the mountains to the Northwest. Delegations from the Plains Indians were sent to inquire and returned to report. Some of these pilgrimages over unfamiliar mountains and across deserts through the land of unknown tribes form minor epics.[5]

In the southwestern Indian Territory the Kiowas were skeptical, and the Comanches only mildly affected. The Cheyennes and Arapahos and the Wichitas and affiliated tribes were caught up in an emotional fervor that swept all before it. They danced until they fell unconscious; revived, they told of visits they had had with their deceased friends and relatives. To these unhappy people, the earth was worn out, the buffalo and the wild horses were gone, the trees had been cut down, the streams were dry. Now a new earth would move slowly from the northwest to cover it; and on it would ride the Messiah, their resurrected relatives, and the wild life. It would push the white men into the sea or back to the place from whence they came. Even the date was set—the spring of 1891 when the grass should be an inch high.

The post commander at Fort Sill detailed Lieutenant Scott to circulate among the Indians and keep himself informed. As the excitement mounted in the fall of 1890, disquieting news came from the Sioux; and General Wesley Merritt, the Department commander, ordered Scott to prepare to stop the dancing and disarm the Indians. Scott earnestly advised against this policy as certain to lead to violence, and Merritt accepted his judgment. When spring failed to bring the

[5] The Kiowa quest with the adverse report is related in Marriott, *Ten Grandmothers.*

expected deliverance, the movement collapsed in defeat and disillusion. A generation later, Scott questioned the Arapaho who had been the most active of the evangelists. He answered, "My father's brother, I hope you won't talk about these things now. I have put them all away behind me, and I pray now only to the Spirit above and go to the white man's church."

The failure of their hopes must have brought unreckoned despair to all the believers, but only to the Sioux did the ghost dance bring tragedy. It came at a bad time for that unreconciled people. Seven years of sharp practice and legerdemain had culminated in 1889 in the dismemberment of their great reservation, cutting away nearly half of its area and dividing the remainder into five separate tracts (as presently constituted). Then the worst drought on record came that same year, wiping out their half-hearted agricultural efforts. (Thousands of white homesteaders abandoned their Dakota farms in 1889, a discouraging reversal of the great rush of settlement anticipated when the Sioux land was acquired; ironically, this date also marked the division of Dakota Territory and the admission of the two states into the Union.) And at that very time, Congress and the Indian administration cut the beef ration. The Sioux suffered from actual hunger, and when a measles epidemic struck them the following winter, their weakened children died by hundreds. A still partially untamed people, uneasy, suspicious, excitable, they were ready to grasp any desperate expedient when word came to them of a Messiah in a western land far beyond their ken. They held councils and sent delegations which returned early in 1890, fully convinced and ready to teach the new rituals.

Apparently Wovoka's exhortations to peace were to apply only to relations between Indians. Even so, hostility to whites was not indicated, since the dances would bring about their elimination. (On the North Plains, it was a dust storm that would cover the white man and his works.) But the Sioux were in a mood to help the business along. Congress delayed their appropriation that year, thus necessitating a still more drastic cut in the beef issue, and again drought destroyed their crops. Soon the men were dancing with rifles strapped to their backs, their bodies crisscrossed with full cartridge belts, and wearing "bulletproof" shirts painted with sacred symbols. Fear of a repetition of the 1862 Minnesota tragedy spread along the frontier. In November troops were sent to protect the agencies. The tamer Indians—who were not very tame—collected around them, while the more fanatic dancers carried on their ceremonies in distant camps, feasting on cattle driven from government herds or from their more progressive tribesmen.

Sitting Bull had returned from Canada in 1881 and was living on the Standing Rock Reservation, which straddled the boundary between North and South Dakota. He had remained recalcitrant, refusing to have anything to do with the agent, and now his log cabin camp with about 475 of his followers forty miles from the agency was a center of the ghost dance excitement. James McLaughlin, the able and experienced agent, sent his trusty Sioux police there, and they returned dazed and believing. They had seen the dancers—men, women, and children—"fall dead" and "come to life" again with ecstatic accounts of meetings with their dead relatives, all alive and happy and preparing to return to earth with vast herds of buffalo.

Soon it was apparent that Sitting Bull was preparing to move his camp. He probably intended to join a ghost dance center in the Big Badlands, a region of fantastically eroded canyons, bluffs, and mesas far from the agency on the Pine Ridge Reservation in southwestern South Dakota. Possibly he planned to put himself at the head of all the ghost dancers. It was a situation of great potential danger. He was a native patriot, valiant in war, great in medicine, and unwavering in his hostility to the white man and his "civilization."[6]

On December 14, McLaughlin on orders from Washington sent thirty-three of his police to arrest the Chief, while two troops of cavalry marched out to support them if necessary. Before dawn the next morning the police quietly entered his house and took him into custody. The camp sprang into life and more than 150 fanatic dancers began to surround them. One of them shot and fatally wounded a policeman, and the wounded man then shot Sitting Bull. A fight followed, in which even the women participated with knives and clubs. Four of the police were killed and another badly wounded, while the ghost dancers lost seven killed besides Sitting Bull and three wounded. The cavalry arrived, and the dancers were subdued. About 250 of them went to the agency and surrendered. The rest, half-clad, freezing, and starving, fled to the ghost dance camps on other reservations.

With the arrival of the refugees, the excitement in these camps mounted to frenzy. But Miles, in command of the army, worked patiently to contain it, throwing a military cordon around the whole

6 The standard biography of this chief is Stanley Vestal, *Sitting Bull, Champion of the Sioux.*

Sioux area and sending troops under officers the Indians knew and trusted to bring the dancers in to the agencies. Surrounded, persuaded, pushed, they came in, frustrated, quarreling with each other, but without the firing of a shot. The fight at Sitting Bull's camp could have been the extent of the violence.

On the Cheyenne River Reservation, which joined Standing Rock on the south, the most distant ghost dance camp was that of Big Foot with about 550 followers. The officer sent out to bring them in was handling them with great tact and patience, and they were moving ahead of the troops down the river toward their agency. Then they were thrown into anger and panic by the arrival of 38 of Sitting Bull's survivors, men, women, and children. At that very time, an infantry force, sent in by an unwise order, appeared ahead of them. Were the soldiers going to surround and murder them? They broke and fled south to the Pine Ridge Reservation. About 65, including 18 warriors, went to the Big Badlands. The others, with Big Foot, were coming in towards the Pine Ridge Agency, most of them ready for peace and security, though there were some fanatics among them. At Wounded Knee Creek, eighteen miles away, they were surrounded by soldiers and surrendered without resistance.

George A. Forsyth of Beecher Island fame, now a colonel, was sent out from the agency with reinforcements and assumed command. He had eight troops—470 officers and men—of the Seventh Cavalry, Custer's famous regiment with its memories of the Little Bighorn. He saw no need of easing the Indians on to the agency, where they would voluntarily give up their guns and settle down. He would disarm them at once and bring them as prisoners. (In his defense it should be noted that these were his orders, but he could have exercised more judgment in carrying them out.) On December 29 he stationed troops all around the camp, set up three Hotchkiss guns trained on their tipis, and ordered the men and older boys to come out and form a semicircle in front of his tent. Numbering 106, they squatted on the ground, wearing their ghost dance shirts under their blankets, and at least one carried a concealed gun. Standing very close was a line of dismounted cavalry holding their carbines at the ready. Then some of the troopers were sent to search the tipis for weapons. The women and children became frightened as they were pushed around roughly by the soldiers, and some of them began to wail.

In such a crisis the Sioux were always likely to give way to panic or blind rage, and in either case to begin shooting. The squatting men became instantly alert. A medicine man jumped up and started dancing about, performing his incantations and reminding the warriors that their shirts were bulletproof. Forsyth sternly ordered him to sit down, but just then a Sioux pulled a gun from under his blanket and shot an officer. The warriors leaped to their feet. At the same instant the troops fired a volley into them, piling up 52 dead in the semicircle where they had squatted, and the Hotchkiss guns rained explosive shells upon the women and children in the camp. The surviving warriors fought the soldiers hand to hand with knives and clubs and then fled up a dry ravine and tried to hide in gullies. The maddened soldiers followed, slaughtering indiscriminately. Dead women and children were strung out for three miles from the place where the massacre started. It is not known how many Indians were killed. The most careful count showed 146, of whom 84 (including Big Foot) were men and boys of fighting age, 44 women, and 18 children. At least 33 were wounded, many of them mortally.

The sound of the guns was heard at the agency, where about six thousand Sioux were camped. Some of them sprang on horses and raced out to investigate. Soon they came flying back with the news that the soldiers were killing Big Foot's people. The whole great encampment went wild with grief and rage. Instantly they began to take down their tipis, family groups began to streak off to the Badlands, and mounted warriors swarmed over the prairie ready to attack any whites they might meet. They set the grass on fire, harassed the returning cavalry, and circled around the agency firing shots. The troopers suffered unexplained casualties of twenty-five dead and thirty-five wounded. Probably some had been hit by their own cross fire at Wounded Knee and the Indians may have managed to kill some with what weapons they could snatch up; others may have been picked off by the avenging warriors who rode out from the agency.

By night only about two thousand of the most peaceable or the most helpless Sioux remained in the big camp near the agency. The military sent out a call for reinforcements, and the Ninth Cavalry, a Negro unit, made an amazing forced march of ninety miles, arriving the next day at dawn. Soon General Miles came with more reinforcements and set up his headquarters at the agency. He handled the situation with restraint and understanding. He placed eight thousand troopers around the Big Badlands stronghold with its thousand-or-so warriors, and sent in messages promising food and peace. (The rations provided by the treaties had been restored as soon as the trouble started.) The Indians were outnumbered, they were hungry, and the sight of ghost dance shirts pierced by bullets at Wounded Knee had destroyed their faith in a supernatural deliverance. Die-hards still urged an attack on the soldiers, but arguing and quarreling as they came, the camp inched its way towards the agency. By the middle of January this last flare of the old Indian spirit had ended in surrender.[7]

It is immensely significant that throughout the excitement of the expected deliverance and the anger following the massacre at Wounded Knee, none of the Sioux, not even the most hostile, had thought of leaving the reservations to raid the settlements. Even to these still half-wild people the area remaining to them had become their homeland.

Thus, with the most widely ranging tribes reconciled to occupying a compact, stabilized tract, the centuries-old conflict over land ownership should have ended. In theory, all that remained now was for them to develop their resources and find a viable life way to replace the old. But the mere existence of a reservation—a piece of real estate reserved for Indians—was an incitement to white cupidity. It was encouraged, it if needed encouragement, by a legal technicality.

In 1871, Congress passed a law terminating the negotiation of treaties with Indian tribes, the system used in dealing with them throughout the history of the United States. It had no effect in making agreements with them; it simply made the agreements easier to ratify— by a simple majority of Congress instead of the two-thirds Senate vote required for treaties. Also, Congress had always had the legal right to abrogate a treaty, though this power had been used reluctantly as a breach of faith. But most of the reservations established after 1871 were set apart by executive order, and it became convenient to assume that the Indian title to them was inferior to other land titles. "The Indians were presumed to be living there on sufferance like so many animals on a wildlife refuge."[8] Thus, as we have seen in the preceding chapter, the Apache reservations were juggled at the whim of the administration, established by the stroke of a pen, and restored to the public domain by another stroke.

This precarious tenure was unblushingly expressed by Congress. The Colville Reservation in Washington had been set aside by execu-

---

[7] An excellent account of the ghost dance and its aftermath among the Sioux is found in Hyde, *A Sioux Chronicle*.

[8] Characterization used in Ruby and Brown, *Half-Sun*.

tive order in 1872. Then in 1891, the northern half was wanted for white settlement. The Indian Office showed some decent hesitation in taking it and negotiated a purchase agreement with the Indians. Congress eliminated the provision for payment and declared that "nothing herein contained shall be construed as recognizing title or ownership of said Indians to any part of the said Colville Reservation, whether that hereby restored to the public domain or that still reserved by the Government for their use and occupancy." President Harrison refused to sign this iniquitous bill, but he allowed it to become a law on July 1, 1892, without his signature. Six years later Congress threw the diminished reservation open for mineral entry. The Indians were still graciously permitted to occupy the surface, while prospectors covered their land "like swarming termites seeking a place to burrow."[9] As it happened, the mining claims proved to be worthless and were eventually abandoned, but that did not change the supposed transience of the Indian title.

Chief Moses of the Colville summed up the situation in a vivid allegory. Two white men, he said, came to look at the stony surface of the reservation. He told them it was a present to him from the whites. One of them picked up a stone. It fell from his hand and broke open, showing gold and silver inside. Then they began fighting each other for possession. They told Moses that the outside of the stone was his, but the inside belonged to them.

The Indians' ownership of their minerals was still in question as late as the 1920s. The Navaho Reservation, instead of following the usual pattern of shrinkage, had been increased by executive order. When oil was struck there, Harding's secretary of the interior, Albert Fall (of Teapot Dome ill fame), ruled that it belonged to the government. Harlan Stone, Coolidge's attorney general, repudiated this interpretation in 1924, and two years later an act of Congress stabilized the Indian title to executive order lands. But the evil results of the old policy persisted. In 1917, intruders entered the Papago Reservation under pretense of staking mining claims, acquired the springs and water holes, and thus controlled the range. It was not until 1955 that Congress passed a law establishing the Papagos' ownership of their minerals. Incidentally, the righting of this wrong illustrates a trend repeated in many states emerging into maturity. Once Arizona pioneers loudly demanded everything belonging to the Indians; in 1955 it

[9] *Ibid.*

was Arizona's delegation in Congress—Senators Carl Hayden and Barry Goldwater and Representatives Stewart Udall and John Rhodes —who pushed the legislation in behalf of the Papagos.

During the whole period when white land-grabbers were hungrily eyeing the reservations, their strongest regard was focused on the solid block of Indian-owned land that constituted the Indian Territory. Not too far west for successful agriculture of the eastern pattern; bounded on three sides by the improved farms and growing towns of Kansas, Arkansas, and Texas; with mile stretching beyond mile of ungrazed grass "as tall as the saddle horn"; and with the unratified bribe of the railroad grants, it seemed to promise a farm to the home-seeker, range to the cattleman, and wealth to the speculator.

There was no immediate prospect of filling it up with Indians. Of the land acquired for that purpose in the Reconstruction treaties, large tracts ceded by the Cherokees, Creeks, and Seminoles—adding up to almost half of the entire ceded area—had not been assigned to any tribe. Congressional policy, as we have seen, had blocked further removals. Admittedly, bringing protesting tribes to die there was too cruel; still, the Indian population could have been increased somewhat by willing immigrants. The Apache captives would certainly have preferred a reservation there to imprisonment at Fort Marion, Mount Vernon—or Carlisle. The Alabamas and Coushattas of Texas would gladly have joined their Creek kinsmen. There would have been others. But it had become apparent by the close of the 1870s that the land was too good for Indians. Predictably, it was the railroad interests that began the new drive to open it to white people.

Their efforts to break down the Indian regime by acts of Congress had finally become discredited—their influence behind these proposals had received too much publicity. In 1879 they changed their tactics. The campaign was launched by the Katy attorney, T. C. Sears, and Elias Cornelius Boudinot, the son of the murdered Cherokee leader. Two years old at the time of his father's death, Boudinot had been brought up in New England by his white relatives. Later he settled in Arkansas and Washington, becoming an undercover man for the railroads and an active agitator against tribal interests. He and Sears, through newspaper articles and interviews, letters, and circulars with official looking maps, gave great publicity to their "discovery" that the unassigned land was public land open to homestead entry. The news swept the country. Leaders—of whom at least some were almost certainly in the pay of the railroads—collected bands of "Boomers" in Kansas and began to invade the area, staking claims and laying out townsites, while all the border towns, in mass meetings, inflammatory speeches, and newspaper articles, applauded their efforts. At the same time invaders, less formally organized, came in from Texas.

President Hayes issued a proclamation stating that the land was Indian land and sent troops to remove the trespassers, while the agitators launched new invasions and the border press urged them to defy the President. In 1880 the most active of the Boomer leaders was brought before the federal district court at Fort Smith, and the Five Tribes employed an able Cherokee attorney to assist the Department of Justice in his prosecution. The government and the Indians won their case. The court ruled that the tribes had ceded the land to the United States for the use of Indians, and whether or not Indians had been located upon it, it was still Indian country. The Boomer leader was fined one thousand dollars for trespass, a sentence that caused him no inconvenience since he did not own one thousand dollars, and he resumed his invasions.

But the Boomers' cause began to win public sympathy and congressional support. After all, they were following the whole trend of American history, cupidity and speculative fervor linked with a creative urge that had inspired all the centuries of white pioneering. During the late 1880s the Atchison, Topeka, and Santa Fe Railroad built two main lines across the area. This time the franchises carried no corrupting land grant, but the construction was all a part of the anticipated development. Also, it was true that the unassigned land was occupied, with or without the consent of the Indians, by cattlemen, and the poor homeseeker versus rich cattleman motif entered into the argument. From 1885 on, bills were introduced in Congress for opening the land to homesteaders, and the Indians saw that they must choose between a forced sale and seizure. Early in 1889 the Creeks and Seminoles made an unconditional sale to the government, and it was opened to settlement at high noon on April 22. The Cherokees held out nearly three more years, consenting to cede their unassigned land (known as the Cherokee Outlet) in December, 1891.

The Creek-Seminole cession comprised nearly three thousand square miles in the heart of the Indian Territory. By this time abundant land free for the working no longer lay beyond the frontier; hence, by the opening date, thousands of prospective settlers waited around the border. Among them were a few of the former Boomers who had been legitimate home-seekers.[10] At the signal all rushed in, driving their stakes to claim their farms, and the same afternoon tent cities sprang up at Oklahoma City and other places.

Thus was broken the barrier that had set the Indian Territory apart for Indian occupancy. Even before this a policy had been adopted for the liquidation of all the Indian reservations in the United States.

[10] I knew one such myself. He established a family on the land, and it became their home for three generations.

CHAPTER SIXTEEN

BREAKING UP THE RESERVATIONS

For more than one-half century, sincere friends of the Indians had been advocating the individual ownership of land as the salvation of any Indian who would accept it. Like other mistaken policies it was all part of the centuries-old aim of changing Indians into white people. Break up their natural groupings, whether by abolishing the governments of advanced tribes or undermining the influence of primitive chiefs, and set each family alone on a farm to develop habits of industry and the pride of possession. Said the agent of the Yankton Sioux (an eastern Sioux tribe with a reservation in southeastern South Dakota) in his annual report of 1877:

"As long as Indians live in villages they will retain many of their old and injurious habits. Frequent feasts, heathen ceremonies and dances, constant visiting—these will continue . . . I trust that before another year is ended they will generally be located upon individual land or farms. From that date will begin their real and permanent progress."

The Indians' friends also argued that only a fee simple title would protect their land from the insecurity of reservation and treaty guarantees. These arguments did not deceive the land-grabbers. They *knew*. The only protection the Indian had came from his tribe; standing alone before the "equality" of the white man's law and courts he was helpless. The Indians who had experienced allotment knew this, too. With the earnestness of desperation the leaders of the Five Civilized Tribes told what had happened in Mississippi, Alabama, Kansas, and elsewhere. Very few people listened. Along with the "benefit" to the Indians was a tempting bonus: after the allotments were made, much land would be left over for white settlement. The philanthropists even reasoned that smaller holdings would advance the Indians' "civilization"; too much land encouraged their roaming tendencies.

Thus humanitarians and land-grabbers united to urge the policy upon Congress. A bill to that effect was introduced in 1879 and again in 1880. But a clear-sighted minority report of the House Indian Affairs Committee stated that even the Indians' well-wishers would have to admit "it does not make a farmer out of an Indian to give him a quarter section of land." It went on to charge that "The real aim of this bill is to get at the Indian lands and open them up to settlement. . . . If this were done in the name of greed it would be bad enough; but to do it in the name of humanity, and under the cloak of an ardent desire to promote the Indian's welfare by making him like ourselves, whether he will or not, is infinitely worse." The National Indian Defense Association, founded in 1885, added its voice to the opposition, but it stood alone among organizations formed to champion the Indian cause.

Succeeding secretaries of the interior and commissioners of Indian affairs supported the policy, and in 1885 and again in 1886 President Cleveland recommended it in his annual messages to Congress. It became law on February 8, 1887. It is generally known as the Dawes Act from its sponsor, Senator Henry L. Dawes of Massachusetts, one of the most active of the well-meaning opponents of Indian nationality.

The Five Civilized Tribes, the Osages, and a few others who held their land under patented titles were exempted from its provisions; otherwise the president was authorized to allot all tribal land in the United States to individuals. The standard share was 160 acres (a "quarter" of the mile-square "section") to each head of a family, smaller amounts to unmarried men and children. But the Indians expressed so much opposition to this alien "head of a family" concept—in their society married women and children had property rights—that in 1891 the act was amended to provide equal shares to all—80 acres of agricultural, 160 acres of grazing land. These amounts were subsequently modified in agreements made with different tribes.

In an attempt to protect the allottees from the wholesale exploitation of former times, the allotments were to be held in trust status, inalienable and nontaxable for twenty-five years. Negotiations were to be carried on with the tribes for the sale to the United States of the land remaining after the allotments were made and for its opening to white settlement. (Another benefit to the Indians; they would learn the superior ways of the white people settled among them.) All allottees were to become citizens of the United States; but in 1906 the act was amended to delay citizenship in future allotments until the expiration of the trust period, and to permit removal of the trust restrictions from the allotments of Indians adjudged competent.

Although Indian consent was not required, it was more convenient to obtain it if possible. During the winter of 1886–87 preceding the passage of the law, Commissioner of Indian Affairs J. D. C. Atkins visited the tribes of the western Indian Territory trying to convert them to the policy. Ne-ka-ke-pa-hah, the principal chief of the Osages, thus summed up his arguments, "if I would do that I would have everlasting home for myself and children and my people and their children and that each one of our people could control at least 700 head of cattle and other stock." But it was Ne-ka-ke-pa-hah's opinion that "as to letting white settlement with our people would soon Disfranchise the poore Indians and as to the stock we only look out to the state of Kansas we see the whites who live on alotments they have two ropes one to lead there cow and one to stake out the calve." (This was, indeed, an accurate characterization of the hard-run white homesteader on *his* 160 acres.)

Atkins met the same determined opposition from the tribes to the southwest. In February, Chief Jake of the Caddos and Lone Wolf of the Kiowas started out to Washington to protest. Their agent, ignoring the Standing Bear decision, attempted to arrest them for leaving their reservations without permission. They managed to reach the Creek Nation, where the Creeks indignantly intervened in their behalf, and they were allowed to purchase a railroad ticket and proceed on their journey. The bill had already become law by the time they reached the capital, but they insisted on seeing Atkins. As Chief Jake later described it through an interpreter, "I told the Commissioner that in former times and up [to] the present time he and all his people had advised us and all the Indians to labor and gain education, etc., and now when my people are just now beginning to realize and accept the benefits of knowledge how to work you are attempting to change our customs and entail ruin on my people."

When they returned, Lone Wolf called a council of all the southwestern tribes of the Territory. They drew up a protest to the Commissioner and appealed to the Five Tribes for support. The Creeks accordingly called a council in their country. It was attended by fifty-seven delegates from nineteen tribes, including the ablest Five Tribes leaders and many of the great war chiefs of the Plains. Chief Jake and

301

Lone Wolf told of their futile trip to Washington. Towaconie Jim of the Wichitas said, "It is now thirty-two years since you five tribes advised the Wichitas to be peaceable and to obey the will of the great government at Washington. And for thirty-two years we have followed your advice, and have sent our children to school, and have made us some farms, and built houses, and raise stock. You also invited us to adopt the Christian religion and we have done so.[1] We have always thought our lands would remain ours, and never be divided in severalty, and *it can never be done with our consent*. The government treats us as if we had no rights, but we have always lived at our present place, and that is our home."

The educated Indians knew that the law had already been passed, but they were deeply stirred by the appeal of these "wild" delegates. The council adopted a memorial to the president entreating him to stay its execution "upon powerless and protesting people" until they were at least given the opportunity to test their rights in court. (It *was* tested in 1901 in *Lone Wolf* v. *Hitchcock*, and the Indians lost.) The council then adjourned to meet the next year in the Cherokee country.

Commissioner Atkins was furious when he heard of these proceedings. In a Washington newspaper interview and in his official report he asserted that none of the affected tribes had attended the council, that in fact they had *sought* the passage of the law; and he fulminated against the Five Tribes, who were exempted from its provisions, for "their insubordinate and unpardonable meddling" and their attempts "to manufacture a hostile sentiment against this solemn act of Congress."[2] The Indians had no means of publicity to combat such official falsehoods. The proceedings of the council were published in a Creek-owned newspaper, but it had a very limited circulation.

Away from the Five Tribes, Indian protests were even more deeply buried. During that same winter of 1886–87, Sitting Bull is said to have visited the Crows in Montana, stirring them up against the allotment of their land. Six days before the act became law, Atkins ordered the Indian agents of the Northwest to forbid their charges to leave the reservations without permission. There, as in the Indian Territory, he tried to prevent the tribes from forming a united front.[3]

[1] The Creeks began sending Baptist missionaries to the "wild" tribes in 1874. In their first congregation were warriors with scalps of white people hanging from their belts.

[2] The whole story may be found in Debo, *The Road to Disappearance*.

[3] Ruby and Brown, *Half-Sun*, 239.

He was, of course, not able to prevent the Indian Territory tribes from holding the council they had scheduled for 1888. The Five Tribes leaders knew their rights too well. It convened on June 19 at the little town of Fort Gibson, which had grown up around the old military post. Delegates from twenty-two tribes were in attendance and two or three thousand people were present as spectators. Chiefs of the western tribes made impassioned appeals to their "elder brothers" against the impending threat. Said White Man, a Kiowa-Apache, "The white people see a great deal further than we do. This may be something that will prove our ruin. We come to you as more intelligent Indians and ask your advice." Said White Wolf, famed Comanche warrior, "We urge you, civilized brothers, use all your wisdom on the road for safety for our lands. With that safe, there is hope of perpetuation."

In their desperation they urged the formation of a united government to resist the danger. "We should live as one family under one Indian government," said Joe Vitter, an Iowa. "If we combine," said Macopia, a Potawatomi, "we shall then be like an island in the waters. We should not be carried away, but should stand. I think if we do our best God will help us." He had visited the Chippewas of Minnesota to invite them to the council and brought back a message of friendship with tobacco and strings of wampum. (This glimpse of Chippewa feeling is significant as an indication of the unrecorded protests of many tribes.)

Pleasant Porter of the Creeks eloquently urged the cause of unity. He admitted the practical difficulties. To the "wild" tribes it would mean the surrender of authority by the old-time chiefs, "the laying aside of all the honors of leadership you have inherited from your ancestors." To the Five Civilized Tribes it would mean the absorption of a less advanced people; but "The civilized tribes cannot escape if they fail to help you. The weak will fall, but not alone." It would be "a policy untried. All past policy has been death to the Indian. I believe this policy must come from us; from within ourselves; from our own minds. All natures grow from within. Communities have the same growth from within, not from without." When the presiding officer, a Cherokee, mindful of the difficulties, temporized, Porter said, "This is an important question—one of life or death." He introduced a resolution providing for a committee to present the Indians' cause to the president of the United States, another committee to draft a constitution, and a council to meet in June the following year to adopt a plan of union to submit to the tribes.

The new commissioner of Indian affairs, less arrogant than Atkins, published these proceedings in his report, with the comment that the Indians would not carry out their expressed aims. Truly they had no opportunity. It became clear in the succeeding session of Congress that the Creeks and Seminoles must choose between ceding their unassigned land and losing it, and Porter himself was a member of the delegation that negotiated the Creek cession. Its opening to white settlement the following April 22 destroyed the last chance for an "Indian commonwealth" projected by the tribes. Only two of them troubled to attend the council in June.

That same June the government authorized a commission—usually known as the Jerome Commission from David H. Jerome who served most of the time as its chairman[4]—to go to the Indian Territory and prepare the western tribes for allotment under the Dawes Act. The next year Congress created the Territory of Oklahoma embracing the white settlement of April 22, 1889, and providing for the extension of its authority to the western reservations marked for liquidation. Thus the Indian Territory was reduced to its eastern half—the area retained by the Five Civilized Tribes in the Reconstruction treaties.

Meanwhile, the allotment of reservations was progressing rapidly throughout the United States. As soon as the Dawes Act was passed, Atkins began to make contracts for surveying the land and to appoint allotting agents. Humanitarians, who had hailed it as an "Indian Magna Charta" and a "Declaration of Independence," had innocently assumed that tribes would be selected on the basis of their advancement, but it was soon apparent that the desirability of their land was the important criterion.

The first allotment began in 1887 on the reservation of the Sisseton and Wahpeton Sioux. These tribes had never gone out on the plains. Crowded from Minnesota, they still owned about one million acres in the rich valley of the Red River of the North, in the northeastern corner of what would soon become the state of South Dakota. When allotments were completed to the two thousand Indians, the 660,000-acre "surplus" was opened to white settlement in April, 1892.

Allotment began on several other reservations—small tracts in South Dakota, Nebraska, even in Oregon—before the year 1887 was over. Others followed quickly. The liquidation of the rich timber lands of the Minnesota Chippewas had already begun when they sent their

---

[4] Also called the Cherokee Commission because it applied the pressure that forced the Cherokees to cede their unassigned land.

message to the Fort Gibson council. (The Chippewas of the Red Lake Reservation were somehow overlooked; they retained their swamp and timber, and in recent times they established a profitable fishing and fish-processing industry, while their forest is operated on a sustained-yield basis.) Within a year after Sitting Bull visited the Crows, their allotment began; it yielded a surplus of 1,800,000 acres. In 1891 the commissioner of Indian affairs could report that in the preceding two years, he had restored to the public domain 12,071,380 acres, or 11½ per cent, of the total reservation area of 104,314,349 acres existing in 1889.

The Nez Percé allotment began in 1889, but progressed slowly because of the mountainous terrain, being completed in 1895. These Indians, skilled horse breeders for a century and engaged in cattle raising for half as long, wanted to keep the surplus for a communal range, but the government and the local land-grabbers finally pushed through the sale. Significantly, their historian concludes that this outcome was probably better for them; otherwise white stockmen would have continued to trespass on their grasslands.[5] In other words, when the land was acquired by white men, it came under legal protection; as long as it was owned by Indians, no laws or courts or the plighted faith of the government could keep it free of intruders. This had been a universal experience since the discouraged observations of Washington and Knox.

The allotment of the Oklahoma tribes proceeded rapidly during the 1890s, followed by successive land rushes as dramatic as the 1889 opening. Some form of agreement was always obtained from the Indians, whether by persuasion, intimidation, or fraud, but in the background was the authority to put the policy into effect without their consent. The Cheyenne and Arapaho buffalo hunters had fifteen years between their warfare on the Plains and their submission to the new order in 1890, two additional years before being swamped by a land rush in 1892. The irreconcilable Kickapoos, from the time when they were dragged protesting from Mexico, had eighteen years until a forged instrument in 1891 purported to be their consent to the break-up of their reservation, four more years before being inundated by another land rush. And so it went as tribe after tribe fell before the onslaught. The allottees became citizens of the United States and of the Territory of Oklahoma, but they suffered an unreckoned damage in the liquidation of their own community organizations. Only the Osages, exempt

[5] Haines, *The Nez Percés*, 302, 309–10.

from the provisions of the Dawes Act, though accepting the division of the surface among the 2,229 individuals on their roll, managed to retain tribal ownership of their minerals, a fact that was to loom large in their history when their former reservation became one of the great oil fields of the world.

The Five Civilized Tribes came next. They still owned and governed the reduced Indian Territory, but they were as badly swamped by white immigrants as the western tribes of the land openings. Some of these were legal residents, allowed to settle there under a system that varied from tribe to tribe according to their own laws and their treaties with the United States. Traders licensed by the government and taxed by the tribes built up lively small towns at the railroad stations. The Choctaws and Chickasaws owned extensive coal fields leased to operators by the Indians and worked by imported miners. Some of the wealthy mixed-bloods laid out large farms and employed white "laborers," who were actually lessees. White men married Indian women. But all this immigration was regulated by tribal law and was kept under some control. Much more numerous and troublesome were intruders, who came in defiance of laws and regulations and fastened themselves on the Indians' property. It was estimated in 1879 that there were 12,287 white people living in the Five Tribes area, and the number continued to increase.

For the first fifteen years after the Reconstruction treaties the government made an honest effort to remove the intruders. The process was somewhat complicated. The local tribal officials reported them to the principal chief; the chief reported them to the federal agent; the agent reported them to the Indian Office; the Indian Office reported them to the secretary of the interior; the secretary requested the War Department to act; and the secretary of war relayed an order through army channels down to the commander at Fort Gibson. A detachment of soldiers then reported to the agent, and if he was still in the same mind, they conveyed the intruder to the border and dropped him down on Kansas or Texas soil. Then he turned around and came back, and the whole process had to be repeated. The Indian Office vainly urged Congress to impose an adequate penalty, but a fine was as far as Congress ever went, and there was no way of collecting it. After 1880 the Indian Office ceased to be concerned; the Indians, in fact, suspected that it encouraged the intruders in order to weaken the authority of the tribes.

There was also an unrecorded influx of "state raised" Negroes, who joined the liberated slaves of the Indians and escaped notice. The first federal census, that of 1890, showed a population of 109,393 whites, 18,636 Negroes, and 50,055 Indians. Some of these white and Negro residents were tribal citizens; but even so, the citizens were in the minority, and the tribal laws and courts, even the tribal schools, were restricted to citizens. Intruders laid out farms, built houses, and planted orchards; published newspapers demanding the opening of the country to white settlement; cut and shipped out the valuable walnut and pine timber; brought in cattle and turned them loose on the range—and the Indians could not touch them.

Fundamentally, the Five Tribes population was not large enough to bring their domain into full production. As early as 1876, Commissioner of Indian Affairs J. Q. Smith questioned whether "an extensive area of fertile country is to be allowed to remain . . . an uncultivated waste" and commended "a very general and growing opinion" that "the strict letter of treaties with Indians" should be disregarded. There might have been some justification for this argument—except that it was never applied to land withheld from production for estates and country clubs by wealthy white Americans.

But the Five Tribes held their land under patented titles, and Congress hesitated to invalidate them. When the long-threatened law was finally passed in 1893, it provided only for negotiation by a commission. Henry L. Dawes, just retired from the Senate, served as its first chairman; thus it is generally known as the Dawes Commission. With frequent changes in membership it continued in existence for twelve years. It published annual reports, and its members testified before congressional committees and made speeches throughout the United States. These statements accurately depicted the inconveniences of the white population, but flagrantly misrepresented the condition and sentiments of the Indians and in a high moral tone urged the abolition of their institutions as a deliverance to *them*. Greed, philanthropy, and public opinion were thus united to break down the tribes' defenses. What might have been advocated as a measure of cold-blooded realism was represented as a holy crusade.[6]

As the tribes continued to hold out, Congress prepared for their dissolution. In 1895 it authorized a survey of their land, the next year it directed the Dawes Commission to make rolls of their citizens, and at every session bills to force the change came closer to passage. Finally

---

[6] See Angie Debo, *And Still the Waters Run,* 24–30, for an evaluation of their arguments and a Cherokee report.

some of the leading mixed-bloods saw that only by negotiating a settlement could they avoid a dictated one, and in December, 1896, the first tribe, the Choctaw, consented to treat. The next year Congress undermined the tribes' governmental authority by extending federal law over their citizens and requiring presidential approval of every act of their councils. In 1898 the final blow fell, when Congress passed the Curtis Act (sponsored by Representative Charles Curtis of Kansas) authorizing the allotment of their land, the division of their other property, and the termination of their governments. Only shadowy principal chiefs appointed irregularly by the president remained in after years as their spokesmen. Also under the Curtis Act the Department of the Interior took over their schools and enlarged them into a public school system.

The Dawes Commission then liquidated their estates under this act or negotiated modifications. The allotment began with the Creeks—on April 1, 1899. The principal chief was Isparhecher, a fullblood committed to passive resistance. Through an interpreter he told a newspaper reporter: "The Saviour of Mankind brought peace and good will to the people and set up the golden rule and the Creeks . . . were still hopeful and believed that eternal right would at last prevail. On these lines they . . . expect to continue the fight." After the next election he was succeeded by Pleasant Porter, who had campaigned on a platform of negotiating with the Commission. Seven years later Porter said he was conscious at the time that he was compelled to accept terms "[that I now know] took the lifeblood of my people."

The Cherokee allotment also began under the Curtis Act and was modified later by negotiations. One proposal was labeled, "Plan for preserving in effect the continuity of Tribal Relations of the full blood Indian." It provided that fullbloods might take adjacent allotments within an area approved by the Commission and hold it as a corporation under communal title. This attempt to preserve a small reservation within the former Cherokee territory received no consideration by the federal officials.

The Choctaw decision to negotiate barely carried in the election for principal chief in 1896. A defeated candidate was Jacob B. Jackson, an elderly fullblood educated in the tribal schools and at college in "the States," who had long been active in tribal politics. Now he became a leader in a Mexican or South American emigration plan, which extended to all the tribes and assumed at one time an official character. To the visiting Senate committee in 1906 he presented a paper requesting permission for this party to sell their allotments and purchase land for a colony.

"Surely a race of people, desiring to preserve the integrity of that race, who love it by reason of its traditions and their common ancestors and blood, who are proud of the fact that they belong to it may be permitted to protect themselves, if in no other way by emigration. Our educated people inform us that the white man came to this country to avoid conditions which to him were not as bad as the present conditions are to us. . . . All we ask is that we may be permitted to exercise the same privilege. . . .

"If the Choctaw and Chickasaw people as a whole were willing to lose their racial status, to become . . . white men in fact, we do not oppose the carrying out of their desires; but . . . we believe that the Great Father of all men created the Indian to fill a proper place in this world . . . a right to exist as a race, and that in the protection of that right . . . we are fulfilling the purpose of the Divine Creator of mankind."

The senators received this appeal with ridicule, and it was disregarded by the administration. All five of the tribes eventually entered into negotiations with the Dawes Commission. In deference to their objections no "surplus" was opened to white homesteaders, but about three and one-half million acres of Choctaw-Chickasaw land was sold at auction. During this whole period white people poured in—it was legal now—settling and developing the area as actively, though not as dramatically, as in the land openings to the west. The tribal citizens were granted United States citizenship in 1901 and became citizens of the state when their Indian Territory was joined with the Territory of Oklahoma and admitted to the Union in 1907. A special census taken that year gave the new state a population of 1,414,177 of which 5.3 per cent was Indian. Thus the concept of an Indian state was abandoned forever. First expressed in the Delaware treaty even before American independence was achieved, it had persisted through the years; but whenever it came up for consideration, it had always been joined with measures destructive of Indian nationality.

Theoretically, the Indians were entering a new composite society. Many of the mixed-bloods even became its leaders. They had more experience in public affairs and more intellectual and cultural stability than the rootless white newcomers. They had defended their small republics with all the resources of law and diplomacy; when they failed, they carried their lost loyalties into the larger society. Even to the present day Oklahoma pridefully accepts the achievements of the Five Tribes as its own historic past. At the same time this sentiment obscured the fate of the Indians who failed to make a successful transition.

To the fullbloods the dissolution of their tribal affairs was the end of everything. Their most eloquent spokesman was Chitto Harjo. He lived in a log cabin in the hills along the North Canadian, cultivated five or ten acres of land with a pony, raised cattle and hogs and filled his smokehouse with meat, and sharpened his neighbors' plowshares and beat out silver ornaments on a little forge he had constructed. When he defended the Indian cause before the Senate committee in 1906, "His speech was like a flower that blossomed and bloomed," as the chief of the Euchee town remembered it fifty years later.

Tracing the history of the Indians from Columbus on—"I am going to make a foundation for what I have to say, for, of course, a thing has to have a root before it can grow"—he came to the land losses and difficulties in the East and finally to the removal. "First, it was this and then it was something else that was taken away from me and my people, so we couldn't stay there any more. . . . Then it was the overtures of the Government to my people to leave their land, the home of their fathers, the land that they loved. He said, 'It will be better for you to do as I want, for these old treaties can not be kept any longer.' . . . He said: 'Go away out there to this land toward the setting sun, . . . and I will give you that land forever, and I will protect you and your children in it forever.' That was the agreement and the treaty, and I and my people came out here and we settled on this land, and I carried out these agreements and treaties in all points and violated none." He told how they prospered, how the Civil War shattered their peace, and how they had supported the Union. "I believe that everything wholly and fully came back to me on account of the position I took . . . for the father at Washington conquered in that war, and he promised me that if I was faithful to my treaties I should have them all back again. . . . and today I am living under them and with them. I never agreed to the . . . allotting of my lands. I knew it never would do for my people . . . I don't know what the trouble is now. . . . I think that my lands are all cut up. . . . My treaty said it never would be done unless I wanted it done. . . .

"All that I am begging of you, honorable Senators, is that these ancient agreements and treaties . . . be fulfilled."

"I know that I have not ever wanted our country to be divided," said Osway Porter, a Chickasaw fullblood. "I love this country as I love my mother, for it is my mother. I love it as I love my own father. I love its hills and mountains, and its valleys and trees and rivers, and everything that is in this country."

Indian-like these fullbloods withdrew from the whole process. They read their treaties and found them reassuring; thus, they reasoned, the Dawes Commission had no lawful authority, and the United States would protect them from its illegal acts. They hid from the enrollment parties and refused to select allotments. When members of their tribes were employed to hunt them out and assist in making the selection, they regarded this as the ultimate betrayal; and they indignantly rejected the allotment certificates and land patents. Eufaula Harjo, a Creek, said that "the half-breed Indians . . . would go out and hunt for the names of the full-blood Indians without their consent, and they would take the names down and go and present them before the Dawes Commission. . . . These people would not know anything about it, but they would find a certificate sent to them at the postoffice. . . . The Indian people did not want these certificates, so they gathered up a whole lot of them and brought them to me and I took them to the Indian agent."

The Cherokee irreconcilables threatened bodily harm to any tribal member who would give their names to the enrollment parties, and United States deputy marshals were then sent out to bring them in. Redbird Smith described this experience. "I was at home enjoying myself in peace when . . . I and several other Indians were arrested and taken together to the Muskogee jail for standing up for our rights—my old treaty with the United States Government. . . . On Saturday evening they put me in jail and they kept me all night in jail and on Sunday morning they let me out, and then they took me to the commissioner's office and made me enroll against my will."

The Commission conscientiously tried to include the Indians' little farms in the assigned tracts, but in view of their refusal to co-operate some mistakes occurred. They lived in constant fear of dispossession, not knowing that they were protected by the patent they refused to accept or, failing that, that they owned an allotment somewhere. And surrounding them with hungry eyes upon their land were the onrushing white men. Even at the best, the neat rectangular survey disrupted their simple agriculture and deprived them of the free range for their livestock.

"The full-blood Indian people are pushed out today," said Eufaula

Harjo, "and they have left their homes and taken what they have, and everything, and are camped out in the woods . . . and they don't know what to do or where to go. It is going to be cold weather after a while, and there is the women and the little children and the old people, and we don't know what to do with them or where to get a house to put them in. All the property such as cattle and hogs and horses—it is all gone, and we have not got anything left. We used to have plenty and more than we wanted and now we haven't got anything."

Asked if this was not because they had declined to take their allotments, and that their land had accordingly been allotted to some-one else, he answered, "They have taken it away from us, and they are in the houses that we built and that are ours."

The following colloquy took place between the senators and a Creek fullblood named Samuel Leslie:

"[Leslie]: Another woman got my farm, and she has sold it to a white man, and they have that farm and have been working on it for two years, so I haven't any farm today . . .

"Q. How long did you work that farm?—A. I had that farm and worked it for a good while. It was about fourteen years that I worked it."

Osway Porter, safe, if he had only known it, told of his plight:

"Q. Have you taken your allotment?—A. No, sir.

"Q. Do you live in the same place you have been living on for the past ten or fifteen years?—A. I am still living on the same place now for twenty-four years. . . .

"Q. Have you been interfered with in the possession of that home? —A. I have been under fear all the time about that home.

"Q. Well, why don't you take . . . your allotment and so remove this fear?—A. I believe the old treaty between the United States and the Indians never told me that I must take a piece of ground."

As late as 1912 nearly two thousand members of the Cherokee tribe alone refused to claim their allotments, and although they were living in the most extreme destitution, they refused to accept the per capita payments to which they were entitled in the division of their tribal funds. In 1915, Creeks were still returning checks mailed to them from the agency. Up to that time and for years thereafter a fullblood intertribal organization worked for the restoration of the old order. A letter written by a Creek to the secretary of the interior in 1912 illus-trates their efforts to present their cause to the government officials.

"This is what your all have said In the treaty your have syned in the year of 1832. June 9. This treaty will be life as long as the sun rise and go down. and as long as grass grew. And as long as the sky dont fell to the earth. As long as the water runs. The home of Indians will be there for ever. . . . To-day the sky is still in the air yet. and grass grew yet. and water run yet. . . . But you the man know all this matter. So fill out what I want and answer. I remain hoping to hear in earliest date."

Such anguished, groping protests were being made by Indians on reservation after reservation throughout the United States as their tribal holdings and their native groupings were broken up by the enforcement of the Dawes Act. Their words went unrecorded, but their desperation can be glimpsed even in the cold statistical reports of the Indian Office. In some instances they succeeded in delaying the work by their opposition. Land surveys were begun on the great Sioux reservations in the Dakotas in 1893—less than three years removed from Wounded Knee—but these Indians received unexpected support from the military officer still in control of the Pine Ridge Agency. He reported that 90 per cent of his people opposed allotment because they wanted to hold their land as a stock range, and he agreed. It was worthless for agriculture, he said, and cutting it up for farms would "result in the degradation of this people and their speedy extinction." The real break-up of these reservations occurred in the years following 1903. As late as 1905 the Cheyenne River allotment had to be discontinued because of Sioux objections.

But the work went relentlessly on. In general, the various allotting agents, like the Dawes Commission, were insensitive to the Indians' feelings and indifferent to the ultimate effect on the allottees; and, also like the Dawes Commission, they honestly tried to make an equitable division of the tribes' physical assets. Every year the published reports listed allotments made, land opened to white settlement, Indian opposition brushed off but apparent. Even deserts were not spared; the White River Utes became so outraged when their barren land was divided that they left in a body looking for a home somewhere in South Dakota. A beginning was made to allot even the resisting Hopis; then public sentiment (for once) became so aroused that the attempt was abandoned. Some few allotments were made to other tribes of the Southwest, but, in general, the Indians of that area escaped. Francis E. Leupp, who served as commissioner of Indian affairs from 1904 to 1909, was the first administrator since the allotment started to show concern for its effect on the Indians. Also by that time, the process had begun to slow down because the remaining blocks of Indian land were not attractive to homesteaders. The last reservation to be allotted was that of the Northern Cheyennes during 1930–31 under special legislation enacted in 1926.

Thirty years later the Cheyenne headman, John Wooden Legs, expressed this judgment: "Our Cheyenne land is cattle country. Sensible people knew it would be wrong to take cattle land like ours and divide it up into little pieces—big enough for grazing rabbits, but not cattle."

The breaking up of the reservations was also paralleled by the removal under the law of 1906 of the trust restrictions from the allotments of Indians adjudged competent. Commissioner Leupp proceeded with caution; the test, he thought, was the Indian's demonstrated success in earning his living. Four years later, Leupp's successor began creating competency commissions to work on the allotted reservations and pass on the individual Indians. He believed that making their allotments available for purchase would "so relieve all proper land-hunger in the regions round about that the pressure to open reservations should lose some of its momentum."

Then in 1913, Woodrow Wilson's secretary of the interior, Franklin K. Lane, and Cato Sells, the Texas politician who served as commissioner of Indian affairs, went at the business with a vengeance. Sells hailed it as "the dawn of a new era" and "the beginning of the end of the Indian problem," and Lane's reports regularly listed the statistics of these grants of competence as the measure of his success in advancing the welfare of the Indians. In 1920 a man who had headed competency commissions in several states explained their methods to a committee of the House of Representatives. They made a house-to-house canvass interviewing all the Indians owning restricted land and, disregarding their protests, ran them through the hopper in fifteen minutes to one-half hour for each. He said he considered education desirable but not essential; some of the best cases he had passed were fullbloods who had no education whatever. Asked what became of the Indian after his land was released from trust, he said this was difficult to answer; the Indian service dropped such individuals immediately and had no further contact with them. A total of 9,894 Indians received fee patents from 1906 to 1917; then as Lane's mills began grinding more rapidly, some 20,000 patents were issued in the four years following.

Thus the allotment policy may be traced in Indian Office statistics, on maps, in land records, and in the extension of new white frontiers. The account of what actually happened when a specific tribe was liquidated is the real story, and that will be presented in the next chapter.

CHAPTER SEVENTEEN

WHAT HAPPENED TO THE INDIANS?

Many excellent histories have been written of Indian tribes, but only two studies have ever been made of the liquidation of a tribe and the fate of the separated individuals that once formed it. As it happens, both of these are of Indian Territory tribes, but they are typical case studies of developments throughout the United States. They represent the greatest extremes of Indian advancement: the Kickapoos, truly "formed out of rock" in their adherence to the native ways, and the Five Civilized Tribes, consciously traveling "the white man's road."

First came the allotment of the Kickapoos.[1] The Jerome Commission made three futile attempts to negotiate with them during 1889–90, characterizing them as "the most ignorant and degraded Indians" it had encountered, though "possessed of an animal cunning, and obstinacy in a rare degree." Their small reservation was one of the richest tracts of land in Oklahoma: "simply a magnificent park," said a local newspaper. Something had to give. The method, according to reports subsequently made by an investigator of the Indian Rights Association and a Senate committee, was as follows:

The baffled Jerome Commission employed two of the floating white population of the Indian country to work on the Kickapoos: John T. Hill, who had grazed cattle there, and Joe Whipple, who spoke their language and was trusted by them. With Whipple interpreting, Hill told the Indians that there was money belonging to them in Washington (this, of course, was false); he believed he could get it for them and could also influence the Commission to drop the allotment. They held a council and chose two chiefs to accompany the two

[1] The whole story is told in Gibson, *The Kickapoos*.

316

white men to the capital. Strangely enough, the government paid their expenses.

When they boarded the train at Oklahoma City, they found the members of the Commission in the same car. When they were taken to the office of Secretary of the Interior John W. Noble, they found these same commissioners there. (Noble was credited by a grateful citizenry with opening more Indian reservations to white settlement "than all his predecessors combined.") They were suspicious, but being threatened with bodily harm, they finally signed something—on September 9, 1891. It turned out to be an "agreement" to accept 80-acre allotments and to sell the approximately 200,000-acre "surplus" to the United States at thirty cents an acre. (The Potawatomis and Shawnees, owners of a hilly, scrub-timbered tract across the river from the Kickapoos, had received $1.50 an acre for *their* "surplus.") It purported to carry the signatures of all adult male Kickapoos. Subsequent evidence indicated that many of the names were fabricated and others were of deceased tribesmen—"a palpable forgery" was the characterization of the Indian Rights Association. The "agreement" was submitted to Congress and approved on March 30, 1893. It carried a payment to Hill of $5,172 from the Kickapoos' money—the $64,650 due them for their "surplus" land.

The Kickapoos were worried when their chiefs came back from Washington with vague accounts of what had happened there, but it was not until an allotting agent appeared that they realized its import. They refused to be enrolled, to accept allotments, or to receive the per capita payments from the "sale" of their "surplus." But the survey went on, a roll of 283 names was compiled, and the allotments were made, the agent conscientiously giving them the richest land in the valley. A band of nearly fifty that had been away on a hunt returned too late to be included and departed to live with their kinsmen in Mexico. Finally, some of the more progressive settled on their allotments, but the majority remained in their communal villages.

They refused to vacate the unallotted land, insisting that they had never sold it, and the administration hesitated to use the military to drive them off, while homeseekers gathering around the border chafed at the delay. Finally the reservation was opened at high noon on May 18, 1895, in a stampede that surpassed anything previously seen in Oklahoma land rushes. The *Kansas City Star*, exulting over every addition to its trade territory, predicted that even the name *Kickapoo* would be "dropped from history and the memory of man. . . . Unfit to

317

occupy the soil they were removed as cumberers of the ground. Such is the alternative offered the races of man."

Soon there arrived a Kansas attorney named Martin J. Bentley, who won the confidence of the conservative band so completely that they petitioned Washington for his appointment as their agent. The harassed commissioner of Indian affairs accepted this solution to a problem that he had found insoluble. The results Bentley reported were too good to believe—except that they were believed. The recalcitrants settled on their allotments, fenced the land and put it under cultivation, sent their children to school, and were rapidly acquiring the use of English. The first suspicion came in 1900 when the Indian Office was apprised by the State Department that Bentley and Kickapoo delegations had made trips to Mexico to negotiate with President Díaz for the colonization of the tribe there. The commissioner ordered him to discontinue these activities; he ignored the warning and was dismissed, and replaced by Frank A. Thackery, a career man in the Indian service. Throughout all the years of controversy that followed, Thackery was upheld by his superiors. The Indian administration, having advocated individual ownership of land, felt obligated to protect this title.

Thackery reported that all Bentley's claims of progress were fictitious and that his influence with the Kickapoos rested on his plan to restore them to their old way of life in Mexico. He said that most of their allotments were leased to white farmers under Bentley's management and that their living came from funds appropriated by the government for schools and farm equipment. He charged that Bentley had become the guardian of all their minors, with control over their allotments and per capita payments, and that he controlled the sales of inherited lands and the custody of the proceeds. (As the Kickapoos were citizens of the United States and of the Territory of Oklahoma, their probate matters were under the jurisdiction of the local courts.) All the money received from these sources was supposedly placed in a "tribal pool" to pay the colonizing expenses. At the same time, an inspector sent from the Indian Office reported Bentley's financial records so chaotic that he was unable to check them.

Thackery charged that Bentley's activities were part of a gigantic plot to acquire all the Kickapoo allotments. Eventually, he began to suspect that members of Congress were implicated. Bentley made frequent trips to Washington with Kickapoo delegations, and bills were introduced in Congress to remove the trust status of the allotments so

318

that the tribe could sell them "and return to Mexico and make a fresh start." Other bills would appropriate $215,000 to compensate the Indians for the "injustices" of the Hill agreement. These proposals failed in 1903 and 1904, the bill to free the land was reported favorably in 1905, but the measure enacted on March 3 that year removed the restrictions of only seven designated allotments.

The thriving city of Shawnee, that had sprung into existence when the Sauk and Fox Reservation was opened by a land rush in 1891, touched the Kickapoos' eastern boundary, and now these seven allotments were required for its westward expansion. Affidavits subsequently acquired by Thackery from these seven allottees stated that even before the act was signed, Bentley transported them to Mexico, where they would be beyond the reach of other land buyers; then he obtained warranty deeds from them at prices ranging from $300 to $1,500 in Mexican money. The Shawnee Townsite Company offered him $43,970, $39,000, and down to the lowest, $28,300 for each of the 80-acre tracts.

All went well until one of the allottees returned to Shawnee in the late spring of 1905, found surveyors platting her land, and was told that the townsite company had bought it from Bentley. She went to Thackery and made an affidavit that she had "touched the pen" to approve a lease and had received a down payment of three hundred dollars. The Indian Office then sent Inspector Charles H. Dickson out to investigate. He found only about one hundred of the more progressive Kickapoos remaining in Oklahoma, while more than two hundred had migrated with Bentley's assistance to Mexico.

An educated Shawnee, Thomas Wildcat Alford, was working as a clerk in Thackery's office. Later he told how rumors were deliberately circulated among the Indians to frighten them into emigration. Almost daily, he said, some Kickapoo would come to the office with his fears. "One would say 'he had been informed' that the government was going to take his children away from him and send them to school, and 'make white people out of them.' Some would complain that they had been told that they would have to pay heavy taxes on their land, and if they failed to pay they would be sent to jail. (The civilized mind can hardly conceive the horror that the word 'jail' means to an Indian.) Others had been told that there soon would be a war, when all the Kickapoos would be killed and their land given to the white people. The poor creatures were in a desperate state of unhappiness."[2]

2 Alford, *Civilization*, 187–88.

Dickson traveled to Mexico, where the governor of Coahuila told him that the Kickapoos long resident near Nacimiento were Mexican citizens, thrifty and law-abiding, but that Bentley's recent immigrants were so demoralized that his government had refused them permission to settle with their relatives. Dickson then visited them in a temporary camp in a pasture Bentley had rented near Múzquiz, and found them drunken, hopeless, and hungry.

His report was so damaging that the secretary of the interior transmitted it to Congress with the recommendation that the deeds to the seven allotments be vacated and that no more land be removed from trust status. At the same time, Bentley wrote to Walter Field, who was associated with him in the Kickapoo business, that he was going "to meet Congressman Curtis . . . to get him to help us out." Somebody did help them out. Congress ignored the inspector's report and passed an act at the next session—in early June, 1906—removing the restrictions on all allotments held by nonresident adult Kickapoos. Henry M. Teller, one of the most powerful members of the Senate, made a vigorous defense of Bentley and a strong argument for the measure just before its passage.

About fifteen men in Shawnee and other Oklahoma towns also had their eyes on the allotments and the acts of Congress. To their Kickapoo victims they were known collectively as the "Shawnee Wolves." Although rivals to each other, they composed their differences to work together against Bentley; thus the nonresident provision of the law did not give him the expected monopoly. He had scarcely begun taking deeds at Múzquiz before the "wolf" pack arrived. In the competition between the two parties the Kickapoos were for the first time subjected to physical violence. The *jefe político* had been happily certifying deeds for a substantial fee; now he added the use of his police and jail. The Indians were beaten, pistol-whipped, and jailed by one side or the other to force them to sign the deeds. The *jefe* was susceptible to the last and best bribe, and the Shawnee Wolves finally won his support. Even Bentley was jailed, and they had a clear field. If an Indian could not be forced even by physical abuse to "touch the pen," they used outright forgery. They also gathered up at least six Kickapoo minors, took them to Eagle Pass, Texas, and had them married, thus conferring majority upon them by Oklahoma law and enabling them to sell their allotments.

After they returned to Oklahoma with their deeds, Bentley was released from jail. He collected the Kickapoos, who had fled in fear to the mountains, and settled them in Sonora across the line from Douglas, Arizona. Then he established a trust with himself, his wife, and a business associate to receive their deeds and use the proceeds for the Mexican colonization. They also employed him as their attorney. He had the satisfaction of seeing the Shawnee Wolves exposed and discredited. The Senate passed a resolution, introduced by Teller, to appoint a committee of investigation. Teller served on the committee, as did also Curtis, now in the Senate.

Bentley took a leading part in building up the case against his rivals. Thackery impartially presented evidence against both parties, but his charges against Bentley failed to convince the committee. The published report condemned the Wolves in the strongest possible language and praised and vindicated Bentley. It recommended that the Department of Justice take action to recover the land "from the parties claiming to hold title" except that held by the Bentley trust. It also described the fraud practiced on the Kickapoos in obtaining the allotment agreement.

The next year Congress undertook to right this original wrong by appropriating $215,000 to compensate the tribe for the inadequate price paid for the "surplus land." The provisions of the act were peculiar. The payment was to be made as directed by a council of the surviving allottees and attested by the Federal District Court of Arizona. Thus the council was held at Douglas, twenty miles from Bentley's colony and a quarter of the distance across the United States from the more progressive Kickapoos who had remained in Oklahoma, with no provision for transportation.

Agent Thackery was determined to keep this payment from Bentley's control. He managed to collect enough money from private sources to buy railroad tickets and food for the Oklahoma Kickapoos. (How these contributors expected to get their money back remains unrecorded.) There were 157 living allottees when the council convened on May 16, 1908. Seventy-five still supported Bentley and colonization; 82 trusted their agent. Indian-like they worked out a compromise settlement. Bentley received 12½ per cent of the award, $26,875, for his services as their attorney in securing the appropriation. The remainder was divided numerically: nearly $90,000 belonging to Bentley's followers was turned over to him for the establishment of the colony; the rest was paid out per capita to the Oklahoma party, each allottee receiving $1,200. Nothing could be more eloquent of Indian constancy than the fact that after all the betrayal, abuse, defeat, and destitution of the past seventeen years, almost half of the tribe still rejected a $1,200 payment to pursue a hopeless plan to rebuild their own way of life.

Meanwhile, in late 1907, the Justice Department disregarded the recommendation of the Senate committee and began court action to clear title to *all* the allotments (approximately one hundred) deeded under the 1906 act removing the restrictions. Federal District Attorney John Embry was in charge of the suit. This time *all* the evidence collected by Thackery and Indian Office inspectors was presented. It makes nauseating reading. The government won its case in 1911, and an appeal in 1914. The allotments were cleared, and the defendants found themselves obligated to reimburse innocent purchasers.

As one looks back on the forces at work, it seems remarkable how easily Congress was influenced to act in Bentley's interest. In 1906, when he was in Mexico waiting to take deeds as soon as it should become legal, his agent in Washington sent him this telegram: "Indian bill signed. No change. Attend to matter of checks by wire." One can only speculate about who in Washington received these checks.

Three years later a former Sauk and Fox agent confessed his own implication in Bentley's plans and testified that at a conference with Bentley and Field in late 1905 to discuss the cost of the desired legislation, the two told him "that Teller would have to be taken care of." He also testified regarding the appropriation act authorizing the council in Arizona, that plans were made at the time to organize a trust company to handle the emigration of Kickapoos and other Indians and issue stock "to the several parties interested." The interrogation proceeded as follows:

"Question: Who were the interested parties or supposed to be?

"Answer: Field, Bentley, . . . some of Field's Washington friends and myself.

"Question: How much did Curtis have?

"Answer: Ten thousand I think it was.

"Question: How much did Senator Teller get?

"Answer: I think it was the same."

Teller, sometimes in conjunction with Curtis, used his powerful position in the Senate to bring pressure on the administration. He wrote a peremptory letter to the State Department indicating that Bentley's deeds to Kickapoo land had better be affirmed by the American consul in Mexico. With Curtis' endorsement, he wrote to Embry requesting that proceedings to terminate Bentley's guardianships of

Kickapoo minors be dropped. He wrote to the secretary of the interior attempting to have Thackery removed as Kickapoo agent. But in general the administration stood firm.

Alford, writing in 1936, told how the same emigration plan nearly succeeded in involving the nearby Shawnees, and he alluded very cautiously to the hidden support behind it. "This scheme was sponsored by powerful men whose influence reached to officials of the national government. In fact there were men involved . . . who are so prominent in the country today that were I to mention their names a national scandal would be raised. This I have no intention of doing, but I do intend to file a true account of the affair with the Oklahoma Historical Society because it rightly belongs to the history of the Oklahoma Indians."[3]

It belongs to the history of *all* allotted Indians. It was repeated many times throughout the United States with immaterial differences in names and dates. True, justice for the Kickapoos finally triumphed—in a measure. They received some financial compensation for land they "sold" for a song under a forged "agreement" with an official commission; and the allotments acquired by conspirators under the act of 1906 were recovered. But unreckoned financial losses occurred in routine transactions, and the spiritual damage they suffered is beyond reckoning. The progress they had finally begun in their Indian Territory refuge was swept away.

After the Arizona council, Thackery, in the manner of conscientious Indian agents, encouraged his Kickapoos to use their per capita payments in improving their allotments. Probably his reports, also after the manner of good Indian agents, were too sanguine, but certainly this party was more prosperous than the Mexican band. The land in Sonora turned out to be a rocky desert, and only token improvements were ever made there. The Indians wandered about over Mexico, stopping briefly to visit their kinsmen at Nacimiento, venturing back to Oklahoma to collect lease money from farmers using their recovered allotments, and living largely on the charity of their relatives. Finally disillusioned, they instituted proceedings against Bentley for the $90,000, but it had disappeared. It was not until the late 1920s that an appreciable number of them settled in Oklahoma.

They gathered in villages in the area of their former reservation, following their own customs, understandably distrustful of the white

---

[3] Alford did write this account, but his family has never released it to the Historical Society.

man and all his ways. They now number about 450. They still own a few allotments; none of them ever adopted the white man's farm pattern, but they value their land and refuse to part with it. As property owners they are ineligible for old-age assistance and other relief, preferring to live in destitution, although some of their 80-acre tracts would easily sell for $25,000 each. It is only in the 1960s that signs of progress similar to that first tentative beginning halted more than three-quarters of a century ago are once more visible in the tribe.

If the assets of one small reservation could spawn a conspiracy that would reach from Oklahoma to Mexico to Washington, the liquidation of the Five Tribes holdings offered a spoliation many times magnified. These landed estates totaled nineteen and one-half million acres, half of present Oklahoma, an area almost as large as Indiana, with rich valleys, extensive pine forests, producing coal fields, and un-tapped oil pools of incalculable value. No other exploiters of Indian property in the history of the United States had ever been offered so rich a prize.[4] The pickings were too plentiful and too widespread to be gathered up in a few hands like the snug little scheme to dispossess the Kickapoos. Even the fullblood emigration plan was too diffuse for manipulation.

The Dawes rolls totaled 101,506 names of men, women, and children.[5] Of these, approximately 26½ per cent were classed as full-bloods, 48 per cent as mixed-bloods, including many fullblood Indians of mixed tribal descent, 23 per cent as Negroes, and 2½ per cent as intermarried whites. The allotments ran from 110 acres of average land for the Cherokees to 320 acres for the Choctaws and Chickasaws (the actual acreage varying according to quality). A stated amount—forty acres of average land in most of the tribes—was designated as a homestead, inalienable and nontaxable for an extended period. The rest of the allotment was designated as "surplus," and could be sold by the allottee after a short time—a substitute for the usual practice of opening the "surplus" of a reservation to white homesteaders. Also, as the allottees died off, the inherited land became alienable.

It was immediately apparent that even these advanced Indians, who had supported themselves thriftily and governed themselves well, had no concept of the written instruments—deeds, mortgages, leases, powers of attorney—that regulated the white man's land trans-

---

[4] The whole account is found in Debo, *And Still the Waters Run.*
[5] This number is much larger than the population; the names of newborn babies were added from time to time as the allotment proceeded.

actions. Theoretically, as United States citizens they had access to the courts, but the entire legal system of eastern Oklahoma was warped to strip them of their property. The term *grafter* was universally applied to dealers in Indian land and was frankly accepted by them. For a generation they monopolized the best land, holding large tracts and leasing it to tenant farmers, who were as helpless as the Indians to break the system.

Their first opportunity came in assisting the Indians to select their allotments. The Choctaw government, in particular, tried to protect its citizens. Before the allotment began, their council attempted to create a commission to visit every settlement with maps, plats, and field notes to assist in the selections; but this act was vetoed by President Roosevelt upon the advice of Acting Inspector J. W. Zevely. Subsequent appeals from the tribal governments were disregarded. Whether or not it was so intended, this policy in effect delivered the Indians to the grafters.

The land offices of the Dawes Commission were perhaps ninety or more miles from the Indians' settlements, and of course they were entirely unfamiliar with the white man's numerical descriptions used in identifying land. The Commission attempted to safeguard each Indian's little farm in the hills as his homestead and to give him his share of choice valley or prairie land as his "surplus." Enterprising scouts gathered up the fullbloods, brought them in, and sold them to the highest bidders among the grafters at ten, twenty-five, or even thirty dollars a head. The grafters then assisted them in making their selections and directed them to sign another paper, which always turned out to be a lease of their "surplus" and usually carried an illegal contract to sell it as soon as it should become alienable. The Indian received perhaps five dollars, perhaps a small rental, and returned to his distant home. The grafters also added to their holdings the "surplus" of the recalcitrants who refused to accept allotments; there was nobody to contest their possession.

Allottees who made their selections without the assistance of grafters were also induced to sign leases carrying sales contracts. Robert L. Owen, who was to enter the Senate at statehood, was an extensive dealer in the rich valley land of Cherokee and Creek allottees. One of his leases to an eighty-acre tract signed by mark by a Creek allottee in 1901 carried a cash payment of $50; and the lessor agreed to deliver a warranty deed for an additional $110, and "hereby contracts and agrees" that default would bring a penalty of $500. Another of his leases, dated December 18, 1901, would run for ninety-nine years and the entire rental was discounted as follows: $10 had been paid November 29, $30 was paid when the lease was made, and $320 would be paid upon the execution of a deed. The lessee might make improvements, which would become the property of the allottee upon the expiration of the lease (in the year 2000). Many thousands of such conveyances were made by land dealers throughout the Five Tribes area. The holders argued that an allottee could sell his equity in restricted land regardless of laws to the contrary.

The most revolting form of grafting was the plundering of children through professional guardians appointed by the probate courts. At first these guardians specialized in orphans; then when it became apparent that parents could not qualify through the legal formalities, their children also became the victims. The grafter reckoned his property by the guardianships he owned. He used up the rental from the agricultural land, or he chose allotments for his wards in the pine belt and sold off the timber.

The grafters also found ways of having restrictions removed from land they controlled. An allottee could apply to the agency and establish his competence to manage his land, but many applications were made without the knowledge of the Indian by dealers who held sales contracts or merchants who had extended extravagant credit. Another method was to have the restrictions removed by special acts of Congress by slipping the Indians' names into the Indian Appropriation Bill. A study of the individual victims named in this act in 1906 shows shocking spoliation in every instance. Some of them had given powers of attorney to a merchant to whom they owed money; then as soon as the bill was enacted, he gave deeds to a fellow conspirator. In another case a guardian sold his ward's valuable oil land without the knowledge of the child's father.

But even with the best efforts of the grafter to circumvent them, the restrictions on allotted land retarded "the development of the country," and the entire citizenship, except for the unrecorded voice of the Indians, demanded their removal. In 1908, in the session of Congress following Oklahoma statehood, they were removed from most of the land, but retained on the homesteads of half-blood and up to three-fourths-blood Indians, and extended on the entire allotments of three-fourths-bloods on up. The Dawes rolls were followed; thus, for example, a Creek citizen of one-fourth Creek and three-fourths Seminole blood would be classed as a quarter-blood. The government undertook to clear illegal conveyances from the land that remained restricted—litigation that lasted many years.

Virtually all the Negroes' released land went to the grafters: the adults' allotments through unconscionable contracts and fraudulent deeds, or forgery if necessary; the children's by guardians' sales. These Negroes had been especially favored during the allotment period, receiving land beyond the stipulations of the Reconstruction treaties. Giving it to them and then taking it away was simply a method of cutting down the Indians' holdings.

With the land status somewhat stabilized, the guardianship business became the most profitable form of grafting. Sixty thousand minors came under the jurisdiction of the courts of the Five Tribes area. The agricultural value of their estates totaled about $130,000,000, with an estimated oil value of $25,000,000, which continued to increase. About 70 per cent of their land was released by the act of 1908, and there were besides the inherited estates of deceased allottees. All this could be sold. The rest could be exploited. Then about 1913 it was discovered that oil-rich adults needed guardians, and they were brought into the probate courts and declared incompetent. The proportion of allottees owning oil land was very small, but a few had wealth past imagining. Oil leasing, unlike agricultural leasing, had been placed by the laws and agreements under Indian Bureau supervision. Thus the agency made the oil leases and collected the royalty. It retained some of the Indian's accumulated wealth, but it had no choice but to turn over whatever was required for the supposed needs of the Indian by the court-appointed guardian. As the children grew up, the guardianship business became concentrated on these oil-rich adults.

Some of the probate judges were in collusion with the guardians. A larger number built up political machines by the distribution of guardianships. Some were simply swamped by the magnitude of the task. A few worked desperately to protect the minor allottees. Some of them were defeated for re-election; one, it is pleasant to record, had a later distinguished career as a federal judge. A few guardians also carried out their responsibilities with integrity, but that was exceptional. The Lewis case, selected at random, is typical of the system.

John Lewis was a fullblood Creek of good character who lived quietly and frugally with his family in an Indian settlement. Then early in 1924 oil began to spout from his allotment and his income rose to $24,000 a month. His estate was uncomplicated and his royalty was quietly accumulating at the agency. He went there in August that year to arrange for the education of his minor son and was killed in an automobile accident. His heirs were his wife to whom he had been married for more than thirty years, an adult son, an adult daughter, the minor son, and a minor grandchild.

His minor heirs, of course, automatically became wards of the court with court-appointed guardians. Five days after his death, a petition was filed to declare the three adults incompetent. While it was pending, a firm of county-seat lawyers secured a contract carrying a 50 per cent contingent fee with a Creek woman ready to claim she had lived with Lewis before his marriage to Mrs. Lewis and was therefore his legal wife; and this contract was approved by the judge. Apparently she had no case, for she was still living with the man enrolled as her husband by the Dawes Commission, and two of their children had been placed on the rolls as the issue of this marriage; but the Lewis heirs became alarmed and employed another lawyer upon a 25 per cent contingent fee to defeat the scheme. The judge approved this contract also. Then he declared the adult Lewis heirs incompetent and appointed two guardians for each.

Thus there were eight guardians for the family. If each followed the usual practice of employing an attorney, there were sixteen persons authorized to draw fees from the estate, besides the attorney with the 25 per cent contract also authorized by the court to quiet title. Then the family in desperation employed another attorney to rid them of the guardians. All these complications arose within two months and five days from the time of John Lewis' death. This was only the beginning. It would serve no purpose to follow the case through its dreary ramifications in the years that followed. In this same county during the preceding two years, thirty adult Indians had been declared incompetent. Any one of the thirty had a story matching that of the Lewis family. This region in which a number of fullbloods had been allotted, had become one of the important oil fields of Oklahoma.

Any attempt to change the system brought concerted opposition from the state's congressional delegation. The abuses began to taper off in the 1930s with the shrinkage of Indian property. By the end of that decade there was little left to excite the cupidity of the despoilers or to exert public support for their activities.

During the entire period the agency (later titles were superintendency and area office) conducted its limited administration over the allottees' affairs with surprising integrity but no effective guidance. In tribal days a Union agent and a clerk or two conducted what was mainly a diplomatic relationship with five autonomous governments; with thousands of bewildered individuals stripped of tribal coherence, now it required a large number of Indian Service employees to give them even minimum protection. Virtually all the agency effort was concentrated on supervising restricted property. Here extreme caution was required; the superintendent was a spoils appointee and so were most of his employees, vulnerable to the dominant local sentiment.

One agency policy popular in Oklahoma was the conditional removal of restrictions: after an examination of each individual case, advertising and selling (always at a fair price) a portion of the allotment, and using the proceeds to improve the remainder. It was supposed to contribute to the Indians' welfare more than the ownership of unused land, but obviously it brought no solution to a complex social problem. Then during the Lane regime the attrition of the Indians' holdings was speeded up by the competency commissions, which freed all the land of hundreds of fullbloods, and by a blanket order which cleared the restrictions remaining on the homesteads of adult half-bloods.

In the statistics of land transactions nobody wondered about what happened to the Indians involved. They withdrew farther into the hills and timber, living in poverty and moral deterioration. The agency maintained contact only with those still owning restricted land. The number in 1926 was 11,386. A whole generation born too late to receive allotments was growing up in illiteracy and squalor with no land and no tribal relations. Even their names were unknown to the Indian service. They squatted on the allotments of friends or relatives, or they settled on their church grounds, using the camp houses they had built in happier days for their week-long services.

The act of 1908 had set 1931 as the date for the expiration of the remaining restrictions. As this time approached, Congress extended it to 1956. Oklahoma objections were vociferous, but no longer unanimous. The Indians pleaded vainly for the inclusion of land inherited by the unallotted generation. In 1930 a Cherokee came from the hills to speak for his community to a visiting Senate committee:

"We have some of these old folks who have restricted lands, and they leave it up to me to say this. . . . The old folks are going to die pretty soon. . . . We are thinking. I have talked it over and over. Just leave the restrictions on it and not let anybody, the State or anyone else, take the restrictions off the land. . . . We have not very much land left now. If we keep on selling it piece by piece, after a while the

Indians will not have any land in this country, not one piece left. Now what are we going to do? Are we going to be turned out like hogs or something like that? . . . If we do not have but one acre, we could live there till we starved to death or just die."

He was not speaking figuratively. In that year of general depression and a drought in the hill country the Indians were living on one or two meals a day of a native gruel made of ground parched corn, and only the disaster program of the Red Cross kept them from starving to death during the following winter, when an average of more than three thousand families received weekly assistance.

By this time the calamitous results of the whole liquidation policy were coming into general notice. When the year 1956 approached, it was the Oklahoma congressional delegation that sponsored legislation extending the restrictions for the lifetime of the original allottees. Thus 316,902 acres of restricted land remain of the 19,500,000 acres belonging to the Five Tribes in 1898.[6] The last deadline for the enrollment of "newborns" was March 4, 1906; thus the youngest allottees are now sixty-four years old. What will become of the Indians squatting on these crumbling fragments of their former holdings is a human problem that transcends statistics.

Meanwhile, the long agony of the Kickapoos and of the Five Tribes was being duplicated on reservations throughout the United States, but only a few glimpses appear. There were the Sisseton and Wahpeton Sioux, first subjects of the Dawes Act in 1887, losing two thirds of their allotted land by 1909 through its removal from trust status and sale to whites. How was this accomplished? And what happened to the Indians in the process? Said a tribal member in 1946: "Our young people get married and have no place to go . . . and so, supposing a certain relative was making his way pretty well . . . they go and double themselves up until the old man is finally broke." There was the spoliation of the White Earth Reservation in Minnesota with its rich timber, and a congressional delegation adept at slipping provisions favoring the lumber companies into the Indian appropriation bills. It erupted into a national scandal through the courage of Warren K. Moorehead of the Board of Indian Commissioners, but what it did to the Indians has never been recorded. And what is the real story of the White River Utes, who struck out across the country searching vainly for an asylum?

[6] About 305,786 acres of inherited land, now unrestricted, is still in the possession of the heirs.

330

It can be shown statistically that Indian holdings declined from 138,000,000 acres in 1887 to 47,000,000 in 1934. But these figures are misleading, for not all reservations were allotted; the huge desert holdings of the Navahos were even increased during the same period. A more accurate indication of what was happening is the shrinkage of Five Tribes holdings from 19,500,000 to slightly more than 1,500,000 acres by 1934 (and most of that worthless, twenty acres of cut-over timber required to support one cow).

Looking back in 1948, the Indian Task Force of the Hoover Commission[7] made this evaluation: "The practice of allotting land and issuing fee patents obviously did not make the Indians 'competent'. It proved to be chiefly a way of getting Indian land into non-Indian ownership." And elsewhere it stated: "The rationalization behind this policy is so obviously false that it could not have prevailed for so long a time if not supported by the avid demands of others for Indian lands. This was a way of getting them, usually at bargain prices."

But the Indian spirit is strong. Speaking out of the anguish of his people in 1906, Pleasant Porter expressed it thus: "There is enough of the Indian in me to take what is coming without repining . . . and sometimes I can see through this cloud that obscures us—this semi-darkness which covers the whole land the dawn of a better hope and a better time." He did not live to realize it, but in the late 1920s a movement began that was to lead to the greatest reform in the history of Indian policy.

[7] Officially "The Commission on the Organization of the Executive Branch of the Government," created by act of Congress July 7, 1947, and headed by former President Hoover. The report of the Indian Task Force was not printed, and apparently it had little influence.

CHAPTER EIGHTEEN

THE WHITE MAN REPENTS

After more than a generation of destruction of the Indian spirit by forced acculturalization and exploitation of the Indian property by throwing it also into the melting pot, it began to dawn on some of the good people who had urged the allotment policy that perhaps the Indians were not exactly prospering under it. Also by this time, the Indian holdings has indeed melted away to the place where despoiling them was ceasing to be big business dominating the economic and political life of the states involved.

It should be pointed out that good or bad Indian administration is not the monopoly of either Democrats or Republicans. The two-party system of the United States rests on other issues. Neither is it entirely dependent on the good will and statesmanship of the president. Some of the greatest presidents, notably Abraham Lincoln and Woodrow Wilson, were so engrossed in other problems that they were unaware of what their secretary of the interior and their commissioner of Indian affairs were doing to the Indians. It is true, however, that presidents of Western sympathy, like Andrew Jackson and Theodore Roosevelt, who took a personal interest in Indian affairs and even cultivated a boyish romantic friendship with chiefs, consistently directed an anti-Indian policy. But the frontier spirit had lost its influence; the Indian wars were past, and the Indians no longer aroused antagonism as obstacles in the march of destiny.

Thus the reform that reversed the forces unleashed by the Dawes Act was nonpartisan and objective. It began in the Republican Coolidge administration (1923–29), was accelerated under the Republican Hoover (1929–33), and reached its culmination under the Democratic

New Dealer Franklin D. Roosevelt (beginning in 1933). It began, logically enough, by attempts to find out how the Indians were faring under the system forced upon them with such uncritical unanimity.

Some members of the Board of Indian Commissioners were the first to weaken. As monstrous abuses appeared in the Five Tribes area, the White Earth Reservation, and other places, they made earnest efforts to publicize and correct them. Now they began tentatively to question the policy itself. In 1921 they sent to eighty-seven Indian service employees questionnaires regarding Indians whose land had been released from trusteeship by the competency commissions. After studying the answers the Board concluded that the policy which had been followed "seems to be a short cut to the separation of freed Indians from their land and cash."

Thus it was becoming apparent that "setting the Indians free" was in effect throwing them to the wolves. Nobody knew this better than the members of Congress from Oklahoma. In the field of general Indian administration, Charles D. Carter and W. W. Hastings, able members of the House, both of Indian descent, warned of the danger of placing the property of minors and incompetent adults under state courts and argued for departmental supervision. The demands of their constituents were too powerful for them to support this policy for the Five Tribes, but they worked for legislation to curb the unholy power of the Osage guardians, which was localized in one Oklahoma county.

Since all Osage allottees shared in the undivided oil wealth, virtually the entire income of the tribe was plundered there. It added up to about twenty million dollars a year. Even murder was systematically employed to channel the inheritance of the headrights into the conspirators' hands—twenty-four unsolved cases, including shooting, poisoning, and blowing up a house with nitroglycerine, in three years beginning with 1921—and the Indians lived in terror of the next strike. Finally, in 1925, Congress gave the Osage Agency joint supervision with the county court in the appointment and the expenditures of guardians. This action ended the racket. It was as easy as that. No scandal has ever touched the Agency.

But government supervision of the Indians' property was destructive of their initiative. It was not yet apparent to their well-wishers that their dilemma—subservience to the benevolent despotism of the Indian Bureau or helpless subjection to the exploiters—arose from the loss of their own institutions. The Hoover Commission Task Force, with the wisdom of hindsight, expressed it this way in 1948: "The destruction

333

of Indian tribal government, the liquidation of tribal organization and tribal property, and the hostility to all Indian ways and culture that characterized so much of Government policy now appears to have been a mistake."

Pleasant Porter could have told them in 1903, but nobody listened: "There is that sense of right and wrong which will bind men together and preserve the peace and maintain virtue and provide for offense without. That is the institution out of which a nation grows ... but you rub that out, you transplant them into what they have no knowledge of," and the end is "dissolution, not growth."

The tribes still intact were saved by a hair in the early 1920s. By that time the reservations that could be conveniently divided into farm-sized tracts had been liquidated. It required a new policy to dispose of the ones remaining. Early in the Harding administration Secretary Fall sponsored the so-called Omnibus Bill for paying the Indians the cash value of all their remaining assets and quitclaiming all further government responsibility. It passed the House and was favorably reported by the Indian Affairs Committee of the Senate. Then Indian leaders enlisted the support of the aged Robert M. La Follette, champion of unpopular causes, and he managed to kill it on the Senate floor. The defeat saved the Indians of the Southwest and the owners of rich forests—notably the Klamaths of Oregon and the Menominees of Wisconsin—from being swept off their land and subjected to a new orgy of plunder.

At the same time, another method was attempted to dispossess the Pueblos. These tribal city-states, old before Columbus, held their land under grants from the Spanish crown confirmed by the United States. But for many years hordes of non-Indians, mainly Spanish speaking and influential in New Mexican politics, had encroached on their property, in some cases acquiring 90 per cent of the pueblo's irrigated land. In 1922, Senator Holm O. Bursum of New Mexico, with the blessing of Secretary Fall and the acquiescence of the commissioner of Indian affairs, introduced a bill recognizing the rights of these squatters. It slid smoothly through the Senate, unknown to the Pueblos and unnoticed by the public.

Then the Pueblos learned about the threatened legislation. They began to hold meetings, analyzing its provisions in English, Spanish, and their own diverse languages. "We must unite as we did once before," said one of the leaders, referring back to 1680. In November, 123 headmen, representing the 8,000 people of the 19 pueblos, met at

Santo Domingo; in a timber-beamed, whitewashed room hung with strings of red pepper, dried meat, and red, blue, and yellow ears of corn—the age-old family dwelling—they organized the first united action in 242 years. "The time has come when we must live or die," they said. They drew up a memorial to the American people and chose 17 leaders to present their cause.

Their appeal to the public conscience was successful. Ethnologists, writers, and artists of Taos and Santa Fe and the influential newspaper the *New Mexican* rallied to their support. The General Federation of Women's Clubs was enlisted. Several pro-Indian organizations were formed, forerunners of the Association on American Indian Affairs. The Bursum Bill was snowed under by this avalanche of protest. Then in 1924, in the reaction following the scandals involving the Harding administration and Secretary Fall, Congress authorized the establishment of a Pueblo Lands Board to pass on ownership. As usual, the squatters retained some of their holdings, but the pueblos were compensated for the land they lost, a total of $1,300,000.

All this contributed to the mounting public interest in the welfare of the Indians. In 1924 a relatively inexpensive reform was effected by blanket legislation extending United States citizenship to all of them who had not already received it. In the First World War, whether citizens or noncitizens, they had enlisted so eagerly and had so distinguished themselves that this legislation seemed a fair recognition. There had been a time when they had resisted citizenship as a device to break down their own nationality. Senator Owen of Oklahoma, in defending his land dealings, said that it was he who induced Congress to grant citizenship to the Indians of the Five Civilized Tribes in 1901 and that the sole purpose of the measure was to end the government's supervision over restricted land. In this he and other land dealers were confusing the freedom of the individual and his unrestricted management of his private property with the terms under which he holds land and other property coming to him from the tribe.

The distinction was clarified in 1911 by the Supreme Court in the Marchie Tiger case involving a Creek allottee. Said the Court, "There is nothing in citizenship incompatible with this guardianship over the Indian lands." Thus there is no restricted Indian,[1] but only restricted property. In general, the Indians value their citizenship as do other

---

[1] The expression is used in common speech as a convenient designation of Indians owning restricted land. Regrettably, I used it in *And Still the Waters Run*, not realizing that it is subject to misinterpretation.

Americans. A few deny it, notably the still-proud remnants of the Iroquois Confederacy in New York.

Another significant step was taken in 1926 when Secretary of the Interior Hubert Work invited the Institute for Government Research (the Brookings Institution) to make a thorough social and economic survey of Indians throughout the United States. This nongovernmental agency, with $125,000 in privately supplied funds, appointed a capable staff headed by Lewis Meriam which spent seven months visiting Indian reservations and settlements and government agencies, hospitals, and schools. Its 872-page report published in 1928 was a shocking revelation.

For forty years, as tribe after tribe was liquidated and thousands upon thousands of individuals entered, in theory, the general pattern of white life and culture, it had all been reported in terms of "progress." Now for the first time deplorable conditions of poverty, disease, lack of social and economic adjustment, suffering, and discontent were uncovered, and the allotment policy was cited as the main cause. "The strength of the ancient system of communal ownership was not realized" was the conclusion.

The survey found the Indian service exclusively occupied with property matters growing out of the new tenure, to the neglect of field work and vocational guidance. It found little to commend in the education of the children. The boarding schools were inadequately financed and badly administered; also, the "policy of removing Indian children from the homes . . . interferes with normally developing family life." No attempt was made at placement of the returned student; thus "in many instances the child returns to his home poorly adjusted to conditions that confront him." Henry Roe Cloud, a Winnebago member of the staff, often quoted Benjamin Franklin: "It is hard to make an empty sack stand upright."

Also in 1928, the Senate launched a full-scale investigation of Indian matters. Its committee traveled to every part of the Indian country over a period of years and published its findings in many volumes. Its visit to the Five Tribes in 1930 was typical of the general pattern. It went out to remote fullblood settlements listening to the Indians, inspected the boarding schools, observed the work of the superintendency, explored the ramifications of the hideous guardianship system (the congressional gift to the state), and held open hearings throughout the area, receiving testimony from all classes of people. Congressional committees as well as the Dawes Commission had made many so-called investigations of the Five Tribes Indians from 1893 on, but it can be stated categorically that this was the first sincere attempt in all the thirty-seven years to find out anything about them.

The debates in Congress during this period show the same aroused concern. There were frequent references to the Meriam study and impatience to know its findings. Even before its publication, Congress, at the request of the Department of the Interior, passed a law in 1927 authorizing the cancellation of fee simple patents issued to Indians without their consent before the expiration of the restrictions on their allotments. The work of the competency commissions had already been discontinued administratively.

When Hoover became president, he ignored the usual political considerations and appointed Charles J. Rhoads, the president of the Indian Rights Association, as commissioner of Indian affairs and Joseph Henry Scattergood as assistant commissioner. Both men were Quaker bankers and philanthropists of Philadelphia, and both had been active in reconstruction work in France. They began at once to improve the Indian service by the appointment of qualified persons.

Dr. W. Carson Ryan, a distinguished educator who had served on the Meriam staff, was placed in charge of the schools. With better congressional appropriations he improved the physical conditions, and he employed competent teachers, applied modern educational principles, and emphasized the value of Indian culture. So far as terrain and transportation would permit, he substituted day schools, with the children living at home, in place of the distant boarding schools and arranged for the attendance of as many children as possible in the public schools.

In 1930 the Extension Service was established, and persons professionally trained in agriculture, home economics, and social casework went out into the field where the Indians lived. Because of the general depression there was not much they could do at the time, but the need for trained personnel was apparent. Previously, a "farmer" in the Indian service was a man who knew how to drive a team of mules but was usually kept at a desk at the agency.

Directing all the work from the central office were highly qualified specialists in their respective fields. Besides these administrative reforms the Bureau issued important policy statements advocating an effective economic base for Indian communities—describing the ruin wrought by breaking up such units and recommending laws to legalize tribal organization. But ironically, following the bureaucratic tendency

337

to continue routine procedures, the Northern Cheyenne allotment was carried out as planned during this enlightened administration.

Further publicity was given to the reform movement in 1932 when most of the Protestant churches through their local women's societies united in the use of a study book on Indians prepared by the interdenominational agency that was the forerunner of the Joint Commission on Missionary Education of the National Council of Churches. Almost three fourths of this text was written by Lewis Meriam, and he brought all the findings of the recent survey to bear upon the problems of the Indians. Although it was published in an election year, he appraised in a factual, specific, and purely nonpartisan manner the great reforms that had already been effected.

Even before Franklin D. Roosevelt took office, he received a petition signed by more than six hundred of the country's leading churchmen, educators, editors, and other civic-minded citizens calling for a complete reversal of the old policy. They received it when John Collier was appointed as commissioner of Indian affairs. Aggressive, fearless, dedicated, he had been for eleven years in the forefront of the fight for the Pueblos, and he was the first commissioner who approached his task from the point of view of the ethnologist and social scientist. He received unwavering support from President Roosevelt and Secretary of the Interior Harold L. Ickes.

The freeing of allotted land from trust status, already slowed down, was stopped completely except in cases of emergency, as was also the sale of inherited land. (This last did not apply to the Five Tribes, whose inherited land came under the local probate courts.) Then in 1934 under Collier's leadership Congress passed the Indian Reorganization Act.

This act prohibited further allotment of land still held under tribal tenure, extended the trust period on restricted allotments until further legislation by Congress, and authorized the appropriation of two million dollars a year for the acquisition of land for Indians. It permitted the organization of tribal governments with control over tribal funds and the expenditures of the Indian service and of tribal corporations for the management of communal property. It authorized a ten-million-dollar revolving loan fund for the use of tribes and individual Indians. It exempted qualified Indians from general civil service competition in appointment to positions under the Indian Bureau.

The law did not apply except in minor particulars to Alaska or Oklahoma. In 1936, Congress extended its essential provisions to

338

Alaska and passed the Oklahoma Indian Welfare Act, an adaptation of its principles to the tribeless Indians of that state, permitting them to organize as corporations and form co-operatives and authorizing a special revolving loan fund of two million dollars for them.

Collier also tried "to break down," as he expressed it, "the monopoly of the Indian Bureau" in services to the Indians. He enlisted the Public Health Service (eventually, in 1954, Congress gave this agency sole responsibility for Indian health) and worked closely with the Department of Agriculture. He sponsored the measure known as the Johnson-O'Malley Act passed by Congress in 1934 authorizing the Indian Bureau to enter into contracts with state and local agencies to carry on various services. The first contracts were made with state departments of education for public school attendance of Indian children. Boarding school enrollment, declining throughout the Rhoads-Scattergood era, was reduced more drastically—from 22,000 to 14,000 during the first two years.

In all these educational, economic, and administrative reforms, Collier—himself an almost fanatical admirer of the Indian spirit[2]—used all the resources of his office to promote pride in what he called "Indianhood." The Bureau enlisted ethnologists and historians to produce texts on Indian history and achievements for use in its schools. For tribes unacquainted with English it even prepared bilingual readers, finding them not only a means of communication but a distinct help in teaching English. Especially with the Navahos, of whom not more than 10 per cent spoke English, linguistic experts reduced the language to writing. Crafts were encouraged and assistance was provided in marketing the products. Studies and publications outside the Bureau were welcomed.[3]

Collier also insisted that the Indians were entitled to the American guarantees of religious freedom: boarding school children were no longer required to attend Christian services, and on the reservations the native religious observances, once forbidden, were freely tolerated.

[2] This is most readily observed in his book *Indians of the Americas*.

[3] I know this from personal experience. When I began to investigate the liquidation of the Five Tribes simply as a historical study, I had never met Collier and was completely uninformed about Indian policy or the effect of allotment. He furnished me a letter that opened every file from Oklahoma to Washington, but not the slightest attempt was ever made by Indian service personnel to influence my judgment. Nobody from Collier down was even aware of my conclusions, until my findings were published in *And Still the Waters Run* under independent auspices six years later.

339

He also influenced Congress to discontinue an appropriation to suppress traffic in peyote. This hallucinatory "button," produced by a small cactus growing in northern Mexico, had long been used by the Indians of that region. It is not habit forming and does not incite to violence, but when taken under harmonious auspices, it produces beatific visions and a sense of religious rapport. In the 1880s the cult was brought—by Quanah Parker, it is said—to the defeated buffalo hunters cooped up in the Indian Territory, and it spread rapidly throughout the Plains tribes. It developed distinctive ceremonials with sacramental eating of the drug in all-night services with some borrowed Christian features. Like the "prophet" cults that preceded it, it is a nativist movement binding Indians together in a sense of racial solidarity, and its appeal is to the baffled and hopeless. Now, it also was accorded constitutional protection.

The reform policy aroused bitter opposition. Some missionary organizations—not all, but some—resented the religious toleration. Theorists of the Dawes days saw their cherished principles discarded, a return to the "degrading tribalism" they had thought to abolish. Exploiters, finding their business destroyed, were still able to enlist politicians, corrupt the press, and appeal to public sentiment. Superpatriots even detected the hidden hand of Red Russia behind the policy, and Collier had to defend himself before the House Indian Affairs Committee against charges of atheism, Communism, and sedition.

More serious was what Oliver La Farge once called "cotton wool resistance," the capacity of insensitive, dictatorial Indian Bureau employees, secure in their civil service tenure, to lie low until a reform dies down. There was also the lag between policy and performance due to bureaucratic inertia. For example, as late as 1949 under one especially enlightened area administration, the education office had 1,637 children's books and 330 books on teaching practice, but not one of the many excellent books about the tribes it served. Even so, the reforms gradually trickled down to the grass roots where the Indians lived.

Bureau employees began very soon to assist the Indians in forming the constitutions for the self-governing tribal societies encouraged to function under the Reorganization Act. Altogether, ninety-five tribes adopted constitutions, and about seventy-four formed corporations for conducting their business. Some relatively undisturbed tribes continued to manage their affairs under their ancient customs. Said one of the Pueblo leaders, "If we had a written constitution and laws, we'd always have to look up what we could do and then maybe ask a lawyer half the time." It was, of course, impossible for completely pulverized tribes like the Five Tribes of Oklahoma to collect their scattered fragments.

The success of these self-governing groups has been uneven. In general, the ones that function best are those with their tribal holdings intact. None ever achieved the economic autonomy, the independence of Bureau control, that Collier envisioned. But in 1948 the Hoover Commission Task Force found their progress "encouraging"—"The dividends from this investment in self-government are just beginning to come in." The beginning years were the hardest—the stumbling, learning years. The San Carlos Apaches made a marked success in ranching, but Clarence Wesley, the chairman of their tribal council, said in 1953, "Twenty years under I. R. A. at San Carlos is actually seven years old."

The strength of the movement was what Commissioner Collier referred to as "the continued survival, through all historical change and disaster, of the Indian tribal group." Answering the objection of white Americans to "tribalism," he said that, ignoring all other phases of this community organization, "At the minimum, the tribe is a legally recognized holding corporation—a holder of property and a holder of tangible rights granted by treaty or statute." He thought some tribes might "remain cohesive social units for a very long time; others will more or less rapidly diffuse themselves among the rest of the population. It is not our policy to force this issue."

The landed property, which became the basis of this collective economy, grew instead of shrinking. Congress never appropriated the full amount authorized for land purchase by the Reorganization Act, but it did make annual appropriations until 1941—a total of $5,500,000 for 400,000 acres of land. In addition, 875,000 acres were added to reservations by special legislation; more than 1,000,000 acres of public domain grazing land was turned over for Indian use, as was also some submarginal land purchased by the Resettlement Administration for the relief of depression-stricken white farmers; and almost 1,000,000 acres of ceded "surplus" land never homesteaded was returned to the tribes. Finally, tribes using their own funds acquired about 390,000 acres at a cost of more than $2,000,000. These acquisitions totaled about 4,000,000 acres. Most of it, of course, was very poor—otherwise it would not have been available—but some of it could be used.

At the same time, much of the land already belonging to the

Indians was not in a usable form. Soon after the damage was done, the Indian service recognized the folly of dividing up many of the western reservations into small rectangular allotments. Always more efficient in developing property than people, it began to form grazing units, larger areas with natural boundaries and access to water. These units were checkerboarded with a constantly increasing number of white-owned tracts; thus it was impossible for an individual Indian without capital to obtain control. White cattlemen owning part of the land leased the allotments, and the allottees lived in idleness and poverty on the inadequate rental.

The leasing evil grew constantly worse as the allottees died off. When, in 1933, Collier put a stop to the easy solution of selling the inherited land, he hoped to bring it back into the tribal estate, giving the heirs a proportionate share in the collective enterprises. The original draft of the Reorganization Act carried such a provision, but Congress was unwilling to go so far. As time went on, the fragmentation became fantastic. One allotment might have hundreds of scattered heirs, and fifty heirship equities might vest in one Indian. The Hoover Commission Task Force recommended the liquidation of such heirships by loans enabling individual Indians to purchase them, or the solution urged by Collier if there were more than five heirs for one allotment; but Congress has never acted, and the chaos of fragmentation at the present time dizzies the imagination.

Much usable land was returned from leasing to Indian utilization by the loan provisions of the Reorganization Act. Congress never appriated the full authorization, but by 1945 a revolving credit fund of about $4,250,000 had been established, and loans totaling $12,000,000 had been made at a low interest rate to Indians unable, because of no security except their personal honesty, to borrow from any commercial lending agency. With this they bought equipment and livestock and, with the guidance of the agricultural extension agents, took over and operated 400,000 acres of crop lands and 7,000,000 acres of grazing lands formerly leased to white men. By 1948 more than 12,000 families had been completely or partially rehabilitated on their own land and were wholly or nearly self-supporting. Even aside from humanitarian considerations, this emergence of Indians from relief clients to tax-payers was an important national asset. And their record of repayment (including some foreclosures) was almost 100 per cent.

Statistics do not tell the whole story. Individual examples of what was happening to real people throughout the Indian country are more revealing. Typical are some case histories in a survey made in 1949 of Five Tribes Indians in fullbloods settlements of eastern Oklahoma.[4]

The first agricultural extension workers sent there spent most of their time giving futile advice to people entirely without capital and distributing Red Cross and other relief. One of these men made a study of a community in the Cherokee hills near the place where the great Sequoyah had lived and taught his people. When the Cherokees settled there, they cleared the level places and raised cotton for their homespun garments, food for their families, and feed for their livestock running the range. Then had come allotment and the disruption of their economic base. There were now one hundred families in the community, of which seventy-five were Cherokee of a high degree of Indian blood, mainly of the landless generation. Only about one fifth of the six-mile-square surveyor's township remained in Indian ownership. One generous old woman was furnishing asylum to six families living in miserable cabins on her sixty acres.

Then late in 1937 the revolving loan fund to Oklahoma Indians became available. It was a perfect system: accessible capital and trained guidance in management, Indian labor, and self-help. The extension agent analyzed the mantle of loose rock that covered the hills and concluded that it would raise strawberries; he studied the Indians and decided they were adapted to the painstaking hand work. He helped one community to organize a co-operative. Their capital totaled one horse and no farm equipment. They borrowed $2,800 with which they bought a team of horses and paid other necessary expenses, and set out twenty acres of plants, which they later increased to forty. They paid off their debt, earned an average profit of $600 a year (their previous income had been $54), and branched out into individual growing.

At the time of the 1949 survey this extension worker had 150 families raising strawberries and expected to double the number the following year. All these ventures were started with small loans. In that hill county there had been 363 loans totaling $168,567.49, of which $120,329.94 had been repaid ($2,773.57 through foreclosure), $47,-821.11 was still outstanding, and only $416.44 had been charged off as lost. A remarkable record by adding machine standards, but more remarkable in terms of contented people living on their land. And it was not only the loans that had been repaid; one elderly fullblood, who

[4] Angie Debo, *The Five Civilized Tribes of Oklahoma: Report on Social and Economic Conditions.* I made this survey at the request of the Indian Rights Association, which became the publisher of my findings.

had cleared $1,500 as his season's profit, had paid debts he had owed at the store for thirty years. (Incidentally, the success of the Indians started an important Oklahoma industry as white people also went into the strawberry business.)

Similar successes were seen in the small farming ventures of full-bloods who had settled on land turned over to their use by the Resettlement Administration and for which they paid a small rental. There was a landless couple of young middle age who had formerly been crowded into the cabin of the wife's mother, a good woman who had trained her daughter in the old-time Cherokee housekeeping. "Now their yard is perfectly kept, their house is modern in taste and furnishings, and beautifully canned fruit and vegetables are on the shelves. The man does his farming with one small well-cared-for horse raising fine patches of beans and strawberries." Farther down the road an elderly couple was farming a small, rich spot of valley in the old way, raising good corn and filling a log storehouse with food. Another settler was a landless son of Redbird Smith, a good farmer, using 160 acres, half in cultivation, the rest in range; he was raising his food and feed for his livestock and running a sorghum mill. Close by was his son, who was also prospering.

At the other end of the scale were Indians who still had access to good land, their own or family allotments. Typical of these was a young landless Creek, a fullblood in appearance. When the loan policy started, he was living on a fine forty-acre tract belonging to another Creek, farming inadequately with one team. Then one of his horses died in the middle of the busy season, and he came diffidently to the extension agent for help. At the time of the survey he had bought the forty acres and was renting another eighty, and his terraced fields were beautifully cultivated. He was living in a comfortable house with butane fuel and electricity, and there was a tractor and other farm machinery under shelter and a sturdy old-model car in the garage. All this was earned through the judicious use of borrowed capital and the advice of an expert in the beginning years. At the time of the survey the extension agent was asking *his* advice in a problem with a new client.

There were gradations all the way between the bean- and strawberry-growing truck farmers in the hills and the mechanized efficiency of those living on good land, but there was the same emergence of independence and self-support. A check of the same individuals seven years later showed that they were still prospering. But there were only fifteen agricultural extension workers in the whole Five Tribes area.

344

In the Cherokee hills only four or five hundred Indians were receiving guidance out of a needy six thousand.

Such were the individual cases that went into the twelve thousand reported successes. There were, of course, some human failures offsetting these statistics. Some loan clients were lazy and shiftless; they paid off their obligation by foreclosure and settled back into poverty. Some communities and tribes failed to grasp the opportunity, for it required a demonstration of success, and how could people who knew only failure make the initial effort? Then there were insensitive extension men who ran the operations themselves, ignoring educational guidance. Probably they accounted for some of the successful twelve thousand. (There was no evidence of this in the Five Tribes.) Also, some of the area offices failed to grasp the relation between the credit decisions and the field experience of the agricultural agents. For example, in one area the loans were supervised by a woman secretary who knew office techniques but nothing about farming. Any agricultural success here was achieved in spite of the administration.

Rehabilitation was probably the least successful on the northern Great Plains, where allotments of uneconomic acreage were distributed through white-operated grazing units. In 1941 the Sioux of the Pine Ridge Reservation were selected as representative of this environment in a joint study initiated by the Indian Bureau and the University of Chicago and carried out by the anthropologist Gordon Macgregor. His findings trace the destruction of a viable life way in the range-cattle industry.[5]

Even during the ill-conceived attempt of the first reservation years to start these Indians in farming, some cattle had been issued to them. Progress had been interrupted by butchering during the starving times and the depredations of the ghost dancers, and they had to start again. A capable agent came in 1900 and worked with them for seventeen years in developing a cattle economy. Their former great camp circle broke up into smaller bands close to water and grass, and by 1912 they owned 40,000 cattle and were developing a new confidence and hope. Their allotment came late—beginning in 1904, completed in 1916—and little "surplus" was left for homesteaders. Thus the inevitable disruption of their range did not occur until about the time the United States entered World War I. Then, along with the ensuing wheat shortage and the patriotic urge to increase the acreage, came a new agent advising them to sell their cattle and plant wheat. Since they lacked the

[5] Published in *Warriors without Weapons*.

capital to buy the mechanized equipment or the experience to operate it, that advice meant leasing to large-scale growers.

Cattle prices were good, and the Indians lived well while their money lasted. Then wheat prices dropped and the land went back to cattle, but the Indians never regained control. With the continuing land losses only a white cattleman could put together the sixteen-or-so Sioux-owned and white-owned tracts to form a grazing unit, and the Indians lived on the shrinking lease money.

By 1930 more than one fourth of their land had been sold and more than half of the remainder was in heirship status. When the sales were stopped, the fractionization went on. Little, if any, rehabilitation was apparent at the time of Macgregor's investigation. He found the Indians frustrated, demoralized, and hopeless. He concluded: "[Their] loss of the cattle herds was the greatest disaster that had befallen the Pine Ridge Indians since the vanishing of the buffalo. For the second time the basis of their economy and the foundation upon which their society rested had been swept away." At that time more than 40 per cent of all the Indian-owned land in the northern Great Plains was still leased to whites.

In contrast, it had been simple for the tribes on unallotted reservations to reclaim their land. In 1923 only 4 per cent of the San Carlos Reservation was being used by its three thousand owners; all the rest was leased to white cattlemen. Under the Reorganization Act the owners set up co-operative livestock associations and took over their entire range. The Indians of the Fort Apache Reservation also developed a successful ranching operation in which they utilized all their land.

One other reform measure aided in the development of some unbroken reservations. In 1946, Congress created the Indian Claims Commission for adjudicating all claims arising out of fraud, treaty violations, or other wrongs done to the Indians by the government. Since that time it has passed on 256 claims, rejecting 133 and awarding judgments in 123. Many are still pending. The most effectively organized tribes have used the awards constructively for long-term economic development. To dismembered tribes, the money has been divided per capita, serving no real purpose except the satisfaction of abstract justice. This last, however, is important. Indians, like other Americans, are entitled to their day in court. Also, the acknowledgment of these claims may possibly have some effect in preventing future wrongs.

346

Besides their income from tribal property, whole or fragmented, some wage work was available to Indians, mainly in relief work during the depression years. The Indian Division of the Civilian Conservation Corps was especially productive, for it familiarized them with trades and the handling of power machinery. Then as the slowed economy quickened with the approach of World War II, many of them graduated to skilled labor in defense plants, where their manual dexterity, color perception, and patient application were decided assets. Outside employment was in fact necessary—and sometimes preferred—even by Indians whose reservations had not been dismembered. About one-half of the San Carlos Apaches, for example, were earning an adequate livelihood with their cattle; the others needed to depend on wage work. Referring to them, Oliver La Farge said: "The development here suggests a possible goal for Indians generally. The reservation itself supports a portion of the tribe, which cannot be increased. To the remainder it is . . . a base of operations for competition with the white world."

The Navahos furnished the most conspicuous example of a people overflowing its reservation resources. Their population of eight or ten thousand in 1868 had increased to seventy thousand by 1947, and in spite of all their thrift and industry they were close to starvation. By the Treaty of 1868 the government had promised to maintain a one-teacher school for every thirty children; but the trackless distances had proved too great, and the Navahos themselves rejected this alien influence. For many years the schools were few and far between.

They had not been forgotten in the period of reform. From 1928 on, Congress had added land to their desert holdings, and a school building program was launched; but the population outran these gains. Also the Indian Bureau had assisted them to weld their scattered settlements into a united tribal organization. Perhaps it was this and the reduction of their language to writing that started a new spirit stirring among them. Then during World War II it flashed into action. Thousands of their young men in the armed services or working off the reservation in war plants found a new way of life, and they had the humiliation of seeing thousands more rejected because of their illiteracy. As early as 1944 they began asking for the schools promised by the treaty.[6]

Their plight aroused so much concern that in 1947 a number of

[6] Probably the best account of this new spirit among the Navahos is in T. D. Allen, *Navahos Have Five Fingers*.

religious and humanitarian organizations sponsored an institute to study their needs and gave publicity to its findings; the Department of the Interior drafted a long-range rehabilitation measure, and President Truman urged Congress to pass it. The act passed April 1, 1950, was for the Navahos and the Hopis, whose ancient homeland forms an enclave within the Navaho Reservation. It authorized an appropriation of $88,570,000 for a ten-year "program of basic improvement," including $19,000,000 for soil and moisture conservation and irrigation, $25,000,000 for education, $1,000,000 for developing industry and business enterprises on the reservation, and $3,500,000 for assisting Navahos to find outside employment and adjust to off-reservation living.

But by then the reform had run its course. The Navaho-Hopi Act was the last important piece of constructive Indian legislation passed by Congress at that time, and the very year it was passed the reaction captured the executive branch also. The decade that followed brought a return to the Indian policy of the Dawes Act and its disastrous consequences.[7]

[7] Probably the best study of the whole range of Indian policy is Harold E. Fey and D'Arcy McNickle, *Indians and Other Americans*.

CHAPTER NINETEEN

BACK TO THE OLD BAD DAYS

The years from 1950 through 1960 marked the most concerted drive against Indian property and Indian survival since the removals following the act of 1830 and the liquidation of tribes and reservations following 1887. There had been ominous portents. World War II had its effect: with the expanding agriculture, envious eyes were again fixed on the Indians' land at the same time that the national attention was focused elsewhere. Strangely, the first attempt to turn public sentiment away from the reform policy came from the churches.

In 1944 the women's societies of the denominations affiliated with the National Council of Churches again turned to a mission study. The executives, busy with other things and unfamiliar with the specialized field of Indian history, assigned the preparation of the text to the person who made the loudest claim to expert knowledge. Throughout the reform era he had used his influence against it, without much effect. Now he had his chance. With plain misstatements of fact he set out to show that the Indians' native traits were all bad, he condemned the "high-sounding cry of 'religious freedom'," and above all he denounced the Reorganization Act as a "revival of tribalism." Throughout the book was a fervent appeal "to release the Indian from wardship" and to free his land from the trust status so degrading to his self-respect.

Actually the Indian had never been a "ward." This legal misconception had crept into the public vocabulary from the court's ruling in *Cherokee Nation* v. *Georgia* that the relationship of the *tribe* to the United States "resembles that of a ward to his guardian." It had been invoked to justify illegal acts against individual Indians, or even to de-

349

fend their vested rights of property, and had been loosely used even by reputable writers unaware of its technical meaning. As for the status of tribal property or the allotments into which it was divided, it is a trust relationship based on contractual agreements. The United States as trustee is obligated to protect the property, but has no control over the person of the beneficiary. But the local church people, already with an uneasy conscience about Indians, were ready to join in an indignant demand to "set them free."

Also the reform spirit was slowing down in Congress. During the session of 1947, for example, eighty-seven bills were introduced to require the issuance of unrestricted patents to all allotments, forty-six for the sale of the submarginal land to white people, and nine to liquidate the property of specified tribes and distribute the proceeds per capita. At the same time, a perennial bill urged by several western senators would repeal the Reorganization Act, break up all tribal organizations and their assets, cover the revolving loan fund back into the federal treasury, and remove restrictions from all Indian land. This proposal would not only "free" the Indians from "slavery," but stop an increasing drain on the public finances.

Such persons never admitted that the greatest cost of the Indian service was the direct result of the policy they were advocating. Allotting the reservations and then clearing the allotments of restrictions was an expensive process, actually a service to white land-seekers but charged to Indian welfare; at the same time it required an increased agency force to protect a modicum of the allottees' property from the worst of the exploiters. Then when the reform movement stopped the attrition of the Indians' holdings, a disproportionate agency effort went into the inheritance bookkeeping. At the very time of these senators' complaints, the Hoover Commission Task Force made its unheeded recommendation for heirship legislation. Just when rehabilitation of the forgotten allottees was succeeding, congressional sentiment was veering back to the same disastrous cycle.

The diverse forces at work were apparent in the progress of the Navaho-Hopi Bill. The missions branch of the National Council of Churches, ignoring its recent study text, joined with other humanitarian groups in holding the Navaho Institute and appealing for legislation. But Congress inserted provisions so objectionable to the Indians when it passed the bill in 1949 that President Truman vetoed it at their request, and they had to wait another year.

Commissioner Collier had resigned in 1945, but his successors continued his policy, albeit less aggressively. Then in May, 1950, a month after the passage of the Navaho-Hopi Act, Dillon S. Myer was appointed to the position. He had been in charge of the internment camps in which persons of Japanese ancestry were placed in the panic following Pearl Harbor, and had carried out a vigorous, even coercive, policy of resettling them throughout the general population. Now he showed the same intention of breaking up the Indian reservations and scattering the people, and he used the same coercive methods. As early as 1951 he officially abandoned programs of Indian development and concentrated on what he called "withdrawal programming." Regarding Indian reactions to Bureau decisions, he instructed his field employees the next year, "I realize that it will not be possible always to obtain Indian cooperation. . . . We must proceed, even though [this] may be lacking."

He interfered with the election of tribal officers on the Blackfoot Reservation, sold some land belonging to the San Ildefonso Pueblo without Indian consent, and for the first time in years challenged the right of tribes to select their own attorneys. (The last was condemned by a special commission appointed by the American Bar Association.) He even supported a bill introduced in Congress that would have authorized Indian service employees to carry arms and arrest Indians without warrant.

Reform administrators in the Indian Bureau resigned or were discharged. There were complaints of administrative actions here and there favoring white appropriation of Indian property. Certainly this happened to the Paiutes of the Pyramid Lake Reservation in Nevada, where white trespassers were using their grazing lands. The Indians took the case to court and won. Their superintendent supported their rights, and Myer moved him to another reservation at the demand of the trespassers' counsel, Senator Pat McCarran. Then the trespassers remained, and the Indians could not dislodge them.

Myer's tenure was short-lived, but it was apparent in the presidential election of 1952 that his philosophy was in the ascendant. The party platforms were identical: the Democrats promised "to remove restrictions on the rights of Indians individually and through their tribal councils to handle their own affairs"; the Republicans asserted that "All Indians are citizens of the United States and no longer should be denied full enjoyment of their rights of citizenship." Good words, to which nobody could object—except that Indian affairs has its specialized vocabulary.

The new word with the old purpose was *termination*. The Eisenhower administration, from Secretary of the Interior Douglas McKay down through the Department hierarchy from Assistant Secretary Orme Lewis to Commissioner of Indian Affairs Glenn L. Emmons (a banker from Gallup, New Mexico) and Assistant Commissioner Rex Lee (holding over from the Myer era), and both sessions of the Eighty-third Congress lost no time in implementing this policy. It began with House Concurrent Resolution (HCR) 108 adopted August 1, 1953, stating "the policy of Congress . . . to make the Indians . . . subject to the same laws and entitled to the same privileges and responsibilities as . . . other citizens . . . and to end their status as wards of the United States, and to grant them all of the rights and privileges pertaining to American citizenship."

A congressional resolution, of course, has no standing in law. It does not require the president's signature. It expresses only the opinion of the current Congress. Even so, it threw Indians throughout the country into a state of shock. They knew that the resolution simply meant that Congress intended to break up the tribal communities authorized by the Reorganization Act to manage their affairs, and in effect to throw their land on the market by abolishing its trust and nontaxable status. These contractual relations with the government no more limited their citizenship than does the ownership by a white man of tax-free municipal bonds or the white community's ownership of a city water system. They would have been still more disturbed if they had known how long HCR 108 would be invoked to destroy them. Five Congresses and eleven years later it was still being cited by the Senate committee as binding on the Indian Bureau.

A few days after this policy statement Congress passed Public Law 280 giving the states power to extend their civil and criminal law over Indian reservations. As "domestic dependent nations," the tribes had once governed their internal affairs, whether under borrowed Anglo-American forms or their own customs.[1] Many of these governments had been completely liquidated, as in Oklahoma, but other tribes still lived under the social controls of age-old practice, except that ten major crimes came within the jurisdiction of federal laws and courts. Some of these latter tribes had become so disintegrated that the extension of state jurisdiction was feasible. Some, like the Pueblo city-states, had functioning institutions that had enabled them to survive

[1] For the smoothly structured primitive law of a Plains tribe, see Karl N. Llewellyn and E. Adamson Hoebel, *The Cheyenne Way.*

through the centuries; others were engaging in reservation-wide economic development and maintaining good order over their people. But the advocates of "freeing the Indians" opposed such separateness. The section of the first Navaho-Hopi Bill that caused President Truman to veto it would have extended state laws over the closely knit Hopis and over the Navaho Reservation, an area the size of West Virginia sprawling over portions of three states.

Public Law 280 extended state law over reservations in Wisconsin, Minnesota (except Red Lake), Nebraska, California, and Oregon (except several tribes on Warm Springs) and gave any other state the authority to assume the same jurisdiction. President Eisenhower signed it, but advised Congress to amend it by providing for consultation with the Indians affected. It is hard to amend a measure after it has been enacted. It was not until April 11, 1968—after it had remained an overhanging threat for fifteen years—that a bill signed by President Johnson required the states to obtain Indian consent.[2]

In Nebraska the Omahas and some of their Winnebago relatives were concentrated in one county. Unlike other Indians they paid taxes on their trust allotments, and these payments totaled 60 to 75 per cent of the county budget. When they lost the authority to police themselves, the state failed to take over, and they had no law enforcement whatever. La Verne Madigan, the executive director of the Association on American Indian Affairs (AAIA), initiated a project to enlist the unhappy Omahas and their well-disposed white neighbors in a community betterment program. Later the AAIA financed a study of law enforcement by the University of Nebraska, and many good citizens became concerned. At last in 1961—after eight years in which crime flourished unchecked—the legislature, by a narrow margin, made provision for the state to assume responsibility.

Of the states permitted to make their own choice, South Dakota took over jurisdiction, an action favored by the small but powerful group of cattlemen who were leasing Sioux allotments. The Sioux then circulated a petition for a statewide referendum, and won enough non-Indian votes to defeat the law. Nevada accepted jurisdiction, but left the choice up to the counties. Nothing was said about the Indians' consent, but most of the counties did follow their wishes. This sums up the response to Public Law 280. The states were not as eager to control the reservations as the advocates of termination had expected. But more than one hundred bills to "free" the Indians were introduced at

[2] Note the difference between *consultation* and *consent*.

that same session of the Eighty-third Congress. Six tribes or groups were terminated in the 1954 session. Several others were threatened.

Among the latter were the Florida Seminoles. In the hearings on the Bureau-sponsored bill to terminate them, it was brought out that 90 per cent were illiterate. The bill was not passed. The nine thousand Chippewas of the Turtle Mountain Reservation in North Dakota were also on the list. This tribe had ceded ten million acres of good wheat land to the government at ten cents an acre, and in 1882 had received a small reservation, cut in 1884 to two six-mile-square townships of untillable brush-covered hills. When allotment came, there was not enough land; thus 2,700 tribal members were given allotments scattered throughout the public domain in the two Dakotas and Montana. Being Indians, they returned to crowd in with their people, where the small land base became complicated with the usual inheritance tangle, while most of their distant "farms" gravitated into white ownership. In 1940 a land-purchase program added 35,000 acres to their holdings before the money ran out. The Indians lived on wages for work they could pick up in the surrounding area and on relief. Because the Department of the Interior found "little prospect for alleviation of [their] social and economic plight," it recommended termination. Their assets, if divided, would have yielded about thirty-seven dollars per capita. North Dakota had advocated termination in general, but now the state joined the Indians in arguing that they should first be put on their feet. Such a program would have cost real money. The legislation was not enacted.

The Osages had a narrow escape. These people had largely shaken off the white harpies that once preyed upon them—after Congress had delivered them from the guardians in 1925 and some criminal convictions had delivered them from the murderers—and they were developing self-direction in the use of their wealth. Although the total income from their mineral estate had declined since its flush production, it amounted to $4,571,644.66 in 1952. Through inheritance their shares had become uneven, but few, if any, were poor. They received the same public services as other Oklahomans, and they paid taxes on everything except the surface allotments still held in trust. Restrictions on the trust property of all adults of less than one-half Indian blood expired automatically. Forty-five per cent of the tribal membership was thus affected, for intermarriage with whites had been frequent since statehood. Others could have the restrictions removed on application. The agency administered the oil estate, and the tribe paid the

Modern Florida Seminoles in front of a chickee with the late Acee
Blue Eagle, Oklahoma Creek-Pawnee artist, in the center wearing his
ceremonial costume.

Children of Tesuque Pueblo.
Tribal city states, old before Columbus.
AUTHOR'S COLLECTION

Fort Apache cattle being loaded into vans after a sale on the reservation. Note the Apache cowhand and the watching Apache boys, while leaning on the chute are the purchasers and the van drivers with their cattle prods.

These Indians developed a successful ranching operation in which they utilized all their land.

COURTESY BUREAU OF INDIAN AFFAIRS

Guy Okakok at a meeting of the Association on American Indian
Affairs, New York, May 7, 1962.
"Now today, the problem is still same, and haven't change much."
COURTESY DR. THEODORE B. HETZEL

John Wooden Legs.
"You would have to be a Cheyenne to know what it meant when the Government in Washington kept its word."

COURTESY DR. THEODORE B. HETZEL

Howard Rock and La Verne Madigan at Athapascan meeting,
Tanana, Alaska, June, 1962.

*Miss Madigan came to help, and Dr. Hetzel was present, but
the Indians organized and conducted the proceedings.*

COURTESY DR. THEODORE B. HETZEL

Chief Andrew Isaac of Tanacross.
Wise in the ways of land and nature but limited in the white man's education.
Photograph by Thomas Richards, Jr.
<small>COURTESY</small> *Tundra Times*

Successful urban Indians, the Fred Tsoodle family, Kiowas of Oklahoma City. The parents hold excellent jobs and their children attend school and college, but they plan to return to their home community after retirement.

Third Annual Oklahomans for Indian Opportunity Youth Conference,
University of Oklahoma, March 29, 1969.

COURTESY OKLAHOMANS FOR INDIAN OPPORTUNITY

Church of Taos Pueblo (above) and altar (below).
"We have to pray for what we receive from the sun that gives us light and the water we drink."

Paul Bernal on the shore of Blue Lake.
COURTESY CHARLOTTE TREGO

Governor Severino Martinez (left) of Taos Pueblo and his interpreter, Paul Bernal, speaking to the AAIA in New York, April 17, 1961.

"We have sacred things we deeply love, deeply believe."

COURTESY DR. THEODORE B. HETZEL

Navaho capitol at Window Rock.
Free to control their land and people are the Navahos.
AUTHOR'S COLLECTION

Guy Gorman, President

Carl Todacheene, Vice-President

Yazzie Begay

Timothy Benally

Howard Gorman

Larry Isaac

Raymond Nakai

Dillon Platero

Wilson Skeet

Chester Yellowhair

Regents of the Navajo Community College, Many Farms, Arizona.
The entire curriculum is oriented towards Navaho needs and culture.

COURTESY NAVAJO COMMUNITY COLLEGE

Zuni women baking their excellent bread.
Thrift and well-being are apparent throughout their village.
AUTHOR'S COLLECTION

entire cost of this operation and of the supervision of the restricted property of individuals. Three fourths of the surface allotments had been purchased by white people, who were not without hope that some lucky whim of Congress would give them the underlying minerals.

"Freeing" the Osages would have meant dividing up their mineral estate or setting up a corporation to manage it. The first would have brought a return to the days when their "freedom" was subject to the county court. The second would have brought unreckoned complications and the possibility of mismanagement. The Osages were not notified that their tribe was on the list. Just before the hearings they were warned by the National Congress of American Indians, an all-Indian defense organization formed in 1944. They put through rapid telephone calls to the state congressional delegation and hurried to Washington to testify. One has only to read the published hearings—the sarcastic remarks of committee members, the excessive courtesy of the Osages fearing to antagonize those in positions of power—to see how real was their danger. But the Oklahoma congressional delegation supported them as a unit, not relishing the scandals, legal tangles, and probable impoverishment of this prospering people; and they were not terminated. Said one of the Osages, "It was a near tragedy for us."

Long after the policy changed, the fear lingered among the Indians. Looking back, Earl Old Person, the Blackfoot tribal chairman, said in 1966 to a new commissioner, "It is important to note that in our Indian language the only translation for termination is to 'wipe out' or 'kill off.' . . . You have caused us to jump every time we hear this word . . . how can we plan our future when the Indian Bureau threatens to wipe us out as a race? It is like trying to cook a meal in your tipi when someone is standing outside trying to burn the tipi down."

The Eighty-third Congress did in fact pass six termination laws. Among the tribes affected were scattered bands in western Oregon, some of whom owned valuable timber. No study has ever been made regarding them. The Alabama-Coushatta Reservation in Texas was turned over to the state. This official change was logical; except for some Bureau help during the reform era, it had always been a state responsibility. At present Texas is giving publicity to this isolated people as a tourist attraction.

A modified act was passed for the Utes on the Uintah-Ouray Reservation; those of one-half or less Indian blood would be terminated in 1961. In 1950 these Indians had won nearly $19,000,000 in a Claims case. Congress had authorized a distribution of $1,000 per capita and provided that the rest of the money should be used in a thirteen-year program of social and economic development to prepare them for termination. Factions developed among them, and the 1954 act was passed at their request, though with a suspiciously small number participating in the decision. The mixed-bloods constituted 27 per cent of the population, 494 persons, mainly descendants of four women once adopted by the group. Most of the "development" of the succeeding seven years was devoted to separating their tribal assets and setting up corporations to manage their released property, these to remain in trust status till 1964. But at the termination date in 1961 they began to sell their stock to non-Indians, some shares valued at $1,500 for as low as $30.93. In 1968 the federal district court ruled that since the trust period had not expired, they were entitled to recover the full value of their stock. The fullblood remainder, with its reservation dismembered, is still torn by factions, its self-government is a farce, and its development program has largely failed. If termination cannot be blamed for all this, it was certainly not the remedy.

Also in Utah four scattered bands of illiterate, poverty-stricken Paiutes numbering about two hundred were terminated. The reason given was that they had never received any appreciable help from the government anyhow. More to the point was the fact that their 46,000 acres of desert might have oil and uranium. Congress, warned of this, in a spasm of concern extended the undivided mineral interest for ten years. If their inhospitable land really had begun to spout liquid gold, one can imagine what would have happened to the Indians at the end of the ten years. They hardly knew about the termination bill while it was pending; if they had known, they had no money to go to Washington to testify. Public-spirited citizens protested to President Eisenhower, but he accepted the judgment of his advisers and signed it. Their arid land was transferred from the Indian Bureau to a bank and trust company in Salt Lake City, 160 miles away. Dissatisfied with the management, they finally collected enough money to make the journey, where they had a brief interview with the trustee, but they were unable to understand his explanation. They are completely baffled by their new responsibilities and unable to exercise any of "the rights and privileges pertaining to American citizenship."

Two wealthy tribes, owners of valuable timber, were terminated by the same Congress: the Menominee of Wisconsin and the Klamath of Oregon. The date set for completion of the work was 1957, but as complications developed, new laws were passed and the deadlines were extended.

The Menominees are an Algonquian tribe numbering 3,270. They owned a 234,000-acre unallotted reservation with the best timber remaining in Wisconsin, effectively managed by the Indian Bureau. They operated a small sawmill profitably and earned adequate wages at work in the logging camps and at the sawmill. They controlled their own finances, with an annual budget of over $450,000 received from their timber and lumber sales. They paid all the expense of the Bureau services, maintained law and order, and appropriated $125,000 for medical care and a hospital built with $750,000 of their own funds and operated by the Catholic church, up to $30,000 for welfare and relief, $60,000 (under Catholic auspices) for their schools, and up to $60,000 for construction and maintenance of buildings, roads, two hydro-electric plants, a steam plant, and so on. They had a tribal loan fund of approximately $40,000. Nine of their people had graduated from college, 328 from high school.

Their successful conduct of their affairs was the reason given for termination. Under duress they gave a sort of consent. They had recently won an award of eight and one-half million dollars from the Indian Claims Commission, and they wanted part of this to be distributed per capita. Delegates they sent to Washington to protest against termination were told by congressional committee members that only by accepting it could they have their money. Then they consented, though it appears that the tribe would have foregone the payment. Rex Lee said, "We did not feel that it was necessary for us to go back to the Tribe or the State Officials." The Wisconsin congressional delegation had in fact warned against the measure without success.

The Menominees were faced with the almost insuperable problem of drawing up a plan that would satisfy a termination-minded administration and hold their property intact. The termination law had provided for a per capita distribution of $1,500; later the Department of the Interior ordered a second $778 payment. This drained away the tribal balance needed to carry out the change. The state gave what help it could. In 1959 a new administration brought in as lieutenant governor Philleo Nash, a business executive, who held a doctorate in anthropology from the University of Chicago and had served as special assistant to President Truman in Department of the Interior matters; and he gave his attention to the last stages of the planning.

With the assistance of the legislature a new county was created comprising the former reservation, and a corporation with a tribally elected board of directors was formed to manage the assets. All services had to be meshed into the state system and supported by taxes, and because these, though as high as the legal limit, proved insufficient, they were supplemented by corporation subsidies. This burden, falling mainly on the sawmill, proved so heavy that in 1966 a remorseful Congress authorized a grant of $800,000 annually for four years in tax assistance. (Typical of the "savings" effected by termination.)

During the long period of transition the Menominees' social services were disrupted; their logging and lumbering industry was at a standstill, with resulting unemployment; and bitter factionalism grew out of their natural dissatisfaction. But by 1965 their corporation had come out of the red, and there was a growing prospect of eventual success. Through constructive statesmanship by Indians and Wisconsin whites they have escaped the exploitation, degradation, and final pauperism that have usually marked the termination of a tribe. Even their forest has been saved as a public resource. The final outcome is not assured, but it seems hopeful.

The Klamaths were not so fortunate. These 2,133 Indians owned a 720,000-acre forest so rich that every predatory interest on the West Coast longed to slash it. It was well managed by the Indian Bureau, and the Indians paid for the service, but they had made little progress in education or self-government, and most of them were content to live on the income—about $800 per capita—from the timber sales. They sent delegates to Washington to oppose termination, but an individual who had been defeated in their election was brought to the capital by Secretary McKay at tribal expense to advocate it. The official delegate testified, "We want to remain a going concern, on the same basis as other going concerns operate," and he asked for an orderly plan to be worked out by the Department, the tribe, and the state. "Because it has to do with the last thing we have got, we cannot be too careful," he said. His appeal went unregarded.

The termination act gave each tribesman the option of taking his share of the assets or allowing it to remain in a block to be managed as a trusteeship under state law. When it became apparent that each share was worth $44,000, understandably 78 per cent elected to withdraw. What happened after the distribution has never been told; it can be easily imagined. The timber at least was saved; one tract was sold to a private purchaser who undertook a sustained-yield obligation, the rest

374

to the government. The block remaining to the 22 per cent is managed by a Portland bank.

All this termination legislation was enacted by the Eighty-third Congress. Then the Democrats won the off-year election of 1954, which brought new chairmen to committees, who, as it happened, were on the side of the Indians. But Commissioner Emmons carried out the termination policy administratively during the remaining six years of his term. To his credit, he continued the educational progress initiated in the Rhoads-Scattergood era, and in general he spared the Southwestern tribes, especially the Navahos, but otherwise his administration was a disaster.

Eventually public sentiment became aroused on behalf of the Indians. The National Council of Churches and the major Protestant denominations came out with strong pronouncements, and articles appeared in Catholic publications. In 1955 the mission study agency of the National Council issued a text that was sound in scholarship from historical background to the recent acts of Congress, all illuminated and colored by religious feeling. At the same time, devastating articles were published in quality magazines of general circulation, and Ralph Nader, in the *Harvard Law Review*, used all his remarkable resources of legal knowledge, ethnology, and spiritual insight to present a comprehensive review of past Indian policy, current trends, and prospects for the future. Also constant in publishing the damaging facts and in vain attempts to influence administrative action were the three major Indian interest organizations: the Indians' own Washington-based National Congress of American Indians (NCAI); the old and influential Indian Rights Association, of Philadelphia; and the aggressive Association on American Indian Affairs (AAIA), based in New York, but under the presidency of the distinguished Santa Fe writer and ethnologist, Oliver La Farge. And the ever dependable Quakers, through their meetings, their circulated material, and their Washington contacts, never gave up the fight. All this influence is illustrated in the d'Ewart incident.

Montana Representative Wesley d'Ewart had been active in termination legislation. In 1954 he was defeated in the Senate race, and a place was accordingly found for him to succeed Orme Lewis, who had recently resigned as assistant secretary of the interior. The NCAI was holding its annual meeting at the time, and it sent an earnest protest to President Eisenhower. But the Indians' wishes were ignored, and he received an interim appointment after Congress adjourned in

1955. When the next session convened, protests began to pour in to the Senate against his confirmation. These had no rubber-stamp characteristics, but were individual expressions of informed concern. The Senate failed to confirm him, and he was forced to retire.

In the presidential election that year the party platforms again were identical, but a complete reversal of their 1952 stand. The Republicans favored the "sympathetic and constructive execution of the Federal trusteeship . . . always in full consultation with Indians . . . and the expansion of their rights of self-government in local and tribal affairs." The Democrats would stop the "erosion of Indian rights, reduction of their economic base through alienation of their lands, and repudiation of Federal responsibility."

During the preceding four years the Department of the Interior had removed restrictions from 1,600,000 acres of allotted land—12 per cent of the Indians' entire allotted holdings—and sold it outright or allowed it to fall into the hands of white people by natural gravitation. Why did the Indians sell? Some of them were irresponsible; more were suffering actual hunger. "We had to sell our land to live," said a Blackfoot woman. "The Indian Bureau is starving us to get our land." The revolving loan fund, which had given individuals and tribes their first economic toehold, had been frozen. Eight million dollars was lying in the federal treasury, and no Indian could touch it. A former Bureau regulation had warned against removing restrictions when the sale of a tract would "destroy or jeopardize a timber unit or grazing area." On May 16, 1955, Emmons sent a directive to all area offices notifying them to abandon this protection. Thus, if a white rancher could prevail upon one Indian to sell the water hole, all the allotments in the grazing area would fall into his hands like so many ripe plums. At that very time, in South Dakota alone there were seven Bureau employees, with five more soon to be added, engaged in what amounted to a real estate business "helping" Indians to sell their land. (All paid for by congressional appropriations for the welfare of the Indians.)

What would become of the Indians when their land was gone? The Bureau had a ready answer. Ship them off to the cities. This movement had always existed just as it had with rural white Americans, but when "relocation" was joined with the drive of the Myer and Emmons era to make reservation life untenable it became part of a sinister pattern. Even Bureau construction work on reservations, which had once furnished employment and job training for Indians, was let to outside contractors, who brought in their own laborers.

The first relocation centers were established in Chicago, Denver, and Los Angeles; and a few others were added later. The Bureau recruited the Indians, paid the cost of removal, placed them in jobs, and helped them in housing and other adjustments. Slightly more than $1,000,000 was used to remove 5,603 wage earners, a total, with their families, of 12,626 Indians during the fiscal year 1956; and the budget was increased to $3,500,000 the next year. Many of those relocated drifted to skid row or returned home. But to some it offered opportunity; they remained and prospered.

The Bureau consciously aimed to separate the relocated Indians from their tribal associations. When Carl Beck, who headed the program, came out to Oklahoma to confer with tribal leaders, a Kiowa asked him, "Why do you send them so far away?"[3] He answered that if they worked in nearby cities they became "homesick" and returned on weekends to visit their friends. At that very time Richard Chuculate, a Cherokee graduate student, was making a study of a fullblood Cherokee settlement. He found Indians working in Tulsa and Muskogee returning to attend church, and in his judgment they needed this steadying influence. One barely literate fullblood from the hills was holding a good job in Kansas City, but he did not move his family there, making the 350-mile round trip home by train on weekends. The effect of his wages was clearly apparent in the family living standards.

An objective outside survey was made in 1956. It found a real need for the program, reported much dedicated commitment by employees in charge, but rejected the "malign" pressure of forcing relocation by destroying the alternative. Even in the Bureau's incomplete statistics of success and failure, a clear pattern was evident: few failures from tribes secure in their home base, an overwhelming number from those whose land was being pulled out from under them. The survey recommended the development of reservation resources and the opening of relocation centers in cities in Indian states.[4]

Thus a program that might have offered the Indians a vocational choice and provided an outlet for surplus population became a part of the over-all drive against their communities. Commissioner Emmons

[3] I was privileged to sit in at this meeting, at Anadarko, June 25, 1956.
[4] The report was published by the AAIA in its *Indian Affairs*, December, 1956. I served as a member of the survey team.

did change his words after the election of 1956, but his policy never changed. The Bureau's large "Realty" branch, with an annual appropriation of over three million dollars, was engaged almost wholly in land sales. And a tribe could be terminated administratively by a simple withdrawal of services. The Omahas knew what this meant.

They had begun to develop hope through their community improvement program. Early in 1958 they learned that plans were afoot to abolish their agency and turn its services over to the state and local government that was still withholding law enforcement. Said Tribal Chairman Alfred Wayne Gilpin: "What can I say to my Omaha people? . . . For two nights I have stayed awake, looking for honest thoughts and true words to say. . . . It is a poor life, but it is the only one they have to live. . . . they will remember the lawlessness that came after PL 280 and they will be afraid, they will sink down lower. If my Omaha people are allowed to make their own change, they will feel brave, they will face the future standing up straight."

When the Northern Cheyennes tried to "stand up straight," they were cut down by Bureau authority. At the allotment of their reservation in 1930–31, they had managed to retain the "surplus" in tribal ownership. Then when the trust period on the allotments began to expire in 1955, the council members—in the words of the president, John Wooden Legs—"went to the five districts of the reservation and asked the people what they wanted us, their leaders, to do. The people told us to find a way for the Tribe to buy the land that foolish or desperate members put up for sale, so that the reservation would remain Northern Cheyenne." Two years later the Bureau advertised 1,340 acres of grazing land, a key area known as the Bixby Tracts, where the streams head and the main water resource of the reservation is concentrated. Three months before the sale, the tribe liquidated a cattle project for $40,000 to buy it. The Bureau, claiming the right of supervision, got control of the money and held it. As the date of the sale approached, the tribe frantically petitioned for its postponement, and members of Congress from Montana added their protest. The land was sold to a white bidder for $22,485; a year later he offered it to the Indians for $47,736, but by that time they had to use their money to bid on other allotments as they were offered. They managed to hold everything but the Bixby Tracts. Said John Wooden Legs:

"To us, to be Cheyenne means being one tribe—living on our own land—in America, where we are citizens. Our land is everything to us. . . . It is the only place where Cheyennes remember same things together. I will tell you one of the things we remember on our land. We remember our grandfathers paid for it—with their life." He had personal cause to remember. In the flight from Camp Robinson, "My grandmother told me she walked holding a little girl by the hand on each side. She had to keep pulling them out of the line of the soldiers' bullets."[5]

But a tribe might be tricked into dissolution. Trickery was tried on the Fort Sill Apaches, a closely knit group of 104 descendants of the prisoners who had chosen to remain in Oklahoma. They owned 4,420 acres of restricted land. Early in 1958, Bureau officials called them to a meeting to discuss "means of bringing about social and economic improvement." This turned out to be a termination plan to which they were invited to offer procedural suggestions. When they started to reject it in its entirety, one of the officials sprang to his feet saying, "The law for termination has already been passed, and there is nothing you can do about it. You may as well accept it now and get what you can, for you may get nothing later." Threatened with this nonexistent "law," the Apaches took time to investigate. Then they wrote a surprisingly moderate account of the incident to Senator Robert S. Kerr. The Senator referred it to Emmons, who justified the Bureau action as taken "in accordance with the desires of Congress as expressed in House Concurrent Resolution No. 108."

This tortured interpretation was expressly repudiated the following fall by Fred A. Seaton, who had succeeded McKay as secretary of the interior. In a broadcast from Flagstaff, Arizona, on September 18 he said that HCR 108 was meant "to state an objective, not an immediate goal," and he declared that "it is absolutely unthinkable to me" to force "upon an Indian tribe a so-called termination plan which did not have the understanding and acceptance of the members affected. I will follow this as long as I am Secretary." His pronouncement did not filter down to the Bureau, but the Indians did find a champion in Assistant Secretary Roger C. Ernst, who now held the place left vacant by d'Ewart. The Northern Cheyennes among others had cause to be grateful.

In 1959 with the encouragement of the AAIA they worked out an "unallotment" plan and submitted it to the Department of the Interior. As they saw it, "The Government divided our land so that it could be

[5] I heard Mr. Wooden Legs tell his story at a meeting of the AAIA in New York, May 2, 1960. His account was published by the AAIA in *Indian Affairs*, June, 1960.

sold to white men in pieces. Now we are willing to buy every piece back again with our own money." They requested a moritorium on land sales except to the tribe and applied for a loan of $500,000 to be repaid over a long-term period by the income from their tribal holdings. (The tribe's credit record was good; during the years when loans were available it had borrowed extensively and repaid all indebtedness with interest.) The Department through Ernst promised to co-operate. But the local area director discouraged it. Said John Wooden Legs, "He wrote me a letter that said my people should not try to keep their land. He said we should let white men buy all over our reservation, so that the Cheyennes could live next door to these white men and learn to be just like them."

In spite of contrary orders from the Department, the director advertised thirteen tracts for sale. Nearly all of them joined the Bixby Tracts. Then a friend of the Indians got the word to Ernst. As Wooden Legs related it:

"The land sale was advertised. Certain white men were wheeling around like buzzards waiting for the bidding to start. The Cheyennes could not talk—they were so angry and sad. Then all at once the land sale was called off—by a telephone call from Washington. You would have to be a Cheyenne to know what it meant when the Government in Washington kept its word . . . I never saw the Cheyennes as happy as that. I was never as happy myself in my whole life. I think all of us had a picture of the Government helping us save our land, then helping us with a plan to make our Cheyenne community a good part of America."

In 1960 they drew up a formal plan. They employed an attorney to work out the technical details, but the ideas and the words were theirs. It began, "Our people are proud to be Americans and Northern Cheyennes. That is all we have to be proud of today, except our honorable past. . . . We think of our past as we write this plan for our future, because we need strength for our spirits if we are to make our future good," and in this past "are the names of great and generous hunters who fed the people, fighters who died for freedom just as white men's heroes died, holy men who filled us with the power of God. Take us together that way . . . and we will have the strength of spirit to decide what to do and do it. We will do good things as a tribe that is growing and changing that we cannot do as individual men cut off from our forefathers." As for the plan, "The goals . . . will be the goals the Cheyenne people want to reach, and not the goals others of good heart think we should want to reach." Then followed involved computations of borrowing and repayment, and the final aim of the tribe to "hold together its lands, either in individual Indian ownership by restricted titles, or as tribal lands. No Indian will at any time be forced to sell his or her allotment. Only when the allottee elects to sell . . . will the tribe stand ready to bid upon and purchase the lands."

By this time the frozen loan fund was beginning to thaw, and other tribes had begun to take hope. But "cotton wool resistance" managed to delay official approval of the Northern Cheyenne plan until well into the next administration—in 1962. La Verne Madigan telephoned the good news to Wooden Legs, comparing him with Little Wolf and Dull Knife. He was so moved he could hardly speak, but he answered, "The Wolf protected our people; Morning Star [Dull Knife] led our people; and Wooden Legs had strong thighs and could keep on walking for a long, long time." Later when the council gave its formal acceptance, a councilman, John Stands-in-Timber, said, "Usually we sit in Council and pass resolutions on little things, silly things. Today we did a big thing. Today we were men."

At the same time, the tribe received an additional loan for developing crafts, tourism, and tribal and individual cattle production. In five years employment and family income doubled and morbidity and mortality rates were cut in half. In 1966 the tribe established a $250,000 scholarship fund and set up another fund to attract industry and develop its timber and coal reserves. It has in fact become one of the most successful Indian tribes in the United States.

Thus the Northern Cheyennes escaped the erosion that was undermining the economy of other tribes. Their progress was matched by the relatively secure tribes of the Southwest. Notable among these were the Navahos.

While the Navahos were still receiving rehabilitation assistance under the act of 1950, they were able to supplement it by income from oil and uranium leases. By 1954 the tribal income totaled $6,000,000. It could have been distributed per capita, $80 each to the then 76,000 desperately poor Navahos; but they applied it to long-term projects. They set aside $5,000,000, later increasing it to $10,000,000, as an educational endowment, using the interest to send their high school graduates to college. Soon their income reached $16,000,000. Their budget for the fiscal year 1959 was $12,639,131, with the following most important allocations: $3,000,000 for construction, using Navaho labor; $619,500 in relief for needy school children (clothing, hearing

381

aids, eye care); $352,000 for welfare; $156,750 for a health committee (layettes for new babies, vitamins, medicines); $860,000 for drilling water wells and providing water storage; $768,766 for law and order (Navaho police force, tribal courts, jails); $185,000 for industrial development including the operation of the tribal business office. At Window Rock, their capital, they built a motel, established a craft center, and launched a program to capture the tourist trade. They built sawmills, employing Navaho labor and bringing an income to the tribe. In 1960 they launched a newspaper, the *Navajo Times*, with the able Dillon Platero in charge. It is an excellent publication reporting on all phases of Navaho life. At the same time, local communities with the encouragement of the tribal council were organizing into "chapters" and building chapter houses as meeting places for local political, social, and educational activities.

Even with these developments the Navahos realized that their reservation could not adequately support their still-growing population, and they looked to relocation to take the overflow. But their spiritual upsurge showed that Indians could cook their own meal in the tipi when nobody was trying to burn it down. In the election of 1960 this hope was held out to other tribes also.

CHAPTER TWENTY

THE WHITE MAN
GETS A NEW CHANCE

In the presidential election of 1960 both parties adopted platform planks favorable to the Indians, and both candidates made enlightened personal commitments. Then when he became president, John F. Kennedy appointed Stewart L. Udall, whose Indian record as a representative from Arizona had been good, as secretary of the interior; and John A. Carver, who became an ardent defender of Indian interests, as assistant secretary.

Besides all the old responsibilities, the administration faced a new obligation of great magnitude, as the unresolved problems of the Alaska natives came to a head during the 1960s.[1] All the conflicts and cross-currents of interest and policy that had marked the history of the "Lower 48" were repeated in this new state, and it seems evident that the same disaster would have overwhelmed the natives except for the crusading zeal of nongovernmental Indian interest organizations.

As had happened in the Lower 48 the exploitation was ameliorated by educational and humanitarian influences. In 1794 the first Orthodox missionaries came with thirty families of Russian settlers to Kodiak Island, and their work with the natives was continued by the local churches and priests after the United States purchased Alaska in 1867. As late as 1900 they were conducting six schools for them. When the Indian Bureau first brought a contingent of two hundred native students to Chilocco, Oklahoma, in 1967, a local Catholic priest was

---

[1] A comprehensive study of the Alaska natives—history, ethnography, primitive economy and its changing patterns, population, and present condition—and detailed information regarding land ownership may be found in *Alaska Natives and Their Land*, by the Federal Field Commission for Development Planning in Alaska, published at Anchorage in October, 1958.

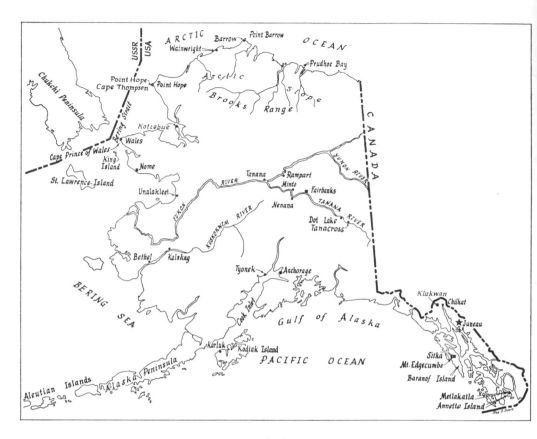

Alaska

qualified to conduct services in the Eastern rite for fifty of the group who held the Orthodox faith.

By the treaty of purchase the "uncivilized native tribes" became subject to the same laws as their contemporaries in the rest of the United States. This, of course, made them eligible for the same educational and vocational training and health services—as soon as it should be possible to provide them. There were no land rushes to this frozen area, hence no wars to complicate these efforts. In 1884, Congress provided a territorial government and authorized the Department of the Interior to establish schools for the children without reference to race. These schools were conducted by the Bureau of Education until they were transferred to the Indian Bureau in 1931. Apparently, the first ones were in the narrow southeastern strip.

Six years after the territory was created, the Bureau of Education opened its first schools for the Eskimos: at Cape Prince of Wales, on Bering Strait; at Point Hope, projecting into the Arctic on the northwest; and at Point Barrow, the northernmost tip. The annual congressional appropriation for white and native schools in all Alaska was then fifty thousand dollars. Substantial buildings were constructed and the schools were operated under subsidy contracts with Presbyterian, Episcopal, and Congregational mission boards. Supplies were brought up annually by a sturdy steamer, first from San Francisco, then from Seattle. The Eskimos, always a friendly people, welcomed the teachers, and the responsive children fulfilled a pedagogue's dream of perfection.[2]

Young William T. Lopp at Wales combined sympathetic understanding of native ways with practical planning. For many generations the Eskimos had been assembling there every summer for a trading voyage to Siberia in seventy or eighty great walrus-skin canoes (umiaks), each manned by thirty to forty rowers. On the point of land visible across the stormy strait lived the Chukchis, a people identical to themselves in language and race, but with a reindeer-raising rather than a hunting economy. There the Eskimos traded whale meat for reindeer meat, skins, and sinews. When Lopp saw the return of the loaded umiaks, he suggested importing a herd of these food-clothing-transportation animals, and the Eskimos approved enthusiastically. The Washington office favored the plan, and the next year the supply ship crossed the strait and brought back 16 reindeer with three deermen to teach the techniques of herding them and breaking them to the sled. Eventually, 1,280 were imported. The project was financed at first by philanthropic contributions until Congress made a small appropriation in 1893. As missions and schools multiplied, the natural increase of the first shipments provided them with herds. (For example, in 1924, Wainwright, a village on the north coast of fewer than three hundred Eskimos, owned four herds totaling 8,000 deer.) At present native-owned herds may be found along the northern and western coast; there is a commercial meat-processing plant at Nome, owned and operated by natives; and the more southern villages, lacking permafrost, are installing electric freezers; but the domestic reindeer has only supplemented, never supplanted, the hunting and dog-sledding economy of the Eskimos.

[2] A charming account of one teacher's experience during the year 1924–25 is given in Eva Alvey Richards, *Arctic Mood.*

As white enterprise increased, the schools in the settled areas were gradually supported by taxation, while the Education Bureau concentrated on schools for the natives. In 1925 it reported 85 schools with 154 teachers, reaching an estimated 44 per cent of the villages. Education is still not universal, but considering the obstacles of climate and distance encountered by the federal administration, the number of natives who are literate or able to express themselves orally in English seems a remarkable achievement. They are requesting local high schools, grieving over their children sent five thousand miles to Oklahoma, half as far to Chemawa, Oregon, or perhaps a mere fifteen hundred miles to the Bureau's only Alaska high school, Mount Edgecumbe, near Sitka. But even so, a surprising number go on to college at the University of Alaska or in the Lower 48.

When the Bureau of Education set up schools in the native villages, it established co-operative trading posts there. To the Arctic Eskimos the goods came up annually in the same ship that brought the teachers and the school supplies, and a native manager in each store traded throughout the year for furs and pelts brought in by the trappers. Thus the economy was gradually modified by these outside products. When the Indian Reorganization Act was extended to Alaska in 1936, these native stores were united under the Alaska Native Industries Cooperative Association (ANICA), and it became possible for them to borrow money from the revolving loan fund. The ANICA still supervises the native stores and acts as their purchasing agent in an annual gross business of more than one million dollars, but it is directed by an Indian Bureau office in Seattle under all-white management. Some co-operative salmon canneries were established under the same act in the area facing the Pacific, but they also never came under effective native control. The natives there find their main livelihood in owning and operating or in manning the boats for the fishing that supplies the canneries. Probably the Indian administration even at its best found Alaska too remote for any imaginative economic planning with the natives.

The most neglected of their problems was the protection of their land. The act creating the territory had provided that they should "not be disturbed" in their possession, but the terms under which they might acquire title were "reserved for future legislation by Congress." Congress made no attempt to define these terms, but in the early 1900s twelve reservations were set apart for native groups by executive order. Then in 1919 a general law, applicable to Alaska, forbade the practice.

386

Finally the law of 1936 specifically authorized the Department of the Interior to establish reservations for Alaska natives and provided that these selections should be subject to their approval in an election by secret ballot. The Indian Bureau assisted the villages to form corporate charters under the act, and six reservations were set aside for them during the early 1940s. One of them was a small tract on Kodiak Island comprising the fabulously rich salmon-spawning waters of the Karluk River and the adjoining coast. Commercial fishermen were accordingly required to procure licenses to fish there, and one of the canneries on the island brought suit. On May 31, 1949, in *Hynes* v. *Grimes Packing Company* the Supreme Court ruled that reservations established under the Reorganization Act "are subject to the unfettered will of Congress" and that the secretary "was without statutory authority" to convey "any permanent title or right" to the natives. Thus these reservations were under the same uncertain status as had once unsettled the Indians' title to executive order reservations in the Lower 48.

The secretary meanwhile was laying out other reservations, but an intensive campaign was launched by local interests to frighten the natives into rejecting them. They were told that they would be "confined" there and would lose the valued American citizenship they had acquired under the blanket law of 1924. They accordingly voted against acceptance. Later, in the early 1950s, ninety villages did petition to have their land reserved, but the Department of the Interior failed to act. By that date the Indian administration under the termination policy was breaking up reservations, not establishing them. Some people of good will in the Lower 48 became concerned, but nothing in the natives' concept of property warned them of their precarious tenure on the land that had supported them for ages.

Then came the statehood act of 1958. It reaffirmed the principle of native possession expressed in the territorial act but made no effort to define it, and it authorized the new state to select 102,550,000 acres of land from the public domain. In all of Alaska the natives held clear title to only two small reservations, both in the southeast: on Annette Island the Indian village of Metlakatla, which had moved over in a body from Canada and acquired its land by a special act of Congress in 1891; and Chilkat Indian village near Klukwan, which was given title to its minerals by an act of September 7, 1957.

By then events were moving to a climax. In 1930 the natives had constituted one-half the population. After World War II came the cold war with the Soviet Union and the multiplication of defense installations in Alaska. Next, statehood brought a surge of development. The census of 1960 showed that the nonnative population outnumbered the native more than four to one—183,086 nonnative to 43,081 native, of whom 14,444 were Indians, about 24,000 Eskimos, and 5,000 Aleuts.[3] Along with this influx of white population came all the ruthless drive and creative power of a new frontier and the eagerness of federal administrators to make their mark on an untouched land. When the Indian Bureau tried to protect the natives, it was thwarted by more powerful agencies in its own department. Notable was the Bureau of Land Management, which gave away land to anybody who wanted it, regardless of the natives' still undetermined claims. As it happened, it was arbitrary actions by such agencies that first alarmed them.

In 1958 the Bureau of Land Management licensed the Atomic Energy Commission to use 1,600 square miles of land around Cape Thompson south of Point Hope as an experimental test site. Nobody bothered to consult the Eskimos who lived in the area—three villages with seven hundred people—and there was the greater danger of contaminating the migrating caribou and the drifting sea animals, which would be hunted and eaten far from the scene. A University of Alaska botanist resigned in protest from the committee investigating the project and communicated with the AAIA. (He was discharged from his faculty position by the university; later, two other scientists who dared to question the project suffered similar penalties.)

La Verne Madigan made a fact-finding trip to the state in the summer of 1960—"to find out exactly what the areas of our ignorance are in order that we may know what we have to learn before we can form an 'Alaska policy'" for the AAIA. She talked with leading Alaskans, finding some concerned citizens willing to co-operate. Out of their concern grew the Alaska Native Rights Association (ANRA). She visited the Eskimos at Barrow, and they said they would call three villages to meet her there if she would come back and explain their status; they could not understand why since statehood they had been required to buy hunting and fishing licenses. At the same time the Eskimos at Point Hope were appealing to the AAIA for help. Council President Paul Frankson wrote, "all and everyone at this village would not like to see this experiment blast . . . with our earnest desire we have

[3] Eskimos and Aleuts were not enumerated separately. "Other races" totaled 28,637.

388

been seeking in someone who would help us . . . for we wish not to be hurted as any kind of race living."

The next year the Interior Department's Fish and Wildlife Service began a vigorous enforcement of the international migratory bird treaty and arrested Eskimos who killed ducks for food. Neither the Canadian nor the American government had previously enforced it against them; their take was small in comparison with that of sportsmen, and the fowl were not even in their area during the open season. Guy Okakok of Barrow wrote to the AAIA: "We just had a meeting yesterday in school[house], right after evening service. We discuss about our ducks. . . . We did not know that we can't shoot ducks when they come through our shore. Anyway, please come so I can let you know everything." Nobody could advise these dwellers on the barren tundra to take 160-acre homesteads and support themselves by farming, but all the hunting regulations were designed for sports hunters. As Okakok saw it, "Why don't they realize that the kids and family depend on meat?"

Dr. Theodore B. Hetzel of Haverford College visited Alaska during June and July that year on behalf of the Indian Rights Association. Miss Madigan and Dr. Henry S. Forbes of the AAIA board of directors came in July. The visitors held conferences with officials of the federal agencies from Juneau to Fairbanks and talked with anthropologists and wildlife experts. They found the Bureau of Land Management busily disposing of the public domain with no notice to the native occupants except an advertisement in an Alaska newspaper, a procedure equivalent to no notice at all to the people of a remote village. There was the selection of the state's 102,550,000 acres, grants to groups needing recreation areas, deeds to wilderness-loving white men under the homestead act—all of which added to the great tracts set aside by the federal government as forest reserves and for other purposes indicated that the land would all be gone before any provision was made for the natives.

They saw a good example of the confused land situation when they visited the Athapascan village of Tyonek in an area of active oil development on Cook Inlet. The 265 Indians occupied a 27,000-acre reservation, established by executive order in 1915 at the request of their Bureau of Education teacher and incorporated under the Reorganization Act in 1939. In 1960, Rex Lee had ruled for the Department of the Interior that it was not a true reservation and that the

Indians had no title to the land or its minerals. Now oil wells were producing and leases were selling at a premium in the state-acquired land adjoining it, and the oil companies were anxious to lease the reservation if only its status were defined. The state also was concerned: if the land belonged to the Indians, all the oil income would go to them; if the federal government still owned it, Alaska, under a provision of the statehood act, would receive 90 per cent. The Indian Bureau favored legislation confirming the Indian title; the Bureau of Land Management opposed it.

The visitors flew to a number of Eskimo villages and talked with the people. They found them disturbed and puzzled, but uninformed about their legal position. Miss Madigan told them that the AAIA would pay the expense (bush plane transportation) of a general meeting where they could exchange experiences and meet government officials, where technical experts would be available, but which would be planned and run by natives. "This idea caught like wildfire," as Dr. Forbes reported it, "and the village councils at once went into action." They decided to hold the meeting at Barrow in November. They were beginning to realize that the atomic threat and the hunting restrictions were only surface indications of their underlying insecurity. Even Barrow was inside a naval petroleum reserve set aside in 1923, and nearby was a large defense installation. Beneath was a great natural-gas field, from which gas was piped through the village to supply the base and other federal facilities, but the Eskimos, huddled in their huts with winds of fifty degrees below zero blowing outside, were forbidden to use it.

Indian Bureau Area Director James Hawkins, with headquarters at far-off Juneau, was sincerely devoted to the natives' interests. When land selected by the state included their villages, he had assisted them in filing protests with the Bureau of Land Management. These were usually pigeonholed or rejected, or the village site with no outlying land was excluded from the state grant; but even so, Hawkins was a nuisance. The Alaska delegation in Congress, especially Senator Ernest Gruening, demanded his removal and the appointment of an Alaskan of their own choosing. The administration yielded and agreed to transfer him to the Lower 48. (After all, Gruening was a powerful Democratic politician and he had served as territorial governor of Alaska from 1939 until the beginning of the Eisenhower administration.) But Hawkins' removal was postponed by the Department of the Interior long enough for him to help the Eskimos set up their meeting.

Miss Madigan had suggested that a committee unhampered by white advisers should prepare the agenda. They met on August 31 at Point Hope. Guy Okakok served as chairman and Frank Degnan of Unalakleet as secretary. The minutes are eloquent of the Eskimos' practical statesmanship, their democratic procedures, and their dawning realization that all the villages had identical problems.

"Chairman, Guy Okakok open the floor, and have started the meeting. He said, men you all know, why we are here to attend the meeting. Meeting where no one will disturb us in our speech. 'First,' I would like each one of you to know . . . we Eskimos have been living on ducks from generations to generations, taking the ducks with slings and other implements of our own devising before the white man ever laid his [eyes?] on Alaska. . . . Mr. Degnan stood up and said, Mr. Chairman, I have heard lots about you Eskimos up at Barrow, its not only in your place Barrow but we have same problems like you have. . . . Chairman asked any more objection? No one stood up and Chairman said to the committees [committee members] this is one of the problems we to discuss about in the November meeting. . . .

". . . Dan? have you any problems you wish to speak about? [Daniel Lisburne of Point Hope:] Mr. Chairman few years ago the atomic have placed a sign up. The Atomic Commission have planned to blow a Nuclear Explosives. . . . I myself as a citizen is against it, not me alone, but the rest of the residents of Pt. Hope. . . . That means our hunting ground will be destroyed. If they do where are we going to hunt the games, and how are we to find food for our families. Mr. Chairman, Dan asked, you better have to talk about this and explain it in the meeting this coming November."

There were some problems of communication in the days following. Guy Okakok went out in his boat to hunt walrus and was icebound for nearly two weeks—"The ocean has been terrible here." Then in October, "I have been away for weeks hunting, Bowhead whales this fall. . . . 3 whales were killed the very same day, but one sink."

The meeting was held on November 15–18. Carver was there to represent the government; he was deeply moved by the experience and gave the natives his wholehearted support. Miss Madigan was present throughout. Now fully informed about the legal basis of their tenure, the Eskimos struggled with a declaration of policy. As Okakok told it later,[4] "Have work 19 hours one day, all these committees and delegates sure were working patiently over on our Statement, had to come home tired and sleepy. When home 3:38 a.m. Following evening at 8:00 p.m. the Native Store Theater opens for General Public meeting. Never did see so many people, attendance during meeting hours. Inupiat[5] Statement was read to the audience." The statement began:

"We the Inupiat have come together for the first time ever in all the years of our history. . . . We always thought that our Inupiat Paitot ["Peoples' Heritage"] was safe to be passed down to our future generations as our fathers passed down to us. Our Inupiat Paitot is our land around the whole Arctic world where we the Inupiat live. . . . Today our Inupiat Paitot is called by white men aboriginal rights. . . .

"The rights of us Inupiat have never been explained truthfully and properly to us. . . . We were told that if the government reserved our aboriginal land for us, we could not be citizens of United States—could not vote—would be tied on reservation like a dog—could not have businesses come on our land or sell products of our land.

"That was a lie told to us Inupiat to take away our aboriginal land and mineral rights. Talking at this meeting, about what we were told about aboriginal rights and reservations, we found that each one of our villages were told the same lies. But we never knew that, because we never before had a chance to talk to each other.

"We did not know before what our . . . rights were, but now we know. . . . Our Inupiat right to own the land and minerals of our ancestors, to hunt and fish without restrictions over this land and sea."

Examples were given: marketable timber of Kalskag on the lower Kuskokwim River, the natural gas under Barrow—"things from which we could get income and royalties. We could use these to develop our people; to improve our education, housing and sanitation; to make employment; to get better transportation for our villages. We could use this income to keep the independence we the Inupiat have always had and want to pass on to our children."

Regarding the hunting restrictions, "The problem is not how to get food. We are hunters and we know how. The problem is game laws and sport hunters. . . . During last half of winter there are light planes that hunt polar bears and line up on ice in front of Kotzebue and other villages. . . . These sport hunters take their kill, take the skin and

4 Speaking to the AAIA in New York, May 7, 1962.
5 "People," the Eskimos' word for themselves.

leave the meat, the food. . . . We find the dead bears drifted shore or untouched on ice with bullet holes in them."

It asked the Department of the Interior to set aside tracts of land around the natives' villages and to permit them to hunt there and on the sea. It requested exemption from the migratory bird treaty and the abandonment of the atomic explosion. It made recommendations regarding education, housing, health, and employment opportunities. Finally, it suggested the formation of a permanent organization with a newsletter to be sent to the villages.

At the very time this meeting was in progress, Alaska's own candidate for area director of the Indian service was in Washington being oriented for his responsibility. But—according to a statement he made at the time—his ideas were in such direct opposition to those of the Bureau that he declined the position. The Bureau then selected one of its ablest employees, Robert L. Bennett, an Oneida Indian from Wisconsin, who had served in field offices and in Washington; and the administration stood firm against Senator Gruening's demands for a political appointment. Then Senator E. L. Bartlett began to show concern for the natives' problems, and under his leadership the congressional delegation obtained legislation authorizing the navy to sell gas to Barrow and championed the duck hunters so ardently that Secretary Udall restrained the zeal of his Fish and Wildlife Service. Even the powerful Atomic Energy Commission dropped its plans, after a stormy confrontation with the natives at Point Hope. But the fundamental problem of aboriginal rights remained unresolved.

Nearly fifty villages, mainly Eskimo, had filed claims with the Bureau of Land Management for land they were using, and Hawkins had presented them as one of his last official acts. This blocking of state selections caused an uproar in Alaska, and great political pressure was put on the Department of the Interior to release them. On February 28, before Bennett had arrived in Alaska, the Bureau of Land Management rejected the protests.

It was very hard for the Eskimos, trusting Carver as their friend, to understand the Department's split personality. Paul Tiulana, the leader of the King Island village, wrote to Miss Madigan that "our very rich land . . . will be too valuable to them, for set aside for us under our aboriginal rights. I might be wrong but thats the way I feel about it now. We are not going to fight with the rifles, but our moral. This is not going to be easy battle because our opponents are train in College and we are don't much in white man language. But we have a very good friends and you are one of them, you know the language and I depended on you." Then with typical Eskimo good nature he added, "I am not condemning the good persons in our government. there always be some bad ones in good government."

Meanwhile, that same spring of 1962, the Athapascans of the interior were appealing to the AAIA for help in *their* problems. Miss Madigan flew to Alaska to confer with both groups. She attended a planning session of the chiefs and leaders of eight Athapascan villages called at Nenana by the Nenana chief, Alfred Ketzler. Then she visited the leaders of the Eskimo organization that had been formed following the Barrow meeting. A craze for tape recording had struck the villages so that they exchanged messages in their own language over miles of tundra, but they still hoped to establish a newsletter. They chose Howard Rock (Weyahok), a Point Hope Eskimo, to edit it. A product of the local Episcopal mission school, he had gone on to attend the University of Washington at Seattle and was now living at Fairbanks as an established painter of Northern subjects.

Another Athapascan meeting was held at Tanana, historic meeting place of these people, during June 24–26, with Alfred Ketzler as chairman. Miss Madigan came back to help, and Dr. Hetzel was present, but the Indians organized and conducted the proceedings. Not all the delegates spoke English adequately—said one, "When I stand up to speak my mind sits down"—but as village after village stated its problems, it was apparent that these Indians, living in more desirable areas than the Eskimos, were suffering greater encroachment.

Minto once had "a good village. Then statehood came and the new State has made a map of our village. Now a man can only own land where his house is. The State is taking land right at Minto. . . . For 15 miles around our village, we hunt [musk]rats and moose. We always did. Now there are 24 white camps there. *Everywhere you turn you are bumping into a white man. . . .* Without our hunting land, our village is finished."

Said the Dot Lake representative: "The surveyors for the State came in and surveyed the property and told the people they had no claim because they had not filed on it. Many of the people do not read or write and speak poor English. They do not understand the laws and no one has explained them."

The Tanacross spokesman told how his village had repeatedly filed claims to their hunting and fishing grounds without result. "We must get together and do something. There must be a way."

394

And so it went, with state and army recreation centers taking up all available land and with sportsmen flying in to build cabins and hunt in areas adjacent to the villages where the Indians hunted for subsistence. The mayor of distant Metlakatka,[6] unrelated to other Alaska Indians, came as a delegate, with the only happy report. There, where the people had control of their resources, they operated fish traps providing jobs for two hundred people, and a native-owned cannery, a store, and other businesses provided more work as well as profit. They also received lease money from an airport located on their land.

The most disturbing report of all came from a plan to build a great dam on the Yukon at Rampart. The Corps of Engineers had made the survey and Secretary Udall ardently advocated the construction as a source of hydroelectric power. It would back up a lake the size of Lake Erie, destroy the ecology of the whole vast region, and flood ten Athapascan villages.

Dr. Hetzel found that the Athapascans had been as thoroughly brainwashed as the Eskimos against reservations. He suggested that they send a delegation to visit reservations in the Lower 48. They finally drew up a statement of policy:

"We have talked for three days about things we did not understand before. We have found that all the Natives of Alaska have many of the same problems. . . . Our people always thought they owned the land where they lived and hunted. They did not lose it by war and they did not sell it. We still feel it is ours. . . . The state is invading and selling our land. There are no jobs in the villages and our hunting grounds are being taken away. We no longer have any way to feed our children."

They made recommendations about schools and the employment of natives on government and private construction projects. They joined the Eskimos in requesting the withdrawal of land around their villages pending settlement of their claims. Finally they said:

"Too often good things are said by men at meetings and when they are together they feel strong enough to carry out great plans. Then they go to their different villages and when each man is alone he finds that he is too weak and discouraged to do what was planned together. We will not let that happen," and they decided to form a permanent organization. They asked for continued help from the AAIA, the

---

[6] His village is so far away that I strongly suspect he was brought there by the AAIA, but the Athapascans welcomed him and were greatly impressed by his report.

ANRA, the Indian Rights Association, and the Eskimo organization.

The Tanana meeting was Miss Madigan's last service to the Alaskan natives, for the next month she was killed in an accident. But Dr. Forbes had become deeply committed to their cause. In August from his Massachusetts home he called Howard Rock and offered his financial backing for a native newspaper—a real newspaper, not a little newsletter—on condition that Rock serve as editor. Rock protested his lack of newspaper experience, but he finally took over the work with some help at first from a local journalist. The first issue of the *Tundra Times* came off the press at Fairbanks on October 1, with the names of the two native organizations on the masthead. Individuals and villages purchased stock in the publishing corporation but Dr. Forbes continued his financial assistance until the end of 1968.

Through objective reporting and discerning editorials the paper has become the voice of an informed native citizenry and has exerted an educational influence on nonnative Alaskans of good will. The very first issue carried congratulatory greetings from Indian Bureau Area Director Bennett—recognition of a government agency that had been reduced to near impotence by Alaskan opposition. Even more significant was a statement given at a press conference by Secretary Udall, who happened to be in Alaska at the time. Courageously he characterized the unpopular ("meddlesome," even "Communistic") AAIA as "a constructive organization," saying that its president, Oliver La Farge, "happens to be a good friend of mine."

That first issue also carried a message from Alfred Ketzler describing the action taken at the Eskimo and Athapascan meetings and inviting the co-operation of other natives. (They took his advice; the paper now represents the other three ethnic groups, the Aleuts, the Tlingits, and the Haidas.)

"Your grandfathers and mine," he said, "left this land to us in the only kind of deed they knew . . . by word of mouth and our continued possession. Among our people this 'deed' was honored just as much as if it was written and signed by the President of the United States. . . . Now things have changed. We need a legal title to our land if we are to hold it."

Their precarious tenure was demonstrated the following March, when the Bureau of Land Management quietly published a notice in the *Federal Register* that it was going to set aside nine million acres of land for the Rampart Dam. Thirty days were allowed for filing protests that could lead to hearings by the Alaska division of the Bureau.

At the same time, this Alaska office gave out informally that "squawks" from the Athapascan villages affected would not count in calling hearings. The AAIA learned of the notice only by accident after most of the time had expired. It notified the villages, and Oliver La Farge wrote to Udall. The Secretary was as surprised as the Indians and assured them of ample time and adequate hearings. Meanwhile, the *Tundra Times* published protests from the villages, protests that would not have appeared in any other Alaska newspaper.

All this—*or something*—apparently stimulated the Department of the Interior to do a little studying. In 1967 it dropped the project on the ground that there was no present use for the power it would generate and that it would destroy the habitat of thousands of moose and the nesting grounds of migratory fowl. Thus incidentally was saved the habitat and nesting grounds of the Indians.

Meanwhile, the natives, with the encouragement of their white well-wishers, continued to strengthen their organizations. Dr. Hetzel was present at the Athapascan meeting in 1963 as was also William Byler, the new executive director of the AAIA. To the Indians the most interesting guest was Lester Oliver, tribal chairman of their long-separated relatives, the White Mountain Apaches, who had been brought there by the ANRA through the initiative of Dr. Hetzel. He showed pictures of the beautiful, unspoiled Fort Apache Reservation and told how his people were developing its resources with Indian Bureau help on projects of their own choosing, hunted and fished on their land without interference from the United States or Arizona, and even required sportsmen to pay for hunting, fishing, and camping privileges. The situation he described was very different from the shrinking economy of his hearers: "Nothing is so sorrowful as for a hunter, empty handed, to be greeted by hungry children," said Chief Richard Frank of Minto.

At that very time the Athapascans received unexpected confirmation of the White Mountain argument. The solicitor for the Department of the Interior, after a review of all the legal questions, ruled that the Indian Bureau possessed authority to lease the Tyonek land for oil and gas development for the benefit of the Indians. The lease was made the following year, and the Tyoneks received a bonus of nearly $12,000,000. One of their first acts was to pay off a mortgage on their village store and to build a community hall. They then adopted a program of road improvement, the expansion of an air strip, and housing, health, and welfare projects; and they set aside a $200,000 trust fund for education. Finally, in 1969, with the assistance of a state agency, they launched a campaign to lure small industry to their village, offering the inducements of abundant gas and power, low taxes, and a capable work force. Their claim to the surface has also been upheld by the courts. All this furnishes an object lesson to other natives, showing what they could do with their land if they had it.

But before she died, Miss Madigan had concluded that Congress would never define the native rights except on terms satisfactory to the members from Alaska. This meant that the natives with their 20 per cent voting strength had to become active in politics. In June, 1964, the AAIA sponsored a two-day conference at Fairbanks of all the native organizations in the state. By then a number of regional organizations had sprung up, so that seven were represented. They made statements about educational and economic development, but they especially stressed political action at the village level—acquainting the people with candidates and issues and instructing them in the mechanics of voting.

Their influence was not apparent in the election that fall, but in October, 1966, three hundred of their leaders from all over the state met at Anchorage and formed the Alaska Federation of Natives (AFN). There they drafted legislation to be presented to Congress, and local politicians of both parties promptly endorsed it. Their ballots that year were credited with swinging the election in some state contests.

Shortly after this election—on a date buried somewhere in Department of the Interior files[7]—Secretary Udall ordered a "land freeze" halting state selections and all other dispositions until Congress should legislate on the natives' claims. This action brought outraged protests of new state builders from recently elected Governor Walter J. Hickel on down. On August 10, 1967, in a letter to the Governor defending this action, Udall closed with an almost wistful appeal for understanding.

"I hope you will agree that these actions are justified. . . . I trust the State is not intent upon depriving the Alaska Natives of the lands they use and occupy and need for their livelihood. The National conscience would be deeply disturbed if it believed we were not upholding our ideals of human justice in dealing with the Eskimos and Alaska Indians.

[7] I have explored every possible source of information without result. Even the Federal Field Commission failed to find it.

"I am sure you will join me in meeting this high expectation."

But the state brought a test case in the federal district court to compel the Secretary to grant it the land used by the village of Nenana. It won in the local court, and the Government and the natives appealed. In December, 1969, the Ninth Circuit Court of Appeals not only upheld the freeze but also affirmed the validity of aboriginal use and occupancy. Thus the natives had a strong legal position.

Meanwhile, with its selections halted, the state was driven to recognize the natives' claims. The state officials and the AFN leaders, with the support of the legislature, drafted a settlement by which the natives would retain 40,000,000 acres (10 per cent of the state area, including much barren tundra) and receive some compensation for the remainder.

Thus in 1968, Congress entered the second century of the undetermined claims with the first serious showing of interest in resolving them. Also, in January of that year the Haida and Tlinget Indians won a court judgment of seven and one-half million dollars for the Tongass National Forest and other land taken for federal purposes without their consent. This decision was a warning of what might happen when aboriginal rights were ignored. The next month the Senate Interior and Insular Affairs Committee came to Anchorage and held three-day hearings, giving the natives the first opportunity they had ever had to present their case.

The natives had come a long way in the eight years since they had groped for outside help to explain their status in a baffling situation. Now it was the native organizations that informed the people. "We have been a little weak in communications with the villages on land matters," said Emil Notti, the president of the AFN; and in June the directors took out six months' subscriptions to the *Tundra Times* for them—227 in all, with names like Afognak, Chowhoctolik, and Ugsonokle. The AFN paid such expenses from voluntary donations of natives and nonnative well-wishers. (Tyonek lent it $100,000 in May that year, and in December it received a grant of $100,000 from the Ford Foundation.)

Twenty-one strongly functioning regional organizations are now affiliated with the AFN. Notti, the president, is an Athapascan who grew up in a village on the Yukon, graduated from Mount Edgecumbe, and then went on to college for a degree in electronic engineering. John Borbridge, the first vice-president, serves as president of the Tlingit-Haida organization and is a graduate of the University of

Michigan. In July, Notti, Borbridge, and nine other native leaders went to Washington and were permitted to testify before committees of both houses of Congress—for the first time in 101 years. Among them were William L. Hensley, an Eskimo of Kotzebue and a member of the state legislature, and Donald R. Wright (descended from an Eskimo grandmother married to a white engineer and an Athapascan grandfather who married a white nurse), president of the Cook Inlet Native Association. Governor Hickel went along and gave them at least qualified support, as did also the members of Congress from the state. They made an impressive presentation, and there were high hopes of a final settlement, but the Ninetieth Congress adjourned without taking action.

The protection of their land means the difference between starvation and plenty in the villages, for subsistence hunting is still the major source of their economy. The natives are hard-working and adaptable—they have to be to survive—but they have few, if any, opportunities for employment in the developing industry of the state. Nearly all the work is done by outside contractors, who bring in their own crews. The situation came to a head in 1968, when immense oil deposits were discovered on the Arctic Slope at Prudhoe Bay on land the state had cannily acquired east of the naval reserve. In December that year John Sackett, an able young Athapascan member of the state legislature, visited the area and reported to the *Tundra Times*:

"It is with great, rapid and thundering strides that the complexities of the 20th century has struck the Arctic Slope. . . . Great regions where a man could travel for miles upon miles in search of furs and food is now criss-crossed by caterpillars [and] trucks, and [there is] the ceaseless noise of carpenters building structures to house the [development]." Not one Eskimo had been hired, although 250, many with the necessary mechanical skills, were available at Barrow.

In September, Governor Hickel appointed a task force to work for the employment of local people, especially natives. The chairman was W. W. Keeler of Bartlesville, Oklahoma, chairman of Phillips Petroleum Corporation, who is also serving as principal chief of the Cherokees and combines the drive and decisiveness of the white man with the Indian's sensitive perceptions and an awareness of native problems. The other members were Alaska industrialists (copper mining, lumbering, fisheries, and contracting), labor union officials, natives (Howard Rock, Emil Notti, John Borbridge), and public leaders in various fields.

The next month the task force held a meeting at Anchorage with seventeen high officials of the major oil companies of the United States. The native members in particular made an effective presentation, combining practical reasoning with eloquence. The Governor aided them throughout. "Employ the people who really understand the area," he told the oil men. "These people have learned to cope with the elements." The officials listened, but up to the present the situation remains unchanged.

Also in October the AFN held its annual meeting at Fairbanks, with 275 delegates in attendance. All the candidates for Congress (for one Senate seat and the state's one representative) addressed the gathering, each advocating the settlement of the land question. The convention avoided making any official endorsement, but certainly native rights was the paramount issue in the decisions of individual voters.

On December 11, after the election of Richard M. Nixon to the presidency, Secretary Udall served notice that he was extending the land freeze until the end of 1970 or until the Ninety-first Congress should settle its status. At the same time, Nixon designated Governor Hickel as his choice for secretary of the interior. Throughout American history from the admission of Kentucky to the Union in 1792 to that of Oklahoma in 1907, appointing the governor of any frontier state to a position supervising native rights would have been equivalent to appointing a wolf as guardian of the sheepfold. This appointment might be different, for Hickel had come to concede the natives' claim and had co-operated with them in advancing it. But now he publicly stated, "What Udall can do by executive order I can undo."

This statement was very disturbing to the natives. When opposition to his confirmation developed in the Senate, he requested the endorsement of the AFN. The organization decided to withhold it until he clarified his position. Emil Notti, William Hensley, and Eben Hopson of Barrow, the executive director of the Arctic Slope Native Association, were sent to Washington, where they conferred with Chairman Henry M. Jackson and other members of the Interior and Insular Affairs Committee. Hickel was closely questioned during the hearings, and he made a public pledge that he would not lift the freeze until Congress should have the opportunity to act. The native leaders then gave their endorsement. "Natives Breach Edge of National Conscience," was the headline used that week in the *Tundra Times* editorial.

401

The breach will have to go deeper than the edge. The history of the one small village of Tanacross is more eloquent than many generalizations of the helplessness of an obscure native group fighting for survival against massed power abetted by indifference in high places. Its first claim to its land base was marked on a map and registered in 1917. Then in the 1940s an Indian Bureau official came and informed the villagers that a road would be constructed across the area—the present Alaska Highway connecting the state through Canada with the Lower 48—and he had them mark another map so that their interests would be protected. They heard no more about it. On November 6, 1950, they petitioned the Department of the Interior to set the tract aside as a reservation "for our exclusive use and occupancy," and on November 30 they presented a formal claim with clearly defined boundaries to the Bureau of Land Management. Both documents were sent to the Indian Bureau area office in Juneau, where they apparently lay unregarded until 1961.

It will be remembered that in the fall of that year Area Director Hawkins was actively assisting native villages to file their claims. The Tanacross claim thus reached the Bureau of Land Management office in Fairbanks. It still lies there, bearing the stamp, "Received November 16, 1961." It was rejected by this office, and on February 24, 1962, the area director's office filed an appeal on behalf of the village asking for a hearing on the 1950 petition. This appeal was presumably sent to the Bureau office in Washington, but nobody ever heard from it again. No hearing was held, and 63,533 acres of the land was approved as a state selection. (This is the experience of only one of the fifty-or-so villages that Hawkins attempted to protect that winter.)

In 1964 the state prepared to sell vacant lots within the village site. Chief Andrew Isaac, wise in the ways of land and nature but limited in the white man's education, thereupon filed a blanket claim to the tract described in the 1950 petition. Then the next year the state launched a plan to sell "wilderness estates" within the area to outdoor-minded visitors at the New York World's Fair, and it became the duty of Richard D. Mueller of its Division of Lands to investigate the title. Working through the region, he learned that it was being used and claimed by the Tanacross natives. According to the story he told later, he informed his superiors and was told to keep quiet. He then went to the Indian Bureau district office at Fairbanks and found that the claim had indeed been marked on the 1917 map, but he was summarily dismissed from his post for leaving his headquarters without permission.

The *Tundra Times* published the whole story, and the resulting publicity regarding this cloud on the title stopped the plans for selling "wilderness estates" and lots within the townsite.

The matter rested until 1969, when the state again offered some of the land for sale. Chief Isaac protested to Secretary of the Interior Hickel, and in the first answer the village ever received from Washington, Hickel replied that he had checked with the Bureau of Land Management office in the Department and with the state's Division of Lands at Anchorage and was informed that they had no record of any native claim.

"We are not a chess game, we are human beings and right now are a very upset and disturbed people," said the embattled old chief; and he went on to say that "our land has fed, clothed and helped us to survive and is still doing so. Do you wonder why we are fighting to keep it?"

The only hope for any village to "keep it" lies in an equitable settlement of the whole question. In addition to the forty million acres of land, the natives are asking, as compensation for the surrender of the remainder, $500,000,000 (payable over a nine-year period from the wealth the government will derive from acquiring it) and a residual royalty of 2 per cent, the monetary settlement to be administered by native regional and village development corporations. They have not been very successful in informing the Lower 48 of their cause. Alaska is off the regular news beat, so the issue is seldom presented by the press or the broadcasting media. Only the Indian interest organizations, notably the AAIA and the Indian Rights Association, have consistently sought to bring it to public attention.

But Secretary Hickel has modified the terms he had consented as governor to accept. The bill proposed by the administration would trim the land settlement down from forty million to about twelve million acres. Each village would be granted from one to two six-mile-square townships with no land to sustain it, a proposal equivalent to securing a white farmer in his house and barns and cutting off his fields and pastures. The present governor, Keith H. Miller, testifying before congressional committees, has advocated a similar settlement. At the same time, some Alaska politicians and newspapers and the state chamber of commerce are working to create sentiment opposing the natives' position.

All this was intensified when, on September 17 at Anchorage, the state held a sale of oil and gas leases on its North Slope land. A wave

403

of excitement swept the meeting when at the opening of the sealed bids the winner of the first tract was announced at a price of $15,528,960. Whistles and cheers and awed exclamations greeted each sale, and when the most desirable tract of all went for $72,300,000, the crowd broke into wild applause. The day closed with a total of $900,220,590, almost six times the state's operating budget from its total tax revenue; and besides this, there is the anticipated royalties from what is believed to be the greatest oil field ever discovered on the continent.

In the wild exultation that followed there were increased demands that no mineral rights should go with any land settlement made with the natives. The argument ran that since they had taken no part in the discovery or development, they had no claim to the revenue—reasoning never applied to the Texas farmer when oil derricks spring up on his land, or even to the state of Alaska itself in its North Slope windfall. But the natives have many staunch friends in Alaska, especially in the churches and in labor organizations.

Thus the issue is still in doubt. But in spite of setbacks it seems possible that the natives will win their fight and that the tragic history of the Indians in the Lower 48 will not be repeated in Alaska. Like their historical counterparts they will have to make difficult adjustments to the new order. They are still an unspoiled people with keen minds and great adaptability—the Barrow Eskimos, for example, now use motors instead of oars to drive their whaling umiaks, and snowmobiles instead of dog teams for their land travel—but even so, they will encounter problems. Trying to think it through, Paul Tiulana wrote to Miss Madigan back in 1962:

"I never rest my mind since we meet at Barrow last fall. I have been try to dig some clue why we always rejected from our tradition living from our ancestor. And now also rejected when we try to enter to your modernize world. We cannot live in two world, we are going to be lost if the pressure getting too much from each aside. Let find a solution before its too late."

Only the protection of their land base will ease them over this transition. If given this chance, they will find their "solution." In some respects it is already "too late" in the Lower 48 as Indians and enlightened administrators struggle with the tangled effects of the good and evil policies that have shaped their history through the centuries. The results are uneven, but with them also there is hope.

CHAPTER TWENTY-ONE

THE INDIANS FIND NEW HOPE

After ten years of systematic oppression the Indians stood to win in the presidential election of 1960, for both candidates were on their side. Richard M. Nixon stated to the AAIA:

"I want to emphasize here my deep and abiding respect for the values of Indian culture and for the undeniable right of Indian people to preserve their traditional heritage. Our overriding aim, as I see it, should not be to separate the Indians from the richness of their past or force them into some preconceived mold of human behavior. . . .

"Every conceivable effort will be made to shape our actions and our policies in full harmony with the deepest aspirations of the Indian citizenry."

John F. Kennedy wrote to Oliver La Farge that if he were elected, "There would be no change in treaty or contractual relationships without the consent of the tribes concerned. No steps would be taken to impair the cultural heritage of any group. . . . There would be protection of the Indian land base. . . .

"Indians have heard fine words and promises long enough. They are right in asking for deeds."

It was Kennedy who had the opportunity to put his "words and promises" into "deeds." It fell to Secretary Udall to implement them. Asked about HCR 108, Udall answered that it had "died with the 83rd Congress and is of no legal effect at the present time." He at once appointed a task force to investigate and report on the Indian situation. W. W. Keeler served as chairman, and Dr. Philleo Nash was one of its members. After its report was in, Nash was appointed as commissioner of Indian affairs, one of the best officials who ever served in that posi-

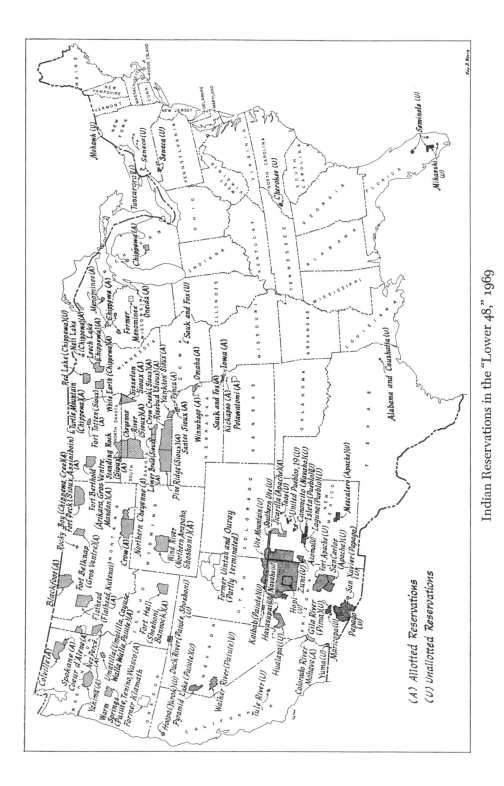

Roy P. Davis

Indian Reservations in the "Lower 48," 1969

(A) Allotted Reservations
(U) Unallotted Reservations

Colville (A)
Spokane (A)
Coeur d'Alene (A)
Nez Perce (A)
Yakima (A)
Umatilla (Umatilla, Cayuse, Walla Walla, Paiute)(A)
Warm Springs (Paiute, Tenino, Wasco)(A)
Former Klamath

Flathead (Flathead, Kutenai)(A)
Fort Hall (Shoshoni)
Bannock(A)

Blackfoot (A)
Rocky Boy (Chippewa, Cree)(A)
Fort Belknap (Gros Ventre)(A)
Fort Peck (Sioux, Assiniboin) (A)
Fort Berthold (Arikara, Gros Ventre, Mandan)(A)
Turtle Mountain (Chippewa)(A)
Red Lake (Chippewa)(U)
Nett Lake (Chippewa)(U)
Leech Lake (Chippewa)(A)
White Earth (Chippewa)(A)
Fort Totten (Sioux)(A)
Standing Rock (Sioux)(A)
Cheyenne River (Sioux)(A)
Lower Brule (Sioux)(A)
Crow Creek (Sioux)(A)
Sisseton (Sioux)(A)
Rosebud (Sioux)(A)
Yankton Sioux (A)
Santee Sioux (A)
Pine Ridge (Sioux)(A)
Ponca (A)
Winnebago (A)
Omaha (A)
Sauk and Fox (A)
Iowa (A)
Kickapoo (A)
Potawatomi (A)
Sauk and Fox (U)
Oneida (A)
Former Menominee
Menominee(A)
Chippewa (A)
Chippewa (A)

Crow (A)
Northern Cheyenne (A)
Wind River (Northern Arapaho, Shoshoni)(A)

Former Uintah and Ouray (Partly terminated)

Kaibab (Paiute)(U)
Havasupai (U)
Hualapai (U)
Hopi (U)
Hopi (Navaho)(U)
Zuni(U)
Southern Ute (U)
Ute Mountain (U)
Jicarilla (Apache)(U)
Taos (U)
United Pueblos, 19 (U)
Canoncito (Navaho)(U)
Isleta (Pueblo)(U)
Laguna (Pueblo)(U)
Acoma (U)
Fort Apache (U)
San Carlos (Apache)(U)
Mescalero (Apache)(U)
San Xavier (Papago)(U)
Papago (U)
Maricopa(U)
Gila River (Pima)(U)
Yuma (U)
Mohave(A)
Colorado River (U)

Hoopa (Yurok)(U)
Duck River (Paiute, Shoshoni)(U)
Pyramid Lake (Paiute)(U)
Walker River (Paiute)(U)
Tule River (U)

Mohawk (U)
Tuscarora
Seneca (U)
Seneca (U)

Cherokee (U)

Alabama and Coushatta (U)

Seminole (U)
Mikasuki (U)

tion. At that time Udall made a policy statement to the Indian Bureau employees.

"At the hearings held by the Task Force it was clear that the Indians were seeing 'termination' lurking behind every rock and every tree. I agree with the Task Force that our goal is maximum development. When we reach that goal, termination will have disappeared as an issue. . . . I firmly believe that the Indian's land base is essential to a sound economic future. I intend to support Indian effort to acquire more land where they need it and use it productively." He mentioned the heirship problem—by that time there were 40,000 tracts worth $180,000,000 in heirship status—and called for a "workable law" to resolve it. (That law still waits.) He also called for an increased revolving loan fund—"More money is needed . . . for all sorts of purposes."

The first session of the new Congress did raise the loan authorization to $20,000,000 and appropriated $4,000,000. In four years the fund reached $27,000,000. The Federal Housing Authority also entered the Indian field. Eventually it became very active, with the Indian's labor credited as his down payment. An increasing number of industrial plants were lured by Bureau and tribal initiative to locate on reservations (or in Oklahoma on former reservations). The total of such investments reached more than $99,000,000 during the one year 1968. Such employment opportunities are proving to be a godsend to depressed communities; among them are the almost hopeless Sioux on the Pine Ridge and the neighboring Rosebud reservations. Throughout the Indian country is a constantly expanding market for crafts products. In that the Zunis have become the most prosperous. They farm the same land they farmed in Coronado's time, they raise sheep and cattle, but their silver and turquoise craft brings in real money with a growing market over the United States. Thrift and well-being are apparent throughout their village. They live in good modern houses of native stone with curtains at the windows; and like their rural white contemporaries they drive their cars to town, while their teenagers ride fine horses around for pleasure on Sunday afternoons.[1]

With these developments the Bureau's relocation program lost its sense of urgency. The Indians have continued to migrate to the cities, finding opportunity or failure there; and the assistance in finding employment and adjustment has been extended gradually to places nearer their homes. (Too gradually: for example, Oklahoma Indians, once

[1] A fairly recent and still valid study of Zuni culture is Dorothea C. Leighton and John Adair, *People of the Middle Place.*

407

shipped to Los Angeles, were given their first relocation services in Oklahoma City and Tulsa in 1967.) Nobody knows how many Indians now live in cities. The Bureau estimates—and this is frankly only a guess—that they constitute 40 per cent of the Indian population. About one third of them have received relocation assistance; the remaining two thirds have come on their own. Many hold excellent jobs and practice the same living techniques as other Americans, but they maintain a close connection with their tribes and have a curious sense of living in exile. Many plan to return to their home communities when they reach retirement age.

The cities have become increasingly aware of the problems of the unadjusted. Minneapolis with about eight thousand Chippewas is the most active. Its school system is developing a plan for parental involvement and bicultural education in Indian neighborhoods, where the Chippewa children have a 65 per cent dropout rate from the junior high grades.

Also, the protest of the intellectual community against the termination policy of the 1950s has enlisted the universities—especially those in Indian states and the University of Chicago—in college scholarships and orientation for Indian students, teacher training in Indian education, and extension programs of Indian community development. One of these programs at the University of Oklahoma was the beginning of a statewide movement that may point the way to rehabilitate all the victims of termination, whether of the Dawes era or of the 1950s.

Oklahoma, with an Indian population second only to that of Arizona (with its proliferating Navahos), had been the slowest of all the states to admit that the liquidation of tribes and of tribal land to which it owed its existence had not brought all the separated individuals into happy assimilation with the dominant society. Even prominent state leaders of noticeable Indian descent were unaware of the problem or brushed it off as a reproach to their pride of race. Finally, in 1963, the University of Oklahoma made a contract with the Bureau area office comprising western Oklahoma to conduct centers in six towns, where white civic leaders and the Indians living apart somewhere on the edge would be enlisted in a unified community program. The beginning was slow. In one town only Indians attended the first meeting; in another, concerned white people came, but few Indians. But in Lawton a successful program was launched, mainly through the leadership of two gifted women of the Comanche tribe: Mrs. Iola Taylor, county home demonstration agent for Indian work, and Mrs. LaDonna Harris, the wife of the rising young politician Fred R. Harris.

The result of all this was a called meeting of Indians and non-Indians at the University on June 14, 1965. It turned out to be the most important gathering of Oklahoma Indians since the last intertribal council had met in 1888 to fight dissolution. Nineteen tribes were represented. They discussed their problems and organized a committee with Mrs. Harris (her husband was now in the Senate) serving as chairman. The unity of the diverse tribes was "downright astounding," a Seminole participant reported; and looking back, the leaders agreed that it was due largely to the ability and enthusiasm of Mrs. Harris. Quickly she appointed key persons to report to their tribes, learn their wishes, and prepare agenda for a statewide meeting. It was held at the University on August 7 with over five hundred Indians present. There they formed Oklahomans for Indian Opportunity (OIO), incorporated under state law as a charitable, educational, nonprofit organization. They elected Mrs. Harris as president and chose a list of forty-one directors that reads like a roll call of Oklahoma tribes.

They spent the next months in generating interest and establishing relationships with existing agencies. Then the following year they received a grant of $240,733 from the Office of Economic Opportunity. Mrs. Taylor (she is now Mrs. Hayden) was employed as full-time director, and the staff was expanded as the work grew. The staff offices are at the University; the field workers are Indians living in the areas they serve. The OIO chose locations of Indian concentration and developed programs of (1) community improvement, carried out by Indians and non-Indians working together; (2) work orientation, enlisting employers in training Indian workers; and (3) youth activities, helping Indian high school students acquire qualities of leadership. The organization selected thirty-one public schools with the largest Indian enrollments and presented their libraries with sets of books, valued at fifty dollars each, dealing with the heritage of the Indian—histories for high school reading, attractive children's books for elementary use.

The emphasis throughout was on self-help and individual effort by the Indians, and the development of understanding and acceptance by the white-oriented community. In October that year the OIO held its first annual statewide Indian Achievement Conference with an attendance of 750 Indians and non-Indians and with John W. Gardiner, secretary of health, education, and welfare, as the featured speaker.

Awards were made to individuals and to the town that had done the most to involve Indians in total community living. The following March the first annual statewide Youth Conference was held, with more than one thousand students representing forty Oklahoma schools and with Senator Robert F. Kennedy as the main speaker.

Back in 1906, Pleasant Porter, grieving over the ruin of his people, could still say to the Senate committee that visited the Indian Territory that year, "Above all things, I would like to live to see the day when, in the great State that will inevitably be here, I would see my people and the white man living side by side in a prosperous land on terms of perfect intellectual and political equality, and each doing his share toward the maintenance and support of that state." The fulfillment of his dream has been long in coming. One can still locate the fullblood settlements by superimposing on a modern map of Oklahoma a map of the tribal holdings existing in 1888, or by driving across the state and marking the areas of poor land and substandard housing; but the OIO may well be the agency that will finally bring his dream to realization.

During the years succeeding 1967, the organization continually expanded its work, with grass-roots activity, leadership training seminars, district meetings, and the annual Indian Achievement and Youth conferences at the University with their special awards and such speakers as Labor Secretary Willard Wirtz and Peace Corps Directors Sargent Shriver and Jack Vaughan. Mrs. Harris was elected as president each year until 1968, when she resigned to serve as chairman of the National Women's Advisory Council of the War on Poverty. James Wahpepah, a Kickapoo, who had been active in the movement since its beginning, then became its president. That year the OIO received a grant of $470,277 from the Office of Economic Opportunity to conduct a comprehensive three-year Rural Development Program in ten hill counties of eastern Oklahoma populated by a large number of Cherokee and Choctaw fullbloods. Wahpepah immediately announced ten job openings for neighborhood workers, and began making appointments; among the qualifications are residence in the county and ability to speak Cherokee or Choctaw.

Wahpepah's own career is eloquent of the new spirit stirring among Oklahoma's long forgotten fullbloods. He grew up in a non-English-speaking environment, was sent to Bureau and mission boarding schools, and, returning home, graduated from the local Oklahoma high school. Through interpreting for his aunt he became interested in education and community development for his people, the leader of a

410

small progressive group of younger Kickapoos. In 1961 its members found their opportunity when the Quakers returned to the tribe fifteen acres of land they had been using in their often defeated efforts to help them. With a federal grant under the Depressed Areas legislation the Kickapoos constructed a community building on the tract. Then, under Wahpepah as chairman of the tribal council, they obtained funds from the Office of Economic Opportunity for Head Start, neighborhood youth corps, and adult training programs, all under their own direction and using the facilities of their new meeting place. The effects these activities will have upon the traditionalist majority in this most conservative of all Indian tribes can be evaluated only in the years ahead; but such an Indian-directed movement is less likely to cause a cleavage than the usual "civilizing" policy imposed from outside.

All these hopeful developments throughout the Indian country have been brought about by Indian initiative and by a growing public awareness under an enlightened federal administration. In 1966, Robert L. Bennett was brought from Alaska to succeed Philleo Nash as commissioner of Indian affairs, with no change in Bureau policy.

On March 6, 1968, President Johnson—for the first time in the history of the United States—sent Congress a special message on Indian affairs. He advocated for the Indians: "An opportunity to remain in their homelands, if they choose, without surrendering their dignity; an opportunity to move to the towns and cities of America, if they choose, equipped with the skills to live in equality and dignity." He promised concerted action by all administrative agencies to assist them—by reservation development, education and vocational training, health services—in attaining these goals. Specifically, he urged Congress to amend Public Law 280 by requiring Indian consent to the extension of state law (he signed this act on April 11) and the settlement of native land rights in Alaska (as we have seen this still waits). Throughout he emphasized Indian leadership and freedom of choice rather than paternalism, and "the rights of the first Americans to remain Indians while exercising their rights as Americans."

On the same day, in order to co-ordinate government efforts, he issued an executive order establishing the National Council on Indian Opportunity, with Vice President Humphrey as chairman, and the six cabinet members heading departments involving land and people (Interior; Agriculture; Commerce; Labor; Health, Education and Welfare; and Housing and Urban Development), the director of the Office of Economic Opportunity, and six Indians or Alaska natives

411

serving as members. These last were Wendell Chino, chairman of the Mescalero tribal council and president of the NCAI; Raymond Nakai, chairman of the Navaho tribal council; Cato Valandra, chairman of the Rosebud Sioux tribal council and treasurer of the NCAI; Roger Jourdain, chairman of the Red Lake tribal council; William Hensley, the Alaska Eskimo leader; and Mrs. Harris.

The influence of this Council was not immediately apparent. Before the month was over, there was Robert Kennedy's entrance into the presidential race and Johnson's withdrawal; then followed Humphrey's campaign, Kennedy's assassination, and all the upsetting events of that turbulent political year. Richard Nixon, who emerged as the victor, promised the NCAI during the campaign that he would "fully support the National Council on Indian Opportunity"; but it was not activated until January 26, 1970, when Vice President Spiro Agnew called the first meeting at the angry insistence of Mrs. Harris. Even so, this concept of a unifying agency illustrates a development that has been growing ever since the days of John Collier—the extension to Indians of governmental services other than those of the Indian Bureau.

The same trend is apparent in the education of Indian children, as is also the continued emphasis on family life. More and more children are attending the public schools or—where these are not available— special Indian day schools and living at home. Boarding schools, where required, are coming closer, although too many teenagers are still being sent to distant places to use plants no longer needed for local tribes. The Bureau has no contact with the children in the cities or in rural areas away from reservations and trust lands. Even in localities where there is Indian-owned land, 152,000 children attend public schools; and these schools receive subsidies to balance the loss in taxes, just as do schools near defense installations or other "federal impact areas."

It must be admitted that Indians in general do not like the public schools. Perhaps Eufaula Harjo's analysis, made in 1906, still stands. After the Department of the Interior took over the schools of the Five Civilized Tribes and enlarged them to admit non-Indian children, he said to the Senate committee, "There has been lots of schools among the Indians ever since we came here, and we were proud of our schools, and our children went to them until the white man came in and crowded us out." And he went on to point out the conditions that placed Indian children at a disadvantage. "I came in here a good while ago, and I was sitting back there a long time, but I couldn't understand what was going on only from what my interpreter would tell me. You saw me sitting back there, and I don't [didn't] like to come forward. Now, when I take a little Indian child to school the white man and the negroes will go before me to school with their children and they will put their children first and they will push mine out of school, and that is the way it will go."

That was the way it did go. The fullblood children virtually dropped out of "the schools that we built with our own money and that once were ours." Eventually their attendance increased, so that now it equals that of white children, but the parents still say, "Indian schools best for Indian children."

For smaller tribes it was Indian Bureau schools that yielded to the public school system, but the same dissatisfaction is evident. Recently it came to a head with the 430 Foxes (Mesquakies) living on their 3,000 acres of purchased land near Tama, Iowa. Since 1938 the Indian Bureau had maintained a school in their settlement, but completely surrounding it is the South Tama public school district. For some time pupils from the sixth grade up had been transferred to this district, with the Bureau paying tuition, and when the kindergarten and Head Start programs began, they also were centered there. Then in 1968, without consulting the Indians, the Bureau suddenly closed its school. The Indians went to court, ready to testify that young children coming from homes where their own language is dominant should not be thrust suddenly into an English-speaking school, that they wanted their children to retain a feeling for their own culture and traditions, and that the public school teachers discriminated against them. The case was settled out of court, and the first four grades were taught during the 1968–69 term by the Bureau school in their own community. A permanent decision is still pending.

In spite of the strength of this Indian feeling—and it is certainly widespread—it seems fairly certain that the public schools will eventually take over. The solution probably lies in the development of an all-inclusive community spirit and the training of teachers in awareness of Indian values, so that the children entering a public school will not find themselves in a completely alien environment. These changes, in fact, have occurred in some communities, and in them the problem has disappeared.

Meanwhile, the Indian Bureau is responsible for the education of 54,000 children living in remote areas or orphaned or otherwise homeless. Of these, 4,000 are brought to the so-called bordertown schools, where they are housed in federal dormitories, but attend the public schools of the district. The others are in Bureau schools—33,000 in 81 boarding schools, 17,000 in 173 day schools. Many of the day schools are in very isolated locations: 83 are in the native villages of Alaska, a large number being one-room schools; others are distributed over the Navaho Reservation and other sparsely settled regions. The church mission boards, once so active in Indian education, have also withdrawn to the areas of greatest need. They now enroll 9,000 children in day schools and boarding schools.[2]

The 1961 task force had recommended that the children's parents should participate in formulating the school programs. The Bureau did set up local school boards and affiliates of the Parent-Teacher Association, but their influence was negligible. Then it finally went the whole way by placing two schools under Indian control—the Blackwater on the Pima Reservation and Rough Rock on the Navaho. The latter has attracted national attention.

It was established in 1966. The first director was Dr. Robert A. Roessel, who had conducted a notable Indian education program at Arizona State University. In 1968 he was succeeded by Dillon Platero, who had been serving as assistant director. Necessarily a boarding school because of the great distances on the reservation, it preserves the values of the good Navaho home life by encouraging frequent visits and by rotating Navaho couples to serve as "parents" in the dormitories. The children are free to return home for weekends, while at the same time, an expanding bus service is bringing in an increasing number of day school pupils from the surrounding area. The happiness and outgoing friendliness of the children are apparent to any observer. Little beginners speaking only Navaho are taught English as a second language, Navaho legends and history are stressed, and Navaho staff members with the native resources of art and poetry and the acquired skills of college training are preparing beautiful books on Navaho subjects to be used throughout the reservation.

The local school board exercises complete authority. Only one of its members has ever attended any school—he alone speaks English— but their policies are wise and statesmanlike. Sometimes they and Dr. Roessel had differences of opinion. He yielded, as he was bound to do, but he kept a private record of these occasions when he carried out

[2] These are 1967 statistics. Any change since that time has simply followed the current trend.

414

their decisions against his own best judgment. After the first year he reviewed them—thirty-two in all—and in every instance he found that the Indians had been right and he himself wrong.[3] The Indian Bureau is now sending other school board members there to train them for similar responsibilities in their districts, and universities throughout the country are studying the Rough Rock plan of bicultural education and community involvement. Thus Indian education has come full circle since some good people in London decided to "reduce this people"—"savage and incredibly rude"—"from brutishness to civilitie."

The present concept found support from a special subcommittee set up by the Senate in January, 1968, for a one-year period to make a study of Indian education. Its chairman, Robert F. Kennedy, in the short time he had before his presidential campaign and then his death, and the minority member, Paul J. Fannin, former governor of Arizona, took their responsibility seriously, visiting schools in remote areas far from newspaper headlines or public knowledge. On February 19 they held hearings in the Oklahoma Ozarks, listening to fullblood Cherokees two generations withdrawn from a state that had passed them by. Looking back on their great history, Fannin marveled at "the resilience and pride of Indian people in their own cultural traditions" and saw as "the implications for today—the absolute necessity for *meaningful participation* and self-determination by Indian people in all programs designed for their benefit." Kennedy declared that "cultural differences are not a national burden, they are a national resource—the American vision of itself is of a nation of citizens determining their own destiny; of cultural differences flourishing in an atmosphere of mutual respect." He concluded that "effective education lies at the heart of any lasting solution . . . an education that no longer presumes that cultural difference means cultural inferiority."

But even in the 1960s there were senators determined to impose their own "lasting solution." Although Udall had announced the death of HCR 108, its ghost still walked on Capitol Hill. In 1964 the Senate Committee on Interior and Insular Affairs professed to be "deeply concerned" about the failure of the Indian administration to implement it, and the next year the entire Senate was not above using it to blackmail the Senecas.

For 170 years this prosperous and progressive people had been living on the Allegheny River reservation in New York guaranteed to

[3] Dr. Roessel told me this with great relish when I visited the school in October, 1967.

them by a treaty made under the presidency of Washington, and on a small tract farther down the river in Pennsylvania. Then a dam being built in Pennsylvania by the Corps of Engineers was flooding it, and they were forced to relocate.

The displacement itself was a major calamity: it broke up their community, obliterated their sacred places, covered their cemeteries, destroyed the loved familiar shapes of land and water. Such loss often happened to Indian tribes, because when their original holdings were reduced, the land they retained as reservations was often located in river valleys. Like other Americans they are required to yield when dams are needed for flood control or other public purposes; but the Corps of Engineers is a powerful, almost autonomous agency, building dams without much thought of natural resources or human needs,[4] and the sum of its projects is so much pork for which members of Congress feel obligated to protect each other.

The dam on the Allegheny was designed to reduce the floods on the Ohio River and to give partial protection to the city of Pittsburgh. In addition, it could be expected to bring many million dollars to Pennsylvania. In 1957 the threatened Senecas, hoping to find an alternative, employed Dr. Arthur E. Morgan, the foremost hydraulic engineer in the United States, who had served as chief engineer and then as chairman of the Tennessee Valley Authority and had many other works to his credit. (The Quakers gave some financial help and he donated part of his time and expense.) He concluded that the river could be diverted into Lake Erie through an ancient channel blocked by glacial action and that the cost would be much less and the protection far greater than that of the original plan. But the Corps of Engineers had face to save and the Pennsylvania congressional delegation needed the pork. That same year Congress began making appropriations for the construction. Many people believed at the time and still believe that the dam was a gigantic blunder victimizing the public as well as the Senecas.

In 1964, Congress voted the Indians $15,000,000 for damages and the expense of relocation, and the Senate tacked on a provision— and refused to give it up in conference with the other house—requiring the secretary of the interior to confer with them and submit within

[4] The Hoover Commission recommended that the Corps be under the direction of the secretary of the interior. An objection strongly expressed by dissenting minority members was that the purpose of employing the Engineers on civilian works was to give them practice to prepare them for war emergencies. Any social or economic benefit seemed to be incidental.

three years a plan for their termination. They could not ask for a presidential veto—the water would soon be lapping at their houses and fields. Commissioner Bennett did "consult" them before the deadline in 1967; they rejected the measure and nothing happened. Except for assistance in relocating they have received few Indian Bureau services for many years, but they have a strong attachment to their treaty. Perhaps it strengthens their insistence that they are not citizens of the United States. (The Iroquois Confederacy declared war on Germany in 1917—that was before the citizenship law of 1924—then absent-mindedly or prophetically they failed to make peace, so that participation in World War II presented no technical problem.)

The Senate finally abandoned its support of HCR 108 in 1968 and adopted a new statement in Senate Concurrent Resolution 11.[5] The committee in reporting it expressly repudiated the old declaration and the termination policy, which "may well have delayed the day when the Indian can become a fully self-sufficient citizen." The new resolution stated the aim of Congress to bring Indians and Alaska natives to the social and economic level of other citizens by educational and health services, protection of their trust property, development of their economic resources, respect for their culture and identity, and the direction of these programs through their own tribal governing bodies. Thus, after fifteen years, the ghost of HCR 108 was laid.

The Indians lost a friend in the death of Robert Kennedy, but otherwise the election of 1968 made little change in the composition of Congress in regard to the rights of Indians and Alaska natives. During the campaign Richard Nixon made a comprehensive statement to the NCAI, which was in effect a summary of the most enlightened tenets and the best policies of the preceding years and a pledge to continue and extend them. It is not possible yet to evaluate his administration of Indian affairs, for up to the present it has been in abeyance. The Indian Bureau remained without a head until August, 1969.

Commissioner Bennett's appointment had not been political—he was in fact registered as a Republican—and the Indians hoped that he would be retained in office. But with Hickel as secretary of the interior he had to go. He had served in Alaska as the Bureau's area director, and there are too many occasions of conflict between the ambitious builders of a frontier state and a federal official entrusted with the protection of the natives. Nixon assured the unhappy Indians that

[5] In the confusion of that election year the resolution was not acted upon by the House of Representatives.

although the appointment would be frankly political he would choose an Indian for the position; but as it happened, all the prominent Indian applicants were Democrats.

After seven months' search Hickel found Louis Rooks Bruce, Jr., of New York's Greenwich Village, the vice president of an advertising firm, who had been an active Nixon campaigner. He qualifies as an Indian, for he has Mohawk and Oglala Sioux blood and was born on the Onondaga Reservation. One can only conjecture about his policy, for he has been out of touch with Indian affairs.

President Nixon himself is informed on Indian matters. Throughout his campaign statement to the NCAI there are glimpses of his awareness of the administrative problem—the creaking bureaucratic machinery, the conflicting aims of separate government agencies, the reluctance to trust Indian control. These have thwarted the efforts of perceptive officials throughout the history of reform. The recent experiences of a few tribes stand out to illustrate these problems and, in some cases, their solution.

There is a still unrighted wrong to the 1,200 Indians of Taos. Near the entrance of their pueblo is a beautiful, well-kept church, where they gather for the Catholic mass, but high in the mountains is a lovely 48,000-acre tract of woodland around Blue Lake, where they observe their ancient rituals, merging both experiences of worship in a common faith. In 1906 the government offered to incorporate their wilderness shrine into the Carson National Forest in order to protect it from commercial encroachment, and the Taoseños consented. Thus it came under the supervision of the Forest Service of the Department of Agriculture, which soon forgot that it did not own the land and proceeded to build cabins and lay out trails, stock the lake with fish, and issue permits to campers. To the Indians the litter of beer cans and pop bottles and the uninhibited conduct of the campers was a desecration equal to piling garbage on the high altar of St. Peter's (their own words) and holding a noisy party within its precincts.

After years of futile appeals to public officials, Governor Severino Martinez went to New York early in 1961 to present their cause to a meeting of the AAIA. Most Taoseños speak Spanish and English besides their own language, but he brought along one of his people, Paul Bernal, as interpreter. "We have visited St. Patrick's today," he said. "We have seen it and we had the privilege to kneel down and pray.

"You have beautiful statues, beautiful figures of representative scenes which we now worship, you and I together. We don't have

418

beautiful structures and we don't have gold temples in this lake, but we have a sign of a living God to who we pray—the living trees, the evergreen and spruce and the beautiful flowers and the beautiful rocks and the lake itself. We have this proof of sacred things we deeply love, deeply believe. . . .

". . . Religion is the most important thing in a person's life because without religion, without a prayer, no individual can exist. We have to pray for what we receive from the sun that gives us the light and the water we drink. They are provided by God. We are taking that water to give us strength so we can gain in knowledge and wisdom about the work we are engaged in. . . . That is the reason this Blue Lake is so important to us."

He expressed some hope in the Kennedy administration. "We already understand he has been choosing people who really understand the Indian problems . . . and we hope that this new administration, with new people in it, with new laws, can expedite that claim."

Recently appointed Assistant Secretary Carver was in the audience. Moved by the appeal, he spoke up to assure the Taoseños that he would see to the return of their land. He had not yet experienced the strength of interdepartmental rivalry. The Department of Agriculture refused to release it, conceding only a temporary "exclusive use" permit to the Indians. They then took their case to the Indian Claims Commission. They won a decision in 1965, but this tribunal has no authority to restore property taken from Indians illegally; it can only grant a money judgment. This they refuse to accept. "We will not sell our religion—our life," they say. From a time centuries before the white man came, the Blue Lake area has been their most sacred place, the source of the sparkling stream that waters their fields and runs through their pueblo and of the strength that comes from earth and water and all the forces of nature.

Next they managed to have bills introduced in Congress for the restoration of their land. Secretary Udall personally testified in their behalf before the Senate committee, as did the AAIA, the Indian Rights Association, and a spokesman for the National Council of Churches; but the Department of Agriculture and its Forest Service opposed it, and they had the backing of powerful New Mexican local interests. "We have been waiting a long, long time," Governor Martinez had said in 1961. They are still waiting.

As sturdy as the Taoseños but free to control their land and people are the Navahos. They took the latest step in their educational initiative

419

by setting up their own junior college. After all, for 100,000 Navahos (130,000 by their estimate)[6] a junior college is no more impractical than the many municipal junior colleges in communities of no greater population throughout the United States. Theirs opened in January, 1969, in temporary quarters—a Bureau school plant at Many Farms, far out on the great reaches of their reservation, surrounded by all the dramatic beauty and color of changing sky and upthrust masses of rock and mountain. It is controlled by the tribe, and receives financial support from the tribe, the Bureau, and private endowments. Ned Hatathli, a Navaho graduate of Northern Arizona University, serves as president and Dr. Roessel as chancellor; and the entire curriculum is oriented towards Navaho needs and culture. It offers academic subjects under college-trained instructors, many of them Navahos; arts and crafts classes and an agricultural course designed to train non-English-speaking Navahos in vocational skills; and a Navaho studies program, with young Emerson Blackhorse Mitchell as one of the faculty. The Navahos are still among the poorest of Indians, but in owning land nobody wanted they have been left free to work out their economic salvation.

Less fortunate are the Pimas, who raised corn and cotton centuries before the white man came, bringing water from the Gila and its tributaries by *acequias* ten to sixteen miles long, and who prospered mightily, selling supplies to the California Argonauts. Now they live in poverty in the dust of their desert, while white farmers monopolize their water. And there is the plight of the Pyramid Lake Paiutes, watching their lake shrink—with the destruction of its fish and the loss of its tourist potential—while the water of the Truckee River that feeds it is diverted by the Interior Department's Reclamation Bureau to a far from successful irrigation project and a duck hunting preserve of the Fish and Wildlife Service. In this instance Secretary Udall supported his other agencies against the Indians. Now there is a new menace. California and Nevada have drafted a compact dividing the water between them and specifically excluding the preservation of the lake. Secretary Udall opposed the plan, and it will require congressional approval, but the Indians are discouraged. "We're just like ants down here," says one. This seems to express it, for at the last report Secretary Hickel was supporting the state compact.

[6] A cartoon in a recent issue of the *Navajo Times* shows two women in conversation outside a hogan in a yard filled with children. One is saying, "Whole country take the pill. We take the country."

In contrast is the success of the Cochiti Pueblo in dealing with the Corps of Engineers in the construction of a flood-control dam on the Río Grande to be completed in 1970. With the aid of an attorney furnished by the AAIA, the Indians worked out a settlement giving them the rights of development along the reservoir in exchange for the flooding of 4,000 acres of their 26,000-acre holdings. Thus the Indians are to continue in control, possession, and administration of the land to be used for recreation purposes.

Said Governor Fred Cordero at the ceremonial signing of the agreement in 1965: "The step we are taking has not been a hasty one. . . . We have talked together, prayed together and planned together, having always in mind the question: What will this mean to our children and their children; what will it mean to our community, to our State and to our country?

"We have a deep love for this land which has given us so many centuries of useful living. The Earth is our Mother, a gift from the Great Spirit, and it has given us the means of keeping alive in spite of all the hardships we have had. . . .

"The people of Cochiti were nourished and sustained by this great river for many hundreds of years before the white man came. . . . It has served us well in simple ways, in growing our crops and supplying our basic needs. But now it will play a new part in our lives, it will provide new and different types of benefits. . . .

"We shall continue to grow our crops, to have our sacred ceremonials. Children will no doubt still splash and swim in the acequias. . . . But gradually changes will come. . . . Today we take a great step forward into an experience that is new and strange to us. . . .

"We are not afraid of change; we know that all people everywhere are experiencing changes. . . .

"Every day, we ask God's blessing upon this land; in all our practices we have a sense of the spiritual values which have been a part of our lives through all the days that we have known."

He was speaking out of an immediate experience, but although living techniques and events have varied widely, the words of the wise old governor of one small pueblo present in microcosm the history, the problems, and the hopes of all aboriginal Americans throughout the centuries. Back in 1900, in a darker, sadder time, when all the white man's power was concentrated on liquidating their tribal existence, humanitarians and exploiters alike assumed that wiping them off the map would as easily erase the identity of their citizens. Even in that hour of despair Pleasant Porter knew better. He addressed the Creek council that year in solemn words that were at once a valedictory and a prophecy:

"The vitality of our race still persists. We have not lived for naught. We are the original discoverers of this continent, and the conquerors of it from the animal kingdom, and on it first taught the arts of war and peace, and first planted the institutions of virtue, truth and liberty. The European Nations found us here and were made aware that it was possible for men to exist and subsist here. We have given to the European people on this continent our thought forces. . . . We have made ourselves an indestructible element in their national history. . . . The race that has rendered this service to the other nations of mankind cannot utterly perish."

Addenda

Since this book was published, Blue Lake with the 48,000 acres surrounding it has been restored to the Taos Pueblo by a bill passed by Congress and signed by President Nixon on December 15, 1970.

The land claim of the Alaska natives was settled by an act of December 18, 1971. It grants them fee simple title to 40,000,000 acres and a monetary consideration of $962,500,000 of which $462,500,000 will be paid by the federal treasury over an eleven-year period, and $500,000,000 will accrue from a 2 per cent royalty on minerals from state and federal land. Twelve regional corporations with natives as the voting stockholders administer these financial grants and any mineral royalties from their land; and a thirteenth corporation without land is provided for nonresident natives.

The Menominees became hopelessly entangled with the problems resulting from termination, Congress restored the tribe to its original status by an act of December 22, 1973, and the Indians are striving to establish a viable life-way on the ruins of their former prosperity.

The members of the Klamath tribe who had retained their trust estate decided by a majority vote in 1969 to divide it. The federal government purchased the forest land on November 15, 1974, and most of the purchase price, $48,700,000, was distributed to the Indian owners. Provision was made for selling some remaining ranch and marsh land and closing the estate.

SELECTED READINGS

(In a book of this scope it is impossible to present a bibliography citing all the original sources I have consulted in nearly half a century of research in the Indian field, or to name all the important books by other writers during the past four hundred years. The appended list of selected works will, it is hoped, encourage the reader to branch out independently. Detailed documentation will be found in most of them.)

Alford, Thomas Wildcat. *Civilization*. Norman, University of Oklahoma Press, 1936.

Allen, T. D. *Navahos Have Five Fingers*. Norman, University of Oklahoma Press, 1963.

American Friends Service Committee. *Indians of California*. N.p., n.d. (Written March, 1956; available from AFSC, 1830 Sutter Street, San Francisco.)

Andrist, Ralph K. *The Long Death*. New York, The Macmillan Company, and London, Collier-Macmillan, Ltd., 1964.

Barrett, S. M. *Geronimo's Story of His Life*. New York, Duffield and Company, 1906.

Benét, Stephen Vincent. *Western Star*. New York and Toronto, Farrar and Rinehart, Inc., 1943.

Berthrong, Donald J. *The Southern Cheyennes*. Norman, University of Oklahoma Press, 1963.

Betzinez, Jason. *I Fought with Geronimo*. Ed. and annotated by W. S. Nye. Harrisburg, Pa., Stackpole, 1959.

Bolton, Herbert E. *Coronado on the Turquoise Trail*. Albuquerque, University of New Mexico Press, 1949.

Briggs, Argye M. *Both Banks of the River*. Grand Rapids, Mich., Wm. B. Eerdmans Publishing Company, 1954.

Brooks, Juanita. *The Mountain Meadows Massacre*. New edition. Norman, University of Oklahoma Press, 1962.

Cohoe. *A Cheyenne Sketchbook*. Commentary by E. Adamson Hoebel and Karen Daniels Petersen. Norman, University of Oklahoma Press, 1964.

Collier, John. *Indians of the Americas*. New York, New American Library, 1947.

Collings, Ellsworth. *The Old Home Ranch*. Stillwater, Okla., Redlands Press, 1964.

Crook, General George. *His Autobiography*. Ed. and annotated by Martin F. Schmitt. Norman, University of Oklahoma Press, 1946, 1960.

Cushman, H[oratio] B[ardwell]. *History of the Choctaw, Chickasaw, and Natchez Indians*. Ed. and annotated by Angie Debo. Stillwater, Okla., Redlands Press, 1962.

Dale, Edward Everett, and Gaston Litton. *Cherokee Cavaliers*. Norman, University of Oklahoma Press, 1939.

Davis, Britton. *The Truth about Geronimo*. New Haven, Yale University Press, 1929.

Debo, Angie. *And Still the Waters Run*. Princeton, Princeton University Press, 1940.

——. *The Five Civilized Tribes of Oklahoma: Report on Social and Economic Conditions*. Philadelphia, Indian Rights Association, 1951.

——. *The Rise and Fall of the Choctaw Republic*. Norman, University of Oklahoma Press, 1934.

——. *The Road to Disappearance*. Norman, University of Oklahoma Press, 1941.

Ewers, John C. *The Blackfeet*. Norman, University of Oklahoma Press, 1958.

Fey, Harold E., and D'Arcy McNickle. *Indians and Other Americans*. New York, Harper and Brothers, 1959.

Forbes, Jack D. *Apache, Navaho, and Spaniard*. Norman, University of Oklahoma Press, 1960.

Foreman, Grant. *The Five Civilized Tribes*. Norman, University of Oklahoma Press, 1934.

——. *Indian Removal*. Norman, University of Oklahoma Press, 1932.

——. *Sequoyah*. Norman, University of Oklahoma Press, 1938.

424

Gibson, A. M. *The Kickapoos*. Norman, University of Oklahoma Press, 1963.

Grinnell, George Bird. *The Fighting Cheyennes*. Norman, University of Oklahoma Press, 1956.

Haines, Francis. *The Nez Percés*. Norman, University of Oklahoma Press, 1955.

Hyde, George E. *Life of George Bent*. Ed. and annotated by Savoie Lottinville. Norman, University of Oklahoma Press, 1968.

———. *Red Cloud's Folk*. Norman, University of Oklahoma Press, 1937.

———. *A Sioux Chronicle*. Norman, University of Oklahoma Press, 1956.

———. *Spotted Tail's Folk*. Norman, University of Oklahoma Press, 1961.

Iliff, Flora Gregg. *People of the Blue Water*. New York, Harper and Brothers, 1954.

Irving, Washington. *The Adventures of Captain Bonneville, U.S.A.* Ed. and annotated by Edgeley W. Todd. Norman, University of Oklahoma Press, 1961.

Jones, Douglas C. *The Treaty of Medicine Lodge*. Norman, University of Oklahoma Press, 1966.

Josephy, Alvin M., Jr. *The Nez Percé Indians and the Opening of the Northwest*. New Haven and London, Yale University Press, 1965.

Kroeber, Theodora. *Ishi*. Berkeley and Los Angeles, University of California Press, 1967.

Leighton, Dorothea C., and John Adair. *People of the Middle Place*. ("Behavior Science Monographs.") New Haven, Conn., Human Relations Area Files Press, 1966.

Llewellyn, Karl N., and E. Adamson Hoebel. *The Cheyenne Way*. Norman, University of Oklahoma Press, 1941.

McCracken, Harold. *George Catlin and the Old Frontier*. New York, Dial Press, 1959.

Macgregor, Gordon. *Warriors without Weapons*. Chicago, University of Chicago Press, 1946.

McReynolds, Edwin C. *The Seminoles*. Norman, University of Oklahoma Press, 1957.

Malone, Henry Thompson. *Cherokees of the Old South*. Athens, University of Georgia Press, 1956.

Marriott, Alice. *Maria: The Potter of San Ildefonso*. Norman, University of Oklahoma Press, 1948.

———. *The Ten Grandmothers.* Norman, University of Oklahoma Press, 1945.

Mathews, John Joseph. *The Osages.* Norman, University of Oklahoma Press, 1961.

———. *Wah'Kon-Tah.* Norman, University of Oklahoma Press, 1932.

Meriwether, David. *My Life in the Mountains and on the Plains.* Ed. and annotated by Robert A. Griffen. Norman, University of Oklahoma Press, 1965.

Mitchell, Emerson Blackhorse, and T. D. Allen. *Miracle Hill.* Norman, University of Oklahoma Press, 1967.

Momaday, N. Scott. *House Made of Dawn.* New York and Evanston, Harper and Row, 1966.

Nelson, Oliver. *The Cowman's Southwest.* Ed. and annotated by Angie Debo. Glendale, Calif., Arthur H. Clark, 1953.

Nye, W. S. *Carbine and Lance.* Norman, University of Oklahoma Press, 1937.

Payne, John Howard. *Indian Justice.* Ed. and annotated by Grant Foreman. Muskogee, Okla., Star Printery, Inc., 1962.

Prucha, Francis Paul. *American Indian Policy in the Formative Years.* Cambridge, Harvard University Press, 1962.

Richards, Eva Alvey. *Arctic Mood.* Caldwell, Idaho, Caxton Printers, 1949.

Richardson, Rupert Norval. *The Comanche Barrier to South Plains Settlement.* Glendale, Calif., Arthur H. Clark, 1933.

Ruby, Robert H., and John A. Brown. *Half-Sun on the Columbia.* Norman, University of Oklahoma Press, 1965.

Scott, Hugh Lenox. *Some Memories of a Soldier.* New York and London, Century Company, 1928.

Seger, John H. *Early Days among the Cheyenne and Arapahoe Indians.* Ed. by Stanley Vestal. Norman, University of Oklahoma Press, 1934.

Sonnichsen, C. L. *The Mescalero Apaches.* Norman, University of Oklahoma Press, 1958.

Thomas, Alfred Barnaby. *Forgotten Frontiers.* Norman, University of Oklahoma Press, 1932.

Thrapp, Dan L. *Al Sieber.* Norman, University of Oklahoma Press, 1964.

———. *The Conquest of Apacheria.* Norman, University of Oklahoma Press, 1967.

Tilghman, Zoe A. *Marshal of the Last Frontier.* Glendale, Calif., Arthur H. Clark, 1964.

Trenholm, Virginia Cole, and Maurine Carley. *The Shoshonis.* Norman, University of Oklahoma Press, 1964.

Tucker, Glenn. *Tecumseh: Vision of Glory.* Indianapolis and New York, Bobbs-Merrill Company, Inc., 1956.

Vestal, Stanley. *Sitting Bull, Champion of the Sioux.* Norman, University of Oklahoma Press, 1957.

Willison, George F. *The Pilgrim Reader.* Garden City, N.Y., Doubleday and Company, Inc., 1953.

Woodward, Grace Steele. *The Cherokees.* Norman, University of Oklahoma Press, 1963.

Wright, Muriel H. *A Guide to the Indian Tribes of Oklahoma.* Norman, University of Oklahoma Press, 1951.

427

INDEX

AAIA: *see* Association on American
Indian Affairs
Ácoma Pueblo: 26, 37–38
Adair, James: 76–77
Adams, John Quincy: 116
Adobe Walls fight: 230
AFN: *see* Alaska Federation of Natives
Agnew, Spiro: 412
Agriculture, primitive: 13ff., 420
Alabama, state of: aboriginal Indians
in, 10; French settlements in, 71;
statehood, 113; extends laws over
Indians, 117; removal of Creeks
from, 118–20; Indian allotments in,
118–19, 299
Alabamas: linguistic relationships, 10;
English-French rivalry among, 73;
in Texas, 97, 130, 296, 371
Alarcón, Hernando de: 24–25
Alaska, state of: Russians in, 82–83,
100, 383–84; purchase by United
States, 384; territorial government
for, 384, 386; statehood, 387–88;
land grant to, 387, 389; population,
387–88; defense installations in,
387–88, 390; frontier attitude of,
388, 401, 403–404, 417; oil development in, 389–90, 400, 403–404;
naval petroleum reserve, 390, 400
Alaska Federation of Natives: 398ff.
Alaska Native Industries Co-operative
Association: 386
Alaska native land issue: provisions of
territorial act, 386; reservations,
386–87, 389–90, 392, 395; native
concept of title, 387, 390–93, 395–
96; provisions of statehood act, 387;
grants to state, 387, 389–90, 394,
402–404; grants by Bureau of Land
Management, 388ff.; natives form
protective associations, 390–93, 395–
400; Tanacross incident, 394, 402–
403; land "freeze," 398–99, 401;
court upholds aboriginal title, 399;
proposed settlements, 399, 403–404;
action of Congress, 399–401, 422
Alaska Native Rights Association: 388,
395, 397
Alaska natives: Indian Reorganization
Act extended to, 338–39, 386–87,
389; schools for, 383–86, 394, 399ff.,
414; under purchase treaty, 384; co-
operatives, 386, 395; in salmon industry, 386–87, 395; population,
388; subsistence hunting, 389, 391–
95, 397, 400; start newspaper, 393ff.;
mechanical adaptability, 400, 404;
unemployment in industry, 400–401;
see also Aleuts, Athapascans, Eskimos, Haidas, Metlakatla, Tlingets
Alcatraz: 277
Alcohol: 43, 48, 69, 89, 103, 106, 114,
129, 275, 279; *see also* tizwin
Aleuts: 9, 12, 82–83, 388, 396; *see also*
Alaska natives
Alford, Thomas Wildcat: 174, 319, 323
Algonquian linguistic stock: 9–10, 373
Allen, Terry: 5

Allotment of land: in Mississippi, 118,
299; in Alabama, 118, 299; in Kansas, 147, 207–208, 299; agitation for,
148, 299–300; Indian opposition to,
148, 299, 301–303, 310–14; under
Dawes Act, 304–305, 313–24, 338,
354, 378; of Osages, 305–306; of
Five Civilized Tribes, 307–309, 318–
30; statistical results, 331–32; evaluation of, 331 & n.; impoverishment
of Indians, 329–30, 336, 345; discontinued, 338; see also land tenure
Alvarado, Hernando de: 26–28
American Bar Association: 351
American Board of Commissioners for
Foreign Missions: with Cherokees,
113–14, 121–22; with Choctaws,
114; school in Connecticut, 120; in
Pacific Northwest, 151–56; in
Hawaii, 151, 153
Amherst, Jeffrey: 81
Anchorage, Alaska: 398, 399, 401, 403–
404
ANRA: see Alaska Native Rights Association
Anthony, Scott J.: 194–95
Anza, Juan Bautista de: 98–99
Apaches: 3, 25, 72; linguistic relation-
ships, 11; early life ways, 14–15, 29;
driven to raiding, 17, 67, 162–64;
Pueblo flights to, 50, 67; Spanish
slave raids on, 50; bounty on scalps,
67, 97–98, 162–63, 269; tribal divi-
sions, 162; agriculture, 17, 199, 267–
68, 281–82; United States policy
towards, 266, 268, 270–71, 273–74;
wars with, 267–83; as scouts, 271–
73, 277–78; as police, 273, 275; see
also names of tribes
Apache Kid: 281
Apache Pass: 164, 198
Apache prisoners: 279–82, 286, 288,
296, 379; see also Fort Sill Apaches
Apalachees: 76
Arapahos: see Cheyennes and
Arapahos, Northern Arapahos
Aravaipa Apaches: 268–71, 275, 281–
82
Arikaras: 11, 16, 103
Arkansas, state of: Indians seen by
De Soto, 31–32; settlement of Cher-
okees in, 88, 105, 112-13, 122;

cleared of Indians, 122, 127; statehood, 127
Arizona, state of: Indians in, 162; during Civil War, 198–200; becomes
separate territory, 200; Apache wars
in, 267–69, 271–76; hatred of Indians, 269, 282; present attitude,
296, 415; Indian population in, 408
Army contracts: 215, 273, 279
Association on American Indian Affairs: 353, 375, 377n., 379 & n.,
388ff., 418ff.
Atchison and Pike's Peak Railroad: 207
Atchison, Topeka and Santa Fe Railroad: 213, 297
Athapascan linguistic stock: 11–12
Athapascans: linguistic relationships,
11–12; form defensive organization,
394–96, 399, 400; see also Alaska
natives, Tyonek
Atkins, J. D. C.: 301–302, 304
Atlantic and Pacific Railroad: 202–203
Atomic Energy Commission: 388, 391,
393
Auchiah, James: 231–32
Aztecs: 11, 21

Bacon, Nathaniel: 49
Bannocks: linguistic relationships, 11;
war against trails, 161–62; scouts in
Nez Percé War, 263; war against
settlers, 264–65; ghost dance among,
289
Baptists: 114–15, 129, 302n.
Baranov, Aleksandr Andreevich: 100
Barrow, Alaska: 385ff., 400ff.; meeting
of Eskimos at, 390–93, natural gas
under, 390ff.
Barry (Captain): 267–68
Bartlett, Edward Louis: 393
"Battle of the Washita": 222–23
Bear That Scatters: 167
Beck, Carl: 377 & n.
Beecher Island fight: 221–22, 292
Bennett, Robert L.: 393, 396, 411, 417
Bent, Charles: 219
Bent, George: 193, 219, 222n.
Bent, William: 192, 193, 198
Benteen, Frederick W.: 238–39, 285
Bentley, Martin J.: 318–23
Bering, Vitus: 82
Bernal, Paul: 418–19
Berthrong, Donald J.: 191

Betzinez, Jason: 271 & n., 276n., 288n.
Bienville, Jean Baptiste Le-moyne, Sieur de: 71 ff.
Big Badlands: 292–94
Big Elk: 103–104
Big Foot: 292–93
Bigotes: 26–29
Big Tree: 226ff.
Biloxis: 10
Bismarck, North Dakota: 235, 239, 264
Blackfeet: 351, 371, 376; linguistic relationships, 10; relations with United States, 102–103, 166; trade with the British, 102–103; enmity to trans-mountain tribes, 103, 151, 166
Black Hawk: 9, 109, 127
Black Hills: Kiowas in, 11; home of Sioux, 189, 235–36; gold in, 236, 240; cause of North Plains War, 236; ceded by Sioux, 240
Black Kettle: 191–98, 212, 217, 222–23, 227, 229, 233; wife of, 194–95, 222
Bloody Fellow: 94
Blount, William: 93–94
Blue Jacket: 92
Blue Lake: 418–19
Board of Indian Commissioners: 8, 270, 330, 333
Bonito: 277
"Boomers": 297–98
Boone, Daniel: 81
Borbridge, John: 399–400
Bosque Redondo: 199–200
Bossu, Jean-Bernard: 80
Boudinot, Elias: early life and education, 120; position regarding removal, 120, 122–23; emigration to Oklahoma, 124; assassination, 128, 296
Boudinot, Elias Cornelius: 296
Bozeman Trail: 233–35, 237
Braddock, Edward: 79–80
Brant, Joseph: 84, 91
Brant, Molly: 79, 84
Brave Bear: see Bear That Scatters
Bribery, as Indian policy: 89, 94–95
Bridger, Jim: 104, 154
Brock, Isaac: 109–10
Brookings Institution: 336–37
Brouillet, Jean Baptiste A.: 155
Bruce, Louis Rooks, Jr.: 418
Brulé Sioux: 196, 210, 212, 233–34

Buffalo: early use of, 15–16; seen by Spaniards, 22, 26, 27, 29; numbers of, 27, 213, 285; robes in trade, 72, 213; slaughter of, 213–14, 219, 230
Bull Bear: 216
Bureau of American Ethnology: 288
Bureau of Indian Affairs: 273–74, 295, 306, 313, 318ff., 339ff., 351 ff., 383ff., 402ff.
Bureau of Land Management: 388ff.
Bursum, Holm O.: 334
Bursum Bill: 334–35
Butler, Elizur: 121–22
Butler, John: 87
Byler, William: 397

Cabeza de Vaca, Álvar Núñez: see Vaca
Cabot, John: 19
Cabrillo, Juan Rodríguez: 32
Cacique: 26–28
Caddoan linguistic stock: 9, 11
Caddoan tribes: 71–72, 130–32
Caddo George: see Washington
Caddos: 11, 229, 301–302
California, state of: coast explored by Cabrillo, 32; landing by Drake, 32–33; under Spanish rule, 82–83, 99–100, 164; acquired by the United States, 158; gold rush to, 158–59; treatment of Indians by, 158–59, 164–65; admitted to statehood, 164; Public Law 280 extended to, 353
California trails: 158–64
California Volunteers: 162, 198, 267, 268
Camass bulbs: 18, 102, 153, 265
Cameahwait: 101
Camp Grant: 271; massacre at, 268–70
Camp McDowell: 268
Camp Robinson: 235, 241, 242, 378–79
Camp Sheridan: 235
Camp Supply: 222–23, 228
Camp Verde: 271; see also Verde Reservation
Camp Weld: 193
Canada: French in, 20, 38–39; ceded to England, 80–81; as fur trade center, 102–103; Red River settlement, 150; refuge for Santee Sioux, 189; Sitting Bull in, 241; Nez Percé attempt to reach, 263
Canby, E.R.S.: 260

Captain Jack: 260
Cárdenas, García López de: 24–28, 30, 38
Carleton, James H.: 198–200, 267
Carlisle Indian school: 231, 280–81, 288, 296
Carolina, colony of: Indian trade, 73; Chickasaws take refuge in, 75; destroys Florida Indians, 76; Tuscaroras remove from, 77–78; Cherokee treaty with, 78; see also North Carolina, South Carolina
Carrington, Henry B.: 233–34
Carson, Kit: 154, 198–200
Carter, Charles D.: 333
Cartier, Jacques: 20
Carver, John A.: 383, 391–92, 419
Catawbas: 10, 76, 78
Catholics: 150 ff., 373, 418–19; see also Franciscans, Jesuits
Catlin, George: 126
Caughnawagas: 49–50, 79, 150
Cayugas: 9, 87; see also Iroquois Confederacy
Cayuses: linguistic relationships, 151; Whitman mission to, 151; Whitman massacre by, 153–56; at Walla Walla Council, 156–57; on Umatilla Reservation, 264
Ceremonials: 13–18, 72, 106, 108, 120; see also ghost dance
Cha-lipun: 272
Champlain, Samuel de: 38–39, 69
Charbonneau, Toussaint: 101
Charleston, South Carolina: 73
Chatto: 277, 282
Cheeseekau: 92
Chemawa, Oregon: 386
Cherokee Commission: see Jerome Commission
Cherokee Nation v. Georgia: 121, 349–50
Cherokee Outlet: 297
Cherokees: 6, 7; linguistic relationships, 9; primitive life ways, 14; seen by De Soto, 30; relations with England and France, 73ff.; wars with frontier settlers, 84–88, 92; first treaties with the United States, 88, 93–94; Arkansas emigrants from, 88, 105, 112, 122, 127; economic progress, 88, 94; visited by Tecumseh, 108–109; in Red Stick War, 111–12,

120; land cession to Andrew Jackson, 112; progress in civilization, 113–14; tribal newspaper, 114, 120, 122–24, 128; removal to Oklahoma, 120–25; Texas emigrants, 123, 129–30; North Carolina remnant, 125; progress in the Indian Territory, 128–29; in Civil War, 168, 169, 171–80, 201–202; Reconstruction, 182, 204; cede unassigned land, 296–97; dissolution of tribe, 307ff.; impoverishment of fullblood, 329–30; see also Chickamaugans, Five Civilized Tribes
Cheyenne River Agency (for Sioux): 235
Cheyenne River Reservation (of Sioux): 290, 292, 313
Cheyennes: see Cheyennes and Arapahos, Northern Cheyennes
Cheyennes and Arapahos: linguistic relationships, 9; emigration to Plains, 9–10, 15, 190; at Horse Creek Council, 165–66; division into Northern and Southern bands, 190; tribal relations, 190; treaty at Fort Lyon, 190–91; in Plains War of 1864–65, 191–98; treaty at Wichita site, 198, 212; in Central and South Plains War of 1867–69, 215–23; see also Northern Arapahos, Northern Cheyennes, Southern Cheyennes and Arapahos
Chicago, Illinois: see Fort Dearborn
Chickamaugans: 86, 88, 93, 94, 105; see also Cherokees
Chickasaws: linguistic relationships, 10; primitive government, 14; fight with De Soto, 31; alliance with English, 73, 76; French wars against, 74–75; Spanish intrigues, 88–89; treaty with the United States, 89; attacks on Tennessee settlements, 92; visited by Tecumseh, 107–108; land cession to Andrew Jackson, 112; progress in civilization, 114, 125; removal to West, 124; progress in the Indian Territory, 128–29; in Civil War, 168, 170, 172–76, 178–80; Reconstruction, 182–83; dissolution of tribe, 307ff.; see also Five Civilized Tribes
Chief Jake: 301–302

Chihuahua (Apache warrior): 278, 282
Children: Indian, in white captivity, 41–42, 287–88, 319; white, in Indian captivity, 288
Chilocco, Oklahoma: 383, 386
Chino, Wendell: 412
Chinook dances: 18
Chinook tribes: 102
Chippewas: linguistic relationships, 9; allotment of, 303, 305, 354; in North Dakota, 354; in Minnesota, 408; see also Red Lake Chippewas
Chiricahua Apaches: 162–64, 271, 274–75
Chitto Harjo: on "discovery" of America, 19, 310; on Indian wars, 36; on treaties, 70, 149, 176, 310; on life in the Indian Territory, 149; on Civil War, 168, 176, 310; on removal, 310; on allotment, 310; life of, 310
Chivington, John: 191–96, 198
Choctaws: 6, 7; linguistic relationships, 10; aboriginal life ways, 14; visited by De Soto, 30; subjected to French-English intrigues, 73–75; Spanish intrigues among, 88–89; first treaty with the United States, 89; decide against Tecumseh, 107–108; in Red Stick War, 111; allied with Jackson at New Orleans, 112; land cessions to Jackson, 112–13; progress in civilization, 114; removal to West, 117–18; progress in the Indian Territory, 128–29; in Civil War, 168–70, 172–75, 178–80, 201; Reconstruction, 182–83; dissolution of tribe, 307ff.; see also Five Civilized Tribes
Chouteau, Auguste: 82
Christianity: 7, 69, 124, 129, 150, 156–57, 186, 188, 261, 289, 290, 302 & n., 308; see also churches, missionaries
Chuculate, Richard: 377
Churches: appointment of Indian agents by, 204–205n.; study courses on Indians, 338, 349–50, 375; see also Federal Council of Churches and names of denominations
Cíbola: 23–30; see also Zunis
Cicúye Pueblo: 26–29
Cincinnati, Ohio: 90 ff.
Citizenship, United States: 148, 300–

301, 309, 318, 325, 335–36, 351, 352, 372, 387, 392, 417
Civil War: 162, 208; in Indian Territory, 168–83; in Minnesota, 184–89; on Plains, 191–98; in New Mexico and Arizona, 198–200; see Reconstruction treaties
Clark, George Rogers: 86
Clark, William: 101–103, 151
Cleveland, Grover: 280, 300
Cloud, Henry Roe: 336
Clum, John P.: 273–75, 278
Cochise: 163–64, 271, 274, 276
Cochiti Pueblo: 421
Cody, William F.: 213
Coeur d'Alenes: 12
Colbert, Jean Baptiste: 69
College of William and Mary: 42
Collier, John: 338–42, 350, 412
Collins, William O.: 191
Colorado, state of: gold rush to, 165, 190; territorial government formed, 190; statehood granted, 265; expulsion of Utes from, 265–66; see also Plains Wars
Colter, John: 103
Columbus, Christopher: 19, 20, 21, 310
Colville Reservation: 264, 294–95
Colyer, Vincent: 270
Comanches: 72, 73, 226, 282, 288, 292–93; linguistic relationships, 11; movement to Plains, 15; Spanish peace with, 98–99; raids in Texas, 130, 224–27; in council at Fort Atkinson, 166; treaty with Confederates, 170–71; raids in Mexico, 178; allied with Cheyennes and Arapahos, 190; in Plains War of 1864–65, 197–98; treaty with, 198, 212; in Central and South Plains War of 1867–69, 218–23; at Medicine Lodge Council, 219–20; reservation in the Indian Territory, 220, 223; in South Plains War of 1874–75, 229–32; at Okmulgee Council, 232; ghost dance among, 289; opposition to allotment, 303; see also Penateka Comanches
Commission to the Five Civilized Tribes: see Dawes Commission
Competency commissions: 314, 329, 333, 337
Concho, Oklahoma: 4–5

433

Confederate treaties, favorable provisions: 170–72
Congregationalists: 385
Connecticut, state of: 46–48, 120
Connor, Patrick E.: 162, 197, 234
Cooley, Dennis N.: 180–82
Coolidge, Calvin: 295, 332
Cooper, Douglas H.: 174–75
Cordero, Fred: 421
Cornstalk: 82
Coronado, Francisco Vásquez de: 14–15, 23–31, 36, 38, 407
Corps of Engineers: 395, 416 & n., 421
Corte-Real, Gaspar: 19
Cortés, Hernando: 21
Cotton cloth: 25, 26, 28
Coureurs de bois: 73 & n.
Coushattas: 10, 97, 130, 296, 371
Coyotero Apaches: 162, 267–68, 270, 275
Crawford, Samuel J.: 218
Creek Confederacy: 10, 13, 74, 80, 95–96, 108, 115–16; *see also* Creeks
Creeks: 4, 6, 8, 422; linguistic relationships, 10; primitive life ways, 13–14, 30, 80, 95; visited by De Soto, 30; consent to Georgia settlement, 70, 76, 116; relations with imperial rivals, 73, 75, 76–77; join English against Florida Indians, 76; encroached upon by Georgians, 81, 89, 95–97; during American Revolution, 85–86; Spanish-American intrigues with, 88–89, 96; attacks on Tennessee settlements, 92, 94; Treaty of New York with, 95–96; visited by Tecumseh, 106–108; forbid unauthorized land cessions, 108, 115–16; in Red Stick War, 110–12, 114–15; adopt "civilization," 114–15; removal to West, 116, 118–20; refugees join Cherokees, 119; progress in the Indian Territory, 128–29, 149; in Civil War, 168–70, 172–79, 201, 310; Reconstruction, 182, 204; economic progress, 201–202, 312; constitutional difficulties, 204–205; invitation to Sioux, 240; cede unassigned land, 296–98, 304; sympathy for "wild" tribes, 301–302 & n.; dissolution of tribe, 307ff.; *see also* Creek Confederacy, Five Civilized Tribes

Crook, George: in Rogue River War, 158–59; in Ponca removal, 211; in North Plains War, 237, 239–40, 274; in Apache wars, 237, 271–73, 276–80; report on Bannock War, 265; use of Apache scouts, 271–72, 282; outfitting of pack trains, 271; efforts for Apache prisoners, 281
Crow Creek Agency (for Sioux): 235
Crows: linguistic relationships, 11; at Horse Creek Council, 165; hostility to Sioux, 190, 284; allied with Crook, 237; refuse sanctuary to Nez Percés, 263; aboriginal life way, 284–85; allotment of, 305
Cufitachiqui: *see* Cusseta
Cuming, Alexander: 78
Curtis, Charles: 308, 320 ff.
Curtis, Samuel R.: 191–93
Curtis Act: 308
Cusseta (Creek town): 30
Custer, George Armstrong: in Central and South Plains wars, 217, 223–24, 225; explored Black Hills, 235–36; in final campaign, 238–40, 285

Dakotas: *see* Sioux
Dakota Territory, division of: 290
Dates, method of reckoning: 50, 110
Davis, Britton: 277–78, 281
Davis, Jefferson: 171
Dawes, Henry L.: 300, 307
Dawes Act: provisions, 300–301; Indian opposition to, 301–304; allotments under, 304–305, 313–14, 316–24, 354; land openings under, 304–305, 317–19; reversal of policy, 332–33, 338–39; *see also* allotment
Dawes Commission: reports of, 307, 336–37; liquidation of Five Civilized Tribes by, 307–309, 311; rolls of, 324, 326, 327; *see also* allotment
Death songs: 167, 188, 194–95, 226
Deer, Bob: 174
Degnan, Frank: 391
Delawares: ethnic relationships: 9, 13; treaty with Penn, 9, 49; meeting with Hudson, 43; treaty with the United States, 86–87, 309; dispersal of, 87, 109, 129–30, 147, 154; on Kansas reservation, 147 & n.; in Civil War, 174, 177; removal to Indian Territory, 206

Delshay: 272–73
Denver, Colorado: as gold rush town, 165, 190; in Plains wars, 193, 195; as relocation center, 377
Denver trails: 165, 191, 215, 217
De Soto, Hernando: 23, 30–32, 111
Detroit, Michigan: 86–87, 92, 109, 111
d'Ewart, Wesley: 375–76, 379
Díaz, Porfirio: 318
Dickson, Charles H.: 319–20
Dinwiddie, Robert: 78, 79
Diseases: 44; see also measles, scarlet fever, smallpox
Dogs, aboriginal use of: 13, 15, 385, 404
Dorchester, 1st baron, Sir Guy Carleton: 92
Dot Lake, Alaska: 394
Douglas (Ute chief): 265
Douglas, Arizona: 321
Drake, Sir Francis: 32–33, 34
Drew, John: 173, 175, 176
Dull Knife: 241–42, 381
Dunmore, 4th Earl of, John Murray: 82
Dutch, in New York: 42–43
Du Tisné, Charles Claude: 72
Dwellings, aboriginal: 13–18, 23ff., 42, 285

Eagle Heart: 226
Eastman, Charles A.: 288n.
Eayre, George S.: 192
Ecueracapa: 98
Education: original aims, 40–41, 47, 90–91, 286–88; reforms in, 337, 339, 413–15, 419–20; Indian control of, 414–15, 419–20; see also schools
Eisenhower, Dwight D.: 352, 353, 372, 375
Eliot, John: 47–49, 114
Elliott, Joel H.: 218–19, 223
Ellis, George E.: 286
Ellis, Joe: 174
Embry, John: 322
Emmons, Glenn L.: 352, 375ff.
Employment, off-reservation: 347–48, 407–408; see also Indians in cities, relocation
England: early explorations by, 19, 32–33; first settlements by, 39–49; colonial Indian policy of, 40–42, 47, 69; in American Revolution, 84–87;

designs on Ohio country, 87–88, 92–93; see also imperial rivalries, War of 1812
Episcopalians: 188, 385, 394
Ernst, Roger C.: 379–80
Eskiminzin: 268–69, 281–82
Eskimos: 9, 12, 400, 412; trade with Chukchis, 385; schools for, 385–86, 394; whaling, 385, 391, 404; reindeer industry of, 385; population, 388; atomic threat to, 388–93; trouble with game laws, 388–93; form Inupiat Paitot, 390–96; see also Alaska natives
Esteván: see Estevanico
Estevanico: 22–24, 30
Euchees: 9, 10, 85, 310
Eufaula Harjo: 4, 311–12, 412–13
Evans, John: 190–93
Executive order reservations: status, 294–96, 387; forbidden by Congress, 386; authorized for Alaska, 387; see also Alaska native land issue
Extension service: established, 337; agricultural achievements, 343–45

Fairbanks, Alaska: 394, 396, 398, 402
Fall, Albert B.: 295, 334–35
Fallen Timbers, Battle of: 92
Fannin, Paul J., Jr.: 415
Federal Housing Authority: 407
Fetterman, William J.: 234
Field, Walter: 320, 322
Finn, Daniel C.: 205
Fish and Wildlife Service: 389, 393, 420
Five Civilized Tribes: progress in the Indian Territory, 127–29, 149; school systems of, 129, 202, 288, 308, 412–13; assistance to "wild" tribes, 130, 148, 227–28, 301–304; in Civil War, 168–80; Reconstruction, 180–83, 201–202; population, 201, 203, 296, 307, 324 & n.; fight to hold heritage, 203; at Okmulgee Council, 224, 227; liquidation of, 306, 307–10, 341, 352; plan for Mexican emigration, 308–309, 324; spoliation of, 324–28, 333; extension of restrictions for, 329–30; present land holdings, 330 & n.; condition of fullbloods, 330, 377; Senate investigation of, 336–37; efforts to rehabilitate, 343–45, 410;

see also Cherokees, Chickasaws, Choctaws, Creeks, Dawes Commission, Indian Territory, Seminoles
Five Nations: *see* Iroquois Confederacy
Flatheads: 12, 150–51, 166
Florida, state of: Spanish explorations in, 21, 30; French attempts to settle, 33–34; Spanish settlements in, 34; Franciscan missions in, 67, 76; ceded to England, 80–81; returned to Spain, 87; purchased by United States, 112–13; removal of Seminoles from, 125–26; Seminoles remaining, 126, 354; *see also* Seminoles
Forbes, Henry S.: 389, 390, 396
Ford Foundation: 399
Forsyth, George A.: 221–22, 292–93
Fort Abraham Lincoln: 235, 237, 239
Fort Apache: 270, 274, 276, 280
Fort Apache Reservation: 270 ff., 346, 397
Fort Atkinson: 166
Fort Benton: 233
Fort Bowie: 198, 278ff.
Fort C. F. Smith: 233–35
Fort Cobb: 147, 177, 222, 223
Fort Dearborn: 109
Fort Duquesne: 78–79; *see also* Fort Pitt
Fort Ellis: 235, 237
Fort Gibson: 128, 175ff., 208
Fort Gibson (town), Oklahoma: 303
Fort Hall: 233
Fort Kearny: 189
Fort Keogh: 259, 263
Fort Laramie: 165–67, 189, 191, 233, 234
Fort Larned: 189ff., 216, 222
Fort Leavenworth: 167, 169, 264
Fort Loudoun: 79–80
Fort Lyon: 189, 190, 193, 194
Fort McRae: 271
Fort Malden: 107, 109, 110
Fort Marion: 231, 279, 280
Fort Miami: 92–93
Fort Mims: 111
Fort Niagara: 79, 81
Fort Phil Kearny: 233–35
Fort Pickens: 280
Fort Pitt: 81, 86–87; *see also* Fort Duquesne
Fort Reno: 233–35
Fort Richardson: 225, 228

Fort Ridgely: 184, 186–87
Fort Riley: 192
Fort Rosalie: 71, 74
Fort Sill: 223, 225–27, 229, 281, 289
Fort Sill Apaches: 379; *see also* Apache prisoners
Fort Smith Council: 180–82
Fort Snelling: 188, 189
Fort Toulouse: 73–74, 80
Fort Wayne: 93
Fort Wingate: 267, 268
Fort Wise: *see* Fort Lyon
Fractionated heirships: 341–42, 346, 350, 354, 407
France: early explorations by, 19–20; attempts at colonization by, 33–34; in Canada, 38–39, 49–50; in Louisiana, 67–68, 71–73; Indian policy of, 69–70, 73–75
Franciscans: with Coronado, 23–24; in New Mexico, 36–37, 50, 67; in Florida, 67, 76; in California, 83, 99–100, 164
Franklin, Benjamin: 336
Fraudulent treaties: 115, 123–24, 207, 261; "agreement," 317, 319, 321, 323
Free, Mickey: 163–64
French and Indian War: 71, 78–81
Fur (and pelt) trade: French in Canada, 38–39; English in New England, 39, 43, 45; Dutch in New York, 43; English with Iroquois, 49; French in Louisiana, 72–73; English in Gulf region, 73, 76, 116; in Ohio country, 78; in upper Louisiana, 82, 101–104; in Alaska, 82–83, 100; in Pacific Northwest, 100, 105, 150 ff.

Gall: 235, 238, 240–41
Gardiner, John W.: 409–10
Garry: *see* Spokane Garry
Gatewood, Charles B.: 280
General Allotment Act: *see* Dawes Act
General Federation of Women's Clubs: 335
Georgia, state of: founded, 76; encroachments on Creeks, 81, 89, 95–97; cleared of Creeks, 115–16; extension of state laws to Indians, 117, 120–22; expulsion of Cherokees, 120–25; historical restitution, 124 & n.

Geronimo: 3–4, 8, 271, 274–80, 286
Geronimo, family of: 274–75, 278, 281, 282–83
Geronimo, Robert: 283
Ghost dance: 289–94
Gibbon, John: 237
Gila Apaches: 98–99, 162, 199
Gilpin, Alfred Wayne: 378
Gold: in Hispaniola, 20; in Cherokee country, 120; in California, 158–60; in Colorado, 165, 190; in Montana, 233; in Black Hills, 240; on Nez Percé Reservation, 266
Goldwater, Barry: 295–96
Gookin, Daniel: 47, 49
Gorges, Ferdinando: 43–44
Grant, Ulysses S.: 204n., 223, 225, 236, 269
Grattan, J. L.: 167
Gray, Robert: 100
Gray, William E.: 151
Great Pueblo Revolt: 50, 99, 334–35
Green, John: 267–68
Grinnell, George Bird: 217
Gruening, Ernest: 390, 393
Guadalupe Hidalgo, Treaty of: 158
Guardianships: 318, 322–23, 327–28, 333

Habeas corpus, writ of: 211, 301
Haidas: 12, 396, 399; see also Alaska natives
Hakluyt, Richard: 40
Hamilton, Henry: 86
Hancock, Winfield Scott: 215–17, 221
Harding, Warren: 333, 335
Harlan, James: 180, 224
Harmer, Josiah: 91
Harney, William S.: 167
Harris, Fred R.: 409
Harris, La Donna (Mrs. Fred R. Harris): 408–10, 412
Harrison, Benjamin: 295
Harrison, William Henry: 105–10
Harvard College: 47
Hastings, W. W.: 333
Hatathli, Ned: 420
Havasupais: 12, 17
Haverford College: 389
Hawkins, Benjamin: 94, 96–97, 108ff.
Hawkins, James: 390–91, 402
Hayden, Carl: 295–96
Hayden, Iola: 409; see also Taylor

Hayes, Rutherford B.: 297
Hazen, William B.: 222–23
HCR 108: see House Concurrent Resolution 108
Head Start: 411
Heirships: see fractionated heirships
Henrico, Virginia: see Henricus
Henricus, Virginia: 41–42
Hensley, William L.: 400–401, 412
Hetzel, Theodore B.: 389ff.
Hickel, Walter J.: 398ff., 417–18, 420
High Plains: 29
Hispaniola: 20
Hitchitees: 10, 85
Hoag, Enoch: 224, 228
Hobomok: 45ff.
Honey Springs, Battle of: 178, 180
Hoo: see Juh
Hoover, Herbert: 331n., 332, 337
Hoover Commission: 331 & n., 333–34, 341, 342, 350, 416n.
Hopewell treaties: with Cherokees, 88; with Choctaws, 89; with Chickasaws, 89
Hopis: linguistic relationships, 11; conquered by Spain, 26, 37; in Great Pueblo Revolt, 50, 67; maintained independence, 67, 99; attempt to allot, 313; rehabilitation measure, 348, 353
Hopson, Eben: 401
Horse Creek Council: 165–66, 186
Horses: 15–16, 72, 153–54, 238–39, 285
Horseshoe Bend, Battle of: 112
House Concurrent Resolution 108: 352, 379, 405, 415–17
Houston, Sam: 130, 212
Howard, Oliver Otis: war with Nez Percés, 262–65, 270n.; peace mission to Arizona Indians, 270–71
Hualapais: 12
Hudson, Henry: 42–43
Hudson River, descriptions of: 20, 42–43
Hudson's Bay Company: 102–103, 150ff.
Hull, William: 109
Hunt, Thomas: 43–44
Hurons: 9, 39, 69; see also Wyandots
Hyde, George E.: 189
Hynes v. Grimes Packing Company: 387

Iberville, Pierre Le-moyne, Sieur d':
71, 74
Ickes, Harold L.: 338
Illinois, state of: admitted to Union,
111
Illinois country: 67–68, 71 ff., 86
Imperial rivalries: 69–74, 76–77, 87–
89
Independence, Missouri: 105, 150
Indiana, state of: organization of territory, 105; Indian wars in, 105ff.;
statehood, 111; see also Tecumseh
Indian agents: 90, 94, 96ff., 118, 148,
225–26, 273, 328–29, 333
Indian Bureau: see Bureau of Indian
Affairs
Indian characteristics: adaptation to
environment, 3–4; religious feeling,
3–4, 7, 80, 124, 207, 279, 281, 339–
40, 380, 418–19, 421; feeling for
land, 3–4, 115, 118, 124, 157, 261–
62, 311, 418–19, 421; thought processes, 3–4; artistry, 4–5; eloquence,
5; creative writing, 5–6; thrift and
industry, 6, 285–86; individual drive,
6–7; refusal to compromise, 7–8, 173,
176, 286, 308, 311–13, 415; physical
diversity, 8–9
Indian Claims Commission: 112, 210,
240, 346, 371–72, 373, 419
Indian culture: attempts to destroy, 40–
41, 286–88, 349; recognition of, 288,
339 & n., 415
Indian life ways: in Eastern Wood-
lands, 13–14; on the Plains, 14, 16,
165, 238, 284–85; in the Southwest,
16–17; in the Great Basin, 17; in
California, 17–18; in the Pacific
Northwest, 18, 100, 102; in southeastern Alaska, 18; war strategy, 79,
187, 234; travel techniques, 239
Indian linguistic stocks: 8–12
Indian Office: see Bureau of Indian
Affairs
Indian police: 273, 275, 291
Indian Reorganization Act: 338–42,
346ff., 386–87
Indian Rights Association: 316, 337,
343n., 375, 389ff.
Indians in cities: 376, 407–408; see
also relocation
Indian statehood project: in Delaware
treaty, 87; in Cherokee treaty, 88;

proposed by Creeks, 89; attempted
by Indian Territory tribes, 303–304;
end of concept, 309; see also Okmulgee Council
Indian Territory: extent of, 127; Indians in, 127–49; designs against,
147–48, 180–81, 183, 203, 205, 266,
296–97; in Civil War, 168–83, 201–
202; Reconstruction in, 181–83,
201–202; cession of western half,
182; settlement of new tribes in,
206–12, 220, 223–24, 231; closed to
other Indians, 240, 266, 280–81;
land opening in, 296–98; Territory
of Oklahoma, 296–98, 304, 306–307;
statehood, 309; see also Oklahoma
(west half), Oklahoma, state of
Ingalls, John J.: 205, 286
Institute for Government Research:
see Brookings Institution
Institute of American Indian Arts: 5
Iowa, state of: statehood, 111; Indians
remaining in, 111, 413
Iowas: 11, 206–207, 303
Iron Bull: 284
Iroquoian linguistic stock: 9
Iroquois: linguistic relationships, 9;
hostility to the French, 39; trade
with the Dutch, 43; trade with the
English, 49–50; in French and In-
dian War, 78–79; economic advance-
ment, 87; help sought by Washing-
ton, 91; visited by Tecumseh, 106;
plans to remove, 126–27; see also
Caughnawagas, Iroquois Confed-
eracy, and tribes by name
Iroquois Confederacy: 9, 13, 39, 78, 81,
84, 87, 336, 417; see also Iroquois
Isaac, Andrew: 402–403
Isparhecher: 308

Jack (Ute leader): 265
Jacksboro, Texas: 228, 229; see also
Fort Richardson
Jackson, Andrew: in Congress, 94; in
Red Stick War, 111–12, 120; cap-
ture of New Orleans, 112; invasion
of Florida, 112–13; obtains land
cessions, 112–13; as president, 126–
27; evaluation of, 332
Jackson, Henry M.: 401
Jackson, Jacob B.: 308–309
Jamestown, Virginia: 9, 39–41, 287

Jefferson, Thomas: authorizes Lewis and Clark Expedition, 101; Indian policy of, 105
Jerome, David H.: 304
Jerome Commission: 304, 316–17
Jesuits: in Florida and Georgia, 34; in Virginia, 34; in Canada, 38–39, 49–50
Jicarilla Apaches: 162–63, 198
Johnson, Lyndon B.: 353, 411–12
Johnson, William: 79, 81, 84 & n.
Johnson-O'Malley Act: 339
Johnston, Albert Sidney: 161
Joseph (Old): 151, 153, 156–58, 261
Joseph (Young): 261–64
Jourdain, Roger: 412
Journeycake, Charles: 147n.
Juh: 275–77
Julesburg, Colorado: 196
Juneau, Alaska: 390, 402

Kalispels: 12
Kalskeg, Alaska: 392
Kamiakim: 156, 157
Kansa Indians: 11, 210
Kansas, state of: Coronado in, 29; Indian removals to, 127; territorial government for, 147; encroachment on reservations, 147; designs on Indian Territory, 147, 205, 230, 240, 266, 296–98; statehood, 168; Civil War refugees in, 175–77, 182; Civil War expeditions from, 176–77, 182; removal of Indians from, 206–10; allotments in, 207–208, 299; Cheyenne-Arapaho depredations in, 221, 223
Kansas-Nebraska Act: 147, 207
Kansas Pacific Railroad: 213, 214, 215
Katy Railroad: see Missouri, Kansas and Texas Railroad
Kaws: see Kansa Indians
Ka-ya-ten-nae: 277, 279, 282
Keeler, W. W.: 400–401, 405
Kennedy, John F.: 383, 405, 419
Kennedy, Robert F.: 410, 412, 415, 417
Kentucky, state of: white settlements in, 81–82, 89; statehood, 93–94, 401
Kerr, Robert S.: 379
Ketzler, Alfred: 394, 396
Kickapoos: linguistic relationships, 9; support of Tecumseh, 107; in Texas, 129; in Indian Territory, 130; in

Mexico, 130, 177–78, 208–209, 318ff.; in Civil War, 171, 174, 177–78; enmity to Texas, 171, 208–209; removal to Indian Territory, 206–209; allotments to, 207–208, 316ff.; at Okmulgee Council, 232; liquidation under Dawes Act, 316–24; present condition, 324, 410–11
Kicking Bird: 229–31, 233
Kieta: 280, 282
King Island, Alaska: 393
King Philip: 47–49
King Philip's War: 48–49
Kiowa-Apaches: 11, 178, 193, 197–98, 212, 223ff., 232, 303; see also Kiowas
Kiowas: 5, 282; linguistic relationships, 9; early migrations, 11, 15; primitive life ways, 15–16; raids in Texas, 130, 224ff.; at Fort Atkinson council, 166; in Civil War, 171; raids in Mexico, 178; allied with Cheyennes and Arapahos, 190; raid of Fort Larned by, 192; in Plains wars, 192–93, 197–98, 218–23, 228–32; at Medicine Lodge Council, 218–21; reservation in Indian Territory, 222; at Okmulgee Council, 232; reject ghost dance, 289; oppose allotment, 301–302; question relocation, 377
Kirby-Smith, Edmund: 180
Klamaths: linguistic relationships, 12; stirred to hostility, 158–59; Modocs settled with, 260; termination of, 334, 372, 374–75
Knox, Henry: 88, 90
Kodiak Island, Alaska: 383, 387
Koluschan linguistic stock: 9, 12
Kotzebue, Alaska: 392–93
Kuskokwim River, Alaska: 387
Kutenais: 150

Laclède, Pierre: 82
La Farge, Oliver: xi, 340, 347, 375, 396, 397, 405
La Follette, Robert M.: 334
La Harpe, Bernard de: 71–72
Lake Erie, Battle of: 111
Land tenure: patented, 127, 305; in trust status, 300–301, 324, 337, 338; increased holdings, 341; leasing, 342, 345–46; see also allotment of land, executive order reservations,

fractionated heirships, removal of restrictions
Lane, Franklin K.: 314, 329
Lapwai Mission: 151–55
Lapwai Reservation: 261, 263, 264, 305
La Salle, Robert Cavelier, Sieur de: 67–68, 69
Las Casas, Bartolemé de: 20–21
Laudonnière, René Goulaine de: 33–34
Lawton, Oklahoma: 408
Lazarus, Arthur, Jr.: 403
League of the Iroquois: see Iroquois Confederacy
Lean Bear: 191–92
Leased District: 128, 130, 147, 171, 177, 180
Leavenworth, Jesse H.: 191, 198
Lee, Jason: 151
Lee, Rex: 352, 373, 389
Leeper, Matthew: 170, 177
Left Hand: 192–95
Leslie, Samuel: 312
Leupp, Francis E.: 313, 314
Lewis, John: 327–28
Lewis, Meriwether: 101–103
Lewis, Orme: 352, 375
Lewis and Clark Expedition: 101–103, 150–51, 161
Lewiston, Idaho: 261
Lincoln, Abraham: 168ff., 184, 188, 332
Linguistic stocks: 8–12
Lisa, Manuel: 103
Lisburne, Daniel: 391
Little Bighorn, Custer's defeat on: 237–39
Little Crow: 185–89
Little Raven: 190, 194–95, 198, 212, 218
Little Turtle: 91
Little Wolf: 241–60, 381
Lituamian linguistic stock: 9, 12
Loco: 270, 276–77, 282
London Company: 41
Lone Wolf: 223, 228, 230, 231
Lone Wolf, Delos K.: 301–302
Lone Wolf v. Hitchcock: 302
"Long Walk," Navaho: 199
Looking Glass: 263–64
Lopp, William T.: 385
Louisiana (province): claimed by La Salle, 67–68; French settlement of,

71ff.; ceded to England and Spain, 80–81; acquired by United States, 101; explored by Lewis and Clark, 101–103; see also fur trade
Louisiana, state of: French settlements in, 71; statehood, 113
Lumbees: 34–35
Lyon, Franklin S.: 204–205

Mabila, De Soto battle at: 30–31
McCarran, Pat: 351
McCulloch, Ben: 171, 172
McGillivray, Alexander: 88–89, 95–96
Macgregor, Gordon: 285, 345–46
McIntosh, William: 115–16
McKay, Douglas: 352, 374, 379
McKenney, T. I.: 192
Mackenzie, Ranald S.: 208, 225, 226, 228
McLaughlin, James: 291
Macopia: 303
Madigan, La Verne: 353, 381, 388ff.
Maine, state of: 39
Mamanti: 225–26, 230–31
Mandans: linguistic relationships, 10–11; life ways, 16; visited by Lewis and Clark, 101, 103; wiped out by smallpox, 103
Mangus: 278, 282
Mangas Coloradas: 163–64, 200, 270, 278
Manhattan Island: 42–43
Mankato, Minnesota: 188
Many Farms, Arizona: 420
Marchie Tiger Case: 337
Marcy, Randolph B.: 16
Marietta, Ohio: 90
Marshall, John: 121–22
Martine: 280, 282
Martinez, Severino: 418–19
Massachusetts (Indian tribe): 45, 46
Massachusetts Bay Colony: 46–49
Massasoit: 45, 47, 49
Mather, Increase: 48
Maus, Marion B.: 278, 279
Measles: 154, 290
Medicine Lodge Council: 218–21, 225–26
Meek, Joe: 103, 104, 153, 154
Meeker, Nathan: 265
Menéndez de Avilés, Pedro: 34, 39
Menominees: forest of, 334; termination, 372–74

Meriam, Lewis: 336, 338
Meriam survey: 335–37
Meriwether, David: 163
Merritt, Wesley: 289–90
Mescal: 199 & n.
Mescalero Apaches: location of, 162;
at Bosque Redondo, 198–99; raiding
by, 199, 276; given reservation, 199;
joined by Apache prisoners, 281–83
Methodists: 114, 115, 129, 151
Metlakatla, Alaska: 387, 395 & n.
Mexico: Spanish conquest of, 21, 23;
independence, 105; Kickapoos in,
130, 177–78, 208–209, 318ff.; Kiowa
and Comanche raids in, 178;
Apaches in, 274–80, 283; plan of
Five Civilized Tribes to emigrate to,
308–309
Miamis: 91
Micco Hutke: 174
Miguel: 267–68, 270
Mikasukis: 126, 287; see also Seminoles
Miles, Nelson A.: regarding Mangas
Coloradas, 200; in North Plains wars,
239–40, 285; receives Northern
Cheyennes, 259; in Nez Percé War,
263–64; takes Apaches prisoner,
279–80, 283; controls Sioux ghost
dance, 291–93
Military, wars started by: 166–67,
189ff., 215–17, 221, 262–63
Miller, Keith H.: 403
Mimbreño Apaches: 162, 163–64; see
also Warm Springs Apaches
Minneapolis, Minnesota: 408
Minnesota, state of: Sioux uprising in,
184–89, 290; statehood, 187; Indian
reservations in, 304–305; spoliation
of White Earth Reservation, 330;
Public Law 280 extended to, 353
Minto, Alaska: 394, 397
Missionaries: sent by Spain, 20;
planned by England, 40–42, 47;
linguistic studies by, 67, 113–14,
152; among Delawares, 87; rejected
by Hopis, 100; among Five Civilized
Tribes, 148; quest for, by Northwestern Indians, 150–51; approved
by Blackfeet, 166; rejected by Kickapoos, 209; sent by Creeks to "wild"
tribes, 302n.; opposition to Collier,
340; see also American Board of
Commissioners for Foreign Missions,

Christianity, Franciscans, Jesuits,
and names of denominations
Mississippi, state of: Indians in, 10;
French settlements in, 71; statehood,
113; extension of state laws over
Indians, 117; removal of Choctaws
from, 117–18; allotments in, 118,
299; Choctaws remaining in, 118;
removal of Chickasaws from, 125
Mississippi River: 31–32
Missouri, state of: Osages in, 10; mi-
gration of Shawnees and Delawares
to, 86–87; visited by Tecumseh, 106,
109; statehood, 127; cleared of Indians, 127; Civil War in, 172
Missouri, Kansas and Texas Railroad:
202–203, 296–97
Missouris: see Otos and Missouris
Mitchell, Emerson Blackhorse: 5 & n.,
420
Mobile, Alabama: 71, 73
Modocs: linguistic relationships, 12; in
Rogue River War, 158–59; war in
lava beds, 260; settled in Indian
Territory, 260; at Okmulgee Council,
260; present location of, 260
Mohaves: 12
Mohawks: linguistic relationships, 9;
friendship for Sir William Johnson,
79; migration to Canada, 84; see also
Iroquois Confederacy
Molalas: 151, 158
Momaday, N. Scott: 5–6
Montana, state of: gold in, 233; terri-
torial government, 235; supports
Northern Cheyennes, 378
Moorehead, Warren K.: 330
Moravians: 113
Morgan, Arthur E.: 416
Mormons: 160–61
Morning Star: see Dull Knife
Moses: 287, 295
"Mother towns": 14, 94
Mountain Lamb (wife of Joe Meek):
104
Mountain Meadows Massacre: 161
Mountain men: 103–104
Mount Edgecumbe, Alaska: 386, 399
Mount Vernon Barracks: 281
Mueller, Richard D.: 402–403
Muskhogean linguistic stock: 9, 10
Múzquiz, Mexico: 320
Myer, Dillon S.: 351, 352, 376

Nacimiento, Mexico: 177–78, 320, 323
Nader, Ralph: 375
Naiche: 276, 278–80, 282, 283
Nakai, Raymond: 412
Nana: 276, 278, 282
Nanticokes: 85 & n.
Narragansetts: 45–48
Narváez, Pánfilo de: 21
Nash, Philleo: 373, 405, 411
Natchez Indians: 10, 71, 74–75
National Congress of American Indians: 371, 375, 412, 417, 418
National Council of Churches: 338, 349, 350, 375, 419
National Council on Indian Opportunity: 411–12
National Indian Defense Association: 300
Navaho-Hopi Act: 348, 350, 351, 353
Navaho Reservation: 295, 331, 353
Navahos: 5, 284, 287, 412; linguistic relationships, 11; life ways, 17, 200; relations with Pueblos, 17, 37, 50, 67; raiding by, 67, 162, 199; relations with Apaches, 98–99; progress of, 99, 200, 347, 381–82; on Bosque Redondo, 199–200; population, 199, 347, 381, 408, 420 & n.; schools, 340, 347–48, 381–82, 414–15, 419–20; government, 347, 382; rehabilitation measure, 347–48; mineral royalties, 381–82; newspaper, 382; junior college, 420–21
NCAI: see National Congress of American Indians
Nebraska, state of: Indian reservations in, 127, 147, 188; territorial government, 147; removal of Indians from, 207, 210–12; statehood, 210; Public Law 280 in, 353
Negroes: Estevanico, 22–24; slaves of white men, 73, 111; slaves of Indians, 128, 174, 176; freedmen in Indian Territory, 182–83, 306–307; Ninth Cavalry Regiment, 293; as allottees, 324 & n., 327
Neighbors, Robert S.: 130, 147
Ne-ka-ke-pa-hah: 301
Nenana, Alaska: 394, 399
New Echota (Cherokee capital): 114, 122, 124
New Mexico, state of: acquired by United States, 158; Indian hostility

in, 162; in Civil War, 198–200; Apache wars in, 270, 274, 276; support of Pueblos by, 335
New Orleans, Louisiana: 71, 112
New York, state of: early explorations, 19–20, 38, 42–43; Dutch in, 42–43; English colony, 49–50
New Ulm, Minnesota: 185, 187–88
Nez Percé Reservation: established, 157; reduced, 261; allotted, 305
Nez Percés: 4, 8; linguistic relationships, 12; help to Lewis and Clark, 102; Christianity, 150–57; relations with Blackfeet, 151, 166; advancement in civilization, 153, 157; at Walla Walla Council, 156–57; in Yakima War, 158; as stockmen, 261, 264, 305; war with United States, 262–64; removal to Indian Territory, 264, 266; return to the Northwest, 264
Nisquallis: 12
Nixon, Richard M.: 401, 405, 412, 417–18
Niza, Fray Marcos de: 23–24
Noble, John W.: 317
Nome, Alaska: 385
North Carolina, state of: Raleigh's settlement in, 34–35; Cherokee wars with, 79ff.; Tecumseh's visit to, 108; Cherokee reservation in, 125; see also Carolina
North Dakota, state of: admitted to Union, 290; Indian reservations in, 291, 354
Northern Arapahos: separated from Southern bands, 190; in North Plains War, 238–41; settled with Shoshonis, 241; see also Cheyennes and Arapahos
Northern Arizona University: 420
Northern Cheyennes: separated from Southern bands, 190; in North Plains War, 237–41; settled in Indian Territory, 241; escape to North, 241–60, 379; present home, 259–60; personal qualities, 285; allotment of, 314; fight to hold reservation, 378–81; see also Cheyennes and Arapahos
Northern Pacific Railroad: 235
North Fork Town, Indian Territory: 170
North Slope, Alaska: 400, 403–404

442

North West Company: 102–103
Northwest Ordinance: 89
Notti, Emil: 399–401

Office of Economic Opportunity: 410–11
Oglala Sioux: 196, 197, 216, 233–34, 418
Oglethorpe, James: 70, 76, 116
Ohio, state of: white settlement, 90; Indian wars in, 91–93; statehood, 93
Ohio country: French-English rivalry in, 78; acquired by England, 80–81; during Revolution, 86; British designs on, 87–88; territorial government for, 89–91; Indian wars in, 91–93; see also Old Northwest
OIO: see Oklahomans for Indian Opportunity
Ojibways: see Chippewas
Okakok, Guy: 389, 391 ff.
Oklahoma (present state area): 4, 6, 7; French in, 71–72; Choctaw removal to, 113, 117–18; Creek removal to, 115–16, 119; Cherokee removal to, 122, 124; Chickasaw removal to, 125; Seminole removal to, 125–26; see also Indian Territory
Oklahoma (west half): land openings in, 297–98, 305, 317, 319; granted territorial government, 304; allotments in, 305–306
Oklahoma, state of: admitted to Union, 309; Indian population in, 309, 408; Indian influence in, 309–10; spoliation of allottees, 324–30, 333, 401; aroused concern for Indians, 330, 333, 371, 408–10; fullblood settlements in, 410, 415
Oklahoma City, Oklahoma: 298, 317, 408
Oklahoma Historical Society: 323 & n.
Oklahoma Indian Welfare Act: 338
Oklahomans for Indian Opportunity: 409–10
Okmulgee (Creek capital): 224, 240
Okmulgee Council: 224–32, 260
Oktarharsars Harjo: see Sands
Old Northwest: 127, 206–207; see also Northwest Ordinance, Ohio country
Old Person, Earl: 371
Old Spanish Trail: 159
Old Tassel: 85–86, 88

Oliver, Lester: 397
Ollicut: 262–64
Omahas: linguistic relationships, 11; white abuse of, 103–104; receive Poncas, 211; under Public Law 280, 353, 378; attempt to terminate, 378
Omnibus Bill: 334
Oñate, Juan de: 36–38
Oneidas: 9, 84, 127, 393; see also Iroquois Confederacy
Onondagas: 9, 418; see also Iroquois Confederacy
Opechancanough: 40
Opothle Yahola: as young Creek warrior, 115; in removal, 119; in Civil War, 168n., 173–76
Oregon, state of: white settlement in, 151; land cessions and reservations in, 156–58; Public Law 280 extended to, 353; termination of tribes in, 371, 374–75
Oregon country: joint occupation of, 150; boundary fixed, 155; territorial government established, 156
Oregon Trail: 150, 153–54, 158, 159, 165, 233
Osages: linguistic relationships, 10–11; life ways, 15; relations with French, 72–73; slave trade, 73; visited by Tecumseh, 106, 109; removed to Kansas, 127; attend councils of Five Civilized Tribes, 148; in Civil War, 172; removed to the Indian Territory, 209–10; opposition to allotment, 301; allotment, 305–306; oil wealth, 306, 333, 354, 371; exploitation of, 285, 306; threatened with termination, 354, 371
Osceola: 112, 125–26
Otos and Missouris: 11, 210
Ottawas: 9, 79, 207
Ouray: 265
Overland Trail: see Oregon Trail
Owen, Robert L.: 325–26, 335

Padoucas: see Comanches
Paiutes: linguistic relationships, 11; life ways, 17; first sight of white men, 160; beginning hostility, 160; influence of Mormons, 161; join Bannocks in wars, 162, 265; start ghost dance, 289; termination of

Utah bands, 372; *see also* Pyramid Lake Paiutes
Palmer, Joel: 156–58
Palouses: 12
Papagos: 11, 162, 269, 284, 295–96
Parker, Quanah: 287, 288, 340
Parker, Samuel: 151
Paternalism: 287, 333, 418
Patuxets: 43–44; *see also* Squanto
Pawnees: 27, 29; linguistic relationships, 11; life ways, 16; trade with the French, 72; Osage hostility to, 73; Sioux hostility to, 190; removal to the Indian Territory, 210; news of Custer's defeat, 239
Payne, John Howard: 123
Peace Commission: with South Plains tribes, 218–21; with Sioux, 218 & n., 234–35
Peace of Paris, 1763: *see* Treaty of Paris
Peace of Paris, 1783; *see* Treaty of Paris
Pea Ridge, Battle of: 176
Pecos Pueblo: 98; *see also* Cicúye Pueblo
Penateka Comanches: settled on Texas reservation, 130; driven to the Indian Territory, 130, 148; in Civil War, 170–71, 174; on reservation, 220, 222, 229
Penn, William: 9, 49, 67, 77
Pennsylvania, state of: colony founded, 49; refusal to admit Tuscaroras, 77–78; in French and Indian War, 78–79; in Revolution, 87; dam displaces Senecas, 415–17
Peorias: 207
Pequots: 46–47
Peralta, Pedro de: 38
Peyote cult: 199n., 340
Philip: *see* King Philip
Pierce, Franklin: 167
Pike, Albert: 170–73, 181
Piman linguistic stock: 9, 11
Pimas: 11, 67, 162, 420
Pin-dah-kiss: *see* Miguel
Pine Ridge Agency: 242, 292–94, 313; *see also* Red Cloud Agency
Pine Ridge Reservation: 290–94
Pine Ridge Sioux: 345–46, 407
Plains wars: of 1864–65, 191–98; of Central and South Plains (1867–

69), 215–24; of South Plains (1874–75), 229–31, 287; in Powder River country (1866–68), 233–35; of North Plains (1876–77), 235–41, 262
Platero, Dillon: 382
Platte Bridge fight: 197
Plural marriages: 287
Plymouth, colony of: 9, 43–49
Pocahontas: 41–42
Point Hope, Alaska: 32ff.
Political platforms: in 1952, 351; in 1956, 376
Pomeroy, Samuel C.: 205, 207–208
Poncas: linguistic relationships, 11; removal to the Indian Territory, 210–12, 266; present location, 212
Ponce de León, Juan: 21
Pontiac: 9, 79, 81–82
Popé: 50
Porter, Osway: 311–12
Porter, Pleasant: *ix*, 6, 8, 303–306, 308, 331, 334, 410
Portugal: 19
Potawatomis: linguistic relationships, 9; converts of Tecumseh, 107; destroy Fort Dearborn, 109; removal to the Indian Territory, 206–207; Kansas remnant, 207; opposition to allotment, 303; allotment of, 317
Potlatch: 18
Powder River country: location of, 197; Sioux refuse to cede, 233, 236; war in, 234–35; ceded, 240; Northern Cheyenne reservation in, 259
Powhatan: 39–40, 41
Pratt, Richard H.: 231
Presbyterians: 113, 114, 129, 166, 385
Prescott, Arizona: 271
Procter, Henry: 110, 111
Prophets: Tenskwatawa, 106, 107, 109; Smohalla, 261–62; Apache (Noch-ay-del-klinne), 276; Wovoka, 288–90
Prophet's Town: 106–107, 109
Prudhoe Bay, Alaska: 400
Public Health Service: 339
Public Law 280: 352–53, 378, 411
Pueblo Indians: 6–7, 9, 284, 340–41; life ways, 12, 16–17, 22ff.; trade, 15, 22, 37, 67; Coronado's conquest of, 25–30; revolt, 50; reconquest, 50, 67; incited against Apaches, 67, 98;

attempt to dispossess, 334–35, 338; government, 340–41, 352–53; *see also names of Pueblos*
Pulitzer Prize: 5–6
Pushmataha: 108, 111, 112
Pyramid Lake Paiutes: 351, 420

Quahadi Comanches: 219, 228ff.
Quakers: 46, 48, 77, 127, 209, 224, 225, 337, 375, 411, 416
Quantrill Band: 178, 179
Quapaws: 11, 31, 76, 127, 172, 181
Queen Anne's War: 70, 76
Quivira: 27–29

Railroads: in the Indian Territory, 182–83, 202–203, 205, 224, 235, 296–97; other lines, 207, 213–15; disabled by Cheyennes, 217–18
Raleigh, Walter: 34
Rampart Dam, Alaska: 395–97
Reclamation Bureau: 420
Reconstruction treaties: 180–83, 206, 224, 296, 304, 306, 327
Rector, Elias: 148, 169ff.
Red Cloud: 197, 234–35
Red Cloud Agency: 235, 236, 242; *see also* Pine Ridge Agency
Red Lake Chippewas: 305, 353, 412
Red Sticks: 111, 112
Red Stick War: 110–11, 114–15
Rees: *see* Arikaras
Reindeer industry: 385
Relocation: 376–77, 407–408; *see also* employment, Indians in cities
Removal, Indian: 7, 105, 117–27, 206–207
Removal of restrictions: 314, 319, 326–27, 329, 376; *see also* competency commissions
"Rendezvous," traders': 104, 151
Reno, Marcus A.: 238–39
Reservations: policy of, 271; defeated tribes on, 284–94; as homelands, 284; cattlemen on, 286; white designs on, 294, 296; liquidation of, 298–315; law enforcement on, 352, 353; industry on, 407; *see also* executive order reservations
"Restricted Indians": 335 & n.
Restricted land: *see* land tenure, removal of restrictions
Revolutionary War: 84–87

Revolving loan fund: 338–45, 376, 380, 381, 407
Rhoads, Charles J.: 337
Rhode Island, state of: 46, 48
Rhodes, John: 296
Ribaut, Jean: 33, 34
Ricarees: *see* Arikaras
Ridge, John: early life and education, 120; position regarding removal, 122–23; emigration to Oklahoma, 124; assassination of, 128
Ridge, Major: in Red Stick War, 120; position regarding removal, 122–23; emigration to Oklahoma, 124; assassination of, 128
River Raisin, battle on: 110
Rock, Howard: 394ff.
Rock Island, Illinois: 188
Roessel, Robert A.: 414–15 & n., 420
Rogers, Will: 201 n.
Rogue River War: 158–59, 165, 260
Roman Nose: 197, 216, 222
Roosevelt, Franklin D.: 333, 338
Roosevelt, Theodore: 282, 325, 332
Rosebud, battle on: 237, 239
Rosebud Sioux: 407, 412
Ross, Edmund G.: 218
Ross, John: elected Cherokee chief, 114; in Cherokee removal, 120–25; as slaveowner, 168n.; in Civil War, 169–78; in negotiating Reconstruction treaties, 181–82; death of, 203–204
Ross, Quatie (wife of John Ross): 122, 125
Rough Rock Demonstration School: 414–15
Russians in Alaska: 82–83, 100, 383–84
Ryan, W. Carson: 337

Sacajawea: 101–102
Sackett, John: 400
St. Augustine, Florida: 34; *see also* Fort Marion
St. Clair, Arthur: 89–92, 96
St. Louis, Missouri: 82, 101–104, 150–51
St. Paul, Minnesota: 187ff.
Salishan linguistic stock: 9, 12
Salt Lake City, Utah: 190, 372
Samoset: 44–45
San Antonio, Texas: 71

San Carlos Apaches: 270–77, 281–82, 341, 346–47
Sand Creek massacre: 194–96, 198, 216, 223, 227, 334–35
Sands: 173–75, 227
San Ildefonso Pueblo: 351
San Juan, New Mexico: 36–38, 50
Santa Fe, New Mexico: 5, 38, 50, 67
Santa Fe Trail: 105, 165–66, 193
Santee Sioux: conditions on reservation, 184–85, 188; uprising, 185–87, 190–91; punishment, 187–89; present location, 188
Santo Domingo Pueblo: 36
Satank: runs off horse herd, 192; at Medicine Lodge Council, 220–21; last raid and death, 225–27; sons of, 225, 228
Satanta: at Medicine Lodge Council, 218–20, 221 n.; arrested, 223; raid in Texas, 225–26; punishment, 228–31; family of, 229, 231–32
Sauk and Fox Indians: linguistic relationships, 9; supporters of Tecumseh, 109; in Black Hawk War, 127; remnant in Iowa, 127, 413; in Kansas, 206–207; removal to the Indian Territory, 206–207; allotment, 319
Scarlet fever: 154
Scattergood, Joseph Henry: 337
Schools: 412–15; see also education
Scott, Hugh Lenox: 281–87, 289
Scott, Winfield: 124
Sears, T. C.: 296
Seaton, Fred A.: 379
Seattle, Washington: 386, 394
Seekabo: 108
Sells, Cato: 314
Seminoles: origin of, 10, 76; in Creek Confederacy, 95–96; cut off from Creeks, 97, 112; converts of Tecumseh, 106, 108, 110; Creek accessions to, 112; raiding from Florida, 112; pushed into swamps, 113; removal of, 125–26; remaining in Florida, 126, 354; life in the Indian Territory, 129; in Civil War, 168–78, 201; Reconstruction, 182; cede unassigned land, 296–98, 304; tribal dissolution, 307ff.; see also Five Civilized Tribes, Mikasukis
Senecas: 6, 78; linguistic relationships, 9; in Pontiac's War, 81; in Revolu-

tion, 87; in the Indian Territory, 127, 147; in Civil War, 172, 181; flooding of reservation, 415–17; see also Iroquois Confederacy
Sequoyah: 113–14, 129–30, 343
Serra, Fray Junipero: 83
Seventh Cavalry: 217, 222, 237, 292
Seward, William H.: 147
Shahaptian linguistic stock: 9, 12
Shawnee, Oklahoma: 319, 320
Shawnees: linguistic relationships, 9, 10; relations with Creeks, 10, 92; early wars with whites, 79, 82, 86; western migration of, 86, 109, 129–30; wars with the United States, 91–93; send emissaries to Creeks, 96; in Civil War, 172, 174, 177, 181; removal to the Indian Territory, 206; allotment of, 317, 323
"Shawnee Wolves": 320–21
Sheep: of Navahos, 17, 200; of Pueblos, 67, 407
Sheridan, Philip H.: in Plains wars, 221–23, 231; policy towards Apaches, 279–80
Sherman, William Tecumseh: plan for Plains Indians, 215; on Peace Commission, 218, 221; contempt for Indians, 222, 234, 260, 264; escapes ambush, 225; arrests Kiowa-Comanche raiders, 225–26; at Okmulgee Council, 226–28; retires, 279
Shoshonean linguistic stock: 9, 11
Shoshonis: linguistic relationships, 11; women of, 101, 102, 104; welcome Lewis and Clark, 101–102; Blackfoot enmity to, 102–103; location on trails, 161–62; join war against travelers, 161; at Horse Creek Council, 165; allied with Crook, 237; on reservation, 241; Northern Arapahos settled with, 241; ghost dance among, 289
Shoshonis, desert bands: 159–60, 162
Shoshonis, western bands: 265
Shriver, Sargent: 410
Shulush Homma: 75
Sibley, Henry: 187–88
Sieber, Al: 273–74, 278
Simpson, George: 150
Siouan linguistic stock: 9, 10–11
Sioux: linguistic relationships, 10–11; movement to Plains, 15; converts of

Tecumseh, 107, 189; at Horse Creek Council, 165; Grattan incident, 166–67; range and tribal relations, 190, 210; join Plains War of 1864–65, 216–17; defend Powder River country, 233–35; reservations of, 234–35, 284, 290; in North Plains War, 236–41; attempted removal of, 240; ghost dance disaster, 289–94; allotment of, 313; *see also* Brulé Sioux, Oglala Sioux, Pine Ridge Sioux, Rosebud Sioux, Santee Sioux, Sisseton and Wahpeton Sioux, Yankton Sioux

Sisseton and Wahpeton Sioux: 304, 330

Sitting Bull: 235–41, 291–92, 302, 305

Six Nations: *see* Iroquois Confederacy

Sky Walker: *see* Mamanti

Slavery, Aleutian: 100

Slavery, Indian: by Spaniards, 20–23, 28–32, 37, 50, 159; by Indians, 27–29, 73, 159; by English, 43–44, 47, 49, 77; by French, 73–74; by Americans, 119, 164–65; by Mexicans, 159, 162

Slavery, of Labrador natives: 19

Smallpox: 103, 154

Smith, Edward P.: 230, 232

Smith, Jedediah: 159

Smith, J. Q.: 307

Smith, John: 39, 43–44

Smith, Redbird: 7, 311, 344

Smoke signals: 25, 30, 239, 278

Sopete: 27–29

South Carolina, state of: attempted French settlement of, 33; Indian trade of, 73; *see also* Carolina

South Dakota, state of: granted statehood, 242; Indian reservations in, 291–94, 299, 304

Southern Cheyennes and Arapahos: at Medicine Lodge Council, 218–20; settle on reservation, 223–24, 284; at Okmulgee Council, 224, 227, 232; in South Plains War of 1874–75, 230–32; ghost dance among, 289–90; allotment of, 305; *see also* Cheyennes and Arapahos

Southern Utes: 266

South Pass: 150

Spain: early explorations of, 19–32; in West Indies, 20–21; Indian policy of, 20–21, 30, 38, 67, 69; in Florida, 34,

67, 112–13; in the Southwest, 36–38, 50, 67, 98–99, 105; imperial rivalry of, 71, 83, 87ff.; in Louisiana, 81, 82; in California, 82–83, 99

Spokane Garry: 4, 150

Spokanes: 4, 12, 150, 153

Spotted Tail: 167, 233, 240

Spotted Tail Agency: 235

Squanto: 43–46

Staked Plains: 219, 228

Standing Bear: 211–12

Standing Rock Agency: 235

Standing Rock Reservation: 290–91

Standish, Miles: 46, 47

Stands-in-Timber, John: 381

Stanley, Henry M.: 218

State (or territorial) government: extended over Southern Indians, 117ff.; guarantees against, 117–18, 148; territorial threats, 148, 182, 205, 224, 232; imposition of statehood, 309; *see also* Dawes Act, termination

Stevens, Isaac I.: 156–58, 166

Stone, Harlan: 295

Stuart, John: 84, 85

Sullivan, John: 87

Summit Springs, battle at: 223

Surveys of land: 88, 97, 207, 230–31, 310, 311

Tahlequah (Cherokee capital): 128, 172, 181

Tanacross, Alaska: 394, 402–403

Tanana, Alaska: 394–96

Taos Pueblo: 26, 50, 418–19, 422

Task forces: of Governor Hickel, 400–401; of Secretary Udall, 405, 407, 414; *see also* Hoover Commission

Tatum, Lawrie: 225–26, 228, 229

Tawakonis: 71–72

Taylor, Iola: 408; *see also* Hayden

Taylor, Nathaniel G.: 218ff.

Tecumseh: 9, 189; as young warrior, 91ff., 96; family of, 92, 106, 148, 174; characterization of, 105–106; crusade to unite Indians, 106–109, 189; as ally of British, 109–11; death, 111

Telegraph line: 190

Teller, Henry M.: 265, 320ff.

Tellico (Cherokee "mother town"): 2, 11, 94

Ten Bears: 219, 228

Tennessee, state of: early white settlement in, 81–82, 86, 88, 89; Indian wars in, 92; statehood granted to, 93, 401
Tenskwatawa: 106–109
Termination: agitation for, 349–50; carried out, 350–54, 371–78; Indian fear of, 352, 371, 407; Senate repudiation of, 407 & n.; see also House Concurrent Resolution 108
Terry, Alfred: 237–40
Texas, state of: Spanish explorers in, 21–22; Spanish settlement of, 71; immigrant Indians in, 97, 123, 129–30; admission to Union, 130; Indian reservations in, 130, 147, 296, 371; Kiowa-Comanche raids in, 130, 166, 224ff.; captures Indian Territory forts, 169; Indian Civil War refugees in, 178–79; Indian Territory intrusions from, 230, 297–98
Texas Panhandle: 29, 230; see also Staked Plains
Thackery, Frank A.: 318ff.
Thames, Battle of the: 111
The Bowl: 123, 129–30
The Ridge: see Ridge
Tiguex pueblos: 26–28, 31
Tilghman, William M.: 230 n.
Time reckoning: see dates
Timothy: 153, 156–58
Timucuas: 67, 76
Tippecanoe: see Prophet's Town
Tippecanoe, Battle of: 109
Tiulana, Paul: 393–94, 404
Tizwin: 277–78, 281
Tlaxcalans: 38
Tlingets: 12, 100, 396, 399
Toby, Willis F.: 7
Tompiro pueblos: 37
Tonkawas: 130, 147, 177
Tonto Apaches: 162, 271–74
Toohoolhoolzote: 4, 262, 264
Towaconie Jim: 302
Trade: primitive, 13, 15, 22, 26; Spanish-Comanche, 98; on Oregon Trail, 153–54; see also fur trade
Trails: Indian depredations on, 105, 193, 196–97, 217ff.; traffic on, 189–90; see also Bozeman Trail, California trails, Denver trails, Old Spanish Trail, Oregon Trail, Santa Fe Trail

Travois: 15
Treaty-making (with Indians), ended: 294
Treaty of Paris, 1763: 80–81
Treaty of Paris, 1783: 87
Truman, Harry S.: 348, 350, 353, 373
Tuckabatchee: 108, 111, 115
Tulkepais: 162, 271, 274
Tulsa, Oklahoma: 408
Tulsa (Creek town): 4, 45
Tundra Times: 396ff.
Turk, the: 27–29
Turkeys: 13, 25–26 & n., 27
Turtle Mountain Reservation: 354
Tuscaloosa: 30
Tuscaroras: 9, 77–78, 84; see also Iroquois Confederacy
Tuskegees: 10
Tyonek, Alaska: 389–90, 397–99

Udall, Stewart L.: 295–96, 383, 393ff., 405, 407, 415, 419, 420
Uintah and Ouray Reservation: 266, 313, 371–72
Umatilla Reservation: 157, 264
Umatillas: 12, 157, 264
Union Pacific Railroad: 217–18
Universities: 408, 414
University of Alaska: 386, 388
University of Chicago: 345, 408
University of Oklahoma: 408–409
Utah, state of: Mormon settlement of, 160–61; territorial government for, 160–61; Mountain Meadows massacre in, 161; see also Paiutes, Utes
Utes: linguistic relationships, 11; Spanish relations with, 98, 159; Mormon relations with, 160; Meriwether's negotiations with, 162–63; hostility to Plains tribes, 190, 198; allies of Kit Carson, 198, 219; expulsion from Colorado, 265–66; present location, 266; see also Uintah and Ouray Reservation, White River Utes
Uto-Aztecan linguistic stock: 11

Vaca, Álvar Núñez Cabeza de: 22–23, 26
Valandra, Cato: 412
Vaughan, Jack: 410
Verde Reservation: 271–74
Verrazano, Giovanni da: 19–20

Victorio: 270, 275–76
Villa, Pancho: 283
Vincennes, Indiana: 86, 105, 106, 109
Virginia, state of: Spain in, 34; English settlement of, 39–42; Indian wars with, 40, 46, 49
Vitter, Joe: 303
Voyageurs: 38

Wabasha: 185, 187
Wahpepah, James: 410–11
Wahpeton Sioux: *see* Sisseton and Wahpeton Sioux
Waiilatpuan linguistic stock: 151
Waiilatpu Mission: 151–56, 158
Wainwright, Alaska: 385
Wales, Alaska: 385
Walker, Joseph Reddeford: 159–60
Walla Walla Council: 156–57, 166
Walla Wallas: 12, 157
Wallowa country: 261, 264
Wampanoags: 44–45, 48
Ward, Nancy: 88
"Wardship," Indian: 349–50, 352
Ware, Eugene F.: 191
Warm Springs Apaches: 162, 270–71, 275–76, 353; *see also* Mimbreño Apaches
War of 1812: 109–12
Warrior, Isaac: 181–82
Washakie: 161–62, 165, 241
Washington, George: in French and Indian War, 78–79; during Revolution, 84, 87; establishes Indian policy, 90–91; defeats Indians of Northwest, 91–92; negotiates with Southern Indians, 93–96; treaty with Senecas, 416
Washington, George (Caddo chief): 226
Washington, state of: land cessions and reservations in, 156–58; in Yakima War, 157–58
Watauga, Tennessee: 81, 88–89
Watie, Saladin: 180, 183
Watie, Sarah (wife of Stand Watie): 179–80, 183
Watie, Stand: early life, 120; position regarding removal, 122–23; emigration to Oklahoma, 124; escape from assassination, 128; in Civil War, 172–80; death of, 203
Wayne, Anthony: 91–94

Wesley, Clarence: 341
West Indies: 19–20
Weymouth, George: 43
Whaling, by Eskimos: 385, 391, 404
Whipple, Henry: 188
Whipple, Joe: 316–17
Whisky: *see* alcohol
White Antelope: 190 ff.
White Eagle: 212
White Earth Reservation: 330, 333
White Man: 303
White Mountain Apaches: 162, 267, 270, 397
White River Utes: 265–66, 313, 330
White Wolf: 303
Whitman, Marcus: 151–56
Whitman, Narcissa (wife of Marcus Whitman): 151–56
Whitman, Royal Emerson: 268–69
Whoa: *see* Juh
Wichita Agency: 147, 170–71, 177
Wichitas: 27, 29, 71; linguistic relationships, 11; life ways, 16; early trade with French, 72; in Civil War, 177; *see also* Wichitas and affiliated tribes
Wichitas and affiliated tribes: visited by La Harpe, 71; accept reservation in the Indian Territory, 147, 222; in Civil War, 170–71, 177; attend Okmulgee Council, 224, 227; ghost dance among, 289–90; oppose allotment, 302
Wild Cat: 125–26
Willamette Valley, Oregon: 151, 158
Williams, Roger: 46, 48
Wilson, Woodrow: 314, 332
Wilson's Creek, Battle of: 172
Winnebagos: 10, 109, 336, 353
Winnemucca, Sarah: 160
Wirtz, Willard: 410
Wisconsin, state of: Oneidas in, 127, 393; Public Law 280 extended to, 372; Menominees in, 372–73
Woman chief: 30
Wooden Legs, John: 314, 378, 380–81
Worcester, Samuel Austin: 113–14, 121–22
Worcester v. *Georgia*: 121–22
Work, Hubert: 336
World War I: 335, 345, 417
World War II: 347, 349, 387, 417

449

Wounded Knee, massacre of: 292–94, 313
Wright, Donald R.: 400
Wyandots: 109, 147; *see also* Hurons
Wynkoop, Edward W.: 193, 194, 212, 216
Wyoming Valley, Pennsylvania: 87

Yakima Reservation: 157, 264
Yakimas: 12, 156–57
Yakima War: 157–58
Yankton Sioux: 299
Yaquis: 11

Yavapais: 12, 162, 271–72, 274
Young, Brigham: 160–61
Ysopete: *see* Sopete
Yuchis: *see* Euchees
Yuman linguistic stock: 9, 12
Yuman tribes: 17, 24–25, 162
Yumas: 12

Zaldívar, Juan de: 37
Zaldívar, Vicente de: 36–38
Zevely, J. W.: 325
Zia Pueblo: 28
Zunis: 23–30, 99, 164, 407